MW00805741

UNCREDITED

Uncredited:

The Life and Career of Virginia Gregg

By Lona Bailey

BearManor Media

2022

Uncredited: The Life and Career of Virginia Gregg

Published in the United States of America by:

BearManor Media

4700 Millenia Blvd.
Suite 175 PMB 90497
Orlando, FL 32839

bearmanormedia.com

Printed in the United States.

Typesetting and layout by BearManor Media

ISBN—978-1-62933-927-6

Contents

Dedication

Virginia Gregg knew how to be a friend. She was fair and uncompromised in her evaluation of others. I worked with her on hundreds of radio shows primarily with Jack Webb and *Dragnet*. She had a sense of humor that was intelligent and sophisticated, but always kind. A woman of many talents, she was a professional musician early in her life, and a supreme actress of great diversity in radio, TV, and film. She was loved and admired by her fellow workers in network radio, film, and television of which I include myself. Loved and respected by her sons and family, she was notably beautiful, physically as well as spiritually. She was dedicated to her sons and family, and lived a full life of grace and dignity. Whenever it was known by cast and crew that she would be part of a project, it was an inspiration to all involved. I met her when I was about sixteen years old; we became friends when I was just beginning in network radio, before television. When I would have a difficult part to play, and we were on the air, live, I would come back to the table where all the actors were seated and Virginia would whisper to me, "You were great!" or "Terrific!" When I realized that women in radio had to be well groomed, I asked her, "Where do you go?" "Well, I go to Max Factor on Highland, off Hollywood Blvd." After saving up enough money to go there, I went, feeling like a queen, because 'Ginny' went there. After a long absence, raising a family and a divorce, I came back to work and was to be married to Irish actor, Sean McClory. Virginia was among the first I called to invite. She said, "Oh Peggy, I'd love to! But, I have this sick old lady I have to take care of." I questioned her about getting someone else to watch her for a few hours, but she said, "No, I have to do it." Virginia, true to her unselfish nature, avoided what she knew would have saddened all on my Wedding Day.

She *was* taking care of an old lady. Without saying so, she was speaking of herself. She died within a week.

Peggy Webber September 2020

Author's Note

After months of researching legendary Virginia Gregg, I find myself writing this introduction at a roll top desk in a quaint, turn of the century bed-and-breakfast much like the house that Virginia grew up in in Southern Illinois. As I type, my iPhone plays a score from Virginia's symphony days. Her instrument is difficult to ascertain on its own, but with enough concentration, I can faintly make out the beautiful undergirding of her double bass viol in these recordings produced more than fifty years before my own birth. These melodies make for a lovely time travel vortex that allows me to feel the essence of a woman I have come to know and to love over the past few months in researching and writing about her life and career that is so far removed from my own here in the 2020s.

She has come to life throughout the researching and writing processes and has taught me many things. I have learned to knit the way she did – the German way. I submerged myself into the Golden Age of radio and film, and the early years of American symphony and media production to find fragments of Virginia she left behind in these worlds. I have connected with fascinating people in whom Virginia downloaded pieces of herself throughout various eras in her lifetime, and I have gone far beyond my comfort zone in examining a virtual stranger's most intimate life details. Though a writer for many years, this is my first official biographic effort, and it has been truly "marvelous" as Virginia would say, and though she passed from this life before my own birth, like so many others, I too can say, "Virginia Gregg helped me get started in my career."

I have had many people ask me throughout the researching and writing process, "You're thirty years old. Why did you choose *Virginia Gregg* to do a biography on?" I love that question, because I'm still trying to come up with the answer myself. In a way, I don't feel like I chose this project; I feel like this project chose me. It was during the Great Quarantine of 2020 in which I "met" Virginia through her frequent roles in television's *Gunsmoke*. Like so many others across the globe during that confusing time of hiding in our homes from the invisible enemy named coronavirus, I found myself with a bit of extra time on my hands and an insatiable need to connect with a seemingly simpler time that had never heard of COVID-19 or task force briefings. My family and I stayed huddled in our home for weeks and then months binge watching our favorite classic shows until we had the all-clear from the powers that be. During this time, I noticed a particular character actress who had a captivating, and yet familiar quality. She appeared in many episodes, but unlike other familiar character actors, she never seemed to play the same type of role. Her range even on this one series was phenomenal. In doing some basic research on her filmography per the Internet Movie Database (IMDB), I marveled at its length, but also the number of decades and great range represented in her television and film work. I learned she was a favorite choice of Jack Webb's, making her one of the most familiar faces within the *Dragnet* franchise. I learned she voiced the infamous "Norman Bates'" mother in all three *Psycho* films. I learned she could do painfully serious, funny, drunk, and desperate all with the same potent believability and charm. There was hardly a television series in which she didn't appear throughout the 50s-80s, but once my research led me to her radiography (what there is documented) I was further convinced she had something very different than her peers, and I wanted to know what it was.

In prying into her personal life online, I was dismayed to find limited, and contradicting information (if there's one thing I've learned from this project, it is just how inadequate the internet truly is when it comes to its history recording efforts). Upon learning she was a small-town gal like myself, I contacted the historic society in her hometown to ask if they might have a biography on her. The response was, "No, but one should be written." I pondered that for a while and thought what fun it would be to not only write about this mysterious talent, but also to exhume the information myself outside of the standard ways to which my generation is most accustomed: Googling ad nauseum. Many biographers have the benefit of certain content guides found among their subjects' personal effects such as diaries, letters, and scrapbooks. Virginia Gregg was an extremely private person and didn't make provisions for a biographer. While a general sketch of her life story can be easily accessed online, she left very few clues beyond the basic facts.

She didn't make the research process easy for me, but she certainly made it rewarding.

As a former therapist, I used to be in the business of helping others find their voices for the first time, or for the first time in a long while. I have been out of that business for some time now and have moved into the work of giving voice to others' life stories who perhaps, for whatever reason, were not given an opportunity to be properly credited or understood before their earthly departure.

Virginia Gregg needs no help with her voice, as she still has a very viable, unique one of her own that can be heard loud and clear in her work and in the personal accounts of her family, friends, and colleagues. In this presentation of her life and career, I in no way attempt to give a voice to someone who already has a great one; I simply attempt to share a composite of a life I personally admire and continue to learn from in hopes that others can more fully do the same. I am removed from Ms. Gregg's story and voice by a few generations, and in no way could assume to understand the true nature of the context of her journey, as the years she lived were before my own birth. This book is no summary, as no one's life can ever be truly summarized. This is merely a collection of recorded historical and personal accounts of an individual who greatly contributed to radio, television, film, and to the lives of her family, friends, colleagues, fans, to the art of art itself, and to the world.

This is a chronicle of research, but as a caveat to readers, Virginia Gregg was and is so much more than any book could relay (as all biographic subjects are). While humanity can be better understood through historic preservation, people themselves are much more than collections of facts, records, and personal accounts. In reading this biography, I hope never to even attempt to speak for Ms. Gregg, but to simply introduce you to her in a way that allows you to better hear her voice for yourself. I'm merely turning up the volume on a compelling story that has many elements of connection, inspiration, and grit from which we all can learn.

This work is published after months of sifting through documents, newspaper articles, radio recordings, and historical records in tandem with countless interviews, phone calls, emails, texts, and snail mail exchanges that helped bring the research points into technicolor. While the research presented in these pages has been carefully conducted and compiled with the utmost intentionality, gaps are present and due to the nature of the historical accounts collected and presented, the entirety of any story can never be shared. I hope you will view this as a showcase of several significant portions of Ms. Gregg's life that have contributed toward the legacy she has left behind, and perhaps consider your own in a new way.

This biography is part record and part experience, as all humanity is. It includes primary and secondary data along with the unique interpretation of the researcher and writer herself. The facts and experiential content found in the following pages are accurate in so much as any historical account can be. There are some discrepancies on certain records and dates, but those are generally detailed on a case-by-case basis. The experiential accounts presented by individuals mentioned in this book have been contributed of their own free will based on their own personal recollections and experiences.

The title of the book is *Uncredited* because while Ms. Gregg was eventually credited in many of her productions, as is evidenced on her IMDB profile, many of those credits were not published until long after the productions' release (and after her death), if published at all. While IMDB does a fabulous job of chronicling filmographies, it may be impossible for anyone to compile an exhaustive list of Ms. Gregg's works (especially with regard to her radio career). She was uncredited in many productions in radio, television, and film because during her active years in those media, crediting policies were not what they are today in the 2020s. No IMDB database existed in the days she was active in the business for fans, colleagues, and potential producers and directors to access in examination of an artist. While many of her works are detailed in the pages hereafter, no exhaustive list of her complete works in any media exists.

As a researcher and writer, I approach this biography with three glaring personal biases that should be mentioned straightaway: First, I never had the privilege of meeting the star of this bio; therefore, I have researched and written from behind a glass, so-to-speak. Second, I am removed from the historical context by a couple of generations; therefore, my postmodern worldview will undoubtedly be evident throughout this work. This is significant in that my worldview as a researcher and writer is an indirect byproduct of the eras I have studied and shared about in the following pages. Third, I am a fan of Virginia Gregg, and my interpretation of her career and life will certainly be based on my overall favorable opinion of her and her contribution to our world. Not all biases are negative, though they should be acknowledged in any effort to share information in an ethical and veracious way.

Some of the contextual information found in this biography may be obvious or even painfully boring to some, leaving readers asking, "What the devil does this have to do with Virginia Gregg?" but in an effort to preserve and further the particular segment of history of which Ms. Gregg was a part, I believe it is important to detail as much context as possible for generations, like my own, who may be unaware of some of the era-related implications that make her story so great.

Perhaps most importantly, a very special thanks to all who made this biography possible. Thank you to all those who have been so kind to contribute their time, memories, and support to this project. I have been so fortunate to connect with many remarkable individuals whose journeys intersected with Ms. Gregg's in unforgettable ways. Empirical research is so important in any project of this nature, but the ways in which we touch each other's lives is truly how "biography" is created. One of the most rewarding elements of researching and writing this book has been connecting with family members, friends, and colleagues of Ms. Gregg who have been so generous to share their stories with me. Due to the disastrous nature of the year 2020 for us all, the quarantine culture and multiple natural disasters throughout the United States prevented me from meeting many of my contacts in person. Many times, we only had a phone or email address through which to communicate, and despite my communication clumsiness through these means, I was fortunate enough to "meet" so many wonderful, wonderful people who helped bring this book to life. A *very* special thanks to Virginia's son, Jaime del Valle and his wife Christine for their support of this writing project and for sharing the lovely memories of Virginia. It has been a delight to get to know the del Valles, and Virginia through them.

Thank you to all the stellar people at SPERDVAC who not only personally directed me to many archive interviews and recordings with and about Virginia, but for being instrumental in creating these archive interviews and recordings in the first place. The grand efforts of organizations like SPERDVAC are so important for later generations, of which I am a part, to experience a bit of time travel through the voices and the stories of previous eras. Without SPERDVAC's vigilant efforts in capturing pieces of history through interviews and recordings, the beautiful, hilarious, and heartbreaking stories (many of which you will find in this book) would have been lost forever. While I so appreciate SPERDVAC as a whole, I also want to specifically name a few people within the entity who have been especially impactful in the creation of this book: Larry & John Gassman, Walden Hughes, Timothy Knofler, and Barbara Watkins.

A special thanks to all the wonderful old time radio researchers who helped guide my own research in this project. Without the preservation work of so many researchers before me, this biography would have been incredibly difficult if not impossible to write. Thank you, John Dunning for your incredible work *Tune in Yesterday: The Ultimate Encyclopedia of Old Time Radio 1925-1976*; J. David Goldin's RadioGOLDINdex; OldTimeRadioDownloads. com; Jerry Haendiges Vintage Radio Logs; RUSC Old Time Radio; and The Digital Deli. Your work is invaluable, and I am ever grateful for your efforts to preserve this wonderful history of the Golden Age of radio.

A special thanks to Karl Schadow for his guidance and encouragement. A special thanks to Chuck Schaden for his preservation work in creating recordings of so many interviews with legendary artists like Virginia, and for making them available on his website. I also want to thank him for his graciousness in allowing me to interview him about interviewing her.

A special thanks to those wonderfully talented colleagues of Virginia's who were so kind in sharing their memories with me: Kami Cotler, Ann Robinson, Ann Dusenberry, Anne Whitfield, Barbara Fuller, Joan Del Mar, Gerald Farber, Samuel "Dubs" Smith, and a very special thank you to Peggy Webber who was not only wonderful to talk with on our phone calls, but who so graciously wrote the beautiful dedication at the beginning of this book.

I also want to thank the "dear hearts and gentle people" in Virginia's hometown of Harrisburg, Illinois who gave me the grand tour of the town along with invaluable sources of information for my research. Thank you, Eric Gregg, Gillum Ferguson, Mark Motsinger, Krystal Wilson, and the Saline County Historical Society. Also, a thank you to the family of Catherine Ames for the photos and news clippings despite the death of her nephew Larry Ames during the course of this writing project.

Finally, a special thank you to Ben Ohmart for believing in this book and allowing me to share Virginia's story through BearManor Media.

To everyone mentioned above, thank you all for being so patient with my nosiness and excavation efforts in gathering all the information I could about one of our favorite voices in media history. It has been a great pleasure partnering with you in these research efforts. Thank you for allowing history to live on through your intimate contributions!

-Lona Bailey

True to *Dragnet* form, the story you are about to read is true.

CHAPTER 1: THE ACTRESS' ACTRESS

"DEAR DICK: How come Jack Webb uses Virginia Gregg in so many of his productions? She got something on him?"

Virginia Gregg has one of the most recognizable faces and voices in American media. Known to her family, friends, and close colleagues as "Ginny," she steadily worked as a character actress in radio, television, and film for over forty years during a pivotal time in American history that had far-reaching implications for the life and death of radio dramas, the emergence of the television series, and the evolution of film. She was versatile enough to fluidly move from medium to medium and bring a wide range of characters to life in a multidimensional way. Many recognize her face or her voice, but very rarely both as belonging to the same individual because she performed in such varied capacities spanning so many decades in so many different media. It is hard to imagine from the same person came the unforgettably eerie voice of infamous "Norman Bates'" mother in Hitchcock's classic thriller *Psycho*, the seductive, throaty voice of "Richard Diamond's" Park Avenue girlfriend "Helen Asher," and the soft, broken English of "Paladin's" ardent Chinese friend, "Hey Girl," in *Have Gun Will Travel*.

Needless to say, in her forty + year career, she was never typecast, "unless it's as a woman," as she said.[1]

The historic misogyny of the entertainment industry is evident in the above role descriptions, as Virginia was often "the mother of . . . ." "the girlfriend of " "the friend of." She also had the artistic tendency to have these roles in support of male leads billed in a descriptive nature using nouns and adjectives more often than character names. It often took an article and a preposition to denote her contribution to a given production (if she was credited at all that is): "Featuring Virginia Gregg as **the** *blank* **of** *blank*." She rarely stood on her own in character portrayals, playing second fiddle to male leads and often having no specific character name at all in many television and film productions. Amanda Blake was *Gunsmoke*'s "Miss Kitty," Jeanette Nolan was *The Virginian*'s "Holly Granger," and Barbara Hale was *Perry Mason*'s "Della Street." While these three women were also subjected to the second fiddle position in relation to their male counterparts, they are generally recognized by specific names rather than descriptions. She was the "the-of" of radio, television, and film for over forty years, which isn't particularly remarkable if you have small talent, but in her case, her talent was so weighty, she seemed to have an unending range, artistic supply, and combination of raw and professionally trained talent.

Fellow character actor and longtime friend, Parley Baer, described Virginia's talent as inexhaustible. He felt she was wasted in many supporting roles, such as "Nurse 'Nosy' Parker" on radio's *The Story of Doctor Kildare*, that did little to tap the breadth of her ability. He said whatever she gave to a role was always merely scratching the surface, and that she always had more to give regardless of the role.[2] She never seemed to mind being harnessed in supporting roles nor being under the thumb of Hollywood's patriarchy. She learned to play the industry game and excelled in whatever was handed to her – a knack for versatility that served her well in both her personal and professional life.

Virginia's range brought her voice into the homes of millions of Americans for over forty years in all mainstream media, in addition to several side projects such as her recordings of countless audio books for organizations such as Recordings for the Blind and her recordings of flight announcements for Trans World Airlines (TWA). I'm wondering how many waiting passengers listened to their flight schedule announced through the airport terminals, and thought, "Gee, that voice sounds familiar. Wasn't she the mom on *Psycho*?" Probably no one.

She could transform her vocal cords into natives of Scandinavia, Russia, China, and Ireland on a dime. She could emulate an eighty-year old charwoman, a Grand duchess of flawless proper British, a gun moll from the Bronx, a loud-mouthed hillbilly, a southern saloon madam, an alluring Spanish señorita, or a ten-year old American boy (sometimes playing a variety of roles such as these even within the same script).[3] In radio she made herself virtually untraceable because of her vocal diversity, and with the help of props and makeup, she became just as untraceable in television and film. She excelled at vocal and physical submersion in her roles, appearing much older or younger than her true age. The portions of her radiography and filmography available are quite confusing when trying to understand their progressions chronologically because her roles often did not correspond with her ages. That, coupled with the industry's tendency to leave certain actors and actresses uncredited during the Golden Age before the development of Hollywood's modern crediting policies, means that a complete list of her works could never be compiled for any media.

SUPPORTING PLAYERS

Virginia was often one of the strongest backbones of productions, providing unconditional, high quality support for the leads, in the process giving viewers some fabulous entertainment experiences, many of which stuck with them years after viewing (i.e. who can't quote at least a line or two of "Norman Bates'" mother in Hitchcock's classic *Psycho*?). In staying so focused on her own role and its broader contribution to a given script, she helped create an on-screen (or on-mic) environment for the leads that allowed them to more fully engage with their own craft, having the full backing of the supporting roles fueling the collective synergy of the production. Virginia had the remarkable ability to calibrate to the energy of her fellow actors and actresses and each particular production in radio, television, and film. She believed in everyone pulling his or her own weight, which allowed for a rich and balanced recording scenario- something that is a rare treat for many in the industry.

While seemingly counterintuitive, if you don't particularly notice the supporting actors and actresses within a production, that usually means they are doing a fantastic job. Occasionally however, someone is so extraordinary within multiple supporting roles that you do notice them, and in those cases, you may have encountered a star, who for whatever reason, just happened to not be billed as such. As Virginia herself described: "I was a character actress from the day I started, and I still am, and that delights me. That's exactly what I want to be. I am pleased with it. That's my story."[4]

There are many remarkable things about Virginia Gregg and her presence in American media. For starters, her linear media presence for over forty years is something to be marveled. She was able to stay between the lines of stardom and burnout riding the waves of media's vast changes from the 1940s-1980s. For her, the goal was not stardom, not the lavish Hollywood lifestyle of so many of her peers, and not even the glamourous roles of the Golden Age. In our current culture we love the pay off, don't we? Sure, I'll put in the hard work, but what will it get me? For Virginia, she needed no guarantee before she signed on hardwork's dotted line. She worked hard not because of an idealistic payoff, but because that's who she was and what she valued. Doing hardwork for hardwork's sake is something that may today seem at best a bit old fashioned and at worst altogether pointless, but it was paramount to her. She became an actress because she wanted to be one, and she became so dedicated to that dream that the personal hardship she faced did not keep her from attaining it. I don't know that she herself would see that as the remarkable thing it is in light of the challenges that threatened that dream so often throughout her life. I don't know that she would agree with my interpretation of her as a pioneer for women and a historical figure to be hailed. She seemed to naturally exude humility, and I don't think she was intentionally trying to crusade or champion any cause with her life story, though she certainly did.

As a woman, Virginia led an incredibly beautiful and tragic life. She persevered as a full-time working mother who pioneered through two divorces, breast cancer, and widowhood during the 1940s-1960s, a time in which women were still wrestling to find their voices in the American justice system, in the media industry, and in the world. She believed so fervently in her dream to be an actress, she overcame tremendous personal struggles while staying steadily dedicated to her children, and to a linear presence in media, which is certainly something to be hailed.

After a friend of mine persevered through a particularly difficult season of life, I once asked, "How did you make it through that?" to which they replied, "I didn't know not to." I think that explanation may also apply to several of Virginia's hardships. She wasn't an intentional pioneer or feministic crusader in how she lived her life; she was simply doing what she believed at the time was the right thing, and thus a story was written that up until now has not been fully told. She was so grounded in herself that she faced adversity with natural conviction and grit in order to continue on toward her decided life goals. In other words, she knew hardship might cause some damage, but she refused to let it derail the dream. In a world where goals and convictions can be so ambiguous and so fluid, I personally appreciate someone of such rigor.

In interviewing many of her colleagues, even if they remembered no specifics of the production in which they worked with her, they immediately recalled Virginia as the consummate professional and ever gracious friend. Her reputation in the industry endures as a grounded dichotomy of professional and friend. She is remembered as a fabulously talented, hardworking, versatile, and committed actress, yet always an accessible motherly confidant ready to be a shoulder to cry on, and the go-to fixer and mender for all malfunctions in media and in the human experience. She could offer a steady shoulder and kind words to keep a distressed fellow cast (or crew) member focused through a script, turn to repair the intricate workings of Stacy Harris' sacred gold cigarette lighter, and moments later flood the airwaves with sobbing sincerity if the script called for it. She could tune the orchestra members' instruments, work out technical kinks for the engineers, brew the studio coffee, and come back to her chair to complete a perfect pearl stitch on her latest handiwork in between her turns at the mic. The consensus among her coworkers in the radio world was: "If it's broken, go see Ginny." The always patient, understanding, collected, and prepared, Virginia was the proverbial girl scout whom everyone considered their best friend. In getting to know her through this research process, I really don't think she had the ability to be any other way.

Even in its very structure, her biography is a reflection of her: perhaps more essence than black and white fact. She was so very private in the way she lived her life, intentionally leaving admirers with more questions than answers many times. As the *LA Times* said in a December 1958 feature on Virginia: she was "recognized by many, known by few."[5] She was so busy tending to the world – perhaps intentionally – that there was no time or space left for the world to tend to her. True to Virginia, I have found she left very few clues behind as to who she was behind the thousands of stories she told through her craft that were not her own. Perhaps she did not truly want to be seen or known despite being in the public's eye and earshot for nearly fifty years in her career.

She hid well behind the media masks, and while I have great respect for her privacy, I believe what we know of her life story too good to keep tucked behind those masks despite any modest objections she might have in the hereafter. I just so happen to be the type of postmodern "Gladys Kravitz" who would dare to unmask her, simply because I think what is underneath is more beautiful and more compelling than any mask she ever wore (*especially* more so than the one given to her character "Emily Harper" in *The Twilight Zone's* infamous episode "The Masks"). Truth is often stranger than fiction and more interesting. It is my hope that through this presentation of her life, certain gaps will be filled even if only by showcasing that rather remarkable essence. Sixty years later in response to *The LA Times* story mentioned above, perhaps this biography can serve to change the headline to "Virginia Gregg, recognized by many, known by a few more."

In her character acting craft, she was focused on the process rather than the outcome, the proverbial journey rather than the destination. Virginia's middle son, Jaime, said his mother never wanted to be anyone's hero, but that's exactly what makes her the perfect archetype for one because she was in fact so dedicated to the very art of art that she accomplished far more than many of her associates who perhaps were more concerned with an end goal of fame and fortune. That's one of the things that sets Virginia apart from others present in the industry during her active years. She had a talent that could absolutely have catapulted her to the proverbial "top," and yet she chose to stay in the laborious positions of character acting with little recognition beyond her immediate circles, as fellow actor and good friend Parley Baer said, "We are known from coast-to-coast as 'what's-their-names.'"[6] While I in no way intend to crusade on behalf of Virginia to posthumously turn her into the Mother Teresa of media, I do believe she has an important story that should be told. After all, passing down personal legacy is where the true recognition lies for us all. Who do *we* want to be remembered as and what are we going to do *today* in order to further our own legacies? (When a former therapist writes a biography, these are the kinds of questions you'll have to wrestle with as you read along).

The great irony of Virginia's story is that she decidedly wasn't a star, but absolutely could have been. In fact, she so greatly resented the insinuation that she was a star that she scolded middle son Jaime when he was very young after overhearing him tell a friend, "My mother is a movie star," to which she immediately pulled him aside and chided, "You don't say that. I am not a star. I am an *actress*," and the "actresses' actress" was an even better title, according to Jack Webb.

JACK

The legendary Jack Webb, most recognized as producer and director of the *Dragnet* franchise, as well as for his portrayal of the show's stoic detective "Sgt. Joe Friday," knew and worked with Virginia for over thirty years on myriad productions. In an interview with prolific broadcaster and historian Chuck Schaden, Virginia estimated she appeared in between 65-75% of the *Dragnet* productions, though in reality that percentage is probably higher. It's rare to see an old *Dragnet* episode in which you don't find her in at least one frame. She might appear as a glamourous, manipulative socialite in one episode, and a homely, religious old maid in the next. She's often hard to spot in some episodes due to the extreme range of characters she played and the dramatic changes required for the submersion process according to each role. Her performances will leave you arguing with yourself for the rest of the day: "Was *that* Virginia Gregg?"

Virginia was a favorite of several kingpin producers like Jack who included her in their productions every time a role offer appealed to her nearly through to her retirement. Ranked among those who continuously cast her were such industry demigods like William "Bill" Conrad, Rod Serling, Alfred Hitchcock, Joseph Cotten, and Blake Edwards.

Virginia and Jack had a particularly grand friendship that was one of the most important of her life. Later in Jack's career, Virginia was once asked to speak at a Civic Pioneer Broadcasters event honoring him and his achievements. She initially declined the invitation to speak, as those sorts of engagements always brought on a bad case of the nerves. After declining, she "got that lousy feeling"[7] of guilt that made her change her mind. By the time she called the coordinator back to say she would be available to speak after all, others had already been booked to speak and they no longer needed her contribution. What she had planned to say on Jack's behalf at the event was better than any other commemorative speech that night I'm sure: "Jack Webb is my dear friend, my director, my producer, my mentor, my father, everything but my lover . . . *dammit*."[8]

Likewise, Virginia was an important person for Jack as well. She was his mooring – a stabilizing presence for him both personally and professionally. Her calm, steady nature was soothing to his high-strung temperament. She was one of the few people who never cowered at his rough, perfectionistic edges, and she could calm him even in the midst of one of his rampages for which he was known – rampages that were usually related to his perfectionistic proclivities in studio and on set. His intensity never intimidated her, and he knew it. Fellow actress and dear friend Peggy Webber gave a great example of Virginia's icebreaking capabilities with Jack during a readthrough once.

During a particular rehearsal of a *Dragnet* radio production, several cast members, including Peggy and Virginia, sat at the reading table going through their scripts in the ever-present cloud of cigarette smoke.[9] Suddenly, mid-scene, Jack shot up from the table in a rage directed primarily at one of the sound men over a technical blunder. As Jack berated the man in front of the cast and other crew members, the room fell quiet with that familiar heaviness everyone felt when a fellow coworker was being devoured by Jack's high expectations. As Jack's angry words flew at the sound man, all eyes at the reading table dropped to the respective laps of their owners. All except Virginia's. Her posture and gaze never changed as Jack loudly raved, tearing this man apart with angry word by angry word. She just sat dragging on her cigarette, unamused at his display. No one said anything, barely allowing themselves to breathe as Jack continued in his lecture about the man's "incompetence." The sound man's head dropped lower and lower with each throaty barrage of Jack's. After several minutes of letting his temper run rampant, Jack's voice stopped just as suddenly as it erupted, and the man stood slumped and humiliated, afraid to move. In true Virginia-fashion, she took the collective silence as her icebreaking cue. She leaned in toward Peggy with one elbow on the table, and simply said, "Jewish" with a facetiously knowing nod. Upon hearing her one-word evaluation of his outburst, Jack turned and saw her sitting tall and assured in her assessment of his behavior, and the rage that had consumed him just seconds before immediately melted with a hearty laugh bursting from everyone including Jack and the man who had just been eaten alive. The laughter was a tension release for the entire room and served as a collective reset button so the air once again was heavy only with cigarette smoke and not the emotional upset of an entire studio. Virginia was funny, and she was very keen on taking opportunities to peace-make in the face of discontent. The best part of the icebreaking zinger Virginia delivered to throw Jack off his angry raid was that everyone knew Jack was, in fact, *not* Jewish.[10]

Born John Randolph Webb on April 2, 1920 in Santa Monica, California, Jack really didn't know much about his heritage. He was born fatherless and poverty stricken; as a result, survival was the only aspiration for Jack growing up on either side of the Great Depression as the sole supporter of himself and his single mother. After high school he joined the Army but was discharged to continue providing for his family during World War II in his work at a steel mill and retail store.[11] His desperate beginnings developed in him an unremitting drive that served him well in becoming a powerful presence in Hollywood and in America media as an actor, director, screenwriter, and producer. Jack created *Dragnet* from the real police records of the Los Angeles Police Department (LAPD) and introduced the world to the inner dynamics of the true crime scene. Using his own production company, Mark VII Limited, he pioneered the development of crime shows that blurred the lines between realism and fantasy. While *Dragnet* storylines were in fact created from actual events found in LAPD files, Jack gave us the often-abhorrent details of our own city streets all across the nation. He gave us the gritty facts in provocative narrative form, so we were being educated while being thrilled, yet too intrigued by the story to know it.

Hailed by both the LAPD and general audiences, Jack became a significant liaison between civil servants and the public at large by providing up-close peeks into the plight of police officers and emergency workers. No other person in the industry had done what he had to that point, though many followed his lead in subsequently developing similar shows. Acclaimed director and producer, Jaime del Valle, (also Virginia's second husband) later expanded on Jack's idea in his development of the 1950's radio show *The Lineup*, but Jack was by all accounts the first to capitalize on this idea with *Dragnet*'s radio run from 1949 to 1957.[12] Jack's innovative approach to creating true-crime radio and television gave the industry an archetype for subsequent series and landed him two stars on the Hollywood Walk of Fame.[13] Plus, his "Sgt. Friday" was just so darn likeable in all of his dry fervency that a powerful cultural mnemonic was subtly created in the minds of the public that perhaps if we could like "Friday," we might could think a bit more favorably toward the cops in our own communities. In recent years, *Dragnet* has faced retrospective criticism for espousing a preachy, right-winged perspective in its depiction of the good guys vs. the bad. Despite this perspective, it was a damn good show and one that forged the way in part for others we enjoy today in the genre of crime dramas. After nearly fifty years in the business, Jack died at 62 of a heart attack on December 23, 1982.

Jack was fiercely loyal to friends like Virginia on whom he could consistently rely, which is why she had such a pervasive presence in his shows, as one avid *Dragnet* viewer so crassly pointed out in her submission to the "Ask Dick Kleiner" column in a 1975 edition of the *Redlands Daily Facts*: "DEAR DICK: How come Jack Webb uses Virginia Gregg in so many of his productions? She got something on him?" Dick's response was a concise dispelling of the notion: "She happens to be a fine actress and she is part of what has come to be called 'Jack Webb's Stock Company.' Like many TV producers, he likes to use many of the same actors frequently, actors he knows are reliable and trouble-free."

Jack's stock company was made up of actors and actresses like Virginia Gregg and Peggy Webber on whom Jack knew he could consistently count to churn out quality, professional performances. Other well-known names in the company were Harry Bartell, Vic Perrin, Barney Phillips, Bill Johnstone, Herb Ellis, and Charles McGraw. This stock company formed organically in his hiring and rehiring the same talents to maintain the high quality of work he demanded. He recruited Virginia over and over for virtually all productions in which he was involved.[14] As she once said:

> I want to tell you a story about loyalty. I did, I guess, about 70-75% of the Dragnet TVs. I did practically all of the radio shows. And he had cast me again in something, and whoever was on the board that approves what they do said, 'Gosh you just used her.' And he said, 'I didn't tell you I'd give you the real person. I told you I would give you the best person I can get for you for this part. And Virginia Gregg is the best person I can get for this part. Don't tell me how to cast.' And that's how he stood up for his people.[15]

Jack said Virginia was one of his all-time favorite actresses and famously dubbed her "the actress's actress."

The LA Times *described Jack's great respect for Virginia's talent in this 1958 vignette:*

Jack Webb was so impressed with her [Virginia's] work that he told her to pick any one of the radio Dragnets *and star in its television version. She chose the only* Dragnet *story that has never been reshown.[16] It was the story of a young war bride who couldn't remain faithful while her husband was overseas and bore an illegitimate child. Virginia's main scene in the show lasted eight minutes, she was the only performer on camera. However, the episode was felt to be too shocking and was never repeated. It is regarded today as a TV-acting classic.[17]*

The story you have just read is true. No names were changed and no one was innocent.

CHAPTER 2: ILLINOIS CORNFIELDS

"A light wind swept over the corn, and all nature laughed in the sunshine."

-Anne Bronte

Virginia Lee Gregg was a small-town girl born in Harrisburg, Illinois on March 6, 1916. A closer neighbor to the Kentucky line than to the state capitol of Springfield, Harrisburg is the seat of Saline County in southern Illinois. Framed by the greens, yellows, and browns of the Illinois cornfields, and the thick foliage of the Shawnee National Forest, Harrisburg is a quaint, industrial town that was originally Piankashaw and Shawnee land.[18] Harrisburg was founded 1853 in part by its namesake, a native Tennessean named James Alexander Harris.[19] Harris was instrumental, along with other founding fathers in expanding the town from a single farmhouse, sawmill, and corn field beginning in the 1820s. The town's economy was primarily driven by agriculture and manufacturing, and soon after its 1853 establishment, coal mining began to define the town and drive its economic growth giving many residents their livelihood.

Harrisburg has many hardships in its history. The flood waters of the Ohio River ravaged the small town in 1937 when record rains that January caused the river to swell and flood surrounding areas, displacing nearly all Harrisburg residents. The historic "Flood of '37" took the lives of over 350 people in and around Saline County and left at least 1 million displaced across Illinois and in surrounding states.[20] The Ohio River waters destroyed countless homes, farms, and commercial structures across Harrisburg's townscape, and flooded portions of its coal mines, which greatly affected resident livelihood and local economy. This caused rebuilding efforts to slow in the face of mass unemployment. Harrisburg steadily rebuilt in the following years just before their coal mines met with another threat: "the progress of man." After WWII, companies like Peabody Energy were roving through rural America with "the world's largest shovel" to plunder natural resources in keeping up with high demand caused in part by the war. Much like Muhlenberg County, Kentucky referenced in the John Prine song, "Paradise," Harrisburg was a focal point for strip mining because of its rich coal resource.

More recently, a 2012 tornado hit Harrisburg on Leap Day of that year and demolished the town leaving eight dead and more than 100 severely injured throughout its eight-mile rampage.[21] Harrisburg made national headlines in the damage it sustained from the F4 category winds, being considered the worst tornado-related disaster in United States history since the Joplin, Missouri tornado of 2011 that took the lives of 160 people and injured over 1,000.[22] Harrisburg's mayor at the time of the deadly tornado, Eric Gregg, a relative of Virginia's, gallantly led the town through the disaster and rebuilding efforts. In the following days, Gregg assured his community they would recover and become stronger than ever before, and indeed they did. Today, there is no sign of any natural disaster ever having visited Harrisburg. It is a green, breathable town with friendly folks and a comfortable mix of postmodern advancement and historic preservation.

Harrisburg has since recovered from the ravages of the past, and today, is a quintessential town reminiscent of small-town America with hometown ballgames, front- porches, and church socials. It is home to a little over 9,000 today and retains the welcoming feel of an earlier time amid the corn stalks, and the oaks of the Shawnee Forest.

Virginia shares her hometown of Harrisburg with two other notables: the "kingpin of the Saline County underworld" during the prohibition era, Charlie Birger,[23] and the Walmart in which the

"Walmart Yodeling Kid" Mason Ramsey was discovered through his viral yodeling video that took the internet by storm in 2018.

CHARLIE BIRGER AND THE SHELTON GANG

Infamous mobster Charlie Birger and his bootlegging regime reigned supreme in Harrisburg during Virginia's early years. After World War I ended in 1918, in a theoretical effort to curb crime and arouse American society's sense of morality, the Volstead Act went into effect in 1920 and nationally banned the consumption, production, importation, transportation, and sale of alcohol. While the nation's evangelicals and temperance groups championed the act, it backfired in a sense, as it gave some the opportunity to capitalize on the liquor market left dry by the closing of saloons and bars across the country. Speakeasies and private underground liquor operations (better known as bootlegging in the North and Midwest and moonshining in the South) sprang up all around the country after the governmental closing of liquor businesses.

Under Wilson, Harding, Coolidge, and Hoover, national prohibition lasted from 1920- 1933, during which many individual bootleggers found unlikely havens, often rural areas like Harrisburg, in which to operate their hustles. The era of prohibition gave men like Al Capone, George Remus, William McCoy, Charles Luciano, and Charlie Birger their start in organized crime and our history books.

Birger was a shadowy contradiction still considered controversial in Illinois history. Among Harrisburg locals in particular, many recall him as a slim caricature of the devil incarnate, others, a well-meaning Robin Hood who just came upon bad break after bad break. The inexplicable dichotomy of Birger manifested through his Dillinger- style MO: cheerily handing out coins to local kids from the window of his Huckster having just returned to town from making a corpse out of a rival associate. A very young Virginia may have in fact been a recipient of one of Birger's random acts of kindness some afternoon while she skipped along the sidewalks of Harrisburg with her schoolmates. Having two girls of his own born around the same time as Virginia, Birger was especially fond of children often giving treats or pony rides to any who were interested. Children of town leaders and law enforcement were among his favorites to treat. He was well-known, and by many accounts, well-liked around Harrisburg and surroundings towns. He was a charming personality with an unassuming countenance, purportedly leaving one to immediately doubt rumors of his rap sheet upon meeting him: *but he's such a nice young man.* Since 1913, Birger was a devoted Harrisburg citizen, endearingly referring to it as "his hometown," though he was actually born in the Russian Empire and had lived in countless states since his family's migration to America in the 1880s.[24] Initially in Harrisburg, he worked as a miner in the coal mines and later became a local saloon keeper, but after WWI ended in 1919, prohibition began, which presented him with another career pivot: bootlegging. Despite this career change, he remained a devoted Harrisburg citizen, husband, and father. He was outrageously generous and civic minded, often coming to the aid of neighbors in supplying extra coal or food in winter.

Birger was an altruistic loose cannon, an impulsive contriver, whose acts of kindness were often grandiose and reckless with little thought given to consequences, in fact, his generosity could be downright unreasonable. Once, he decided to treat Harrisburg to the exotic cuisine of "real Oriental food."[25] Not bothering to see if a market for that type of food existed in the small rural community, Birger hired a Chinese chef from St. Louis to give Harrisburg residents the progressive delicacy of an authentic Chinese restaurant – something only available in the swanky big cities in the 1920s. Needless to say, the restaurant didn't last long, as Birger's need to impress was far greater than Harrisburg's need for Chinese food.

From his first visit to Harrisburg, Birger could be seen in local parades, chatting downtown with town officials on the square, gallantly opening doors with a tip of his hat for local ladies, or gaily helping a box boy with his loading duties.[26] He was an ever- philanthropic who just happened to carry a machine gun.

No kingpin mobster is any good without the loyal support of a gang. Birger collected quite a troop of local men in his bootlegging gig and made headquarters at Shady Rest – a roadhouse hideout halfway between Harrisburg and Marion on Route thirteen. Birger and his gang blazed through the Midwest leaving behind a sordid trail of much more than receipts from their manufacturing and distributing liquor. Prostitution and gambling came with the bootlegger's territory, and if one is successful in any type of business, he will undoubtedly face a little market competition. In Birger's escapades, he and his gang quickly developed a heated rivalry with the equally infamous Shelton Brothers.

Ben and Agnes Shelton were a rural Illinois couple who had ten children on a Wayne County farm in the late 1800s. Three of their children Carl, Earl, and Bernie made up what a 1950's article in *The Saturday Evening Post* famously called "America's Bloodiest Gang." The three began their spree of crime in small-time scrapes with the law, and eventually saw great potential in Prohibition, much like Birger had. The Sheltons initially ran their bootlegging operation out of St. Louis, but gradually encroached on other prime territories closer to their Wayne County homestead. Southern Illinois' "Little Egypt" region, which includes Harrisburg, was prime real estate in the eyes of both gangs, and a mutual hate grew into bloody gang wars.

In addition to hating each other, Birger's boys and the Sheltons had two other common enemies: the law and the Ku Klux Klan. For all their lawlessness, the one shining credit to both gangs was their mutual attempt at overthrowing the KKK's heavy presence in "Little Egypt." Though founded in 1865, the KKK made a resurgence during Prohibition. In the 1920s, the KKK was preoccupied with eliminating Blacks, Catholics, and immigrants, all of whom were perceived threats to "White Protestant nationalism."[27] In their crusade against these people groups, the KKK used Prohibition to accuse, raid, torment, and kill those they targeted.

Though on rampages of their own, the Birger and Shelton boys vehemently opposed the revival of gruesome Klan rampages that permeated through southern and midwestern communities in the early 1900s. As immigrants themselves, Birger's Russian heritage and the Shelton's Irish heritage undoubtedly influenced feelings toward the Klan, though conscience evaded them when it came to their own cruelties. Many believe the gangs' interest in eliminating the KKK may have had more to do with self-preservation and capital than social justice. If the KKK raided their customers or tipped police off to their own operations, that meant less market share for them and the potential for their own arrests. Though the gangs committedly hated each other, if nothing else, it was a smarter business move to join forces against the Klan than to risk possible incrimination as individual entities. Chicago may have been gangland headquarters in the 1920s, but the cornfields of Southern Illinois saw just as much bloodshed as the streets of Chicago.

Despite Birger's valiant position against the sadistic acts of the KKK, he himself had his own flavor of sadism. He stole, blackmailed, gambled, coerced, bombed, bribed, kidnapped, and killed all across Southern Illinois leaving a path of corpses and terrified townspeople. To him, all was justified in his philosophy: "I've killed many men, but never a good one."[28]

He was shrewd in not only warring against his enemies and conquering land and market he saw as his own, but also in dodging the law on technicalities. As far as law and order were concerned, Birger was the Harry Houdini of Harrisburg. He escaped the gavel on numerous occasions and managed to charm his way out of close scrapes with government nearly all his life. After myriad shootouts and failed sneak attacks on his rivals (and even a failed costume attack on Earl Shelton during a brief hospital stay of his in which some of Birger's men dressed as lady visitors to do him in), Birger briefly put down the machine gun and used a different weapon to ultimately bring down the Sheltons. He used the Scales of Justice themselves. He heroically tipped off police to the Sheltons' involvement in a mail carrier robbery in 1925 in which the gang killed an elderly mail carrier and made off with $15,000. Thanks in part to Birger's testimony, the brothers were tried and convicted of the murder/robbery and each sentenced to twenty-five years in prison. The Sheltons' sentence was a grand victory for Birger, as he could finally claim Southern Illinois as his exclusive territory with the competition out of the way. With their leaders behind bars, the gang's momentum slowly dissipated, and Birger and his boys reigned supreme.

It was a short-lived reign, as those same Scales of Justice that found the Sheltons guilty, finally found Birger himself guilty too just a few months into his term as bootlegging czar of Illinois. West City Mayor Joe Adams allegedly had involvement with the Shelton gang, and thus was one of Birger's targets. In December 1926, Birger hired two of his boys, brothers Elmo and Harry Thomasson - who at the time were mere teenagers - to kill Adams. They did, but then fingered Birger for their hiring. Birger was arrested in June 1927. The law was much more lenient with the Thomasson boys than Birger; they were handed down prison sentences, but Birger was sentenced to death by hanging.[29]

On April 19, 1928, at the age of forty-seven, Birger was hanged in Benton, Illinois, some thirty miles northwest of Harrisburg. More than 500 people bought tickets to attend the public hanging and watched as this legendary Angel of Darkness was proven by a rope to be a mere mortal after all. Many were glad to finally see this mad delinquent brought to justice, while others were outraged at the law's heavy hand against a misunderstood martyr. There are many legends around Birger's behavior the day of his hanging. By many accounts, he calmly allowed himself to be led through the crowds to the platform, shaking hands with townspeople as he made his way to finally shake hands with his own mortality. As a black hood slipped over Birger's head – he refused the usual white hood lest he be associated with the KKK – he gallantly said, "It's a beautiful world. I've forgiven everybody."[30] True to the mobster's code, he died without pleas, emotion, or even a sound. Birger was the last man to be publicly hanged in Illinois state.

With Birger's gang and the Sheltons shooting over the heads of townsfolk, Harrisburg was anything but the peaceful, rural Midwest town it appeared in the 1920s. A passerby might not have noticed the latent tension of violence and gunpowder, but locals lived among the unease until Birger was assuredly pronounced dead. While Virginia's family was certainly aware of the constant threat of the gang wars like everyone else in town, because of the Greggs' prominence in the community, they may have understood and encountered Birger from a unique vantage point. Virginia's second cousin, Thomas Young "T.Y." Gregg, Sr. was president of The Harrisburg National Bank, of which Birger was a frequent patron when bootlegging was good. T.Y. was also mayor of Harrisburg from 1915-1919 like his descendant Eric Gregg many years subsequent.[31]

T.Y. humored Birger like any savvy banker would do to keep the money rolling in, however ill-gotten it may have been. No doubt Virginia's family knew Birger and his family, though the Greggs happened to be on the opposite side of the law.

ROOTS

Virginia's mother, Dewey Alphaleta Todd Gregg, was born July 15, 1898 in Saline County Illinois to Hugh Erwin Todd and Luella "Tennessee" Ross Todd. Virginia's family roots through the Todd line run deep in the South and Midwest states even intersecting with the family branch of Mary Todd Lincoln, wife of the 16th President of the United States, Abraham Lincoln. The Todds have a rich English and Scottish heritage, with many of Virginia's ancestors settling in New England in the 1600s before subsequent generations migrated south to Kentucky, Tennessee, and eventually backtracking north a bit to Illinois. Virginia's family's Ross line originally settled in Virginia in the 1700 and early 1800s, moving to North Carolina in the 1830s making the southern sweep into Missouri, Kentucky, and Tennessee before Hugh and Luella, called Saline County home. Dewey was the baby of ten children.

Virginia's father, Edward William Gregg, was born June 23, 1890 in Harrisburg, Illinois to William Gregg and Alcesta Cornelia "Nelia" Grace Gregg both of Saline County. The Greggs are of thick Irish blood having migrated from Ireland to the Newberry County South Carolina settlement in the 1700s. The Greggs eventually moved north to Illinois in the 1860s. The Graces migrated from Middlesex in the 1600s to New England with subsequent generations making a southern sweep similar to the Ross line, eventually ending up in Illinois as well. Edward was the youngest of four boys: Thomas, Roy, and an infant boy that died shortly after birth. Both the Todds and the Greggs were upper-middle class families in Saline County, and their lineages still have enduring visibility in the community today.

Dewey married Edward Gregg on December 12, 1914 in Saline County when she was sixteen and he was twenty-four. Two years after marrying, Dewey gave birth to their only child on March 6, 1916. While almost named "Georgia Rose," "Virginia Lee" was ultimately chosen for the lanky blonde-haired, blue-eyed girl full of English, Irish, and Scottish legacy. Virginia's name was developed from a host of namesakes on both sides of the family. There were many ancestral "Virginias" before her, and the moniker "Ginny Lee" fit the little golden girl just right.

Virginia's family in Harrisburg was close. Virginia's grandparents, the Greggs, lived in the center of town on E. Poplar Street in a monstrous, picturesque plantation home of the 1800s.[32] Virginia lived with her parents at 325 E. Locust Street where a historical marker honoring her stands today. Her home on E. Locust Street backed up to her paternal grandparents' E. Poplar home. After the death of her maternal grandfather, Hugh Todd in 1919, when Virginia was three years old, "Grandma Luella" aka "Tennessee Todd" came to live with Virginia and her parents. She had one grandparent in her living room and from her backyard, could peek through the fence slats alongside the chickens and see her other grandparents' towering mansion. Many of her aunts and uncles lived within blocks of each other around the square that housed many of their family-owned businesses. Virginia grew up in a lively extended network of family. They did life together daily, with church choir practices, Sunday suppers, and songs around the family piano. Harrisburg was a happy place with many "dear hearts and gentle people" who loved "little Ginny Lee Gregg."

Dewey, Virginia, and Edward Gregg, circa 1917.
Photo courtesy of Jaime del Valle.

Virginia's paternal second cousin, T.Y., Sr. was president of Harrisburg National Bank and mayor for a period of time, as mentioned in the section on Charlie Birger. Her paternal uncle, Thomas "T.D." Gregg, was a well-known pharmacist in Harrisburg.

Around 1910, he bought out the Rexall drugstore around the square and was known as the quintessential friendly neighborhood druggist and optometrist for the next forty years. He and Virginia remained close after she left Harrisburg, and he often traveled to California to visit her and other family members who also preferred sunny California to the Illinois cold. Upon one particular trip, "Uncle T.D." was given the VIP treatment and shadowed Virginia throughout her typical studio workday, and the local paper, *The Daily Register*, reported on his experience when he returned. He sat in for several of Virginia's radio shows while there and even met the legendary Jack Webb. T.D. was of a softer sort than Virginia's

Virginia Lee Gregg, circa 1920. Photo courtesy of Jaime del Valle.

father Edward, and she found his gentle nature a bit more relatable than Edward's stoicism. Much like Virginia, T.D. was ever the caretaker, remembering her in his will when he died in 1959 at the age of eighty-one. Virginia's other paternal uncle, Roy, was a banker in Eldorado, and for a time ran a car business in Harrisburg. Roy and his wife Olive "Ollie" moved to California not long after Virginia's parents did with their son William, and two daughters, Helen and Dorothy, who were close to Virginia's age.

The girls were close friends while growing up and were housemates in the 1940s.

It was typical for Virginia to see her family's name headlined in the local Harrisburg paper whether for their dinner parties, social events, civic contributions, or even their health updates. Her family's culture was understood through a White, upper-class lens with Kiwanis Club elections, town hall meetings, sewing classes, rotary

Virginia Lee Gregg, circa 1920. Photo courtesy of Jaime del Valle.

events, and choir practices. The women in her family were home-makers and civic leaders in local women's clubs, knitting circles, and church friendship classes. The men of her family were self-starting small-business owners who served on the county boards and councils in their down time. Before the proverbial "Joneses," there were the Greggs. The family's prominence made it difficult for Virginia to go anywhere as a young girl without happy greetings from locals who also seemed like family.

She grew up around the piano with her mother and father both trained pianists and singers and learned to play and sing very early herself. Her aunts and uncles regularly performed together in a local quartet, and T.Y. Gregg Jr.'s wife Gretta, gave piano lessons to children in the community and often performed at the First Presbyterian Church. Those early years with music as a constant surely influenced Virginia's symphony career years later in Pasadena. With symbolic piano accompaniment, Virginia's early life was a slow swirl of family suppers, lazy Sunday afternoons, backyard chickens, and sidewalk jump-rope with neighbor kids, making her childhood the conventional reflection of small-town America in the early 1910-20s.

As an only child, Virginia and her mother, Dewey, were very close. Dewey was a homemaker, and community caretaker. She was a kind and gentle spirit, cooking and mending with an easy, even tempo. The two had a grand friendship as mother and daughter; Virginia often recalled their merry times around the piano teaching the family dog to play for grapes. She also recalled the fun they had feeding the chickens in the backyard. Dewey was Virginia's caregiver, playmate, companion, and ever-present anchor, while Edward was the pragmatic. He was focused, and brooding, distanced by his stoicism. Virginia admired her father and his commanding way, but her mother was her solace. After Dewey's untimely death when Virginia was just nineteen years old, Virginia still treasured Dewey's jewelry, proudly wearing many of her pieces as part of her every day. In several studio prints and television and film productions a ring of Dewey's can be seen on Virginia's left pinky. She also often wore her mother's cameo necklace and single dangling pearl until her own death.

Virginia and Dewey Gregg, circa 1920. Photo courtesy of Jaime del Valle.

CHAPTER 3: SUNNY CALIFORNIA

"It's the artist's business to create sunshine when the sun fails."

-Romain Rolland

In 1921, at the age of twenty-three, Dewey was diagnosed with tuberculosis.

Virginia was only 5. A TB or "consumption" diagnosis even in the 1920s was practically a death sentence – often a slow one. Certainly, consumption's peak of the 1800s had passed with improved living conditions, hygiene, and medical research in the United States, but it still was a deadly condition that struck impartially among social classes with grave prognosis. The death rate of TB patients had slowed compared to its earlier peak, but alongside cardiovascular disease, influenza, and pneumonia in the early 1900s, TB was still considered one of the leading causes of death in the United States. Many who were diagnosed lived less than five years, as treatment options were still in their infancies or unavailable in particular regions.[33]

Just shy of a year after Dewey's diagnosis, the Greggs packed up their E. Locust home in Harrisburg along with the only world Virginia had ever known, and with six- year-old Virginia in tow, they moved to California. Virginia's "Grandma Luella" stayed behind and moved in with other Harrisburg relatives. It was a pilgrimage to the hope of prolonged life. Like many other families of the early 20th century, the Greggs believed in the Promised Land narrative of "Sunny California." With limited medical treatment compared to today's world, California was a mythological beacon of sorts for those with incurable ailments, the proverbial "Pool of Bethesda" in curing conditions of the body, mind, and even soul, including consumption. The idea was that the California sun and dry climate had healing properties untold, and if one could just make it to the West, they would see vast improvement in their symptoms and even prolong their life. Leaving Harrisburg was undoubtedly difficult for the family of three, not just because of the reason for the exodus, but because they would be leaving behind the only hometown the three of them had ever known. It must have been terribly difficult for a six-year-old Virginia to close the door for the last time and bid farewell to many family members she would never see again. California was lightyears away from the comfortable sanctuary of Harrisburg that held the sum of little "Ginny Lee's" existence. It's unclear how much her parents initially told her about her mother's diagnosis and the true reason for their move, but certainly it is difficult for all children to depart from everything they have ever known and move a world away with no prospect of return. Moving meant no more sidewalk frolics with lifelong neighborhood friends, no more backyard games with peeks through the fence at Grandmother and Grandfather Gregg's house, no more playing with chickens, no more strolls around the town square, or afternoon visits to Uncle T.D.'s drugstore for an ice cream soda.

Until the 1930s, air travel was primarily for mail, not families migrating across country, so most likely the Greggs had to leave behind a good portion of their larger belongings, including the beloved family piano that Virginia had played with her mother for hours on end – the piano that had symbolically accompanied all her favorite childhood memories. The three loaded what they could and bade farewell to family and neighbors in a tearful, but hopeful journey toward the healing that so promisingly lie at the end of the 1,937-mile course. Relatives drove the trio to the Chicago train station where they boarded the *Californian* for the West.

The Greggs arrived in Altadena, California after days of seeing the countryside from a boxcar view. They didn't have the dense familial connectedness that they were used to in Harrisburg, but they did have some Saline County family who had made a similar migration to California so they weren't entirely lonewolfers. They had arranged for life to resume as normally as possible upon their arrival in California. Edward worked for the railroad in Harrisburg but got on as foreman with Richfield Oil at the Signal Hill plant after the move where he worked for the next twenty-two years, and Virginia started school at John Fremont Grammar School in Long Beach. It is reasonable to assume that the Greggs may have chosen an Altadena address due to the proximity of the La Vina Sanatorium, a promising, innovative facility that specialized in the treatment of tuberculosis, incorporating those romanticized benefits of California's climate.

It is unknown if Dewey was actually a patient in La Vina, or any sanatorium for that matter, but the Greggs were certainly affluent enough to afford treatment from such a facility, and with it so near to their California settlement, it is plausible. If she were a sanatorium patient, she did not have prolonged stays, as she would have wanted to be involved with Virginia's daily life at all costs, and it is documented that she was indeed functional enough at the beginning of their California move to go about some of her normal duties around the house and within the community, as she was listed among the first women to vote after the 19th amendment to the Constitution was ratified in 1920.

From 1922 to 1935, the Greggs moved from house to apartment to bungalow to boarding house with one change of address after the other. Most of their listed addresses were all within a ten-mile radius. Edward maintained the same position at his job during those years, so it seems the frequent moves were not job-related. It is plausible to assume the moves may have had something to do with Dewey's diagnosis, as the multiple residence listing stop upon her death in 1935.

In the 1920s, a great stigma was attached to tuberculosis. There was still limited understanding around the disease and many cultural rumors developed from that limited understanding that caused TB patients to experience serious reproach if their condition were known. The primary outward symptoms of the disease can include fever often causing rosy cheeks, fatigue, weight loss, and of course the distinct cough. If "the cough" was heard in public, a subtle panic raced through the crowd, even in sunny California.

The cough was something to be stifled at all costs because it could mean your job, your home, or even your freedom. Because Edward remained with the same company and job site during their family's moves, it is plausible that the frequent moves may have been in part due to landlords or neighbors discovering Dewey's condition through the persistent, heavy cough that is impossible to mask for long. After her mother's diagnosis, Virginia was beginning to understand a strange form of prejudice that she had never encountered, all the while she watched as her mother faded a little more each day into the grasp of this incurable disease. Writer Constance Manoli-Skocay describes it most poetically during its 19th century reign: "It was a disease that reflected the culture of its time: the victim slowly, gracefully fading away, transcending their corporeal body, their immortal soul shining through." Surely, Virginia felt as though she were having to hide her mother's condition and as children tend to unknowingly carry the burdens of their family systems, the happy, golden girl of Harrisburg was becoming a hardened adult far too young.

Certainly, there was a looming fear that Edward and/or Virginia might also be infected with the disease, so there were rigid protocols the family had to follow birthed out of assumptions of the day: TB patients had separate beds, dishes, and personal effects from other family members to reduce the spread. They also followed strict guidelines for hygiene and housekeeping to avoid infecting others. Gone were the days of Virginia being able to run to Dewey in childlike freedom and impulsivity for a warm embrace or deluge of kisses. Edward in his pragmatic stoicism did little to fill the gap of affection Virginia had left by the drastic changes in the family.

As Dewey weakened, Virginia assumed more and more of the household responsibilities, and with Edward's focus on providing for his family and making sure Dewey had everything she needed, he had little consolation for his young daughter's grief. There's no doubt Virginia fell asleep many nights to the sound of her mother's cough, wishing for the former days of childhood of backyard adventures, Illinois dandelions, and the sweet sound of her mother's busy singing coming from the kitchen while she fiddled with jacks at Grandma Luella's feet in the living room. Life in California for "Ginny Lee" was fraught with loneliness and worry. She grew up under the dark cloud of that dichotomy; where there was once cheerful piano accompaniment to life's narrative in Harrisburg, there was only silence in California.

Virginia's solace was school, for at school, she could be exactly what she was: a kid. She threw herself into her schoolwork, extra-curricular activities like sports and music, and learned to balance her roles as child by day, adult by night. She had two distinct trainings: school and homelife, and a great chasm existed between the two. She learned the academic basics all children learn, but she also learned about urban life, crime, self-sufficiency, public transit, budgeting, laundry, cooking, and the constant, anxious housekeeping to reduce any potential transfer of germs that the TB infection might produce. The Greggs were certainly well off enough to afford a housekeeper, but with Dewey's condition, they were hard pressed to find someone willing to work in close quarters with a TB patient, so the responsibility fell on Virginia. Beyond learning arithmetic and spelling, she managed two different identities during her formative years.

California taught her a great deal about phenomena she had never experienced in Illinois. She learned about earthquakes, urban labor strikes, multiculturalism. She was introduced to colorful people and cultures. Harrisburg in the 1920s was a primarily middle to upper class White community, and Southern California was one of the most diverse areas in the United States. Virginia's new home introduced her to people of all colors, races, religions, lifestyles, and socioeconomic statuses. Southern California has always been greatly influenced by the Latin and Hispanic peoples in myriad migration waves through the decades, and Virginia's Irish-blood suddenly stood out among her schoolmates and neighbors. This early education in diversity served her well, as she developed an early unconditional respect for all cultures and ways of life. She made no difference between people groups in terms of her friendship and sense of fairness. She treated the new kid in school who happened to be a Jewish immigrant the same as the popular Black girl who was her senior classman. She had a large, diverse friend group that seemed untimely for the 1920s-1930s. Virginia had a unique vantage point of segregation and discrimination (even with regard to the prejudice shown to her own family with her mother's diagnosis), which developed in her a lifelong passion for human rights, equality, and social justice. She was by no means color blind; she was an intentional human lover, and that meant making no difference in humans of all sorts. She didn't care if you were gay, straight, religious, agnostic, Black, White, Asian, or ascribed to no particular identity at all, if she was your friend, she was your friend for life. Although it seems as she got older, she did show a bit of favoritism toward heterosexual, tall, dark, and handsome men in her lover selection, but that would have been her one and only partiality, and who could blame her?

STREET-SMART

The education she received in her new home was hard-earned and perhaps not always age-appropriate, though later in life those lessons seemed to serve her well. Because of her family's situation, she became street-smart too early in finding her way to and from school in Southern California's flat, wide region where everything was scattered. In Harrisburg, everything Virginia needed and knew was within a few blocks' walk from her home. In California, her Long Beach school was at least a thirty-minute drive from her homes in and around Altadena. Streetcars were the primary means of Californian's public transportation in the 1920s, and as a small child she was navigating the streetcar lines and times to ensure she was at school on time in the mornings, and back home on time in the evenings to care for her mother before Edward got home from work. Edward's work was also quite a trek from their home addresses in the Altadena area, so as Virginia was boarding one streetcar for school, he may have been boarding another in the opposite direction toward Signal Hill. The Greggs eventually bought a motorcar to navigate the geography a little more independently, but in the early days of the western-move, Virginia was charged with a necessary self-sufficiency far beyond her age even in the practicalities like getting herself to and from school. It wasn't an ideal education for any young girl, but it was all she had.

After Virginia's family had called Altadena home for those first few years, Edward's brother, Roy, joined them in sunny California with his wife Ollie, and their children William, Helen, and Dorothy. Virginia was great friends with first cousins Helen and Dorothy who were close in age. No doubt their presence in the West was more than welcomed.

Despite her hardships, like most people, Virginia grew up anyway. She excelled in school, sports, music, and social aptitude. She was friendly and well-liked among her peers even at an early age. She was a tall, calm presence in the school crowd, but approachable and blended in well with her peers as a team player. Since before she could remember, she had dreamed of becoming an actress and was dedicated even at a young age to learning all she could about the craft, so she picked up dramatics and humanities courses every chance she got.

Virginia first attended school at John Fremont Grammar School in Long Beach, and then went on to Washington Junior High School where she met her best friend for the next several years: the double bass viol. She started in seventh grade at Thomas Jefferson High School in Los Angeles and graduated in 1933. Afterward she went on to attend Pasadena Junior College, now known as Pasadena City College, where she majored in dramatics. After junior college, she studied at the Pacific Academy of Dramatic Arts where she won a scholarship for acting.

During her schooling at Washington Junior High school, Virginia showed interest in joining the orchestra, not through the assumed means of great musical intrigue, but through necessity: like any red-blooded American girl, she wanted to get out of a particularly boring class, and the orchestra seemed like an easy alternative. Her assignment was the tall, bulky, less than glamourous double bass viol. It might not have been her first choice, but rising to the occasion, she learned it and apparently became so good throughout junior high, high school, and college that she was hired by the Pasadena Symphony and Pops in the 1930s. Being a symphony player is quite an accomplishment even for musicians who have been committed to an instrument for entire lifetimes, much less a few years in school based on a random instrument assignment.[34]

Virginia recalled her seventh-grade year as the highlight of her schooling.

Reporter Tom E. Danson wrote the following based on an interview with Virginia in her early radio days:

It was while in the seventh grade at Jefferson High that Virginia remembers having the most fun. She loved sports and excelled as pitcher on the baseball team. Her specialty was a fast curve and Long Beach teen-agers had their own particular version of the tragedy of Casey-at-the-Bat when they stepped to home plate to face the blue-eyed Gregg gal with the super-duper pitch.

Baseball was far from the only sport she showed promise in. She was an avid sportswoman in athletic competitions of all types throughout high school. She enjoyed swimming, basketball, tennis, and track. Tennis was a particular favorite she continued playing well into her 60s.

Thomas Jefferson High School in Los Angeles was founded in 1916 and is considered one of the oldest public high schools in the LA school district. On March 10 of 1933, a Long Beach earthquake of 6.4 magnitude demolished several buildings on the Jefferson High campus. At age seventeen in 1933, Virginia would have been a senior at the time of the earthquake. According to the *LA Times*, following the earthquake, the school remained closed for nearly two months while the school board decided how to proceed with the remainder of the school year without certain buildings. On April 6, the school reopened with fifteen to twenty tents erected on the football field in place of the buildings that had been demolished. Students attended classes in the tents on a rotation schedule, so the entire student body was able to fulfill their school requirements.[35] I'm sure as an Illinois-native, the California earthquakes were other foreign forces to be reckoned with for a young Virginia, much like other phenomena of the era: The Great Depression and the Dust Bowl.

After graduating high school in early 1933, she began junior college in the Fall of that year. She was accepted into the symphony orchestra at Pasadena Junior College – she was second seat from principal even as a freshman. She was also an active member of the Shakespearean Club[36] receiving grand reviews in pre-women's liberation-style, "Virginia Gregg, sharing honors with the men, presented a dialogue between Katharine and Petruchio from Shakespeare's 'Taming of the Shrew.'[37]" Victors were each given a leather volume of Shakespeare's works. She won Pasadena Junior College's "Forensics Doolittle Contest" – a contest sponsored by the parents of a dramatics student, Ruth Doolittle, who died in 1925 while a student in the dramatic arts at Pasadena Junior College.[38]

Pacific Academy of Dramatic Arts is no longer in existence, but Virginia was trained in dramatics there after her time in junior college and continued in her work at the Pasadena Playhouse. Virginia was the ever-focused and dedicated student, and a favorite of both her instructors and peer group: you know, the stereotypical "good-at-everything-gal." Even though she was quite popular, she didn't date much in her high school and early college years. Virginia described her younger self in less than flattering terms:

> *I was quite overweight when I was younger, and I felt I couldn't look attractive no matter what I wore. So I went to the extreme with this attitude. This can develop into a problem, because eating becomes a kind of self-defense.*[39]

Though she did seem to naturally excel at almost everything, Virginia was a quiet and divided young person with little time for the frivolity of teenage nightlife of the 1930s. She spent what little downtime she had reading and practicing either the bass or her latest acting role either for her coursework or for the Pasadena Playhouse. She was referenced in the papers for certain performances and accomplishments even during her high school and college years such as her first-place win for her Shakespearean interpretation in an artist course presented with the Woman's Club of Hollywood in 1937.[40]

In addition to her acting classes and performances in school, her part-time acting work with the Pasadena Playhouse began in her teens. Since her early high school days, she often performed as a volunteer in roles on the Pasadena stage because not only was it great experience, but having one's name associated with the PP was compensation plenty. As she progressed in her craft, she landed many paying parts too.

PASADENA PLAYHOUSE

The Pasadena Playhouse is a big deal. It's not just your average live theatre venue; it is the official State Theatre of California. This place is steeped in the prestige, history, and vibrato of California's elite heritage. It was established in 1917 by a troupe called the Gilmor Brown Players in a rented "derelict old burlesque house" until 1924 when the community funded the much more permanent and opulent building where it sits today.[41] The Pasadena Playhouse has been instrumental in the launch of many notable acting careers. Virginia is in good company with other alumni such as Robert Young, Charles Bronson, Nick Nolte, Rue McClanahan, Leonard Nimoy, Dustin Hoffman, Gene Hackman, Jeanette Nolan, Tyrone Power, Jamie Farr, Raymond Burr, Barbara Rush, Eve Arden, and more recently Ariana Grande. Virginia treasured the memories of her time at the Pasadena Playhouse where she met many of her industry comrades in their own career infancies like Joel McCrea, Victor Mature, and Eve McVeagh. In her own Californian backyard, Virginia received world-class theatrical training that some travel the country to find, and even still don't make the cut.

By her dedicated efforts toward her dream of becoming an actress even as an adolescent, Virginia's shining path was sure. She earned wonderful opportunities hand over fist throughout her teens due to her incredible focus and talent; the newspapers already knew her name as an industry hopeful by the time she finished high school. As her dream was being realized more and more, surely her heart was full as she considered the path she had single-handedly paved for herself with little more than a dream, but there was a catch, a forlorn catch that stifled this budding prime. Dewey's condition greatly deteriorated in Virginia's late teens. The frail figure in the room next to Virginia was a waning distortion of the vibrant mother she remembered from her youth. Virginia still tended to Dewey and maintained all her household duties despite her additional obligations, but it was becoming clearer by the minute that the end was imminent.

MURDER

Then in June of 1934, there was the family's ax-murder matter. "Dear Dad: I have killed mother and Bob. I am going to tell the police."[42] It sounds like a line from *Yours Truly Johnny Dollar*, but it wasn't fiction. The Rude family from Harrisburg were intertwined with the Gregg family a few times over. The Rude's closest connection to Virginia was through her father's brother, Roy Gregg. He married Olive or "Ollie" Rude Gregg and eventually joined Virginia's family in California in the 1930s. The Rudes were a large family with deep, sprawling roots in Saline County much like the Greggs.

Virginia's Aunt Olive's sister Carrie was one of the Gregg's well-to-do "California kin" living in ritzy Westwood Hills. Carrie's husband Lucius Payne was the president of a utility company in St. Louis where the family lived with their two sons close to Virginia's age, Louis Rude Payne and Willis Robert "Bob" Payne. The Paynes were a well- respected family in both their heritage region of Illinois and their own settlement in St. Louis.

In 1931, Carrie's health began to fail, and like their cousins, the Greggs, they believed the California sunshine would be a sure remedy. Lucius bought a home near Huntington Beach, and the family spent the next year in sunny California while Lucius travelled between Missouri and California with the executive position he still held. In 1932, eldest son Louis was accepted to Washington University in St. Louis, and he and his father moved back to Missouri. Louis was a grand reflection of his father in having been a decorated boy scout and military academy graduate. He had a bright future, and Lucius took every opportunity to make sure he knew it. In 1933, when Louis was nineteen, he killed an elderly pedestrian in a hit-and-run while driving the family car late one evening. While he fled the scene initially, Louis turned himself in the next day to police. He was fined $200, and after pleading guilty, the judge released him.[43] The accident supposedly weighed heavily on young Louis and put the family in a tight reputational spot, so Lucius sent Louis back to California – into the sunshine and out of the spotlight – to be with his mother and brother. At first, the move seemed promising for Louis' heavy mind, and for the entire family. Carrie's condition had improved with the California climate, little Bob was doing well in junior high school, Louis' college studies transferred to a university close to Westwood Hills where he continued his studies, and Lucius didn't mind the travel for work. It was difficult for the family to only see Lucius for a few months at a time with his responsibilities still primarily in St. Louis, but the arrangement was the best money could buy.

On May 29, 1934, upon one of Lucius' trip back to St. Louis, Louis, then twenty- one, woke in the middle of the night one night with an unthinkable objective. He got out of bed and found twine and his boy scout ax. He then calmly walked into his mother's room where she was soundly sleeping. He bound her to the bed, stripped her naked save a pillowcase he placed over her head, and hacked her to death with the ax. Louis then went into his brother Bob's room, who had not been roused by the monstrous attack in the next room. Similarly, he tied Bob to the bed and axed him to death in the same manner. Carrie was forty-six. Bob was fourteen.[44]

After brutally killing both his mother and his brother, Louis returned to his own bed and fell back asleep. The bodies were discovered a few days later when neighbors became concerned with the lack of usual activity at the home. Louis stayed in the home with his slain family until the day before he turned himself in to the Huntington Beach Police Department after neighbors alerted the police to possible foul play. In a letter he wrote to his father, Louis said, "Dear Dad: I have killed mother and Bob. I am going to tell the police." On the first of June, he sedately walked into the police station and confessed to the double murder. When notified, Lucius immediately flew from St. Louis to his son's side and was depicted in the papers as the long-suffering, supportive father throughout the trial. When questioned, Louis flatly gave a barrage of the typical excuses heard when cold-blooded killers feign remorse in these situations: "I don't know why I did it; I was being possessed; I couldn't help it; I am sorry; My parents only gave me $1 allowance a week; School was stressful" etc. etc. etc. Louis' trial was highly publicized in both California and Missouri and in papers all along the way. Lucius hired attorney Charles Rude, another Harrisburg relative to represent Louis. Charles apparently knew his way around the courtroom so-to-speak, as Louis was ultimately found "insane" and sentenced to Mendocino State Hospital for one year after which he was to be reevaluated and if found "sane" at the end of a year's stay, he was to be released.[45] When a year had passed and Louis was reevaluated, his psychiatrists' recommendation was for his permanent residency in Mendocino. He was diagnosed with "epilepsy" during his first year's stay behind Mendocino's walls, and the recommendation of non-release was never contested.[46] He spent a miserable ten years in the asylum before his death in 1944 at age thirty-one.

Cousin Louis was three years older than Virginia, and as they were cousins through two marriages and not by blood, it isn't clear if they were well-acquainted prior to the events of May 29, 1934. Virginia's family no doubt felt the horror that Westwood Hills had seen, the loss of Aunt Carrie and Cousin Bob, the media frenzy, and the trial.

Virginia's father Edward and her uncle Roy both testified during Louis' trial, and several Gregg relatives were interviewed by police and quoted in the papers. Louis' attorney "Cousin" Charles Rude and his family temporarily moved from Harrisburg to California throughout the duration of the trial. Undoubtedly this was an unsettling time-period for Virginia and her parents. Even if the Greggs were not especially close with the Paynes, it was still a family drama that engulfed their conversations and headspaces for months and months from Pasadena to St. Louis, and back home to Harrisburg. For an eighteen-year- old Virginia, that certainly didn't help an already strained family life. No one wants to even know an ax-murderer, much less be related to one. At eighteen, with the latent tension of her family situation, Virginia probably felt like the load she shouldered couldn't get much heavier, but it did - a lot heavier.

MORE DEATH

Dewey Alphletta Todd Gregg died on June 13, 1935, at the age of thirty-seven. Virginia was nineteen. It's difficult to say whether Dewey's thirteen years after her diagnosis were attributed to the California move, but assuming they were, Virginia would certainly have traded all of Illinois and the rest of the world for just a few more memories with her mother. Living thirteen years beyond a consumption diagnosis was quite remarkable in the 1920s-30s, so in that regard, the pilgrimage to California's proverbial "Pool of Bethesda" had indeed been a success. In one way it simply prolonged the inevitable, but in another way, thank God it did.

Dewey was buried in Mountain View Cemetery and Mausoleum in Altadena, California just two blocks down the way from their North Marengo Ave home where the Greggs were living at the time of her death.

Dewey's death wasn't a surprise of course, but it was a bitter blow just the same – one that Virginia carried with her until her own death. The death of her mother meant the death of an entire way of life. Virginia had developed a keen ability for juggling the daily norm for a teenage girl in the 1930s with the shadowy home-life duties so cloaked in secrecy to prevent neighbors and landlords from learning of Dewey's stigmatized diagnosis. Virginia was having to say goodbye to her best friend, and the two-dimensional living that had been the necessary and only way of life she had known since early childhood. When Dewey's heart stopped so did a part of Virginia's. The frequent moves stopped. The duality stopped. The music stopped.

CHAPTER 4: LIFE IS A SYMPHONY

"Life is a symphony, and this action of every person in this life is the playing of his particular part in the music."

-Hazrat Inayat Khan

The music eventually began again, but with a different score and tempo. Virginia and her double bass viol joined the Pasadena Symphony Orchestra just after college at the age of twenty. The bass was a bulky instrument quite literally bigger than she was. She stood a slender 5'7, but it towered her at 6 feet.

Though the Pasadena Symphony is a historical icon in the classical music world now, it was a fairly new venue when Virginia joined. The City of Pasadena funded the founding of the Pasadena Civic Orchestra in 1928 (later known as the Pasadena Symphony and Pops) under Conductor Reginald Bland. Its first concert was presented on April 29, 1929, by its original orchestra made up primarily of volunteer musicians.

Steeped in prestigious musical tradition, the Pasadena Symphony has seen only three musical directors from 1936-2010, and still delights Southern California, now in the Ambassador Auditorium, with its rich classic series each season in tandem with Pops.[47]

From her role as a symphony player, evolved her place in "The Singing Strings," a stringed orchestra comprised of six female musicians. The group organized in 1936 with Harriet Wilson as leader and first violinist, Evelyn Hirsch and Josephine Harvey also as violinists, Catherine Ames as celloist, Leone Turnbow as pianist, and Virginia Gregg as double bass violist. The troupe was under the direction of Dr. Leonard Stallcup, who established the California Mounted Band Girls' Troop (CMBGT) in the early 1900s, and later was the president of Miss California-USA pageant.[48] Dr. Stallcup was an affluent renaissance man of California. A retired Air Force lieutenant colonel, he was a dentist by trade, but an avid musician and photographer. He was a civic-minded businessman, but a rigid and demanding taskmaster with the girls he directed in both the CMBGT and later in Miss California USA pageants. The troop was a military-ordered group in which girls learned equestrian skills and Roman-style riding. On many of the Westerns such as *Gunsmoke* and *Sugarfoot* that Virginia appeared in, she is often seen riding in a buggy or horseback. It is interesting to imagine her years before taking on two horses at once with a foot in the saddle of each. During Virginia's CMBGT days, she learned Morse Code, a skill in which she was fluent.[49] She also picked up another skill fluently: smoking.

THE SINGING STRINGS

"The Singing Strings" were first heard over the airwaves on station KHJ in Los Angeles in 1937, and audiences raved over the all-girl orchestra. The group, given great attention by the press, gained quite the followership for their unique feminine composition and great talent for "sweet and swingy" musical scores that could be heard from coast-to-coast on their weekly show, as well as their spot performances used in the dramatic background scores of popular radio shows.[50] They were one of the first all-female orchestras in the country, as women did not yet have an empowered presence in the classical music world in 1937. It was only seven years earlier that harpist Edna Phillips had caused a national (if not global) stir when she was hired by legendary conductor Leopold Stokowski as the first female principal player in The Philadelphia Orchestra, a move that also made her the first female principal player in any orchestra in the country.

In addition to their standard in-house performances at the Pasadena Symphony and Pops, "The Singing Strings" could be heard over AM and FM airwaves in the late 30s and early 40s through all major broadcasting networks. The girl troop performed majestically, but they were also pioneers in the great feat of establishing the female voice in the classical music industry. They lasted for a five-year run, with Virginia present for the first four. During those four years they made beautiful music together – literally. They cut several records, were presented at the Hollywood Bowl, performed with idols of the day such as Rudy Vallee and the Glen Miller Band, and were hired on as staffers for two different networks: CBS and Mutual.[51] Virginia was with them for a year at CBS and a year and a half with Mutual. It was through her work at Mutual that she did a few on-air commentaries and MC spots that led to her ultimate decision to break away from the music business to pursue acting fulltime.

The experience with the Pasadena Symphony prepared her for radio in myriad ways. In radio, much like the symphony, if everyone is dedicated to her own instrument, the melody is beautiful and balanced, but if one player is over or underplaying, the entire score suffers. Virginia was indeed a team player regardless of the game.

"The Singing Strings," circa 1936. From left to right the photo features Leone Turnbow, Catherine Ames, Josephine Harvey, Harriet Wilson, Evelyn Hirsch, & Virginia Gregg. Photo courtesy of Larry Ames.

LOU

During her symphony days, Virginia became enamored with a fellow musician named Louis "Lou" Butterman, who was tall, dark, handsome, and eight years her senior. Lou was an impressive 6'1 at 195 pounds when Virginia met him, with brown eyes behind his glasses, brown hair, and an olive complexion. He was born of Russian immigrant parents who moved from Colorado to California when he and his siblings were small. Lou's father spoke no English, only Yiddish, and his mother was a large, attentive woman who spoke several languages, though primarily Russian. Lou was recently divorced, and became smitten with the tall, fair, and attractive bass player, who by her 20s had become a slender, dark-haired beauty.

Virginia's family life had drastically changed since her mother's death. Her father Edward remarried shortly after Dewey died. Gertrude Dooley Harris was a divorcee twelve years younger than Edward (and only fourteen years older than Virginia).

Gertrude had a young daughter only four years younger than Virginia. Edward may have wanted to recapture some of the years lost to Dewey's diagnosis with a similar family constellation, but with different players. Ironically enough, Gertrude was also a Harrisburg resident before moving to California. The world must have been smaller then.

As Edward seemed to move on with his life after so many pinched years of preemptive grieving, Virginia moved on in her own way, too. She got a place of her own and committed herself even more fervently to her now dual career: actress and musician. She was never a social dater, but there was something about this Lou. After a brief courtship, they married on August 16, 1937, in Orange County when he was twenty-nine and she was twenty-one, the same year in which "The Singing Strings" organized. Music was in Lou's blood, just like it was in Virginia's, though it may have run a bit thicker in his. He played the bass, guitar, and violin for almost every studio in Hollywood including NBC, MGM, Warner, and was a longtime member of the Hollywood Studio Orchestra.

He held a leadership position in the musician's union – American Federation of Musicians – for years, and if you'll pardon the pun, was instrumental in ensuring Hollywood musicians in the Golden Age received their dues. Lou was well-known in the industry and was a regular in Rudy Vallee's orchestra for many years.

ECHO PARK

As newlyweds, Virginia and Lou lived just two miles from downtown LA in one of the city's first suburbs: Echo Park. Since the 1860s, Echo Park has been a unique residential area of Los Angeles that showcases the man-made Reservoir No. 4, or as it is more commonly known, Echo Lake. Its thirty-three acres were officially established by the city of Los Angeles as "Echo Park" on February 26, 1892. The moniker was reportedly chosen by the park's superintendent and architect, Joseph Henry Tomlinson, after hearing the reverberations of his shouts across the ravine of the Arroyo de Los Reyes that encompasses the man-made lake. The city's hope in establishing Echo Park was to use Echo Lake as the nucleus of the city's new drinking water system. Because of its location in the underdeveloped area of west Los Angeles, the city hoped having an innovative and conveniently located water system for its residents would encourage a real estate boom in the hilly, underdeveloped west. It eventually worked in part, because residential development boomed in the 1910s-20s around Echo Lake, though the intention for the lake to be used as the area's domestic drinking water system was abandoned and it became more of a visual attraction occasionally used for recreation.

In the 1920s-30s, the farmhouses of the 1800s were replaced by new, Spanish-style houses and bungalows that were hedged with courtyards, and other European styles brought in part by the memories of the WWI soldiers returning from their stations in Europe, and in part by the Spanish migration. While California has always had a rich Spanish presence, there were several significant Spanish migrations throughout the 1900s, especially during the industrial boom of LA in the 1910s-1930s; thus the influence of the beautiful Spanish architecture can still be seen in many of its historic buildings.

Greenery was planted by Tomlinson's lead to recreate "The Garden of Eden" with the grounds adorned with palm trees, lotus flowers, and lush foliage that made it a restorative oasis in the desert.

Echo Park was a popular spot in the 1910s-1920s for filmmakers. Many silent films such as Charlie Chaplin's 1914 film *Twenty Minutes of Love* were filmed in Echo Park in the 1910s-1920s. Because of its beauty and convenient location to LA, it became a hub for people in the entertainment industry. Many celebrities have called it home through the years including Steve McQueen, Ann Robinson, Kirstie Alley, Leonardo DiCaprio, and Linda Ronstadt among many others. It began as a White, middle class area of LA county, and after WWII, many Latinos migrated to the area and now represent the population majority of Echo Park.[52] Today, the area is known as a melting pot of architecture, cultures, topography, and history. In Angelino Heights one might see a Victorian brownstone or bungalow next door to a Spanish-colonial cottage. The area has undergone many transformations over the years, yet still retains a unique presence in the city with its art deco influences including the "Lady of the Lake" statue that still stands.[53]

Virginia and Lou lived in an Echo Park apartment as newlyweds just two miles from downtown LA where they both frequented musical rehearsals. With Echo Park's rich historical essence, even in the 1930s, many of their neighbors were those well-established in the industry. No doubt the restless actress/musician was greatly influenced by the vibrant bohemian culture of Echo Park, to which neighboring actors, actresses, musicians, filmmakers, writers, and artists contributed as early industry pioneers.

Virginia and Lou's apartment was right next door to LA's first female City Council member, Estelle Lawton Lindsey, who was hailed as a prolific journalist, socialist, and feminist of the early 1900s.[54] Lindsey is also renowned for her title as first female Mayor of Los Angeles, for thirty-six hours. When Mayor Charles Sebastian left LA for San Francisco in 1915 for the Panama Pacific International Exposition, he appointed Lindsey as acting mayor during his absence, a move that touted LA as the first major US city to appoint a female mayor. Virginia "borrowed cups of sugar" so-to-speak from several colorful neighbors like Estelle in her Echo Park days, although perhaps most noteworthy was evangelist Aimee Semple McPherson.

SISTER AIMEE

She was born Aimee Elizabeth Kennedy on October 9, 1890, in rural Ontario, Canada. Her mother, Minnie, only eighteen years old when she had Aimee, was a devout Salvation Army disciple and obsessively interpreted God's signs in everything from the idiosyncrasies of daily farm life to the star constellations – interpretations she freely shared with her only child, Aimee

Aimee grew up under odd, lonely circumstances, bearing the weight of her mother's own desire to be an evangelist on the world's stage as the focal point of her flowering identity. Minnie was convinced her daughter was "chosen," and took every opportunity to remind her. Aimee grew up under the assumption that God had selected and anointed her to serve Him on behalf of the masses in evangelistic subjugation for the duration of her time on Earth. She was conditioned to believe she was touched, hand-picked, and divinely appointed for the betterment of others – and there was no room for negotiations or autonomy in the matter.

Minnie was a constant presence in Aimee's life as she burgeoned from a raw prodigy on the farm to a charismatic figure head for the masses to follow. Aimee married her first husband, Robert James Semple in 1908. Together they had one child, Roberta Star Semple, while missionaries in Hong Kong. Robert died of dysentery and malaria just before Roberta was born.[55]

Back in the states, Aimee married her second husband, Harold McPherson, in 1912 and had her second child, Rolf Kennedy McPherson, in 1913. Believing God had instructed her on precisely how He wanted her ministry to progress, she left Harold in the dust of domestic life while she and her two children travelled from state to state preaching the gospel anywhere she could draw a crowd: parking lots, community centers, outdoor pavilions, etc. They were divine nomads sometimes sleeping in tents, or in Aimee's trusty Packard, to win souls to Christ. Harold and Aimee divorced in 1921, but by then, she had more than started her ascent into celebrity as America's first *glamourous* preacher. She incorporated a bit of everything into her infamous gospel meetings: music, dance, costumes, theatrical pieces, faith-healing, and speaking in tongues. Throngs of followers would gather around whatever makeshift stage she had to clap, cheer, and sometimes swoon at "Sister Aimee's" compelling messages. After several years of nomad grunt-work, her self-organized tent meetings soon turned into invitations to preach in brick-and-mortars, initially being a bit more well-received by the charismatic denominations than the fundamentals, because after all, Aimee was not only glamourous, outspoken, and theatrical in her preaching of the gospel, she was a *woman* - the most scandalous of her attributes in the 1910s.

After several years of wandering the country in that old Packard with two children and eventually a financial manager named "Mother," the foursome settled in "Sunny California." She began to draw more and more crowds to her California settlement – which meant more and more donations. In 1921, she began construction on the massive, opulent Angelus Temple in Echo Park that still stands today. For a larger-than-life preacher like "Sister Aimee," only a larger-than-life headquarters would do, seating over 5,000 when it was founded in 1923.[56] From magnificent Angelus Temple, she established her own denomination, which still thrives today: The Foursquare Church.

"Sister Aimee" as she was known to the world seemed to make history time and time again in her strong convictions about her place and purpose in the world. In 1922 "Sister Aimee" made history as the first female evangelist ever to preach over radio airwaves. Shortly after, she made history again as the second female ever to be given a broadcasting license when she started her own Christian radio station, KFSG.[57] The Foursquare Church grew by leaps and bounds with "Sister Aimee" at the helm as America's first female megachurch leader. She acquired many critics and skeptics along her journey to stardom, but the thousands of supporters from all classes more than made up for occasional bad press.

"Sister Aimee" was surrounded by scandal almost as much as she was by the Spirit Himself. Some scandals only defined as such by the times, but not all. Take for example "The Case of the Vanishing Evangelist."

On May 18, 1926, during one of the first peaks of her fame and followership, Aimee disappeared. She and her dutiful secretary, Emma Schaffer, were enjoying a sunny day at Venice Beach outside Los Angeles, about twenty miles from the hallowed Angelus Temple. After Aimee had gone for a swim, Emma suddenly realized she was nowhere in sight. After a panicked, thorough search of the area with the help of a gathering crowd, Emma reached the only plausible explanation: Aimee had drown. Efforts to recover her body proved unsuccessful, leading many to hope that their beloved "Sister" was in fact still alive.

The disappearance caused a media frenzy when the news broke that the world's beloved prophetess who had performed so many miracles herself, was unable to overcome either the merciless waves of the Pacific, or some other unnamed misfortune. Followers were sad, enraged, confused, and shocked.[58]

Aimee's mother, Minnie, stepped to the platform in Aimee's absence to lead the masses in some type of closure for the devastating disappearance. Initially, elaborate vigils were held in intercession for "Sister Aimee's" miraculous resurrection or at the very least eternal peace for her soul. Another theory began to circulate, however, that death perhaps wasn't to blame as much as kidnapping. This theory was fostered by an alleged ransom letter Minnie received demanding a half a million dollars for Aimee's release.[59] There were rumors of Aimee-sightings from coast-to-coast leading some to persist in their belief that she would in fact return and return she did.

In June of 1926, one month after her disappearance, Aimee reappeared just as suddenly and mysteriously as she had vanished, and she came back with quite a harrowing tale.

Aimee made colorful claims that two men and a woman had kidnapped her from Venice Beach that day in May and had taken her hostage to Mexico where she was drugged and tortured for ransom. After an agonizing month in captivity, she allegedly escaped her captors fleeing by taxi to Douglas, Arizona where she phoned her mother. The details were winding and dramatic without much to substantiate her claims, though her physical condition did suggest some type of trauma for she was dirty, disheveled, and dehydrated when she reached Arizona. She was hospitalized in Douglas where her family joined her in glorious reunion.[60]

After a respite to regain her strength, Aimee returned to Los Angeles and was met with a queen's welcome. There were reportedly between 30,000 and 50,000 people waiting at the train station for "Sister Aimee's" miraculous return.

Aimee's story was incredible, with vague and outlandish details that didn't always add up, but many were so relieved at her return, they ignored the gaping holes. While her family and followers maintained that she in fact was abducted for that month in 1926, others speculated a good old-fashioned hoax.

"Sister Aimee" resumed her ministry work not long after her return with prophetic insight from her experience that she shared with the masses in reflection on her journey's biblical application. Though she was back on the Angelus Temple stage in all her glory, she was put through the wringer by the media and by the courts when charges were brought against her and some of her inner circle in suspicion of conspiracy among similar charges, as her kidnapping tale proved unsatisfactory to a good portion of the world.

After a draining, lengthy trial in 1927, all charges were dropped, but during proceedings, another theory emerged that many believe to be the real reason for her month-long absence. Kenneth Ormiston was a radio engineer for Aimee's station KFSG. The two became close during their work together. He was also married.

There were rumors the two were lovers even before her disappearance, but the trial spotlighted their relationship. Many believed Aimee was simply a hostage of a conflagrant love affair rather than a criminal's scheme and had spent the month basking in her romance with Kenneth. A hiatus of this nature could certainly damage her ministry if discovered, so creating a fantastic tale of kidnappers, chloroform, and daring escape seemed to be somehow more palatable than the truth. Despite the courtroom drama, no definitive explanation was ever determined, and that month of absence remained shrouded in mystery and speculation the rest of her life.

Aimee continued in her ministry at Angelus Temple for years beyond this bizarre season of her life and managed to push through the ridicule maintaining her status as a pious messenger of God to thousands. On September 27, 1944, "Sister Aimee" was found dead in an Oakland, California hotel room. She was 53. The papers initially cited a heart attack as cause of death, but later reports claimed an accidental overdose on the insomnia drug Seconal was ultimately to blame.[61]

Foursquare Church is still in existence today thanks to her pioneering work over so many decades. Her son Rolf went on to carry the ministry torch, and many followers branched out from the Angelus Temple founding their own replicas of her original design.

To some "Sister Aimee" was just another Bible-thumping charlatan, to others, a contemporary prophetess sent to edify the masses. Regardless of whether one was particularly religious or not, everyone knew who "Sister Aimee" was in the 1920s-1940s.

For all the scandal surrounding her ministry, she was in fact a benevolent who generously supported community needs in and around Los Angeles. She was also a social influencer who openly disagreed with every type of prejudice. She lovingly welcomed minorities into her flock and preached a gospel that accepted everyone unconditionally – a theology not necessarily popular at the time of segregation, even in the progressive West.

Just after the Long Beach earthquake of 1933 that destroyed hundreds of buildings including Virginia's high school, "Sister Aimee" and her Foursquare Church led relief efforts throughout the community to help those affected. It is unclear whether Virginia and "Sister Aimee" ever met, but Virginia was undoubtedly influenced by her presence on the world's stage and in her Echo Park backyard. With almost thirty years between the two, Virginia must have been among Aimee's young admirers – not necessarily for her religious assertions, but at the very least for her example of dynamic, proud, loving womanhood. Young girls in the 1920s and 1930s must have seen Aimee's ascent as a bit shocking but terribly encouraging – a glimpse of what was possible for women.

Despite any particulars of Aimee's theology and flashy, unconventional display of her beliefs, she was a pioneer for women. She was outspoken, driven, and proud of her femininity despite the 1920s' and 1930s' cultural repression that systematically told her to "quiet down." Virginia certainly must have heard her over the airwaves and watched her acts of altruism benefit their mutual community. She must have watched and listened in intrigue at Aimee's rise in the public's eye, on radio, and in the world and thought her own dream's realization might be a bit more possible thanks to forerunners in the feminine fight like "Sister Aimee."

Letting the dicey particulars fall by the wayside, Aimee's story is really about a young girl who had a dream and blazed a trail across the entire world to realize that dream to the great benefit of hundreds and thousands of others.

Generally, Virginia wasn't particular about types of roles she was given in terms of content or genre. She always said, if a role was well-written, she wanted it. There was, however, one role she placed above all others: Aimee Semple McPherson. According to an interview by entertainment journalist Charles Witbeck Virginia's greatest desire was to play evangelist Aimee Semple MacPherson in film. While she never achieved that particular goal, she did have the opportunity to channel a bit of "Sister Aimee" in her portrayal of "Bonnie Bates" in the *Dragnet* episode "Pyramid Swindle" complete with Aimee's signature white, flowing, wide-sleeved gown and occasionally accompanying tambourine.

RADIO ACTING DEBUT

"The Singing Strings" were often hired by radio networks to perform dramatic scores for shows. In the 1930s, detective dramas, westerns, and soap operas were the hot genres in the radio waves, and orchestra music was an integral part of their entertainment composition. Though today, radio often relies heavily upon soundtracks and digital assistance, in the 1930s, music, much like the acting performances themselves, was live. Performing with "The Singing Strings" was a fulltime gig with radio and in-house symphony performances and rehearsals for their 20+ shows a week, but unable to ignore her desire to become a fulltime actress, Virginia still took small roles for radio and for the Pasadena Playhouse.

Virginia's first on-air acting role was arranged somewhat by coincidence. Even though she carried a musician's identity, because of her great interest in the *art* of acting, she paid close attention to the radio actors' performances and the script during rehearsals. While some might have used that downtime in between their musical spots to chat or relax, Virginia occupied her time by studying the mechanics of the shows themselves and how the actors brought the storylines to life over the mic. In 1938, while Virginia and "The Singing Strings" were in studio prepared to play for a CBS radio drama, news that the show's leading lady suddenly fell ill ran through the studio, making even the janitor a nervous wreck. With the clock racing toward on-air time with no replacement, the director went into a panic. While Virginia was rehearsing the musical scores with her troupe, she overheard the director's dilemma and asked if she could stand in for the lead. Recognizing Virginia as a studio musician, you can imagine the director was less than confident in agreeing to let her, as the part called for a serious, dramatic actress, not a bass player, but out of desperation he agreed. While the director shakily handed the script over to her, and the show began, he soon learned it was unnecessary to have given her a script at all. During rehearsals over the days leading up to showtime, Virginia had managed to unintentionally memorize the script in her study of the dynamics of the show and actors. She delivered a flawless performance and expertly took the proper cues from the director throughout the show. I imagine his heart began to beat a bit more steadily and his panic soon turned to wonderment as the script unfolded before the mic. Not only had he found an excellent replacement who saved the show, but he might have also accidentally found radio's next star behind the strings of a double bass viol no less.[62]

With Virginia's radio debut in acting a smashing triumph, the double bass viol suddenly paled in comparison to the other instrument she had spent just as long learning: her voice. After four years (1937 – 1941) with "The Singing Strings," at the age of twenty-five,

Virginia made the leap from music to acting fulltime.[63] She had been well-known as a musician in Los Angeles for nearly ten years and abandoning her musical identity for the love of acting wasn't easy. In an interview with radio historian Chuck Schaden, she described a less than accommodating industry when she began her transition from music to acting, as she facetiously said, "I was known as a musician and everyone knows you can't do *two* things."[64]

The decision to pursue acting fulltime climaxed on a particular day for Virginia when she knew there was only one person who could provide the push she needed to scale the next wall of her dreams: Virginia Lee Gregg Butterman. When she made up her mind to pursue what she truly wanted to do, she had no guarantee, no contract, no agent promising fame and fortune, only a dream. She didn't want the split identity she had carried through her youth with the perpetual pull of both worlds. She was good at music, and she was good at acting, but in order to be great in either, she had to leave one behind. She felt success could only be possible if she fully devoted all of herself to the one that meant the most.

If we're serious about our dreams, there has to be sacrifice. The same day she made the decision, she solidified it by selling her bass. She said it was painful, but necessary so she wouldn't go back on her commitment to herself. That was the end of an era in Virginia's life. While there's no way to know if she shed tears as she parted with her instrument, or simply handed it over with unyielding resolve, it is still a tremendous scene to imagine that after years of tending to the emergence of her musical identity, she gave up her loyal friend and livelihood: the double bass viol. The same instrument that she used to perform private concerts for her mother while she lounged in weakness from tuberculosis. The same instrument that led her to her symphony family, to Lou, to her "The Singing Strings," the California Mounted Band Girls' Troop, and Dr. Stallcup.

She never played a bass again after that day. There was one instance however in which she described finding a bass leaned against the corridor in the studio that she picked up to tune years later.

That sacrifice had to be difficult, because after all, there were no guarantees her acting dream would ever be realized. To give up the practical, for the dream is a tremendous gamble and it takes a helluva lot of moxie – especially during the middle of a world war. As of 1941, Virginia Gregg was forever known as "actress."

Aside from a six-month stint in New York in 1942, Virginia remained dedicated to the Los Angeles scene. Lou and Virginia were married eight years through a volatile time in our nation's history. Together they weathered the prodigious changes America underwent in the late 1930s and 1940s. The volatile climate fostered by historic events such as the Hindenburg Disaster, Orson Welles' *War of the Worlds*, WWII, and the death of President Franklin D. Roosevelt had millions reeling, and the Buttermans were no different. Like many other men aged twenty-one to forty-five in the 1940s, Lou was drafted. He was a part of the United States Coast Guard, and left Virginia's side to serve. A Harrisburg cousin moved in with Virginia and her beloved cat, Abdul, during Lou's absence. While he was away, Virginia volunteered her spare time to the war effort and became very dedicated to veteran's affairs even volunteering for Recordings for the Blind, Inc. a few years after, which was established as a resource for veterans.

In 1948, Anne Thompson Macdonald founded Recordings for the Blind, Inc. Originally, its mission was to help World War II veterans further their education through the opportunities fostered under the G.I. Bill. This was an innovative organization that met a very practical need for so many. Recordings for the Blind, Inc. eventually broadened in serving the veteran demographic and became instrumental in providing educational resources that had never previously existed to vision-impaired individuals.

Today, Recordings for the Blind, Inc. is known as Learning Ally. They continue in their mission to provide equal, high-quality educational opportunities to individuals all over the nation through innovative technology that meets the needs of those who may experience learning differences. Learning Ally is still committed to the philosophy Anne Thompson Macdonald espoused in her founding efforts: "Learning through listening is a right, not a privilege." Virginia did countless volunteer recordings for Recordings for the Blind, Inc. from its inception until her death in 1986. She also served as a board member for the organization later in her life.

HOME FROM WAR

When Lou returned home from his service in 1944, the relationship he and Virginia had never quite managed to pick up the same cadence it had before. The war changed everyone in some way or another, and the fallout was often most noticeable in relational scores. The Buttermans moved from their Echo Park newlywed nest and into a brand-new California bungalow on the flip side of East Hollywood – with Lou's widowed mother. I have to wonder how many times Virginia sat across the dinner table from her mother-in-law studying her mouth in its delivery of her rich Russian accent and stored the nuances away for future use in parts that called for a character of Russian heritage.

Virginia and Lou divorced in June of 1945 at her filing. Like Virginia, Lou went on to remarry and have children years after their newlywedded musician days in Echo Park before the war drowned out the song of new love. Lou died July 27, 1992 at the age of eighty-four.

Divorcing in any era is never easy, but in 1945, it was especially *not easy*. Even in progressive Southern California, there was a certain bruise that went along with the title of "divorcee" for a woman, because as with most things, a man's reputation could stand divorce better. Virginia changed her course again and just like she exchanged her musician's ticket for actress, she exchanged her married ticket for divorced just before her 30th birthday. In the 2020s most of us are socialized in this postmodern era to innately choose our directions based on where we want to go – we have been inundated with the cliché dogma that *we* control our own destiny – if we don't like where our ship is headed, set a new course, try on a new identity, start over as many times as it takes. No one thinks twice today if we say, "That corporate job just wasn't for me, so I just quit to open my own small business." We're met with congratulatory "good for yous" and automatic understanding. In Virginia's day, entire families turned their backs on their own for less serious offenses. Our ability to choose more freely what best suits us as individuals is a modern convenience that was not always available to previous generations. The 1940s were fraught with bristly societal norms analogous to nose-to-the-grindstone theology, traditional gender roles bedrocked by misogynistic ideals – a woman choosing to trade in one career for another or filing for divorce because the relationship simply wasn't working were decisions of our time, not Virginia's. What she must have been up against in an institutional sense must have taken tremendous nerve. She was a long way from the Prohibition days in Harrisburg, but independent, working women who divorced were considered just as threatening to America's fundamentalism as bootlegging, if not more so. For a young woman of thirty in the 1940s to grab her own lifeship's wheel with both hands to set a new course just because she simply *wanted* to, was unheard of. Always subtle and always classy, Virginia was the original, "I don't give a damn what you think" gal, and the 1940s couldn't have appreciated that like we can today. She was far ahead of her time. If these major life changes got her down, it sure doesn't show in her recorded trajectory. She moved out on her own again, leaving Lou with his mother, and began life as a post-war single gal determined to make it big, and setting a course for the nearest microphone seemed like the best way to do it.

CHAPTER 5: ON-AIR

"Radio is my medium of choice."

-Virginia Gregg

After Virginia's coincidental radio acting debut in 1938, she gradually got more radio work starting small in supporting and/or commercial roles, but it wasn't easy. She still frequented the stage of the Pasadena Playhouse, and kept her name in the hat so-to-speak of radio producers until the offers picked up speed. As determined as she was, competition was stiff, and she quickly learned that in order keep the offers coming in, she had to be willing to be uncomfortable.

On one of her first radio gigs, she noticed the script called for an Irish accent, and she adamantly announced to director Jack Johnstone, "Oh, I don't do Irish accents." Without ever looking up from the script he was thumbing through, he said, "Yes you do," and she did. Having been musically trained through her family and the Pasadena symphony, she learned to use her voice as an instrument just like her double bass viol. If a song requires a certain tone or chord, the instrument has it within its mechanism, you just have to determine the right combination of manual manipulations to find it. She found that not only could she in fact do a beautiful Irish accent, but, with the help of dialect coaches like Robert Easton, she could also do Scottish, British, African, Chinese, Russian, Filipino, and practically any other dialect a script called for. She started becoming a hot commodity for directors because of her versatility as a character actress and knack for cold reading on air.

The character actors of the Golden Age of radio (roughly 1920s – 1950s) and the early days of television were often the highest quality artists around. Most were professionally trained in the arts with rich backgrounds in theatre, opera, and/or symphony. Who could ever guess comedian Howard Morris who made famous the unforgettable "Ernest T. Bass" on *The Andy Griffith Show* was a classically trained Shakespearean actor before giving us the rowdy rock throwing hillbilly "Ernest T.?" Character acting wasn't for the faint of heart. This group of artists cultivated a deep traction within the industry that leads often could not. They also were able to live more well-rounded lives perhaps, as they were not subjected to the "fishbowl existence" that leading names often were, as Virginia herself so eloquently said.[65] There was no university major to become a "character actor;" the training was organic through the studio system and stock company formations. It was a type of training that is truly a one-of-a-kind that can really never be replicated outside of the Golden Age.

Radio listeners and television viewers came to feel as if they knew these actors and actresses they recognized time and time again in various roles. These players had a familiar essence and audiences felt more connected (whether consciously or subconsciously) to productions and storylines based on that familiarity. Individuals like Denver Pyle, Lurene Tuttle, John Anderson, Jeanette Nolan, Parley Baer, Harry Bartell, Peggy Webber, and many others like them gave us such a wonderful gift in assuming these capillary roles that pumped the lifeblood into our favorite shows, and American media is all the better because of their contributions.

THAT GOLDEN AGE

Virginia began her acting career during a time in American culture when radio had a very different purpose than it does today. Radio during the Golden Age (1920s-50s) provided an escape from war, poverty, and domestic existence. It provided faceless stories that taught, entertained, inspired, and spiritually fed a nation of media consumers. Virginia and other actors and actresses of the time served as a flare of sorts for listeners and perhaps also for themselves. Their engagement with the imaginations of American listeners was better in some cases than therapy. The old-time radio shows had a significance beyond entertainment – they let the masses know that despite the world being thrown on its head, things such as romance, mystery, creativity, and fantasy still existed in that mythical beacon that is Hollywood, and the hope was that if these things indeed still existed there, one day they could exist again in the rest of the world too.

Virginia credits *Calling All Cars* as being the first radio show to give her the first few steady roles of her career. The show wasn't in the habit of crediting performers, so it is difficult to determine which episodes she is in, but she most likely joined the airwaves through that popular crime show (of which *Dragnet* was its protégé some ten years later) in the late 1930s.

Virginia started burning up the lines with her voice on one show after another in the 1940s in such productions as Arch Oboler's *Lights Out, The Screen Guild Theater, Wings to Victory, Lux Radio Theatre, Cavalcade of America, The Rudy Vallee Show, The Count of Monte Cristo, Play for Tonight,* and *The Whistler.* All the studios wanted her, and most were within walking distance of each other, so she spent her days in zigzags going from ABC, to NBC, to Mutual, to CBS, and back again. It was grueling work for the emotions, as she quickly earned her wings in all genres. She could do comedy just as well as drama and thrillers just as well as westerns, and because of her great versatility, she often landed multiple roles within the same show. Virginia's dear friend and nearly lifelong colleague, Parley Baer, once joked that Virginia was the main cause of the spike in unemployment rates in the 1940s because she hogged most of the radio jobs.

Virginia took each of her roles very seriously, no matter how "small" they were, and diligently worked to perfect the delivery and emotive essence each part called for. As one radio actor recalled his experience working with her:

Had the privilege of working with Virginia Gregg on [sic] radio series, years, years ago. Shortly before, she and I were to start recording, noticed her sobbing in the hallway and I went over and asked her what was the matter and then she smiled and said, 'Oh nothing, I am just rehearsing my lines.' Incredible talent of an actress and unforgettable.

FAMILY OF RADIOERS

In honing her craft as an actress, she quickly learned how to play the industry game, and I believe she (almost) always won on her terms. She already had many connections in the industry due to her musician work and knew her way around most studios in Hollywood. The radio studio system was old hat to her by the time she stepped up to the mic in acting roles. The directors, producers, and fellow artists had known her in her capacity as a musician playing background scores for radio shows, but as they grew to know her as an actress, they soon learned she had been wasted behind the bulky bouts of the double bass viol.

Just like in school, she was well-liked by most everyone in the business from studio executives to studio custodians. She calibrated herself to whoever and whatever was in front of her. She was still the transcendent empath and team-player. With the men, she cracked crude jokes. With the women, she talked about all things domestic: sewing, recipes, and skin care. She impressed the radio technicians with her Morse Code skills, and the directors with her spot-on performances. Everyone considered her "their best friend."

Samuel Franklin "Dubs" Smith, a colleague of Virginia's recalled working with her in those early radio days and later in film:

Directors and cast members found Ginny a joy to work with. She was down to earth. No diva qualities. Always. Not that she didn't flub once in a while. She would stand with the crew hav-

ing coffee with them. Those she knew would ask about their families and they returned the questions to her. She fit in as one of the guys. Rough talk and joking she joined in unless really crude and then one of the men would chastise that crew member. All around nice lady.

Dubs also said Virginia wasn't above looking and admiring "something pretty" (a phrase reportedly coined by *Gunsmoke's* Amanda Blake, meaning a very nice-looking male specimen on set or adjoining sound stages). "Just like one of the guys. Always tickled the guys on the crew," he recalled laughing. Dubs is now 102 years old. He recalls many of the old days of radio, television, and film for which he had a backstage view for many decades as an actor and stuntman.

For actors and actresses, there was quite a bit of downtime in radio. Today, production processes are quite different compared to those of the Golden Age, as many actors and actresses today are able to record or shoot at separate times with less intersection than their predecessors. While downtime is certainly involved in the making of modern productions, the nature of it is quite different. Today it is perhaps more regulated with less open-ended interaction among cast members compared to that time period. Supporting cast members in the Golden Age might put in an entire workday at a studio for just a two-minute on-air spot; essentially *everything was live.* They often had to wait through live recordings of other show portions before the episode called for their performance, and time for breaks and unavoidable interruptions were also factored into downtime spent. In some ways the downtime might have been more exhausting than the performance itself. This time gave performers opportunity to become well-acquainted and share in each other's experiences. Some of the grandest friendships developed out of those between-cue times. Virginia described radio performers – especially in the early days – as a family. A family made up of newcomers who were still wobbly and finding their way to their respective chairs in the industry, with such members as Parley Baer, Peggy Webber, Vic Perrin, Carlton Young, Olan Soule, Stacy Harris, Harry Bartell, Art Gilmore, Dick Powell, June Foray, and even Jack Webb. These radio family members (and many more not listed here) became an integrated clan that shared the same dream and the same blood for years. They carried each other's secrets, rejections, triumphs, and inspiration each steering their own vessel in this fleet of young American dreamers.

Parley Baer was perhaps one of Virginia's closest friends in the group. Parley had a broad career in all media, beginning with radio, that spanned more than fifty years. He is perhaps most remembered as the loyal deputy "Chester Proudfoot" on radio's *Gunsmoke*, and the cantankerous "Mayor Stoner" on *The Andy Griffith Show*. Parley and Virginia spent decades together sharing the mic and screens (both big and small) with their equally impressive resumes and reputations. For all of Virginia's diplomacy and tenderness, Parley could be her curt, oblivious antithesis. Despite his somewhat surly disposition, he won Virginia's heart early on with a story that serves as a wonderful abstract of Parley.

Parley's circus background was as odd and interesting as his Mormon-given name. He was a lion trainer in his twenties before his radio days. The circus is also where he met Ernestine, his wife of fifty-four years, as she was an acrobat and equestrian "trick rider." One day on break from training at the circus, Parley happened to be walking through the animal exhibits on the circus-goer side when he noticed a man by the monkey enclosure. Parley watched as the man offered a monkey popcorn from his bucket to lure him within his reach between the bars. When the monkey reached for the treat, he burned the end of the monkey's nose with his cigar. Upon seeing this sadistic display, Parley decided the man would benefit greatly from a few lashes of his training whip. He lashed the man on the back before he had a chance to torture another monkey and drove him off the lot with the whip at his heels. Parley nonchalantly said,

"I just helped him out to the parking lot with that whip all along the way." As an empath and animal-lover, Virginia adored Parley all the more for the sneak peek of heart stuffed back behind his typical cynicism.

The family that formed in the wings of the amber studio light was tight, loyal, and truly *for* each other. Those were the days before agents were really a viable thing for radioers. Virginia described an organic system in which players would advocate for each other among producers and directors. If the clan knew one fellow member was struggling to pay his rent on time, they would go to the director and say, "Could you give Dick an extra role this week, or my spot in this next script?" The troupe struggled together, seasoned together, and gloried together. These friendships that the amber light fostered literally lasted entire lifetimes and perhaps beyond.

Legendary actress Peggy Webber was one such radio family member who first met Virginia in her teens. At ninety-five today, she still recalls so many happy memories of her friendship with Virginia and was gracious enough to write the foreword for this biography.

MAX FACTOR

Some may remember Virginia as a frumpy, washed out housewife or unkempt, dingy Appalachian medicine woman from her television and film days, but in the radio studio and in real life, she was like any Hollywood society gal of the 1940s and relished in regular beauty treatments by the king of makeup: Max Factor. Max was the makeup king of Hollywood's royalty, something that emerged as a residual of his time as beautician for Russia's royalty: Czar Nicholas II and family. Max was born Maksymillian Faktorowicz on September 15, 1877, in Poland and came to America in 1904. In 1916, the year of Virginia's birth, Max launched his makeup line from his Hollywood Blvd location and rode the film industry's rising tide of the late 1910s and 1920s.[66] He built his line on an unfamiliar concept: "makeup" a phrase he himself coined, was for *all* women, not just royalty and high society. His philosophy can be best understood in his famous line: "You are not born glamourous. Glamour is created," and create he did! He was the stylist behind some of the most glamorous and well-known faces in Hollywood. He developed the unforgettable looks of our favorite stars, giving us Lucille Ball's red hair and false eyelashes, Joan Crawford's lips, Clara Bow's bob, and Jean Harlow's famous blonde do.[67]

Max died August 30, 1938 at the age of sixty, and his son Max Factor, Jr. took over the business not long after until his death in the 1990s. Through his creativity and innovative approach to beauty, Max Sr. left behind an enduring legacy that has shaped media, the cosmetic industry, and the worldwide culture of femininity. Younger generations may see the "Max Factor" label in the cosmetic aisle as just another brand among the lot, but his name carries much more than marketing value even so many decades later.

In those Golden days, Virginia was regularly pampered at the Max Factor Studio on Highland off Hollywood Blvd in LA. Peggy recalls being in awe of her older colleague's beauty routine and feeling as if she had truly "made it" in the Hollywood scene upon her own first visit to Max Factor when she was around eighteen. She said as she sat through her own first Factor beauty treatment, she thought to herself, "I'm doing what Virginia Gregg does!"

PEGGY

Peggy and Virginia were great friends all throughout their careers. Peggy, Virginia, and Jeanette Nolan made a delightful trio, as they shared the microphone and their private lives for years and years. Peggy considered Virginia a friend and a mentor always cheering her on with those prodding winks and nods of encouragement during recordings. A Texas native, Peggy was simply born for show business. As a toddler, she began performing in local movie theaters during intermissions, and began in radio when she was still a teenager. She blazed through a fine career in radio, television, and film during the Golden Age, and championed in writing, directing, and producing, which she still does today. Like Virginia, she was a favorite of Jack Webb who dubbed her "his lucky rabbit's foot." Peggy was a part of Jack's stock company for the *Dragnet* franchise in all three media and performed in hundreds (if not thousands) of his productions. In addition to *Dragnet*, she gave brilliantly sincere, agile performances in many of the same productions as Virginia in both radio and television such as *Lux Radio Theatre, The Whistler, Escape, Let George Do It, Family Theatre, Richard Diamond, Private Detective, Sears Radio Theatre, Gunsmoke, Trackdown, Laramie, The Waltons,* and *Project U.F.O.* Though she and Virginia were technically of different generations and different personalities, they shared a rich friendship for over fifty years. When Peggy needed to talk, Virginia's number was the one she dialed.

In 1984, Peggy founded The California Artists Radio Theatre, where she still serves as executive producer and director. She is not only one of the most prolific actresses of the Golden Age, but she has invested her experience and talent into countless up-and-comings who carry on her legacy.

In addition to Peggy's own personal memories of Virginia, she also echoed what fellow radio family member John Dehner always claimed in that Virginia was the one who gave him his start in acting. Virginia saw great potential in the curious disc jockey and promised to put in a good word for him when she herself arrived on a higher rung. That was a catchy social promise lots of folks in the industry made, but John soon found out that "Ginny" was true to her word months after he himself had forgotten her promise.

John had a legendary career in his own right, in all media, but started out as a Disney animator. He remained another lifelong friend of Virginia's, despite his irreverent way, and occasional practical jokes of which she wasn't terribly fond. She never let him forget his bad behavior in a particular radio show where his whimsy got the best of her. On either side of the mic, John and Virginia were doing a scene in which she had a lengthy monologue confessing her love for him. She was looking down at her script for most of her monologue and became so engrossed in the part that tears began to stream down her face. At a line break, she looked up at John across the mic holding with that intense emotion and tear-streaked face only to find him *cross-eyed*. She said listeners probably thought she was merely taking a dramatic pause in between lines, but in reality, she was trying not to laugh into the mic. John got an earful after the broadcast.

JOAN

Acclaimed actress Joan Del Mar is another who fondly remembers Virginia from those early radio days. Joanne Delmer was born in 1934 and later became known as "Joan Del Mar" later in her career, upon a recommendation from fellow actress Anne Baxter during their work together in the 1941 classic film *Swamp Water*. "I don't like my name," Joanne told Anne one day on set in between shooting. "Well how about trying *Joan*?" Anne Baxter suggested. Anne herself had been born "Cornelius Anne Baxter," and knew too well the benefits of having an abbreviated name for industry purposes. Joan began her acting career at age six and climbed the proverbial show-biz ladder through the Golden Age in all media.

She made her radio debut on none other than *The Jack Benny Show* on radio, and as an AFRA member, she often performed on Armed Forces Radio with Virginia. Joan went on to appear in films such as *The Devil and Daniel Webster, The Curse of the Cat People, The Wedding Planner, Along Came Polly, Bad Santa, Armageddon, Bulworth,* and *The Man Who Wasn't There.* She was also the "five minutes to go" girl in the Laurel and Hardy film *Nothing but Trouble.*

Though they belong to different generations, Virginia almost twenty years her senior, Joan has fond memories of her from the early radio days that she was able to share when the two reconnected at a SPERDVAC convention in 1984, two years before Virginia's death. After exchanging reminisces, Joan presented Virginia with a photo of an AFRS performance titled *Operation Little Vittles* with Jack Kruschen and Michael Miller. Virginia autographed the photo with the poignant inscription: "When we were very young. Love to you, Joan, Virginia Gregg."

It wasn't uncommon for Virginia to mentor younger actors and actresses. Bob Bailey's daughter, Roberta Bailey-Goodwin, is another who remembers Virginia "taking her under her wing" as she fondly recalled in an interview with John Dunning.

Everyone considered Virginia their best friend. She was everything to everyone she encountered, yet somehow could stand firm on her own private identity. That's a remarkable balance that is most difficult to achieve in one lifetime. She was a warm refuge among the underdogs, the high-rankers, and the all-betweens.

AFRS recording of *Operation Little Vittles*, circa 1944, featuring from left to right Jack Kruschen, Joan Del Mar, Virginia Gregg, and Michael Miller. Photo courtesy of Joan Del Mar.

PICTURES

Radio kept Virginia incredibly busy in the 1940s, and she was fulfilled in her new family of fellow-radioers, and in her rising status as a Hollywood commodity, but being in "pictures" was of course always the ultimate for any acting hopeful. The stage and radio had given Virginia the confidence needed to try her hand in big screen productions. In 1946, she made her film debut in Alfred Hitchcock's *Notorious* starring Cary Grant, Ingrid Bergman, and Claude Rains. She herself never counted that as her film debut, as she had a non-speaking, non-credited background role titled on the International Movie Database as "file clerk." The next year she appeared in similar background roles in both Elia Kazan's *Gentleman's Agreement* starring Gregory Peck, Dorothy McGuire, and John Garfield and Leigh Jason's *Lost Honeymoon* starring Franchot Tone, Ann Richards, and Tom Conway. She considered 1947's *Body and Soul* as her true start in film thanks to colleague William "Bill" Conrad, though 1946 is technically when the big screen first saw the face that belonged to the voice millions around the country had been hearing so often on radio. The next year, 1948, brought with it more film roles first with John Berry's *Casbah* starring Yvonne De Carlo, Tony Martin, and Peter Lorre, and two lower budget films: Bernard Vorhaus' *The Amazing Mr. X*, and Ray McCarey's *The Gay Intruders*. If the screen and big-name co-stars intimidated her, she hid it well. Even in her early productions, she carried enough innate confidence that her greenness barely showed.

1940s

The 1940s was the decade in which Virginia established herself. It was more blood, sweat, and tears than accolades then, but the struggle and the challenge seemed to prod Virginia on making it one of the most memorable stretches of her career. A string of early 1940s radio series borrowed Virginia's talents on the regular from *Lux Radio Theatre* and *Cavalcade of America* to *The Count of Monte Cristo* and *The Whistler,* and like her colleagues, fans loved her too. Listeners of *Family Theatre, Let George Do It, The Adventures of Philip Marlowe,* and *The Unexpected* enjoyed guessing which role Virginia Gregg would be featured in each week. And then came a singing gumshoe by the name of "Richard Diamond" who was in desperate need of a Park Avenue girlfriend. Virginia knew just the gal.

With each performance, another industry root went down. Virginia was making connections, fans, and history. In the 1940s, she fought hard for many of the offers she received, and it wasn't until the 1950s that much of that fighting started to pay off in regular offers for which she didn't have to cold audition. Taking interval visits into the film world was thrilling, but radio had become a comfortable haven that still offered just enough challenge and more than paid the bills. Virginia had lived as a single gal for a few months post-divorce, and had managed to cogently refute the nuclear family rhetoric of depending on a husband for survival. The industry paid well, and she was frugal with her earnings. Healing from the fraying of her first marriage wasn't easy, but her new radio family and sense of accomplishment in her career had eased the pain and helped her regain some of the pieces she feared had been lost for good when she left Lou. Only a year after their divorce, as Virginia was blossoming in her new career, another tall, dark, and handsome man caught her eye.

CHAPTER 6: CALIFORNIA ROYALTY

"Royalty is completely different than celebrity. Royalty has a magic all its own."

-Philip Treacy

Jaime del Valle was an esteemed director and producer in radio. Everyone knew and respected him. His work was impressive, but he also hailed from one of the wealthiest and most affluent native families in all of California. Virginia and Jaime first met in the 1930s during her musician days, but she was the only one who remembered their introduction.

In their 1930s prime, "The Singing Strings" were hired by then Mutual Broadcasting producer Jaime del Valle to perform bridges for a theatre spot and a few radio shorts. "She played a bass fiddle bigger than she was," Jaime recalled in meeting Virginia for the first time.[68] She had a very direct approach to pursuing her goals even in her 20s, so in seizing an opportunity during her initial spot work for Jaime as a musician she privately asked if he had a speaking part she could fill. According to an interview with Jaime in *The San Francisco Examiner*, he wasn't very taken with her abilities in those early days, but her professionalism and punctuality seemed to make up for any greenness he noticed in her. He gave her a small role in *The Phantom Pilot* serial with Howard Duff and thought nothing more of the young bass player whom he referred to then as "just a kid" who was "average . . . not bad, not great."[69]

Jaime was stationed in Europe for eighteen months during World War II. After his service, he returned to Mutual to continue in his directing role. During his direction on the radio adaption of O. Henry's *Cisco Kid*[70], in which Virginia often performed, the two were reintroduced in a different context.[71] During Jaime's service, Virginia had been hard at work establishing herself in radio after the transition from music. When they reconnected in the late 1940s, she wasn't the unmentionable green kid any longer. She had not only established her name with producers, directors, and fellow actors, but she was also a fan favorite with a budding identity as a dynamic actress, and she caught his eye too.

Some ten years since their first meeting, after finishing a performance on *Cisco Kid*, Virginia noticed Jaime in the wings. When the "on-air" sign flashed off, she took that as her cue to reintroduce herself. "Mr. del Valle? You don't remember me, do you? I'm Virginia Gregg," she said. According to him, he immediately lied and said he most certainly remembered her. "I don't remember if I took her out to dinner that night or not, but shortly after that we were married," Jaime recalled.[72] They married in Las Vegas on Oct 15, 1947. A second marriage for them both, Jaime was thirty-seven and Virginia was thirty-one.

Rich Spanish pioneer blood ran through Jaime's veins. The family roots of both sides of Jaime's family ran as deep as the Santa Clara River. Jaime's great-grandfather Antonio del Valle was a decorated soldier in the Mexican army, and for his service in the Mexican War of Independence in 1810, Ferdinand VII, King of Spain, gave Antonio "The Rancho San Francisco," a 48,612-acre land grant in an effort to foster American frontier settlements.[73] Antonio readily accepted and relocated from Guadalajara to the area now known as Santa Clarita, and per the grant's requirements, he worked the dustland until he soon fashioned it into a thriving ranch with cattle and sheep. Antonio had been given "the largest single tract of land" out of all the grants given to private individuals.[74] Antonio was a devout Catholic as an ambassador for what is now known as the San Fernando Mission established in 1797, and a lifelong rancher after his family's migration.[75] Following in his father's footsteps, Antonio's son, Ygnacio Ramón de Jesus del Valle, also joined the Spanish army and quickly moved up the ranks as a gleaming young lieutenant. Conflict arose, however, between father and son over their political ideals, as Ygnacio had advanced in the army as Antonio's contemporary under new leadership that opposed the former order of Antonio's military career. After Antonio learned that Ygnacio served in a particular battle in the 1830s, of which Ygnacio's side won, the two never spoke again.

In 1841, Antonio died without determining what would happen to the ranchos he had poured his lifeblood into for so many decades. Supposedly, on his deathbed he softened toward Ygnacio after years of animosity and penned a letter to him detailing his wishes for Ygnacio to have the Rancho San Francisco and a few other properties he had purchased through the years. The letter failed to reach Ygnacio before his father breathed his last, and an ugly lawsuit was brought between the remaining family members including Antonio's second wife Jacoba who felt exclusively entitled to her husband's land. After great contention, a settlement was finally reached, and the land was divided in the mid-1840s.

Another claim to fame of the del Valles' family is the Gold Rush of 1848, as that precious element was first discovered (in the region) in the dusty sediment of the del Valles' ranchos. Ygnacio worked his father's land until flooding conditions made it nearly impossible to continue, so he moved to Los Angeles and went into politics. He devoted the rest of his life to serving the community in civic capacities. Among many of his contributions to Los Angeles County was his establishment of "The Los Angeles Rangers," the first police force in LA history organized to thwart the crime sprees of "Mexican bandits."[76]

Antonio and his wife Isabel had many children – by most accounts, twelve, though a few did not survive to adulthood. One of the del Valles' sons, Reginaldo, served as California State Senator during the 1880s, and was instrumental in the founding of the University of California Los Angeles (UCLA), and the preservation of the Mission of San Fernando where his grandfather was once ambassador.[77] Another of the twelve, Ulpiano, married Clara Dowling, who came from the equally prestigious Carrillo family. This marriage only thickened the royal bloodline.

The Carrillo family line also originally hailed from Spain, and like the del Valles, migrated to Mexico sometime after the 1500s. One of Jaime's direct ancestors was Alonzo Carrillo, Archbishop of Toledo who was involved in arranging the marriage of Ferdinand of Aragon and Isabella of Castile in 1469 – the couple who would go on to give birth to Catherine of Aragon, the first wife of the infamous Henry VIII. Another Carrillo, Luis, was an explorer on the 1513 expedition that led to discovery of the Pacific Ocean.

The Carrillos first called California home beginning with Jaime's third great- grandfather, José Raymundo Carrillo Pasos. José came to California as a solider in the 1760s with an expedition group scouting out the frontier. He climbed the ranks in the Mexican army, much like Antonio del Valle did years after, and made captain. He married Maria Tomasa Ygnacia Martinez Lugo, the daughter of a soldier in José' troop, and the first Carrillo family settled in San Diego. The Carrillos' had seven children, two of which were, like the del Valles, given land grants by the King of Spain. The Carrillo children were rancheros, but with José being a decorated military captain, they were also involved in the political scene of the 1830s. Many of the seven also became military heroes and politicians in the early California settlements of Alta and Santa Barbara. The Carrillos are credited with building the first story-two home in the state: the Carrillo House. They are also the settlers of what is known as "The Old Town" outside of San Diego. Jaime's first cousin, "Leo Carrillo, The Movie Star" as he was known, who was a good thirty years older than Jaime, built what is now known as "The Leo Carrillo Ranch, Inc." in Carlsbad, California about forty miles north of his family's settlement in San Diego where he grew up.

Several historic landmarks are scattered throughout Southern California territory recognizing various members of both the del

Valles and Carrillos, two families paramount in California's early establishment.

The imperial Spanish bloodlines of del Valle and Carrillo clans intersected through the marriage of Jaime's father, Ulpiano del Valle, and his mother, Clara Arcadia Dowling del Valle, whose mother was a Carrillo. The two prestigious pioneering DNA sets culminated first in Jaime's sister Estella, then in his brother Ulpiano, and finally, in 1910, in Jaime.

Jaime and his siblings grew up in the heart of LA and the society column's centerstage in the early 1900s. Jaime's immediate family was just as prominent as his ancestors, and they constantly made the headlines and gossip columns of Southern California.

Jaime had gone into radio not long after graduating from Stanford University, but he enlisted in the service and was called to duty in the 1940s like so many others. Like his ancestors before him on both sides of the family tree, he was a decorated war hero. In the Air Force, Jaime had moved to major by the end of the war.[78] As a pilot in the Battle of Normandy, he was shot down– a nightmare he carried with him the rest of his life.

Before WWII, Jaime worked for a number of studios in producing such shows as *The Phantom Pilot*, and upon his return, he went to CBS and produced and directed countless others such as *Cisco Kid*, *Let George Do It*, *Family Theatre*, *Richard Diamond, Private Detective*, *Yours Truly, Johnny Dollar*, and *General Electric Theatre*, though the show he is most well-known for perhaps is the radio and television series *The Lineup*.

Jaime was a charming, commanding man, fluent in French, Portuguese, German, Italian, Spanish, and of course English.[79] He was an avid fisherman, and a natural in the kitchen, and Virginia adored the elaborate Spanish dishes he made. He was a Stanford graduate who spent several seasons as a celebrated halfback at the university.[80] He had a magnetic essence, and a set of piercing black eyes that were hard for Virginia to ignore.

Jaime and Virginia seemed a splendid match. They both came from prominent families in their own right and were accustomed to similar upper-class lifestyles. They had countless mutual friends, and many of the same interests. They were both making it big through different means in the same industry: Jaime orchestrating shows from the dim of the recording booth, and Virginia front and center at the microphone. He was the stubborn, contemptuous, taskmaster taking to his third-floor executive office and the recording booth like the cockpit of his fighter-jet. She was the softer, gentler, experiential who loved to dance in whatever beauty or tragedy that lie within the scripts from which she read. He was the mechanics; she was the humanities. Neither were big on the Hollywood nightlife, though they had standing invites to all the hippest joints in town. They made a well-rounded pair in constant compliment of the other . . . well, for a while.

The two bought a sizeable Los Angeles villa less than a mile from Sunset Blvd and settled in as newlyweds in the heart of LA prestige. They had bright beginnings in their new-found love, and each continued paving their own way in entertainment history.

FAMILY ADDITIONS AND SUBTRACTIONS

On October 10, 1948, at the age of fifty-eight, Virginia's father, Edward William Gregg, died. While his exact cause of death is unclear, he had been sick for some time and died in a local hospital in Bakersfield not far from his home. He was laid to rest in Forest Lawn Memorial Park in Glendale, California. Just a month after Edward's death, nearly to the day, Virginia gave birth to her first child, Gregg Bandini del Valle. He was born on November 11, 1948, a little over a year after Virginia and Jaime married. A beautiful combination of family names was given to the first offspring. Details of the birth spread through the papers like wildfire, as photos of the proud father and adoring mother with their new bundle made front and center in the lifestyles. Gregg was the first of two dynamics bloodlines represented in the powerhouse couple of radio. The papers called him "the prince of California's Royal Family."[81] Gregg made his radio debut at two months old. Jaime recorded his gurgles and goos at home one afternoon and played them back in the studio on a live episode of *The Count of Monte Cristo*. Carleton Young had stiff competition in "Baby del Valle."

Virginia took to motherhood like she did most everything else-with poise, grace, and commitment. She loved little Gregg dearly, and crooned over the unmistakable reflection of his father seen in his thick, black baby-hair and olive skin. She continued to work up until the week before Gregg had been born, and she resumed work not long after they were back home and settled into their new routine as a family of three.

Jaime and his family were devout Catholics, and Virginia was raised Protestant. The mixed marriage posed various points of dogmatic conflict, most prominently, the question of birth control. Contraceptives weren't widely available in the 1940s-1950s anyway, but within a traditional Catholic marriage even if one spouse hailed from Protestant beginnings, birth control was prohibited. Jaime told Virginia that in order to satisfy his religious convictions, Virginia would have to agree to domestic life without modern reproduction conveniences. Always the appeaser, Virginia agreed to abide by Jaime's conviction, after all, she was in love with the dashing Spanish prince turned king, and she had always wanted children. His convictions led to her "dates with the stork" as the newspapers said it. Three dates to be exact.

RADIO ANTICS

Virginia's radio work continued despite the additions and subtractions in her family. Her radio range increased and so did her paychecks. In 1949 she began regularly performed in supporting roles for detective dramas including *Let George Do It* starring Bob Bailey, *The Adventures of Philip Marlowe* staring Gerald Mohr, and *Richard Diamond, Private Detective* starring Dick Powell. She also continued to dabble in television and film when opportunity arose.

Jerry Farber, son of Les Farber, who wrote many radio shows back in the Golden Age, recalls a wonderful story of his intersection with Virginia in 1949, during his early industry days as a teenager:

> *[Jim] Hawthorne was putting together what I guess was a pilot for a TV show – a sort of sit-com. And amazingly, they called me to play a part on the show. As it turns out, though he did do television eventually, this particular show never got picked up. But, OK, so here's the pilot episode. I'm—I don't know—fourteen, maybe? I got cast as—I think it was his nephew. And my character was supposed to be kind of like him. So the scene is that this woman comes by to visit. She was another one of his sisters. She's sitting on the couch; I come in, and Hawthorne tells me 'Kiss your Aunt' [whatever her name was].' And the script calls for me to actually kiss her—on the mouth. That was supposed to be the joke, I guess—that my character took him at his word. So OK, it was maybe a little embarrassing, but in the rehearsal (actually, I think we only had one rehearsal before the show), I just—you know, went for it and laid one on her. What else was I supposed to do? He said to kiss her. (And I knew about kissing. That was the year when Royene Tripp was having these little parties at her parents' house, where we played Spin the Bottle, and Post Office, and Seven Minutes in Heaven.) OK, so I kiss her; she sort of—I don't know, stiffens her back a bit, and we finish the scene. And then people are smiling and looking at each other, and someone—I guess it was the director—takes me aside and explains to me about 'stage kisses' and about how I was supposed to place the kiss not actually on her mouth, but off center in a certain way in*

relation to the camera angle. I think I've blotted out the details because it was kind of embarrassing. What was I supposed to know about stage kisses? I was a radio actor.

DICK BEALS

"She gave me my start in radio," was a common descriptor for Virginia Gregg del Valle. Along with John Dehner, others fondly remembered when Virginia gave them a boost to the mic so-to-speak. Child actor, Dick Beals, was another who recalled her generosity.

"Ginny," as he referred to her, saw him in CBS' crowded lobby one afternoon and after the usual pleasantries, asked who he had met with "upstairs," meaning which executives on the third floor had he talked with about roles with CBS. "Well, nobody," Dick said. "Why not?" Virginia asked indignantly. "I tried to get an appointment with Mr. del Valle, but his secretary said, 'Don't even bother, you don't stand a chance. Mr. del Valle's wife does all the children's parts in this town,'" Dick explained. With her Irish temper flaring, Virginia grabbed Dick's arm leaving the rest of him no choice but to follow her into the elevator for the third floor. With a bang of the number three, they sailed toward the executives' offices, starting with Elliot Lewis'.

Virginia barged in with Dick's arm still in tow. "This is Dick Beals, don't ever use me again, he's twice as good as I am, goodbye." Elliot readily agreed after the two were already sailing down the hall toward the next office. One by one the executives met Dick through Virginia's unexpected introduction. Finally, the two made it to "Mr. del Valle's" office. Virginia marched right passed his secretary's feeble objections and Dick found himself face to face with the man he knew could advance his career in just the way he wanted. "This is Dick Beals, use him for all the children's parts, do you understand?" Virginia said to "Mr. del Valle." Jaime looked Dick over and smiled,

"Yes, Dick that's a promise, thank you." Dick was floored. Ginny Gregg was a magician. What kind of pull could she have with this radio god? Turning from Dick to Ginny, Dick heard Jaime ask, "So, honey what are we having for dinner tonight?" Little did Dick know that "Ginny Gregg" was in fact "Mrs. del Valle."

THREE STORKS

A little over two years after baby Gregg joined the del Valle clan, the couple's second child, Jaime Carrillo del Valle, was born on March 10, 1951. Like his older brother, he too made the papers – along with his 9-pound birth weight. The del Valle's third child, Ricardo Bandini del Valle, was born on August 17, 1953, and like his brothers before him, announcements of his arrival were also print-worthy in the lifestyle sections of all the rags in town. Virginia self-described as "extremely pregnant" all three times but continued on with her career despite the long hours and fatiguing conditions of having three children within a five-year period.[82]

The del Valles' Parkwood Drive villa was brimming with three boys and menagerie of pets. Virginia loved animals – especially dogs and had many different furry pals over the years, most of which were Boxers and Great Danes.

Her radio work remained steady throughout her new role as "mom." She did stand out a bit in the family of radioers, because she was "always pregnant" as fellow actress Anne Whitfield described. Despite her "delicate conditions," Virginia wanted to be treated no differently and continued the long hours and draining emotional work.

Actress Alice Backes, known for her work on *This Is Your FBI*, *The Whistler, and Family Theatre*, recalled working with Virginia in those early glory days:

Our paths first crossed on the Dr. Christian *shows. Through the pregnancies of her three sons, there she would be on the other side of the mike, always the pro, giving always the unique and special quality that each character required. Her versatility, of course, was always legend. Beyond her professional life she was always interested in the other person and how one was coping with life's challenges. She always seemed to meet what life dealt her without rancor.*

Virginia's flubs were few and far between, not because she was invincible, but because of her immense focus and knack for smooth ad-libbing when the occasion called for it. A bad case of pregnancy-brain may be to blame for her most infamous flub, however. Though this is generally attributed to other radioers from Cathy Lewis to Jim Burton, Virginia swore she was the guilty party despite what history recorded. As her confession went, this flub hit the airwaves on the *Dr. Christian* radio show. In this particular episode, she played the role of an assisting nurse during a surgery scene in live recording with a live audience. Her script called for her to administer various essentials to the good doctor during his treatment of the patient. One of her lines read, "Here's your hypodermic needle, Doctor," but she accidentally transposed a few letters and said, "Here's your *hypodeemic nerdle*" instead. At first, she didn't realize what she had said until several more lines down the page when Jean Hersholt began to chuckle through his own lines and couldn't stop. As bad as that was, radio announcer Harry von Zell's infamous "President Hoobert Heever" during a broadcast once might have been worse.

While Virginia was usually the one tending to others, she did find herself in dire need of help during another recording of the *Dr. Christian* show while pregnant.

Reportedly Parley Baer came to her rescue, though Art Gilmore swore *he* was the hero who prevented the near mishap rather than Parley. The *Dr. Christian* show was recorded live weekly in front of an audience of around 300. During the show, the very-pregnant Virginia sat among the other cast members awaiting her cue.

In her third trimester, she was dressed in a smart maternity skirt typical of the day that had a cutout for the baby bump with elastic bands that tied on each side to hold the skirt up. Halfway through the show before her own cue, she felt a subtle *boing* at her side. The elastic had broken all the way around. She knew when she stood up, her skirt would not stand with her. Her mind and heart both undoubtedly raced as she tried to think of a solution. She had to act quickly because her part was fast approaching, and with a live recording in front of a live audience there could be no retakes or stalls. She leaned to her left and nudged *Dr. Christian* regular Rosemary DeCamp and asked if she had a safety pen. Rosemary of course said she didn't. She leaned to her right and asked Parley if he had one. He of course said neither did he. Hearing her cue, she told Parley to grab one side of her skirt and then the other and walk up to the mic with her so she could do her part. He didn't ask questions, he just followed her cue. If it hadn't been for Parley, the live audience would have experienced a very different kind of show that day. According to Parley, that was the most useful he had ever been.[83]

Because of Parley's (or Art's) heroic act that day in the "The Case of the Busted Elastic," the show continued fluidly and even the live audience was never the wiser. Even after all these years, it wouldn't be too hard to imagine Parley and Art in the afterlife still arguing over which one actually held Virginia's skirt up that day. To be fair, perhaps Parley held one side and Art the other.

Lionel Barrymore was a wonderful hurricane of a man. Just after Virginia discovered she was pregnant with her third child, Ricardo, Parley Baer was the first to hear the good news. After her doctor's appointment, Virginia had gone straight to the studio for a recording of *The Story of Doctor Kildare* starring Lionel Barrymore as the ornery old "Dr. Gillespie." Virginia and Parley were alone in the studio wings when she whispered the news to him. From some twenty feet away slumped over in his wheelchair, eyes closed, with a cheek dropped in one palm, sat Lionel seemingly dead to the world. After Parley had offered his congratulations, the two walked out of the wings past Lionel to get to work. Still slumped over with his eyes shut tightly he said without moving anything but his lips, "Ginny, are you pregnant *AGAIN*?" Virginia and Parley both turned white at his question. It's unclear whether Lionel had the hearing of a moth, or was simply part clairvoyant, but his question stunned both Virginia and Parley. "Yes, Lionel I am pregnant *AGAIN*," Virginia answered, meeting his tone. It's also unclear what Lionel's retort was to her "yes" because it was probably not something suitable for the radio air waves, but I'm sure he had a brilliantly crude comeback to let Virginia know exactly how he felt about her news – as he aged, his feelings of course were never held back in the spirit of decorum.

It was a bit unusual for a woman in the prime of her career to have three children within such a short amount of time and still continue in her chosen career. Many women were forced to choose families over careers or vice versa, because "nobody could have both," though Virginia sure tried. Parley Baer recalled, "Aside from consistently magnificent performances, I remember Virginia constantly embroidering, sewing, 'fixing' for other people. Even during her pregnancies, she was forever making something for those of her friends who were also expecting." She somehow managed to create a work-life balance before that was even a thing.

ANNE

Though pleasant and social, Virginia liked to stay busy during her downtime in the studio, possibly espousing the well-known Proverb of "idle hands are the devil's workshop." She couldn't sit still for long and no longer had the strings of the double bass viol to fidget with. Like many of the women of her generation, Virginia was skilled in various types of handwork: sewing, knitting, cross-stitch, embroidery, crochet, etc. In between her cues, she busied herself with creating and mending. Actress Anne Whitfield was a child actress when she first met Virginia who was at least twenty years her senior. Anne recalls her mother making the long drive on Route 66 from Georgia to California in an old Ford with bald tires for her to have the chance to be in "pictures." Anne played "Penelope Lacey" in the beloved family drama *One Man's Family* on radio. When Anne first came to Hollywood as a small child, she brought her southern accent with her. One of her first directors told her to learn German and that would take care of the southern accent. She did, and it did. In addition to *One Man's Family*, she and Virginia did other radio productions together such as *Cisco Kid* and *Romance of the Ranchos*. Anne recalls Virginia as "warm, friendly, and always pregnant."

She recalls one of the first times she met Virginia without a mic standing between them. Anne enjoyed knitting like Virginia did, and one day during studio downtime, Virginia sat down next to her to pass on a "faster way" to knit. She pulled her own project from her purse and taught Anne "the German way" of knitting. Anne said, "There's no telling how many hours and hours Virginia Gregg saved me in knitting by taking the time to pass on a faster way to accomplish the same thing." During the Great Quarantine of 2020, Anne passed on Virginia's knitting trick to me thousands of miles away over the phone. I feel privileged to have a lifehack of Virginia's very own up my sleeve. Anne has had a grand career in the industry from radio to television to film and is an accomplished writer and activist.

ONE MAN'S FAMILY

A favorite role of Virginia's to play was "Betty Barbour" on *One Man's Family*. This was a terribly influential show in the Golden Age, known as "the longest-running uninterrupted dramatic serial in the history of American radio." It ran for an astonishing twenty-seven years on radio from April 29, 1932, until May 8, 1959. The series was created by Carlton E. Morse in the 1930s about the San Francisco family, the "Barbours," whose typical American family sagas amid the fast-changing nation in the early 20th century were cathartic to many listeners. The weekly stories of the "Barbours" were told through life chapters, making it an airwave novelty at the time. The show survived the Great Depression, WWII, and even the radio-to-television transition with Morse at the helm. Virginia's character "Betty" first joined in the cast in 1950 and remained throughout its radio run until 1959, as daughter-in-law of main characters "Henry and Fanny Barbour."

Virginia once recalled a trip she made to a dime store on break that convinced her of just how significant the show really was to audiences. After browsing a bit, she approached the counter with her findings. The clerk said, "I'm sorry Miss, we can't ring up your purchases right now." Virginia looked around, seeing no other customers or obvious reason why not, and before Virginia's aggravation could answer, the clerk explained, "It's time for *One Man's Family* to come on, and we never miss it. We stop working every day at this time to listen."

With an understanding nod Virginia joined the small group of workers that had gathered around the radio, and they all listened intently to the show. Afterward, the clerk rang up Virginia's purchases and she left without ever letting on that she was in fact one of the show's key players.

THE E WORD

While she certainly had her flaws, ego was something that never personally plagued Virginia. Perhaps one of the greatest struggles she faced in the industry for her duration in it was that flagrant "e" word as antediluvian as time itself. That was something present in every facet of the industry that didn't seem to dim over time. Columnist Lydia Lane once asked Virginia:

'What do you think makes a person difficult to get along with?'
I asked. 'Egotism,' she replied. 'Seeing everything from your
point of view without attempting to understand the other. You
can't consider yourself mature unless you are prepared to give
and take.'[84]

While show business has its big breaks and its big breakdowns, the real threat to the functionality of the whole thing was (and is) perhaps, as Virginia said, "Egotism" – the kind that permeates the system from the inside out.

The competition present in the industry was just as cut-throat in the Golden Age as perhaps it is today – competition that was often perpetuated by that infamous "e word." While Virginia was offered the majority of the parts she played without a cold audition in the traditional sense, she still dealt with the rejection and tough blows that all artists experience. Stock companies weren't ego-free of course, but generally the model was about relationships, crafting, training, and the growth of the actor or actress.

She wisely stuck with the stock company model as long as it lived, and even benefited from it in its death with people like Jack Webb and Bill Conrad who continued to operate under the artistic approach of the stock company's ghost. Supporting players were doing well to be in one stock company, much less multiple. She remained in Jack Webb's, Bill Conrad's, Blake Edwards', Alfred Hitchcock's, and Rod Serling's stock companies until either her retirement or theirs.

CHAPTER 7: ENDING AND BEGINNING AGAIN

"And to make an end is to make a beginning."

-T.S. Eliot

It was October 1958. Virginia had just fastened the clasp of her last bracelet before leaving for the studio. She was scheduled for a taping of *The Barbara Stanwyck Show*. She had just surrendered to one more lipstick check before leaving her vanity when a frantic vacillation of pounding on the front door and the insistent ringing of the doorbell interrupted her thoughts. *Pound, ring, ring, ring, pound, pound.* She ran from her dresser and opened the door to the sight of a strange woman in terror. "Do you have a son?" The woman asked breathlessly, her words seeming to hang in the air between them. "Yes, yes I have a son," Virginia stuttered back.

"There's been an accident," the woman cried.

The stranger ran from the doorstep and Virginia instinctually followed, as the woman flew back toward the street where she seemed to come from. Not far from the end of their Parkwood driveway, in a mangled heap in front of the woman's car was Virginia's middle son, seven-year-old, Jaime.

The world narrowed as Virginia saw Jaime below the nose of the car. She heard a scream – it must have been her own, but she couldn't be sure. Time froze, and she was suddenly running in slow motion to get to him. She fell at his side trying to make sense of his disfigured position in the car's shadow. The strange woman stood helpless over the two, "I'm so sorry, I didn't see him on his bike until it was too late," she stammered.

Virginia gently touched his face, afraid to move him. She fought the urge to grab him in her arms and rock him like she had for so many hours when he was smaller. The extent of his injuries was unknown and snatching him up even in a loving embrace could mean even more agony for him. It was obvious Jaime's little legs had taken the brunt of the impact, as they lie contorted and motionless. Barely able to catch her breath, Virginia directed the woman to phone for help. "Run to the neighbors and have them call the ambulance. He's gotta have help quick --- I can't leave him," she said. The woman robotically took the orders and ran for the next door.

Looking into the yellowed face of her middle child as he lay lifeless on the hot pavement, a million thoughts flashed through her mind. He was moving in and out of consciousness, and as badly as she wanted to crawl through the pavement itself in hysterics, she knew she somehow had to stay calm. She gently brushed the black hair back from his forehead where sweat and blood had begun to bead together. He was limp. "No. No, no, no. You'll be just fine, Jaime," Virginia told him. "I'm here honey, and you'll be alright. Help is coming, and you'll be alright. You've just got to be," Virginia quietly insisted.

A crowd of neighbors had gathered to see the commotion, but to Virginia, the world consisted of only she and her seven-year-old. Jaime's brothers, Gregg ten, and Ricardo five, had come out from their own playing to see what had happened. She instructed them with one finger and two raised eyebrows to stay in their yard back out of the way. Gregg hung his arm around Ricardo's little shoulders as they helplessly looked on.

It felt like hours before the wail of the sirens pierced the air. Virginia closed her eyes in relief as the wails drew closer. She stepped back as the EMS workers surrounded Jaime, her dress spotted with blood and her mind devoid of all prior engagements. Barbara Stanwyck who?

Virginia watched every move as the EMS workers carefully loaded Jaime on to the gurney. She loaded Gregg and Ricardo into her 1955 Ford Ranchwagon to follow the ambulance, and just before she flattened the back of her skirt to get behind the wheel, she noticed a familiar car careening through the narrow street a bit too close to the scene.

It was that ambulance chasing reporter Virginia and everyone else in LA knew. He and his obnoxious yellow Montclair had slowly crept up Parkwood Drive to get a piece of the action the ambulance surely would lead to. His hat did little to disguise him and his intruding camera. He had that excited, coy look all cartoon wolves have just after they put on their bibs to devour the nearest cartoon piglet – and of course the paramount trait any good reporter must have: no shame.

Virginia furiously beat on the window of his Montclair. "There's no story here, Rob. And if you think there is, the del Valles'll be going in the paper business. Now get the hell out of here!" He took off his wolf bib, and suddenly remembered a previous engagement far from Parkwood Drive. She convinced him; the accident stayed out of the papers.

Jaime spent weeks in the hospital recovering from his extensive injuries. His seven-year-old body had been broken to pieces and spent day after day in excruciating traction. Besides the constant physical agony he was in, being away from home furthered his suffering. He looked forward to his mother's phone call each morning and her visit every afternoon. It was a terrifying, confusing, and lonely time for the seven-year-old.

The last thing he remembered was riding his bike down his home street like he had done hundreds of times before, and then pain – incredible pain. He had been plucked from his home and family and confined to a colorless hospital room full of things that seemed to only cause more pain.

Just because Jaime was across town in the hospital didn't mean Virginia was any less attentive to him. One morning when she called, Jaime told her of a nurse who had been particularly rough with him the night before. She calmly listened and told him she was sorry that happened, and casually asked for a description of said nurse. They moved on in the conversation, and Virginia promised to visit later in the day like always. When she arrived at the hospital, instead of her usual beeline to his room, she made a detour.

She stalked the halls until she found the nurse with the terrible bedside manner. In summary, the nurse apologized profusely after Virginia's conversation with her, and Jaime never saw that nurse again.

Jaime recovered, but only after multiple, lengthy hospitalizations and myriad restorative procedures. He still suffers residuals from the accident even today but remembers fondly the care his mother showed him during those terribly black months.

RISING

Like many artists, Virginia continued to channel her own personal hurts into her acting craft from the dusty shootouts of *Tales of the Texas Rangers* to San Francisco police headquarters of the *Lineup*. Her personal struggles aren't obvious in her body of work of course, but the scripts serve as sound euphemisms for her own grief, worry, and struggle. As author and film critic Michael Wood says, "It seems that entertainment is not, as we often think, a full-scale flight from our problems, not a means of forgetting them completely, but rather a rearrangement of our problems into shapes which tame them, which disperse them to the margins of our attention." That certainly must be true for those on both side of the screen.

You could turn the dial on almost any major station in the 1950s and hear Virginia in multiple shows on any given day – at the height of her climb in radio, she was doing five different shows a day. For all the industry sowing she did in the 1940s, the 1950s was a decade of industry reaping. In addition to her standing roles with shows that bled over from the 1940s like *Dragnet, Suspense, Yours Truly, Johnny Dollar, Romance,* and *Let George Do It,* she was also regularly featured in popular series such as *Gunsmoke, The Six Shooter, Have Gun, Will Travel,* and *CBS Radio Workshop.* She was in high demand in radio, and the doors of television and film were also opening for her developed expertise.

In the 1950s, television was quickly becoming a threatening competitor to its radio predecessor, as America became more and more fascinated with the moving pictures they could enjoy from the comfort of their own homes. Some actors and actresses – like some shows – made the radio-to-television transition smoothly while others did not. Virginia was in the aforementioned category. She adapted well to the small screen and vacillated between the two competing media until radio breathed its last in 1962. *Dragnet* was the first to feature Virginia on television. *Dragnet* had a wildly successful radio run from 1949-1957 and began on television in 1951 running concurrently with its radio series until 1959. Virginia alternated between studio and set in the 1950s getting her sea legs in yet another medium. *Dragnet* appearances led to spots on early episodes of other emerging television series like *The Danny Thomas Show, Alfred Hitchcock Presents, Lassie,* and *Perry Mason.*

Some in the radio world were hostile toward television's looming success, as it potentially meant the death and burial of radio as they had known it. Many radio series made the jump to television often with brand new casts, leaving radio actors and actresses to feel more than deserted. Holding to no particular medium loyalty, others embraced the new media: where the work was, they went. Getting in on the ground floor so-to-speak, Virginia was a part of the group of actors and actresses who first introduced television to audiences, thus being among the first to win the world over to television.

Split between radio and television, Virginia still found time to accept film roles. If the script was good, she was interested. She appeared in several films in the 1950s that were a far cry from her description-roles of the 1940s. She was starting to get hearty film roles that better showcased her aptitude and range. In 1955, she appeared in Henry King and Otto Lang's *Love is a Many-Splendored Thing* starring William Holden and Jennifer Jones. Later the same year, she appeared in Daniel Mann's *I'll Cry Tomorrow*, the tragic, yet inspiring biopic of Broadway's Lillian Roth starring Susan Hayward, Richard Conte, and Eddie Albert. The *Dragnet* feature film in 1954 did more than remember Virginia in its casting. A role was fashioned in the script especially for her, and a helluva role it was, nearly earning her an Academy Award nomination.

In those early days of film initiation as "simply" a radioer, you might think Virginia was prone to reticence or an occasional case of awestruck in working alongside veteran film stars, but she was so confident in her own skill set that working with the bigs wasn't threatening. Many stars were neighbors and personal friends with the del Valles, like Steve McQueen, whom Virginia played opposite of in *Wanted: Dead or Alive*. Other film A-listers she wasn't as acquainted with were still no immediate threat. She recalled many who guest spotted on radio shows, and out of good old-fashioned stage-fright, had to rely on patchwork gimmicks to manage their nerves. For instance, to combat their shaking, radio regulars would help nervous film star guests staple their scripts to a cardboard cut out near the mic to prevent them from shaking so uncontrollably they couldn't read their lines. Virginia also recalled having to look the other way when these silver screen heroes sweated through their clothes, needed multiple glasses of water to get through a reading, or let their voices shudder on air. Since she experienced the "Great Oz" phenomenon when "celebrities" visited her radio world, I suppose visiting theirs in film didn't make them any less human.

For all of Virginia's training and talent, she was a pragmatist. She was steeped in the traditions of theatre and housed many methodologies of the dramatic arts, but she was practical in her approach to roles. An enormous amount of preparation went into each role given her – especially for television and film in which appearance was a significant variable largely absent in radio aside from promotional shoots. In prepping for a role, she didn't just memorize lines and try to understand the obvious motivations of her characters, she fussed over the character's context, drives, internal climate, and she let her pen bleed all over television and film scripts' margins. She internalized the very world each script represented and channeled real emotions into the plight of her characters.

Late thespian and acting coach Stella Adler described the modern acting tendency as "bringing great characters down" to the level of the actor, while the true craft requires the actor to "raise themself to the level of the characters."[85] While Adler's commentary almost exclusively derived from stage work rather than television or film, the "raising" process described is certainly one Virginia practiced in her own approach to self-submersion in character portrayal. She never thought of characters as vessels through which to express her own suffering – though of course that is always a byproduct of the craft itself – rather she put the character's plight above her own and rose to the ambitions, tragedies, ugliness, and refinement of any role she was given. This "raising" process is perhaps one of the reasons she was able to have such a diverse range, and perhaps why she always convinced us so.

Virginia dissected every script she was given. She absorbed it, defended it, became a product of its world. She submerged herself in role after role, harnessing whatever emotion was necessary for the part, yet never quite fully giving in to its full expression. The great dichotomy of self-submerging yet withholding a "character's" own emotions is a balance few can create. It can be seen and felt in the beautiful tension in many of her performances. She produced the necessary emotion yet fought with it on screen.[86] She intentionally held back just enough to get the audience's buy in. Her performances were controlled and driven, with hints of her own story scantily bleeding through. One of the novelties of the Golden Age of media is that directors often allowed actors and actresses to create their own character within the parameters of the script. Acting of that era was often a creative process even in the interpretation of a script or character.

The ever-pragmatic, creative Virginia also used tangible props available to her in support of her character's viability regardless of how long her role could be seen or heard. Fourteen seconds or 45 minutes – the camera and the paycheck might have differentiated, but not Virginia's preparation. The camera has a menacing tendency to shorten weeks of prep-work into a few one-dimensional scenes in a film or half-hour show, but to Virginia, it was all part of the experience, as "Hollywood Report" noted:

Virginia Gregg is an actress who looks mighty attractive when she shows up for a radio part but usually looks as if life gave her several swift kicks when she appears in motion picture or on TV. It's a comparatively rare audience which is permitted to see that Miss Gregg is really on the pretty side and resembles very strongly a happy human. Most of her roles call for what is known trade-wise as de-glamorization. Her latest is no exception, but it does demonstrate her continuing versatility. Now she's a hard-work waitress and slum mother in Allied Artists' 'Crime in the Streets.' Her in for the role was typical of her attitude about her work. 'True, I've never lived in a slum or worked as a waitress,' *she said.* 'I knew what it meant to be tired, I guess. Well, to get things right for this part, my clothes were aged and soiled with about five special substances to give the right effect I rubbed and scuffed my shoes against a curb till I liked them. Then a dulling lacquer was sprayed on my hair—made it look drab and frowsy. I used just a line of lipstick under my eyes for makeup to make them look very weary.' *Miss Gregg added to her generally fatigued character by carrying bags full of groceries to make her arms sag—she*

could have used lightweight, padded bags— and then deliber-
ately limited her sleep so she would seem genuinely tired. 'I'm
not exactly typed,' she said, 'unless it's as a woman.'[87]

Virginia underwent a similar process for the role of "Ethel Starkie"
in the *Dragnet* feature. *The LA Times* says she came close to an
Academy Award nomination for her compelling portrayal of the
life-worn lush.[88] Jack Webb and Jim Moser co-wrote the part specifically for Virginia and feveredly called her for a read-through.
Even a cold first reading caused the hairs on her arms stand up, she
recalled. Her prep work for the role met the intensity of the role
itself:

> *For the right kind of red eyes, Virginia merely takes out her*
> *lipstick and goes to work. Then when Jack Webb wanted her*
> *as a drunk on* Dragnet, *Virginia went at it this way: The night*
> *before she had three or four drinks and then went to bed. Then*
> *she set her alarm for 4:00 a.m. When she got up she looked*
> *terrible –who wouldn't! In the morning on the set before doing*
> *her long scene she had two drinks, well spaced. Then she went*
> *on camera with the slight, boozy feeling of one, but with her*
> *mind still sharp. The scene was done in one take, and Virginia*
> *says it was one of her best performances.*[89]

Virginia also recalled having to pass a sobriety test on set from a
consulting police officer who watched her "Ethel Starkie" performance before she was allowed to leave the lot to drive home.

Legendary Golden Age actress Ann Robinson is most well-
known for her famous portrayal of "Sylvia van Buren" in the 1953
film adaptation of H.G. Wells' *War of the Worlds*, though her acting
resume is quite lengthy in both film and television beyond this block-
buster. Ann appeared in the *Dragnet* feature film with Virginia the
year after in 1954. She played the attractive, dedicated "Officer Grace

Downey." Ann wanted the part because like so many of Webb's and Moser's parts, it was wonderfully written and because working with Jack Webb meant exciting possibilities for a rising star. By the time Ann's audition slot for "Officer Downey" came around, Jack apologetically told her he had already signed another actress for the role. Ann wasn't dissuaded. Even at 25, Ann had had enough industry experience under her belt to confidently persuade him to give her an audition, futile as it may have been in his opinion. In a matter of a few minutes into her audition, Jack immediately booted the original actress from the role, paid the broken contract penalty, and Ann became "Officer Grace Downey." What compelling audition won hard-nosed Jack over causing him to break a newly signed contract with his first choice? Ann gave a remarkable impersonation for her audition that made the ever-composed Jack Webb *laugh*. She impersonated *him*.

Like so many other colleagues of Virginia's, Ann Robinson has fond memories of Virginia's performances and finds her portrayal of "Ethel Starkie," the one-legged lush, to be particularly captivating. She recalls Virginia as a fine actress who needs to be remembered: "Virginia is far too important to be forgotten. She needed a biography."

Acting is a relative expression that represents different things for different people. For some, acting is about the audience – what can I make them feel or sense about the world? For others, it is about communicating the stories of the humanities. How can I persuade, convince, or educate the society on the other side of the screen? Generally, regardless of what motivates a person to give in to that draw of the craft, acting is a connection point to the masses (whether 5 or 5 million) that serves as an agent of awareness, change, or exposé. To reference Adler once again, she described theatre as the ultimate X-ray machine of society. She believed that to understand previous generations, we can know no more than what their playwrights and performers left for us in terms of theatrical productions. She believed the theatre could capture what the history books couldn't. I agree with that perspective to a certain degree, but I would also add other media to the list along with theatre including books, music, radio, film, and television. Good, bad, or indifferent, they are all a time-capsuled "X-ray" of the generation in which they were created. Virginia was a part of those Golden Age X-rays, and while she may not be referenced in many history books, she significantly contributed to those time-capsules that inform future generations. While many pieces of art are timeless and can resonate with audiences decades after its creators are dead and gone, there are those time-capsules that can only be truly understood and appreciated by those who evolved within the same context as the work itself. Virginia's crown jewel of her 1950s film-work is just such an example: *Operation Petticoat*.

With a powerhouse cast, Blake Edwards' *Operation Petticoat* was a wild success and quickly became somewhat of a 1950s cult classic with bad boy heartthrob Tony Curtis playing opposite the all-around posh gentleman Cary Grant. Blake was a young radio writer when he and Virginia first met on *Richard Diamond, Private Detective*. They remained friends for years after with Blake always recruiting her for his television and film productions until her death. *Operation Petticoat* was a technicolor X-ray of women's presence in World War II and post-war America. Through a romantic comedy set in the opening of WWII, Blake sent the PSA that women had indeed arrived in a man's world, and men, however they felt about it, had better find a way to accept it. As "Major Edna Heywood," Virginia leads a troop of female army nurses on a friendly ambush of a submarine on a Pacific Ocean operation – an ambush that quickly turns to mayhem as the men must make room for their unexpected feminine guests aboard. In the 2020s, the film may seem at best cheesy, and at worst utterly obsolete, but in its day, the film carried an important message beyond the slapstick in the 1950s. Though Blake used the euphemism of WWII, the film really is much more about war between the sexes – female empowerment and man's response to that inevitable phenomenon in America that only grew louder on the other side of WWII. Who better to play the female lead in a film about that than Virginia Gregg?

Virginia generally refused parts that would require her to travel further than a county over, as she made it clear through her agent her priority was her three boys. After Blake's insistence on this particular film, however, she accepted the role in *Operation Petticoat* though it required her to be on location in Florida for several weeks. It is perhaps one of her most memorable roles, as I repeatedly heard from several of her later-career colleagues during interviews for this book, "If only I had known that was *her* in *Operation Petticoat!*"

THE RIPPING

As Virginia skimmed the morning paper over the breakfast she had made, the ashes from the cigarette between her fingers became long overdue for a flick into the ashtray as her eyes focused on a particular signing announcement of a fellow actress for a new series. A heavy sigh and fold of the paper resounded all around the breakfast table and she remembered her cigarette.

"Your team lose again?" Jaime asked from behind his own section of the paper.

"No, Jim signed somebody else for the part in his new series. I can't understand it. When I talked to him last month, he said I was a shoo-in." She sighed over the clanking of the dishes she collected, wiping a mouth or two as she made her way to the sink. "That's show biz, for you," she said more with her eyebrows than her voice, turning to wipe the chubby little hands beating on the highchair tray.

As Jaime stood for his sharkskin sport coat, he took one more gulp of coffee, and said toward the sink, "Well honey, like I told Jim, there's always next time."

"You talked to Jim?" Virginia asked, rising from between two of the three still sitting at the table all with little feet dangling high above the floor.

"Yeah, that agent of yours is no good. I had all your calls forwarded to me. I just told Jim you couldn't possibly take that part with everything else you have going on."

"Jaime, do you know how much I wanted that? Do you know what that part would have meant for me, for all of us?" Virginia asked with tears starting to gleam over her blue eyes.

"Well, you can't win 'em all, Ginny," he said flatly as he made his way out the door without goodbyes.

Virginia's agent understood her desire to have a reasonable work-life balance and had generally been fair in contract negotiations. She was busy, but busy was how she lived best. She knew it would be of no use to try and reason with Jaime about letting her agent handle her offers instead of him, because as Virginia had learned not too long after their wedding, what Jaime wanted, Jaime got.

The del Valles were a Hollywood power couple. Through the 1940s-50s, they were radio's answer to film's Joan Crawford and Douglas Fairbanks, Jr. and television's Lucy and Desi. By all appearances, they were the archetype for the modern LA family in the entertainment industry. They had made a grand life together with three beautiful children who lived in their home, and countless airwave masterpieces that lived among the masses with Virginia at the mic and Jaime at the controls. They had it all.

Virginia knew from early on that Jaime could be stormy and willful, but that was part of his alpha charm, and as the doting wife of the 1950s, she overlooked his outbursts and readily accepted his "I'm sorry"s the next morning. The bruises usually weren't visible, so she carried the familiar duality of daytime identity and nighttime identity that was perhaps reminiscent of her adolescent days when she worked so hard to conceal her mother's condition and continue as a seemingly carefree schoolkid who didn't have the responsibilities of a grown adult at home.

As the fights became more frequent, the apologies became fewer. The brighter the spotlight in the industry, the darker home became. Jaime and Virginia both worked long, draining hours, and constantly overlapped in their studio work. Jaime continued micromanaging her schedule and books and by his own casual admission in the papers, turned down offers she received as he saw fit – without consulting her.

Those first days of coy romance and exciting pursuit were long since over. The dashing Spanish prince turned king had charmed his way into Virginia's heart, and conquered more and more of her identity's territory as the years of marriage ticked by. The only small corner of her former self she had managed to preserve was her stage name. While Virginia legally took Jaime's name after they married in 1948, she wanted to maintain the name she began her industry climb with: Virginia Gregg. That was the name by which everyone in town knew her, and fans never did take too well to name changes of their favorite performers' years into their careers. In her prime, a last name change in entertainment, could mean career suicide. Despite agreeing she would maintain "Gregg," Jaime continued to pressure her to take "del Valle" before the public eye even going so far as to, against Virginia's wishes, instruct announcers to credit her as "Virginia del Valle" in a few episodes he directed. Virginia was prime, fertile land he had conquered, and he wanted everyone to know it.

After ten years of marriage, at the age of forty-two, Virginia filed for divorce from Jaime in 1958 on the grounds of "grievous mental and physical cruelty" according to the headlines and divorce records. The news of their divorce ran in all major newspapers in nearly all fifty states. From *The Miami Herald* to *The Detroit Free Press* and throughout the rest of the country, the story broke that the great love affair of radio's power couple was finished. And the undertones of why it was finished was probably fairly shocking to the public in the 1950s, and to the couple's friends and associates as troubled affairs of the domestic weren't topics of casual conversation.

Virginia and Jaime both were very accustomed to having all their life details shining from the newsstand each week. They both were considered favorites among entertainment journalists and readers alike. Countless articles were written featuring them individually and as the power couple following the trajectory of their respective careers and the family they had made. Since the 1930s, the media had covered their individual rises in the industry, and readers loved to follow along with news of Virginia's upcoming roles and announcements of Jaime's directing and producing projects. Their names were always before the public's eye with birth announcements of their sons, interviews with Virginia about her beauty secrets, Jaime's behind-the-scenes production drama on *The Lineup*, and promotional anecdotes of studio antics in radio, television, and film. The papers had followed them both as individuals before they were married. They had relayed to the world their marriage announcement, the births of their children, their grand successes in media, and now their divorce under allegations of "grievous mental and physical cruelty," a term most analogous with the umbrella term we use today: domestic violence.

Suing for divorce in the 1950s was, as you might imagine, very different than it is in the 2020s. The system was different, laws were different, and the terminology was different. It wasn't Virginia's first rodeo, but this divorce was a bit stickier than her first. After ten years of melding bloodlines, careers, identities, contacts, and dreams, the ripping process began, and nothing about it ever rips evenly.

With Jaime's family trust fund combined with the paychecks he earned in the industry he seemed to have more money than God. As a man, he also had more pull in the industry and in the court system than she or her testimony did. She was up against a dynasty and a system that didn't think much of the plight of the domestic violence survivor.

Twelve years had passed since divorce documents required Virginia's signature, but the system, and public opinion were slow to change. Divorce was still stigmatized, though it was becoming a bit more accepted as inevitable for Hollywood couples' love affair trajectories.

In the 1950s, the majority of women in situations similar to Virginia's stayed – silently stayed. It was far too risky to try and forge a new life on the other side of a toxic marriage, especially with children. She knew very well what she would be up against in coming forward with allegations of such a nature. There was the risk of the courts not believing her. There was the risk of Jaime barging into court with cannons and the best lawyers money could buy stripping her of everything, including her children. There was the risk of the bad press, what it might mean for her career, what it might mean for her livelihood to support her boys. She had taken the stand countless times on *Dragnet*, *Perry Mason*, and *The Lineup*, but the thought of taking the stand as herself and having all the private details of her ten-year marriage smattered across the world was almost unbearable. The private details she herself had worked so diligently to conceal for ten years. The private details that would be embarrassingly extracted on the stand just for the public to feast upon.

However black and white our current system is in the 2020s, those black and white colors have significantly faded since the 1950s. The system then was black-black and white-white with little understanding of the implications for women caught in that terrible question of staying or leaving. That was a decision women often had to make alone at great cost to personal and professional image. Today, while the system still isn't perfect, we are fortunate to have better resources and psychoeducation surrounding the issues of domestic violence and just how hard it is for women to use their voices in filing for divorce in the face of marital toxicity, but in the

1950s, all things domestic were largely considered private matters between husband and wife. Wives' cheekbones were societally conditioned to become familiar with the back of their husband's hand as a part of typical marital discord. There weren't resources for the specifics of those types of intimate partner violence, and women who found themselves within those diabolical home environments were charged with simply enduring. There were those, like Virginia, who fought their way out for the betterment of their stories, and as much torture as it was to stay, the process of getting out was often harder – temporarily harder, but still harder. Getting out from under misogynistic hostility in a marriage was largely uncharted waters in the 1950s. Sure we had the right to vote then, but not always the right to say "no" in our own homes.

Facing the ramifications of staying or leaving with three children was undoubtedly difficult for Virginia. Much like she had to choose acting over music, she had to choose her future and her children's futures over the present. There were no guarantees that the future would be any better, but she made the hard resolve once again to change the trajectory of her own story. In the divorce suit, Virginia asked for sole custody of their three sons along with monthly alimony, child support, and a percentage of Jaime's future earnings. Pragmatically, the filing and related requests could also have meant the very death of her career, as Jaime was a very influential executive who had the power to make things difficult for Virginia in getting work on the other side of the divorce. She certainly weighted these potential consequences in her choice to sue for divorce along with many others unmentioned, yet she chose to pursue a different life on the other side of a marriage dissolution with the man she had worked with, lived with, loved with for perhaps the most crucial ten-year period of her career, and perhaps of her whole life.

The divorce was as messy as one can get – both in and out of the courtroom. So messy in fact, Virginia was granted an order of protection against Jaime in May of 1959. Not long after Virginia filed for divorce in 1958, Jaime moved out of the Parkwood Drive home while she and the boys remained until after the divorce was final in December 1959. According to court record, the restraining order was necessary because Jaime felt comfortable coming back "home" to take whatever he wanted, whenever he wanted and to do whatever he wanted, whenever he wanted.

Virginia had a tremendous number of friends who rallied around her during that time. They didn't ask questions, they didn't prod for the gory details. They just smiled and nodded her on toward a better way. The only part of her testimony in court that was published was the way she described Jaime after filing as being "cold and indifferent to her."[90] After giving her emotional testimony on the witness stand, the court granted all her requests. Jaime apathetically signed off on everything, and Virginia and her three boys left the warzone of Parkwood Drive and got on with living.

The del Valle's divorce was final on December 21, 1959. True to her private nature, the only public statement Virginia made about the divorce was: "He [Jaime] chose to live his own life."[91] The press was hot once again when the news of the finalization broke. Syndicated coast-to-coast – often on the front page – papers read "*Virginia Gregg Granted Divorce.*"

December of 1959 was not, however, their last trip to the courthouse. Jaime stopped paying child support not long after the divorce was granted and quit work allegedly to avoid paying Virginia the percentage of his earnings the courts granted her. He lived off his trust fund, and worked here and there, but never again to the degree he had before. The back and forth court battles dragged on for years into 1964, with no obvious win for either. Jaime continued to use the only weapon he had left against his former family: indifference.

Jaime went on to marry a third time. He died from pancreatic cancer on September 16, 1981, at the age of seventy-one, five years before and one day after Virginia died on September 15, 1986.

I of course never met Jaime del Valle. Much like the controversial Charlie Birger of Harrisburg, I can't say whether he was a mad delinquent or just a misunderstood martyr, but I do know that whatever he was, Virginia had had enough. Especially given the era, she had to have some pretty convincing evidence of the "numerous acts of grievous mental and physical cruelty" she alleged to receive everything she requested from the courts. So once again, she started over, but this time she wasn't alone. She had three little handsome fellows of eleven, eight, and six to forge forward with into the next decade. And surely, it would be a better one.

CHAPTER 8: AFRAID OF TOMORROW

"When casting people have a call for a woman who looks like the wrath of God, I'm notified."

-Virginia Gregg

Better it was in some ways. Virginia continued to work and to care for little Jaime in his long recovery. The four moved to a lighter, brighter residence in which to start over, and in her most accomplished role as "single-mom," Virginia led the family of four's effort to salvage what they could of all the ripped threads. It was hard, but the hard on the other side of such a ripping seemed much more tolerable and rewarding.

The thorny, exhausting divorce proceedings seemed to have had virtually no effect on Virginia's workload at the time regardless of how public the situation became. The radio work continued to come in steadily, with television offers increasing more and more in threat of the airwaves. Film casters also offered Virginia roles in the 1960s, though much to the chagrin of her agent, she often turned them down due to the travel requirements for filming on location for weeks or even months at a time. As a single-mom, Virginia stayed close to home and close to the radio and television roles much more conducive to her personal priorities. Most studios and locations for radio and television were nearby and did not require intensive time commitments, which allowed her to spend more time with her three boys and make the occasional family ski trip to the slopes of Mammoth or Big Bear – a trip that would often result in a happy lodge run-in with good friend Peggy Webber.

HOLLYWOOD AND THE SINGLE MOM

There were very few single moms in the 1950s and 1960s Hollywood scene. Actresses Joan Crawford and Lana Turner are two of the most notable single moms of the Golden Age, but even they were a bit scandalous in how they chose to head up their own families. This type of feminine empowerment was an ominous threat to the tradition (or superstition) of the American nuclear family that heralded a masculine bureaucracy. It had to be a lonely experience for Virginia and so many women like her who had to essentially hide their dual role as both mother and father in the shadows of the broader more socially accepted family ideals. In the Golden Age, the nuclear family was ballyhooed in all media as the glowing expectation of women everywhere, and if somehow a woman was unable to live up to those expectations, personal failure must somehow be to blame. It wasn't until years after Virginia's three boys were grown that society gradually began to acknowledge that single mom status was in fact the very antithesis of failure, and that it takes the ferocity of ten scorpions and five bobcats to uphold it.

Today, the single mom is openly celebrated and marveled, but society's acceptance of her was slow. It wasn't until the late 1980s and 1990s that film and television caught up to the growing phenomena of mothers playing the role of both mother and father in the typical American family. The 1987 hit film *Baby Boom* starring Diane Keaton was one of the first films to depict the modern woman's unique struggles in chosen single motherhood. The film depicts that dichotomous desire for children and a career – the dichotomy she increasingly faced alone as the sole provider of the family. In 1988, the television sitcom *Murphy Brown* was one of the first to herald the plight of the single, career mother with Candice Bergen's portrayal of the hard-nosed journalist who juggled work and family life. For some audiences, these feminine portrayals were cathartic composites the media's acknowledgment of their own personal struggles; for others, they were threats to the traditional American family.

The wage-gap between men and women still exists in almost every field, and for all of Hollywood's progressive ideals, they too still support an unfair compensation system that places women at a historical disadvantage. Virginia, like her female peers, had always endured the male-dominated industry that paid its women workers far less than its men. By the 1960s, the gap had closed a bit from its 1940s industry peak, but the percentage scale was still tipped in favor of the male species. In 1963, President John F. Kennedy signed off on the Equal Pay Act as a Fair Labor Standards Act amendment, which was a huge step toward the closing of the archaic gap, but in some ways, we have yet to close it completely.

Even in the 1960s, actresses were still bound by the skeleton of the old studio system that took years to truly die after its official collapse in the 1950s. The system may have collapsed, but many of the same industry heads hadn't, so the spirit of the awful thing continued far beyond its technical demise. The contract game had dissolved, but actors and actresses were still viewed as property by some executive kingpins. This unspoken order discouraged players from developing their own set of terms and conditions in negotiations. Actresses confident in their *own* parameters in guiding their *own* careers were still a novelty in the few years after the death of the studio system, and industry executives' ears weren't always primed for the voice of female empowerment.

Despite the old studio system's influence on her career beginnings, Virginia was gutsy enough to set her own parameters in the industry. For all the voice she didn't have in her marriages, she was heard loud and clear by industry executives. Some might argue her austere approach to sifting through offers may have ultimately been a self-constructed fetter limiting an otherwise "bigger" career, but according to her, her career was so satisfying in part because it was self-made. She was one of those rare birds who got to have her career and keep herself too.

THE 1960S

The 1960s were frenzied with political and cultural friction spilling over into the homes of the American people – a spilling over that certainly showed up in media's cultural "X-ray." Media gave either composites of or reprieves from the turmoil of the 1960s with wars of nearly every kind echoing each other across the world: the Vietnam war, civil rights movements, battle of the sexes, and the breakdown of more traditional nationalistic dogma that previous decades had so rigidly ballyhooed. The 1960s in all its tumultuous glory were inevitable after years of stuffy fundamentalism. New generations were finding their voice and media was gradually giving them more and more airtime.

For all the minority oppression of the previous decades in American history, the 1960s began to resound with ricocheting movements balking at the old system – *every* old system. The uprisings of the 1960s were about the righteous indignation of so many who had been suppressed – including women. In tandem with the civil rights movement, women began to advocate for their rights in a new way. Feministic movements go back to the suffrage days in the first wave of American women's liberation, but the second wave of the 1960s might be considered the loudest of the two. We had the right to vote, but we wanted more. We wanted equal pay, equal opportunities, and a wider berth for our role in society, and slowly we began to get it thanks to those who so courageously paved the way over those ugly misogynistic potholes.

With all the changes of 1960s, television played it safe, sticking to escapism in family sitcoms and variety shows. This effort in escapism brought a barrage of roles to Virginia's door. Her radio work began to slow immensely in early 1960 and 1961, but television and film role offers remained steady. *Have Gun, Will Travel* was the last radio series she hung in with; she and John Dehner stayed until the bitter end. It became painfully clear in the early 1950s that radio was terminal. In preparation for radio's untimely death, television picked up many of radio's most popular shows and genres for their rebirth on the small screen. Westerns and detective dramas were among Virginia's favorite genres – and no surprise also among audiences'.

Before the official death of radio, much of Virginia's television work was similar to that in radio, though she was never really typecast. Westerns such as *Gunsmoke* and *Zane Grey Theater* were popular primetime series that made the transition to television rather well, taking with them many radio actors and actresses including Virginia. She also spent the last few years of the 1950s and early 1960s appearing in newer, similar productions such as *Sugarfoot*, *Wanted: Dead or Alive*, and *Bat Masterson*. Detective dramas were of course a viable genre on television just as they had been on radio with popular 1960s shows such as *Bourbon Street Beat*, *Checkmate*, and *Hawaiian Eye*, and of course *Dragnet*, on all of which Virginia appeared.

Her late 1950s film work was also within similar genres, with her performances in *Portland Exposé*, *Twilight for the Gods*, *The Hanging Tree*, and *Hound-Dog Man*. These were the last few films she did before the legend of *Psycho* was created in the next decade, as the 1960s started giving way to a new era of thrillers, to which she adapted fluidly.

Though she adored radio, she didn't let it bind her. When it was time to pull the plug on it for good, she was already established in both the new media of television and the old media of film. Both welcomed her as a supporting character actress, and she quickly became a favorite among producers just as she had in radio. She wasn't alone in this. Radioers were disciplined professionals with loads to offer television and film – if of course they could push aside their resentment in radio's dissolution and open themselves to pivoting. Parley Baer, Jeanette Nolan, Agnes Moorehead, Mary Jane Croft, Gale Gordon, Eleanor Audley, and John Dehner were with Virginia in this category, just to name a few, who gracefully boarded the lifeboats while a handful of their comrades chose to go down with radio's ship.

These players and many others like them may not be remembered by mobs of fans like A-lister stars are, but they earned enormous respect from their superiors, peers, and audiences in all three mediums spanning multiple decades, and in the process, helped make American entertainment history. These were the steady, workhorse players who didn't burnout like the shooting stars surrounding them. In film, Virginia worked with some of the greatest leads in the business and never seemed to be intimidated. She shared the screen with Cary Grant, Ingrid Bergman, Henry Fonda, Claude Rains, John Garfield, Lilli Palmer, Gregory Peck, William Holden, Susan Hayward, Caesar Romero, and the list goes on. She never got those star-struck butterflies when working with the big names because she simply understood them as more visible cogs in the same machine of which she was also a part. Plus, she remembered a few shaking at the microphone in all their glorious humanity years before.

Of all her 1960s work, the most infamous film role of Virginia's among all her decades in the business was perhaps the film that kicked off the 1960s: Alfred Hitchcock's *Psycho*.

MRS. BATES

"I'm not even gonna swat that fly. I hope they are watching. They'll see. They'll see and they'll know, and they'll say, 'Why, she wouldn't even harm a fly.'" Her words poured eerily into the microphone and its spinning recorder reel. The room was small and so was her audience. One tech sat holding gum in his mouth in the corner with a limp clipboard in his lap. Another fiddled with wires while glancing at the script scattered across the bare table, as "the Master of Suspense" himself, Alfred Hitchcock, stood poised in his unmistakably swollen silhouette with his hands barely able touch one another behind his back. As Virginia sat channeling his interpretation of Robert Bloch's "Norma," he paced. If his totalitarian pacing made her nervous, you would have never known. It was no secret that Hitchcock was an obsessive with major mom-issues of his own according to his own statements through the years. He was a brilliant writer, director, and filmmaker with a knack for teasing audiences' psychological recesses with untraditional, spooky, and downright bizarre themes.

Hitchcock's calculated, tyrannical tendencies didn't faze Virginia. She had first worked with him in 1957 in an episode of *Alfred Hitchcock Presents*. He took to her versatility like so many other producers had and earmarked her for subsequent roles on the same series, and in 1960 chose her for perhaps his scariest character: "Norma Bates" in his 1960 flagship film based on Robert Bloch's 1959 novel *Psycho*. Hitchcock continued to request her for another series of his, *The Alfred Hitchcock Hour,* later in the 1960s.

Throughout the film, "Norma Bates'" disembodied voice can be heard at various points in the film either in exclusive conversation with "Norman," or in running commentary on the storyline. The disembodied voice sounds most like Virginia's portrayal of the old, deranged mother, but the voice is actually a combination of voices spliced together at Hitchcock's bidding to increase the spooky factor for audiences. The only part Virginia voices entirely herself is the last monologue after "Norman" is apprehended just before the credits roll, and her tones are noticeably higher and lighter. Paul Jasmin and Jeanette Nolan also individually recorded for "Norma," and Hitchcock mixed Jasmin's heavier tones with Virginia's higher ones, while Nolan voiced many of the film's blood-curdling screams.[92]

This may have been Hitchcock's unintentional effort at manual "auto-tune." In addition to Virginia, Hitchcock hired several former radioers for various parts in *Psycho* including Lurene Tuttle, John McIntire, Jeanette Nolan, and John Anderson.

It certainly wasn't radio, but the steely ridges in the table microphone were a happy sight for Virginia. Producing the crackling, spine-chilling voice of "Norma," the decrepit, controlling mother of unassuming sociopath "Norman Bates," came easily for her, as "playing old" was a favorite of hers in radio from "Nurse Parker" on *The Story of Doctor. Kildare* to the countless character spots she did on shows like *Suspense, Yours Truly, Johnny Dollar,* and *Have Gun Will Travel* in vocally channeling women three times her age. Prior to *Psycho's* release and simultaneous enchantment of movie lovers, "Norma" wasn't an icon waiting to be illuminated, she was just another "mother role" or "old lady part" to Virginia, albeit a demented one. As a matter of fact, "Norma" wasn't actually named in the film, but mostly referred to as "Mother" by "Norman" himself.

To fulfill her role was fairly straightforward compared to the rest of the on-screen cast. "Norma" is never seen on screen, until the ominous ending, which of course is *not* Virginia. She recorded separately from the rest of the cast in a small recording room on the lot with rudimentary audio recording equipment. She could keep her script and cigarette with her and still manage to make film history behind the microphone's curtain.

Virginia pulled back from the mic when she came to the end of her lines on the last page. She looked up over her glasses that had slipped to the bridge of her nose during the recording and waited for Hitchcock's pacing to stop. The recorder's wheels continued to spin with the hum of the reel still threading despite the silence. "I think that's all the lines I had for this scene," she said out of character.

"Fine, fine for now," Hitchcock nodded, stopping his pace. He may have smiled, but it was always hard to tell. "We'll let you know if we need more after the edits, won't we boys?" he prodded the techs who just nodded. Hitchcock stopped her now and again for cuts and suggestions while recording, but nothing compared to the way he allegedly micromanaged his on-screen cast members. He trusted Virginia and for all his pacing, his ears had detected very few correction points in her portrayal overall. So her contribution to the legendary film was, for her, straightforward and simply another well-written, convenient voiceover role, however controversial the film itself was. "Norma Bates" wasn't a particularly sought-after role. She wasn't supposed to be iconic. She wasn't supposed to be a cultural reference for decades after the film's release. As a matter of fact, players took a risk in their signing on, as all the topliner studios wouldn't touch the film due to the plot's violent and suggestive themes leaving Hitchcock to foot the production bill. The risks paid off because not only did *Psycho* go down in history perhaps as Hitchcock's greatest work, but audiences are still fascinated by the story and characters with the more recent development of a number of spin-offs such as Tom Holland's 1980s continuances of "Norman Bates'" plight in *Psycho II* and *Psycho III*, and more recently the A&E television series *Bates Motel*.

Everyone remembers Janet Leigh's infamous shower scene, and even sixty years later, we all still take an extra peek around the shower curtain sometimes just to make *sure* no knife-wielding killer is waiting for us in our own bathrooms, but everyone *really* remembers not "Norma Bates" necessarily by name, but "the mom in *Psycho*." Pop culture is still fraught with the film's references and parodies, and even a more modern in-depth look at "Norma" in the hit television series *Bates Motel* that premiered in 2013 as the prequal to Robert Bloch's original novel. The series stars Vera Farmiga as "Norma" who is understood in her pre-mummified days separate from Hitchcock's limited interpretation of her viability found exclusively within the shadowy memories of "Norman."

Despite her years of radio show work in the crime genre, *Psycho*, may have been Virginia's first role as a dead body. Additionally, despite her legendary performance as "Norma Bates," she was uncredited at the time of the production's release. For years after the role, she enjoyed channeling "Norma's" voice on occasions when her sons were particularly rowdy.

A LUMP

A lump. To her body, it was small, but to her mind it weighed 10,000 tons. The white hospital gown did little to conceal her tremor as the doctor came back in the cold room with his chart. "It's breast cancer," the doctor said. Virginia hadn't practiced her lines for this role, and there was no script or director to consult. It wasn't "Dr. Kildare" or "Dr. Christian" in the white coat, and Virginia wasn't emoting on behalf of a fictious patient. Virginia Lee Gregg was the patient, and at forty-five years old, she was diagnosed with breast cancer.

Any cancer diagnosis in any era is unspeakable, but a breast cancer diagnosis in the early 1960s was often synonymous with a death sentence. By today's standards, only primitive and inhumane options existed for patients in terms of detection, treatment options, prognosis, resources, and support. The medical community has greatly evolved since the 1960s with respect to its response to the disease, but only because of the millions who have gone before us to make improvements possible. Today, in American culture, there is a significant amount of awareness surrounding breast cancer that was virtually nonexistent at the time of Virginia's diagnosis.

If breast cancer was detected in time, which often it wasn't in the 1960s, women had very few treatment options, with mixed outcomes. All treatments were risky and came along with detrimental residuals they carried with them for the rest of their lives – however long that might have been. Understanding the great consequences of treatment, Virginia chose to pursue the thing that would give her the greatest chances of survival despite the great physical and emotional cost.

In the 1960s, there were no pink ribbons, no community walks, no support groups for families, no paid medical leave. Breast cancer was not something that was talked about; it was a very private condition with private implications – if it didn't kill you, of course. Diagnostics and treatments were crude with lifelong residuals. There was no patient care consultant, medical advocate, or counselor to help women (or men) weigh their options in tandem with their doctor's recommendations and talk through their feelings about treatment trajectory. There was no specialized aftercare for patients and their families to help assimilate back into full functionality after treatment, if of course they lived. There was only diagnosis, and treatment – the rest was up to the patient and God's mercy.

In one radio episode of *The Story of Doctor Kildare* featuring Virginia, "Dr. James Kildare" spoke of his patient "Jane Dane" who had just received a cancer diagnosis. The way he described her attitude toward her diagnosis, I believe, was also true of Virginia years later when she herself sat in the patient seat: "The smile of a woman who is convinced she's going to live. A woman who's just *got* to live." And live she did.

As she did about many things in her personal life, Virginia kept her diagnosis very private. Certain family members knew of her battle, but even many close friends weren't told. Knowing how dedicated Virginia was to her career, her secrecy may have been twofold: 1. She was of course a naturally private person, and 2. She may have concealed her diagnosis out of self-preservation as far as the industry was concerned. She may have thought having her diagnosis public would cut down on her hiring opportunities, which would reduce her livelihood and ability to support her sons. In reviewing her filmography during the early 1960s and the few years subsequent, her workload didn't slow down tremendously except in 1961 during and immediately after treatment, which in and of itself is pretty incredible. Not to say she didn't turn down roles during recovery, but she had few obvious gaps in her work history, which further guised her condition.

The treatment she underwent worked, but it took a lifelong toll on her physically and emotionally, and on her sons. She gracefully recovered without audiences and even many friends ever being the wiser. Through the screen, it is nearly impossible to see the debilitating toll it took on her, which says a lot for her personal tenacity, acting ability, and costuming. The process of treatment and recovery aged her as it would anyone who fought that hard, but she continued on and without many knowing of her close call.

FLAVIUS

In Virginia's recovery, radio's impending death was clear, but offers continued to come in for television and film, which further motivated her recovery. One can only turn down so many offers before they stop coming in altogether. There certainly was no shortage of work for her. There was also no shortage of tall, dark, handsome men. Not long after her divorce from Jaime, Virginia found a bit of tea and sympathy from a younger man – a *much* younger man. Her first husband Lou was eight years older than she, and Jaime was six years older. This new love interest was twelve years her junior, and unlike her previous two husbands, an industry-outsider.

Flavius Otto Burket was a professional in early education with a master's from the University of California. After graduating with honors, he became an elementary school teacher in and around the Los Angeles school district and moved to principal in at least two different schools in the Redondo Beach district including Leila M. Andrews Elementary and Prospect Heights Elementary.

Flavius was born in Southern California in 1929, though his family originally hailed from Topeka, Kansas. He was the third Flavius Otto Burket, and the shining progeny of his German/Scottish bloodline as his parents' only child. He carried the generational namesake proudly – a name which historically has been recognized in relation to the dynasty of Roman emperors. The name, as it had the two generations of men before him, fit his good looks, confidence, and impressive resume that undoubtedly drew Virginia to him. For all his higher education, he was the eternal frat boy who loved football, fishing, and females.

He came from an affluent family which was made up of an interesting mix of show biz people and white-collar professionals. He had no personal interest in the entertainment industry, so he was a nice contrast to Virginia's industry saturated circle.

Flavius and Virginia were an unlikely pair beyond the age gap. They almost seemed to have been shuffled together by an old gypsy matchmaker they pulled out of retirement. He was outdoorsy, adventurous, and free-spirited, while she was practical, conscientious, and overly responsible. They met when Virginia's eldest son, Gregg, had Flavius for a teacher in elementary school, and the two took things a step farther than the typical PTA meeting after Virginia and Jaime divorced.

Their romance was mysterious even to those close to Virginia, but everyone knew, when she decided on something, or someone, that was that. He had obtuse tendencies on certain subjects, but he was patient with her post-cancer condition and helped foster an easier recovery. On August 12, 1962 the two married in Orange County. He was 33, she was 46. Though Virginia's boys knew "Mr. Burket" from school, marrying their mother was an entirely different thing. At the ceremony, one fainted beside the bride in subconscious protest of the choice in stepfather, yet the knot had been tied despite any protest – subconscious or otherwise.

She was the single mom no more. At least not for a while.

THE DEATH OF RADIO

On September 30, 1962, old time radio was officially pronounced dead, and television had risen to take its place in the favor of American entertainment.[93] Television did not take kindly to all former radioers and vice versa, but Virginia, having quite an extensive television resume by the time radio flatlined, had bridged the transfer quite nicely. She may not have always assumed the most desirable roles, but she worked steadily and didn't seem to take any unflattering casting personally, as she once famously quipped, "When casting people have a call for a woman who looks like the wrath of God, I'm notified." By 1962, she was forty-six years old and fully immersed into television and film with nearly twenty years of radio experience under her belt. She quickly found that an exclusive television and film career offered very different roles than radio had.

The great irony of Virginia's identity in television and film vs. radio lie in her appearance. *The Hollywood Report* said it best in a 1956 spread: "Virginia Gregg is an actress who looks mighty attractive when she shows up for a radio part but usually looks as if life gave her several swift kicks when she appears in motion picture or on TV."[94] Radio knew a very different side of Virginia than did television or film. Through the radio she could engage with audiences as a sultry twenty-year-old vixen, a ten-year-old boy, or an ailing eighty-year-old woman. Mel Blanc may have been the "Man of a Thousand Voices," but Virginia was his female answer.

She could mimic any age and any dialect. Her range was virtually endless, and the work was abundant because of it. Great Italian actor Salvini was once asked, "What is acting?" to which he promptly replied, "Voice, voice, voice." Though Salvini and Virginia were too divided by time and space to meet, *she* was the very embodiment of his definition on radio, though television might have had a very different answer to "What is acting?" : "Looks, looks, looks."

Virginia was attractive and fit, no doubt, but an actress delivering a Filipino accent with her Scottish/Irish features glaring on screen wouldn't be a great casting decision. Range was calculated much differently for television and film, and for all her girth of talent, suddenly she once again had to pivot her skill set in order to fit industry pace for a new, unchartered season in her life and career.

If there was any reluctance to appear before the screen again post-cancer treatment, Virginia never let on. She flew back into both the big and small screens as soon as she was able and enjoyed a barrage of memorable television roles in the early 1960s like the gunslinging "Clootey Hutter" in *Lawman*, bad, bad "Phoebe Strunk" in *Gunsmoke*, colorful characters on the medical drama *The Eleventh Hour*, and a long running stint as the brassy "Maggie Belle Klaxon" on *Calvin and the Colonel*. Her reintroduction to film after recovering began with Edmond O'Brien's *Man-Trap*. She went on to do several other early 1960s films including *Gorath*, *House of Women*, *Shootout at Big Sag*, and perhaps most memorably, Delmer Daves' *Spencer's Mountain* based on the Earl Hamner Jr. novel that originally inspired *The Waltons* television series.

Virginia proved more than capable of exclusively tackling television and film. Radio had given her her sea legs, but she eclipsed all three mediums. She excelled in comedy, drama, horror, and romance. On the big and small screens, she played the lonely prairie widow just as convincingly as she did the dull but efficient bank secretary who hadn't missed a day of work in twenty years. She mastered the art of taking one-dimensional roles and unfolding them multidimensionally. Just as she had in radio, she became part of the support system that made it possible for the leads and the stories to shine. She was a part of a group of supporting actors and actresses who were the very scaffolding of media during some of the most volatile years in American media history. Audiences forever associate these scaffolders with certain roles and certain seasons in life that provide a very important connection point that crosses all barriers of time and space. Why else do we so vividly remember "Mrs. Bates" and "Phoebe Strunk" so many decades later?

Another supporting television role that has also acquired a bit of a cult following is her portrayal of "Emily Harper" in Rod Serling's

The Twilight Zone in the episode "The Masks." Virginia was a part of Rod Serling's stock company, as were many of her colleagues. She appeared in several episodes throughout the show's five season run from 1959-1964. The most memorable of her work on the show is perhaps in "The Masks," as the greedy, whining daughter of wealthy "Jason Foster" (Robert Keith) who on his deathbed gives his family exactly what they deserve in lieu of the inheritance they are so openly expecting.[95] This *Twilight Zone* episode was written by Rod Serling and is the only one of the series directed by a female: Ida Lupino.

Rod's work was a favorite of Virginia's, as anything "well-written" was her first choice, and *The Twilight Zone* is one of those timeless series that certainly falls under that category.

US DO PART

"They've taken him by helicopter, Virginia. You've got to get to the hospital," came the urgent voice from the other end of the phone. Throwing the receiver in the direction of the phone base, Virginia flew out the door into her car. The usual fifteen-minute drive from Manhattan Beach to Torrance seemed to take hours with her heart pounding above the traffic. When she arrived at Little Company of Mary Hospital, she bolted through the emergency doors frantically searching for familiar faces. Finally seeing one in Bill Smith, she froze as he came dejectedly toward her in wet clothes and a towel, looking completely out of place in the crowded lobby. "He's dead, Virginia. Flavius is dead," Bill said. He held her shoulders in the spirit of consolation as water droplets continued to fall from his wet shorts between them. The room was spinning, and she didn't believe what she had heard. "I need to see him. Where is he? I need to see him," She pulled away from the dripping man and lunged at the front desk for information – information she hoped to God was different than what she had just been told.

It was a silvery Sunday morning in April 1965. Flavius and three friends had planned a boating trip off Point Vicente in Rancho Palos Verdes for the day to do a bit of sun-soaking and skin-diving. Flavius loved the water and almost every type of water sport, though skin-diving was a favorite.

He was accompanied by an older Manhattan Beach couple, I'll call "Bill and Flora Smith," and a nineteen-year-old girl I'll call "Sue" whose relation to Flavius is unknown.[96]

The trip was routinely pleasant aboard the Smiths' vessel *Arbee*, as the foursome sailed off from picturesque Point Vicente. Around noon, Flavius went for his first dive. He was in excellent physical condition and as a seasoned diver he had gone on countless excursions in almost every wave of every popular bay off the coast of Southern California. He suited up in his skin-diving ware and equipment and dove into the familiar Pacific waters while his three comrades lounged in *Arbee* watching as he disappeared under the waves several yards from her hull.

After having only been under for about ten-minutes, Flavius suddenly surfaced farther out in obvious distress. He called for help through gurgles of seawater and disappeared under the waves again. The three instinctually rose to their feet and Bill dove into water. He swam out in Flavius' initial direction, but the choppy waves made it difficult to keep a steady line on him. Flora and young Sue stood frozen in horror and anticipation.

As Flavius sporadically resurfaced enough for Bill to get to him, he feared the worst as he dragged him to the side of *Arbee*. The women helped pulled both men aboard and Bill quickly began resuscitation efforts on deck. Flavius was lifeless.

Flora steered *Arbee* toward shore at Bill's insistence as he continued trying to revive Flavius. Though his bluish color told Bill it was hopeless, he seemed to sputter on occasion, which encouraged him to continue trying.

Once *Arbee* docked, the women quickly found the Coast Guard hub, and a helicopter was deployed for his transport. The trio met him at the Torrance hospital where they were given the news: despite all rescue efforts, Flavius was pronounced dead on April 25, 1965 at thirty-six years old.[97]

Virginia had just finished two films that Spring: Bill Conrad's *Two on a Guillotine* starring Connie Stevens and Cesar Romero, and Alex Segal's *Joy in the Morning* starring Richard Chamberlain and Yvette Mimieux. After wrapping on *Joy in the Morning*, she took a hiatus to process Flavius' death until going back to the small screen in an episode of *The Legend of Jesse James* that September. Flavius' death was very difficult for her. The two had been married just shy of three years and she herself was barely recovered from her primeval war with breast cancer. She never remarried after he died. She was once again the single mom, and now a widow at forty-nine years old.

Virginia didn't seem to fear anything. As much tragedy as she had endured in her life, she seemed to have no obvious hang-ups or phobias that kept her constrained. I once asked Jaime what Virginia was afraid of, and he replied, "With raising three boys on her own, I guess the only thing she was afraid of was tomorrow."

CHAPTER 9: THE SHOW GOES ON

"Afterall, tomorrow is another day."

-Scarlett O'Hara

Even in the cascading grief, Virginia did what she always did when tragedy struck: she went on. She took a few months off of work to process the death of her third husband, and then jumped back into offers with both feet. Not all actresses could take weeks or months off without suffering some level of fallout because everybody knows Hollywood doesn't wait for anyone or anything, but because of Virginia's reputation in the business and great talent to more than back it up, after breaks, she always managed to find her place again as if she never stepped away.

She continued character spots in many of the same television series in which she was already a familiar face: *Dragnet*, *Perry Mason*, *Gunsmoke*, *Hazel*, *The Big Valley*, *The Virginian*, *Ben Casey*, *The Story of Doctor Kildare*, along with a few she was newer to like *My Three Sons*, *The Addams Family*, *Bewitched*, *Bonanza*, and *The Guns of Will Sonnett*. She accepted film roles in what was left of the 1960s in such productions as Fielder Cook's *A Big Hand for the Little Lady* starring Henry Fonda and Joanne Woodward, *Prescription Murder*, *The Bubble*, *Madigan*, and *Heaven with a Gun*. The 1960s were a rollercoaster for Virginia in her personal life and career, but some of her most memorable work developed out of that labored decade.

The 1960s is when Virginia Gregg really became recognizable to television audiences who perhaps were unaware of her vocal familiarity in radio a few years before. Audiences may not have known her name, but her familiar face and voice put them at ease when they recognized her on either screen. She was often recognized in public too, but never for the right reason: "Didn't we meet last year in the Hamptons?" they might ask, or "You're a friend of my sister Susan's aren't you?" She said when she had the time to play along it could be rather fun until some would say, "Oh you're a television actress aren't you?" Yet they never got her name right and would even argue with her when she introduced herself. "Oh, that's right! You're . . . you're" they would think aloud. "Virginia Gregg," she would reply. "No that's not it," they would argue.

Even decades later, when we see Virginia in an episode of *Dragnet* or *Gunsmoke*, she feels familiar, and we are automatically more sympathetic toward her character and her agenda. She makes us feel kinder toward the "Phoebe Strunks"[98], the "Dirty Donnas"[99], the "Ethel Starkies"[100], and even the "Bonnie Bates"[101] of the world. She makes us see their humanity, see beyond their seemingly singular dimension that on the surface may not be relatable. How many of us automatically identify with an upper-class insurance scammer or a Wild West female buffalo skinner? Maybe not many, but because these characters come to life through Virginia, we sympathize with them a bit more than we perhaps would otherwise. She played characters we might not have even noticed had they been portrayed by a different actress. Whether she intended to or not, she spoke up for the underdog in her performances. She gave us an alternate way to understand and accept the intersection between femininity and grit. She gave us such a gift in her storytelling and in her portrayals and we are all the better for it. In experiencing a performance of hers even fifty years later, we might find a bit more space in our hearts for the "Jessie Coppertons"[102] and the "Ada Corelys"[103] of the world. She submerged herself into these stories and presented them for us in a way that brought us closer to ourselves and to each other. She ultimately underwent these submerging processes for the world's benefit as much as her own whether intentional or not. As any Virginia Gregg fan knows, she often played roles that were responsible for lighting the tiny match that set a production's entire plot ablaze. She did it with grace and confidence that we can only attribute to her own artistic genius combined with that rare, quality training of the Golden Age. She readily accepted roles that exhibited those hard, scary parts of ourselves that we prefer to push down and over-compensate for. In her performances, she had nothing to prove and nobody to impress, she simply brought the character to life using whatever means she had available to her. She was versatile enough to move with and adapt to the fluidity of media from radio to television, to film to animated voiceover roles spanning over forty years. She rode the capricious industry out for those forty + years at a steady pace that is more than remarkable for the period. We can all name countless one-hit-wonders, those who perhaps peaked too soon and faded into obscurity, or those who had extreme highs and lows in their industry careers that give way to satire in the post-modern era, but Virginia was able to stay relevant for decades in a business known for its fickle, double-crossing nature.

Character actor David White, who is most remembered for his portrayal of "Darrin Stephens'" greedy, silver tongued boss "Larry Tate" in *Bewitched* once described acting as a process in which the actor must push aside his own needs in order to fulfill the needs of his character however difficult it may be. In Virginia's case, she did just that in most, if not all performances to an astonishing degree.

She was once quoted as saying she had no identity as an actress. To the casual television viewer, perhaps she didn't. She was certainly recognized as a familiar face, but often not much more to some, as many supporting people are overlooked. In true Gestalt-fashion, Virginia's whole identity was certainly greater than the sum of its parts. Her identity as an actress was found in her range and dedication. As the old adage goes, people may not remember your name or the specifics of how they met you, but they always remember how you made them feel. In conducting interviews with those touched by Virginia Gregg, that is certainly true of her. I have noticed in collecting memories of her through interviews with her remaining family members and colleagues who knew Virginia intimately more freely recall how she impacted their lives rather than specific memories and/or facts about the woman herself. While that is a testament all of its own, it makes for a somewhat tricky writing process, hence making this biography more essence than cold hard facts, something about which our "Sgt. Joe Friday" wouldn't be thrilled.

As a character actress, Virginia's own personhood was submerged in countless figures and stories, always placing the story within the script above her own, though I believe her own story may be the most compelling of any character she ever portrayed. She could sit with and express the ugly emotions we don't want to admit we too have within us. Those emotions we so committedly try to avoid, push down, and numb out: the hurt, anger, loneliness, sorrow, and helplessness felt in so many of her character portrayals are difficult to process when those are the same emotions we too are looking to escape, yet her performances often make us feel those things anyway and somehow appreciate it.

"Phoebe Strunk" is just such a character. "Phoebe" is a crude, crass, vulgarian who leads her band of equally offensive sons in crimes of greed and convenience on the frontier. In television's *Gunsmoke*'s eighth series, Lynn Stalmaster cast Virginia in the role of "mean old Phoebe" who, with the help of her boorish sons, ruins the life of "Annie" (Joan Freeman), a young woman they meet in their travels to whom they take a fatal liking.

Jaime recalls being on set with his mother while filming portions of "Phoebe Strunk's" episode. Virginia let Jaime shadow her on the *Gunsmoke* set, as he himself considered a career in acting when he was young.

Several of the episode's scenes are physically rowdy with bouts of tussling and slapping among the "Strunk brothers" and "Phoebe." Even at 5'7, she rules all with an iron fist. While Virginia was before the camera beating up on her 6'0+ sons as "Phoebe," Jaime, eleven at the time, sat particularly still watching the scene. Though never explicitly stated, he said he got his mother's subtle message loud and clear: if she could beat up on these big six-footer sons as "Phoebe Strunk," she could easily handle her three as "Virginia Gregg."

WORK IN THE 1970S

The 70s brought more roles, but with different terms. While Virginia had convincingly played aged parts since she was twenty-one years old, before the 1970s she generally had the freedom to vacillate between older parts and those more consistent with her actual age at the time. One of her many industry tricks was concealing her age. She knew sharing her age could potentially reduce the number of roles offered if they called for a younger or older actress. She adapted to a rigid system and refused to be boxed in even by immovables such as age. In a 1981 interview with the *LA Times*, she said, "Until now, I never told anybody my age. Everybody in the business said not to because if they want somebody thirty-five and you tell them you're forty-two, they're not going to look at you. So I said, 'One day, I'm not going to mind telling my age.'"[104]

She turned fifty-four in March of 1970 and the love interest roles dwindled more and more. In her fifties, audiences began to see Virginia more consistently in matronly characters in television and film. She was just as attractive and talented in her aging, but Hollywood isn't notorious for accommodating women over a certain age no matter how much talent they have.

With its historically standard lag, media went into overdrive in the 1970s trying to keep up with all the changes the 1960s had initiated. Television was shifting from exclusive escapism with revolutionary writers and producers like Norman Lear who created a brand-new type of family sitcom to correspond with all America was facing in the aftermath of the 1960s and welcome of the 1970s.

Lear managed to brilliantly meld escapism and timely PSAs into some of television's best shows like *All in the Family, Sanford and Son, Maude,* and *The Jeffersons.* Virginia never appeared on these particular Lear shows, but television began to change under others like him who saw great opportunity in using prime time entertainment to respond to the world's real-time changes rather than using its exclusively as a one-dimensional happy hideout. This new utilization caused themes to emerge in scripts that had been nothing but taboo before. Suddenly Virginia and her peers were faced with weighty topics in their scripts like racism, homosexuality, birth control, abortion, and rape. Film changed too in adapting to these once-forbidden themes, but audiences perhaps have generally been more forgiving of film in comparison to television – after all we can walk out of a movie theatre if we don't like the weight we're given, but we tend to expect more of our television since it lives with us in our homes. Ellwood Kieser's dramatic anthology television series *Insight* was similar to Norman Lear's in slowly introducing home audiences to heavier themes. Virginia appeared on two episodes of *Insight* in the 1970s in a raw portrayal of life in the ghetto for an immigrant family and the struggles of their engagement with the "American Dream" of the 1970s.

Virginia wasn't personally threatened by these content changes in the least. She had always embraced weighty issues in her personal life and championed social and political causes without a hint of reticence, but the dynamics of the roles she accepted involved more intensity than before – intensity that she had dealt with in her personal life plenty, but not so explicitly in dramatic portrayal. Certainly radio had hinted at the darker side of humanity, but generally in a distanced and fantastical way. The 1970s brought these topics down from the attic and spotlighted them for us all to consider.

Dragnet was similarly influenced by the times in that Jack Webb began to write more and more updated subjects into his plots beyond the stereotypical "jewel thief," in the series' 1967 revival. Virginia remained in Jack Webb's stock company – one of the last standing of its kind – throughout her career. Jack continued to offer her roles through the 70s in *Dragnet*, and other shows he wrote and/or co-produced like *Adam-12, Emergency!, Hec Ramsey*, and *Project UFO*.

Raymond Burr had been a colleague and friend of Virginia's since their Pasadena Playhouse days, and like Jack, he also made sure to bring her with him into the 70s. She often appeared with him in *Perry Mason*, and he continued to offer her roles in his contemporary spin-off of the show: *Ironside*. Another nearly lifetime friend of Virginia's, Bill Conrad, recruited her for his 70s detective series *Cannon*, in which she frequently appeared.

These men weren't in the habit of handing out roles to friends. They were seasoned artists who knew they could count on players like Virginia to complement their latest production. They knew her ability and grounding and continued to recruit her until her pseudo-retirement in the mid-1980s.

In the 70s, she was also able to do more voiceover work warmly reminiscent of the old radio days, even with several members of the old gang at times like Vic Perrin, Jeanette Nolan, Harry Bartell, and of course Parley Baer. Radio reprised some of its airwaves, in novelty rather than in competition with television in the 1970s. Virginia enjoyed doing *CBS Radio Mystery Theater, The Ray Bradbury Theatre, Sears Radio Theatre*, and the Salvation Army's *Heartbeat Theatre*. Of course, nothing could compare to those old Golden days, but the work brought back many happy familiarities of the 1940s and 1950s, though many of these contemporary radio shows presented the same heavy themes found on television in the 1970s. Virginia also enjoyed animation voiceover work which she tried her hand at first in 1961 and 1962 in Charles Correll and Freeman Gosden's series *Calvin and the Colonel*. For the last two decades of her career, she gave voiceover performances on popular animated series like *Yogi's Space Race, The Scooby-Doo Dynomutt Hour*, and *Captain Caveman and the Teen Angels*, and *Space Stars* in 1981.

In 1978, Virginia accepted a role in David Lowell Rich's television adaption of Louisa May Alcott's timeless classic *Little Women*. She played the Marchs' devoted housekeeper, "Hannah." Accomplished actress Ann Dusenberry, known for her work in *Jaws 2* (1978), *Lies* (1983), and *Life with Lucy* (1986), played "Amy March" in Lowell Rich's mini-series as a young, up-and-coming.

Anne fondly recalled working with Virginia in two productions in the same year: *Little Women* (1978) and *Goodbye, Franklin High* (1978). She remembers her as being "so focused" when the cameras were rolling and when they weren't. Even in her 60s, after decades in the business, Virginia was just as diligent about the roles she took on, albeit more selective. Anne said she remembers Virginia generally staying to herself in between her scenes. Television in the 1970s and 1980s wasn't quite like the early days in which stock company players mingled in between their lines, forming life-long friendships that felt more like family than anything else. It was a different culture. The stock company model was outdated, and many players knew they could work intensely with a group of their peers for a particular production and then quite literally never see them again. With the variety and breadth of the industry, it was every person for themself, and socializing wasn't a priority for players of any age. Virginia wasn't terribly keen on the drastic changes in the business in the 1970s and 1980s, giving way to her increased selectivity to sign on for projects. Despite any misgivings she had; however, she adapted and when she was on the set to work, work she did.

Another 1978 role Virginia accepted with rancor was the brutish medicine woman "Ada Corley" in season six of *The Waltons*. The episode is a particularly intense one for the Walton family when "Elizabeth" (Kami Cotler) falls from a wood pile and breaks her leg. Doctors doubt she will ever walk again, so in desperation, with the help of good friend "Aimee Godsey" (Rachel Longaker), "Elizabeth" accepts the less conventional help of "Ada" to restore her ability to walk. Virginia gave a terribly convincing, albeit terrifying performance, nearly scaring her younger colleagues to pieces. Kami and Rachel were both only thirteen years old when filming this episode, and Kami remembers Virginia using an old industry gimmick to help foster the right emotions in the young actresses. Virginia purposively steered clear of the youngsters on set only allowing them to interact with her as "Ada," to help produce a more organic fear-response for their scenes. The gimmick worked, because the climaxing scene of "Ada" treating "Elizabeth" with her potions went down in *The Waltons'* history as one of the most memorable (and perhaps creepiest) of the series.

PERSONALS

Beyond the changing landscape of her work, Virginia's personal life was also very different in her 60s. She was an empty nester for the first time and had no immediate caretaking duties to tend to – something that left her feeling a bit lost, as caretaking was her lifelong specialty. Work was steady, but not overly demanding, so she suddenly had new-found time for her own personal hobbies of sewing, gardening, volunteering, and spending time with friends – both human and non-human alike, as she only seemed to fall more in love with furry creatures as she grew older.

She continued to lend her voice to Recordings for the Blind, Inc. which she had done nearly since its inception in 1948. She was elected to their board of directors, on which she proudly served until her death in 1986. She also enjoyed giving her time and energy to the Special Olympics during the first few years after its 1968 founding through the late 1970s.

Another gig she picked up in the late sixties and maintained throughout the seventies was her work with Howard Hughes' Trans World Airlines (TWA). Though the airlines began to fizzle in the early 2000s, and finally dissolved under American Airlines' acquisition of TWA in 2003, it had been, since its founding in 1930, one of the most prominent airlines in the world. Virginia's voice could be heard echoing in TWA hubs in airports world-wide. She was the guiding voice that provided flight information for waiting passengers, a gig her middle son, Jaime, learned about upon a departure from Los Angeles International Airlines (LAX).

While waiting for a flight, Jaime suddenly heard a familiar voice resounding through the terminal. A bit stunned, he laughed when he realized the voice was "Mom's." He said, "Usually someone who recorded for something like TWA would come home and say, 'Hey I did this!' It's an international airport. It's kind of a big deal, but I only knew about it when I heard her for myself at LAX, and I thought, 'She really *is* everywhere!'"

She also reserved time for her close group of friends, and one more tall, dark, and handsome man. Though she never remarried after the death of Flavius, in the 1970s, she acquired the proverbial "secret lover" who was the first of her life to be her equal. The two were the same age, in the same industry, had many of the same friends and interests, and seemed to want the same things from life. He was spoken for during the week, but on the weekends the two enjoyed swims and playing tennis and keeping up with the Dodgers. More than just lovers, the two were grand friends and remained close until Virginia's death.

For all her toiling as the single mother for most of their adolescence, her three sons had grown up, and couldn't have been more different from one another.

The eldest, Gregg, moved away from Sunny California to Oregon for several years and later settled in Wyoming as the superintendent of a soda ash mine. The next to eldest, Jaime, moved out on his own at fifteen years old and lived in a number of places including Boulder, Colorado and even England. In his younger years, he considered entering the industry as an actor himself, but ultimately decided against it. Instead, he attended gunsmithing school, and became a successful gunsmith for over two decades. The youngest, Ricardo, attended private school in Iowa, and joined the military. He served in Vietnam, and settled in Quincy, California. All three preferred more open regions of the country to the city-life of their childhoods.

Virginia stayed in touch with her sons no matter where they were on the map, and eventually did the same with her grandchildren.

WORTH IT

In the late 1970s, Virginia was asked by longtime friend and colleague, Art Gilmore, to speak at the University of Southern California for a radio education workshop. She accepted the invite a bit begrudgingly, as teaching, according to her, was not her forte. She said she had tried her hand at teaching little children a few times and "they just always ended up in my lap like puppies," so she wasn't especially confident as the lead in a classroom even with university age students. Art asked her to share her wisdom with these anxious up-and-comings upon reflecting over her forty + year career as a radio professional. So, like any living legend, when she stepped to the podium before all the eager faces of industry hopefuls ready with pens in hands to devour every word of her sage advice, she began, "I think you all ought to give it up right now. Get out of the business and go home." The classroom went dead silent and the eagerness she had seen in the sea of faces before her had turned to horror with moderators in the back of the room standing up with raised eyebrows to relieve her of the podium. She continued,

> Unless . . . unless you want to eat, breathe, sleep acting. Unless you're willing to be rejected every time you turn around. Unless you have a thick enough skin to tolerate it and not cry through most of your life. Even if you are terribly talented, you [sic] have to be made of the proper stuff to take what this business dishes out . . . . It's a difficult business but it's worth it.

WORK IN THE 1980s

"Virginia has never considered herself a beauty, but she is one of the most active actresses in the business" columnist Lydia Lane described in a feature on Virginia in 1959. "I've had as many as 104 bosses a year. I work practically every day, and I love it. Acting is my hobby as well as my livelihood," Virginia said.[105] More than twenty years after that feature was published, the same was true. The 1980s brought even more changes that are certainly evident in media's X-ray from that era, and Virginia and her generation of industry players once again pivoted.

Virginia considered the industry in the later years "big business rather than an artform." She remembered the Golden days of crafting with voice, body, and even soul, in acting artistry, something that she believed deteriorated after the Golden Age. She was exceedingly selective in her work in television and film in the 1980s. She liked to accept work with people and entities where mutual trust had been established. In the 1970s-1980s, she selectively worked with those like Hanna-Barbera Productions, Tom Holland, and Blake Edwards.

Hanna-Barbera offered Virginia several animated voiceover roles throughout the 1970s and 1980s. She did a number of television and film parts with their production company, with her last ever television role being in an episode of their series *The Greatest Adventure: Stories from the Bible.*

Blake Edwards wrote and produced a film called *S.O.B.* in 1981 starring William Holden, and Blake's wife, Julie Andrews. He requested Virginia join in on the film, and simply because it was Blake, she agreed. She and he went back as far as *Richard Diamond, Private Detective* when he first started getting his feet wet as a young writer.

Unlike "Norma Bates," Hitchcock's *Psycho* just wouldn't die. In 1983, writer Tom Holland furthered the twisted tale of "Norman

Bates" in *Psycho II*. Holland needed a mother of course, and he called upon Virginia to resurrect "Norma." She accepted, this time having vocal autonomy throughout the role compared to Hitchcock's melding of three voices for one. Three years later, in 1986, Anthony Perkins (who plays the infamous "Norman") directed the final film of the trilogy written by Charles Edward Pogue. And what is a *Psycho* movie without "Mother?" *Psycho III* was Virginia's last film role.

SPERDVAC

Another organization Virginia became heavily involved with later in her career worked to preserve that artform of the Golden Age: The Society to Preserve and Encourage Radio Drama, Variety, and Comedy (SPERDVAC). Since 1974, SPERDVAC has been working to preserve old-time radio shows to which Virginia and her peers gave so much of themselves. Radio historians and founding members like Jerry Haendiges, Gene Ward, and Jim Coontz collaborated to establish SPERDVAC as a non-profit that celebrates and archives these shows for all those who missed out on their real-time airing. If it weren't for organizations like SPERDVAC and their phenomenal archiving efforts, younger generations (like mine) might not be able to even access these wonderful pieces of art that the world got to enjoy over the airwaves during the Golden Age.

SPERDVAC elected Virginia as an honorary member along with several of her radio colleagues. She often appeared at SPERDVAC conventions as a panelist answering audience questions and entertaining with recollections, behind-the-scenes stories, and general perspectives on the industry. Personal interviews were not a favorite of Virginia's, but she stomached the butterflies because she so enjoyed reconnecting with many of her old friends and recalling the old days of radio.

THE MEN

All three of Virginia's sons had grown into men by the 1980s and went on to have their own families and careers outside of their family of origin's spot in Hollywood's limelight. Virginia was proud of them all and their life pursuits, and while none were close with their father, Jaime, they stayed in touch with "Mom," even when hundreds of miles away.

Gregg died in Wyoming in 2001 at the age of fifty-three. Ricardo died of brain cancer associated with Agent Orange exposure from his service in Vietnam. Virginia and Jaime's middle son Jaime is the only living of the three boys. He now resides in Sunny California and has worked as a fire chief for many years.

Virginia was incredibly proud of all three sons. She loved them dearly and remained available to them as an immovable anchorage until her death.

CHAPTER 10: SIGNING OFF

"We all die. The goal isn't to live forever, the goal is to create something that will."

-Chuck Palahniuk

Peggy Webber and Sean McClory were another one of those powerhouse Hollywood matches. She the gentle beauty and he the gallant Irishman. Both veteran entertainers, they had much in common and fell hard and fast for each other becoming engaged in the 1980s. It was a second marriage for them both in their 60s, but with Peggy's excitement, you'd swear they were eloping teenagers. Peggy recalls phoning Virginia to invite her to the wedding several weeks in advance. Virginia was delighted in the news of Peggy's upcoming betrothal but said she could not attend the ceremony. As they talked on, Virginia hesitantly revealed the reason for her "no." "Peggy, I wish I could, but I'm taking care of this old lady who has cancer. I would love to come, but I'm afraid I just can't leave her alone." Always the caretaker, it wasn't unusual for Virginia to be helping someone in a difficult situation, and it also wasn't unusual for her to be quite vague about the details. Peggy thought nothing of the decline and after a typically lovely phone conversation, hung up without a second thought of Virginia's "no." That was the last time the two spoke. Peggy heard the news just a few short weeks later that Virginia had died – on Peggy's 61st birthday. It was only after Virginia's death that Peggy realized the "old lady with cancer" Virginia said she had been caring for was in fact herself.

Virginia Lee Gregg Burket died at age seventy on September 15, 1986, in Encino Hospital. Like most actors and actresses in the Golden Age of radio, Virginia was a smoker and not much was known then about the consequences of a life of drags until it was too late. It is common knowledge to our world in the 2020s that smoking can lead to cancer and a plethora of other health maladies, but in the 1940s, smoking was thought to be as safe as ice-cream sundae. It seemed a harmless pastime that "everyone did." In many of the old radio show recordings, original commercials have been retained that exhibit society's (and Hollywood's) attitude toward smoking in the 1940s-1950s:

> *What cigarettes do doctors themselves smoke? In a nationwide survey, a few years ago, 113,597 doctors – doctors in every branch of medicine were asked, 'What cigarette do you smoke, doctor?' The brand named most was Camel. Again and again in repeated surveys the same preference was shown. Yes, these surveys show that more doctors smoke Camels than any other cigarette. Why don't you smoke Camels, too?*

Smoking was par for the course in the entertainment industry, with many stars endorsing cigarette brands across all mediums. In the Golden Age, no one could have guessed that decades later they would experience dreadful residuals from this common habit. In 1982, television's *Gunsmoke* star Amanda Blake, who portrayed Dodge's fiery, saloon-owner (and Matt Dillon's *true* love in my humble opinion), "Miss Kitty," spoke at a hearing with the House Subcommittee on Health and the Environment on behalf of her own experience with the dangers of smoking. Diagnosed with cancer of the mouth in the 1970s, Amanda underwent surgery and a series of difficult treatments in an effort to reverse the damage the cancer had caused. "I believe that I would not have smoked had I seen a label on a cigarette package or in a cigarette ad that said, 'Warning: Cigarette smoking may cause death from heart disease, cancer, or emphysema.'" Blake said.[106] After together Blake, John Forsythe, and Robert Keeshan spoke to the committee as former smokers who had suffered from years of striking the match, legislation was eventually passed that required more explicit warning labels on cigarette packs. Those old Camel's commercials of the 1940s are caricatures to us today in our "informed" culture of the 2020s – informed of course only through the adversities of those before us like Amanda Blake, who because of her own diagnosis, probably helped to save countless others from similar fates. Of course, for many, the warnings on the cigarette box came far too late.

Virginia's decline must have had echoed that of her mother's. The cough. The fatigue. The dread. In the haunting memories of her mother's fight against tuberculosis so many years before, she must have seen fractal reflections of her own condition. Typically attentive to her health, Virginia tried her damnest to ignore this. She had beat cancer once and perhaps didn't want to face the possibility of a similar war again. Who could blame her?

She constantly blamed the ever-increasing dry, weighty cough on "sinus issues" or "allergies" from spending too much time in her garden tending to her night-blooming jasmine. When her sons would call, the cough interrupted their chats more and more. For more than forty years, her voice had been her superpower, meal-ticket, and identity. Suddenly, at the age of seventy, it was being slowly taken from her and replaced with an uncontrollable hacking that left her weary. She had fought battle over battle for seventy years and won most of them, but she was tired.

Virginia worked less and less as 1986 progressed. Her last film was *Psycho III* in the reprised role of "Norman Bates'" mummified mother. The film was released July 1986, but Virginia could have recorded her voice-over work as early as 1985. Her last known television role was in the Hanna-Barbera children's show *The Greatest Adventure: Stories from the Bible* for the "Samson and Delilah" episode in which she voiced the supporting role of "Miriam."

While never keen on talking about herself in her own character, Virginia was interview-shy for most of her career compared to her peers. She did however give several interviews in the months leading up to her death, as if she knew the end wasn't far off.

She must have found value in leaving those interviews behind for people like me who never would have known her story otherwise. Thank God she was willing to be uncomfortable to pass her story down through these recordings. And thank God for SPERD-VAC for recording them.

A biopsy confirmed her lung cancer diagnosis early in 1986. With essentially no particularly promising treatment options for late-stage diagnoses in the 1980s, she did her best to manage her symptoms at home, knowing there was little that could be done beyond that without extreme interventions reminiscent of her previous battle in the 1960s. Her condition continued to worsen over the next few months, and in September of 1986, much to her chagrin, a family friend insisted she go to the hospital. The cancer had progressed far beyond her self-care methods, and she had been a bit too stubborn to make the trip to the hospital on her own. It was only after her hospitalization that her family officially learned of her diagnosis and quickly fading state. True to her nature, she kept the news from the world as long as she could. Once hospitalized, she declined to the point of requiring intubation and after several days, went into cardiac arrest. She was pronounced dead at 10:50am on September 15, 1986, at the age of seventy.

Though death eventually comes for all of us, that flash between this life and the next is mysterious, personal, and inevitable. No one knows what those last moments were like for Virginia, but of one thing I am certain, I can almost guarantee she faced death like she had faced everything else for seventy years: eye-to-eye.

News of her death quickly flew around LA County to all the media outlets, with the headline: "Versatile Character Actress Virginia Gregg dies at 70." The same newspapers that broke the news of her marriages, divorces, births of her children, her many career successes, beauty tips, court battles, and behind-the-scenes industry insight for over fifty years, also broke the news of her death. Her obituary reads,

"She is survived by sons Gregg, Jaime, and Ricardo del Valle. The family requests that memorial donations be made to Recordings for the Blind, Inc., where she made many recordings as a volunteer and served for many years as a member of the board of directors."[107] She wished to be cremated, and her ashes were given to her sons.

Death can be too quick, too slow, or somewhere in the middle, but the legacy a person leaves behind in those they loved is everlasting. The chapter on Virginia's death should really be on the life she left behind in others, which has been passed on through a couple of generations now, and my hope is that her legacy will continue beyond that in her work, her strength, her love, and her inspiration.

Virginia and fellow actor and founding member of the American Federation of Radio Artists (AFRA) Frank Nelson died 3 days apart in 1986, making it a terribly "black weekend" as Parley Baer described. As both were honorary SPERDVAC members, the November/December 1986 edition of the SPERDVAC newsletter was dedicated to their legacies. Radio colleagues of Virginia and Frank were asked to write their tributes to these two greats. The rest of this chapter is made up of beautiful legacy fragments from those Virginia knew, worked with, and loved. Virginia may not be with us on this earth anymore, but she is so very present in these first-hand remembrances, which reflect the composite of her essence every time they are read. She did not write her own biography, but with the way she touched so many lives, she certainly wrote her own legacy.

Virginia was once asked by columnist Lydia Lane, to what did she attribute her success. She answered:

I studied and worked, but I'm fortunate to have a versatile voice. This was especially helpful on radio because I could play several parts and sound completely different. And another thing which has helped is being able to get along with people.[108]

That ability is more than obvious in the following tributes.

LEGACY

Virginia, a classical musician, a devoted wife and mother of three fine sons, a charitable lady who devoted much of her time and talent toward those less fortunate than she and a deeply loving and emotional friend who always had a big smile and hug and a warm kiss waiting for those she cared for. Above all else, however, was her great talent. Never a bad performance, always an incisive, deeply penetrating and sensitive interpretation of each character she played, even when it was in a scene where she was talking to herself! As she did in the next to last radio show I did with her, the SUSPENSE performance we all did for you "SPERDVACKIANS" a few years ago. And what fun that was. All of you at SPERDVAC have always made us feel we're special . . . and that's always very soul-satisfying. Virginia was superb in that show, as usual . . . as she was when we last worked together in my latest effort (which I'm rather proud to say is a 'Les Tremayne Production'), Please Stand By – A History of Radio. *As always, Virginia played several parts in the same script . . . but you'd never have known it . . . each one was a little gem. And she loved her work, which, of course, is one of the main reasons she was so great. One of a kind, bless her.* – Les Tremayne

As for the lovely talented Virginia Gregg, my memory goes also to her other talents. She was a string bass player and horserider, at the age of twenty. Virginia was in a troupe [sic] of girls (late teens and early twenties) attractively uniformed and guided through their riding programs by Dr. Leonard Stallcup, a demanding taskmaster, also a member of AF of M. – Ivan Ditmars

Our paths hadn't crossed for years, not since the last time on the Stan Freberg show, after which we traveled different tangents of

our profession. Virginia made an untroubled transition from being a consummate radio actress, inordinately talented in any role that she assumed, to a graceful film and television performer. Her personality charmed the pants off of people, and besides all these multiplicity of perquisites, she had physical beauty, a necessary adjunct to young ladies to compete in the celluloid jungle. Her friends and fellow workers were delighted to have participated in her life and feel that the actor's profession has been enhanced because of her presence. – June Foray

I think the greatest thing that can be said about Virginia Gregg is this: I never heard her say a disparaging or mean thing about anybody! Even those who in our lesser sight deserved it. A loving friend to all of us. She laughed with us, rejoiced with us, sympathized with us and wept with us. And now we're left to weep alone. She wouldn't want us to weep. But how can we not? Particularly do I remember Virginia diligently bent over the reading table, repairing a cigarette lighter between scenes. Did you know she was a genius at repairing cigarette lighters? Well she was. The late Stacy Harris, always impeccably dressed, sported a gold 'Norma' pencil (we more proletariat folks had chrome 'Normas'), gold cufflinks (from Maurice's) and a gold cigarette lighter. 'I wouldn't let anyone but Ginny touch it,' Stacy used to say. She kept it going. I wonder what became of the little repair kit she had. God! How these guys are missed.

- Parley Baer

She was an inspiration forever for me and a friend. Her greatest pride was in her sons. How I will miss getting on the phone to her about any subject. She always had the answer for me.

-Alice Backes

It is hard for me to accept the reality that my dear friend Virginia Gregg is gone. I never expected to think such a word since she had always been a kind of presence alive and ongoing in my mind. I can never forget that she had been solely responsible for spurring my career as a professional actor in Hollywood radio. It was in 1943. I had been discharged from the Army and had taken a job as announcer at radio station KMPC, then in Beverly Hills. Every Sunday night KMPC broadcast a local show called The Hermit's Cave. *It was a weird program of murder and suspense. Despite its outrageous format it attracted something of an audience which would tune in and listen week after week to our ghostly shenanigans. I was "The Hermit," a crazed and cackling character who kept the nutty stories moving. It was then I met Virginia Gregg.*

Every Sunday she joined us in our capers and it was during these sessions that this ebullient, outgoing girl began to take an interest in my possibilities as a radio actor. She decided to do what she could to improve my career. How lucky for me. She was already fairly well on her way to building her own name in West Coast radio. She began to make my name known to producers she regularly worked for, taking me around to their offices and introducing me here and there. Out of this it became my great good fortune that, one by one, these producers began to hire me. From then on, it was the usual one thing that led to another and another and another. All exciting. Virginia did it. That was 1943.

I could stop there and have that be the story of my gratitude to this wonderful woman. But beyond setting in train my professional progress I must say she introduced me into an atmosphere I needed as much as I needed a job . . . the warmth and security that comes with making new friends. What a bonanza I found. A welcome into a gathering of dear, good natured, caring, bright people who became my fast friends. For years this lasted and radio was our life with all its ups and downs. Then it all came to an end and we went our sepa-

rate ways, remembering, I'm sure, each other and the days we worked together. For me it was Virginia Gregg who started it all. Now it is forty-three years later and she is no longer with us. For what it's worth I take comfort in believing that she had taken something of me with her – my affection and my boundless gratitude.

-John Dehner

I remember her as not only a fine artist but as a willing and cooperative worker.

–Carlton E. Morse

We who are left here on Mother Earth turn out to be the big losers when we consider angels like Virginia Gregg. Memories are our treasures as we look back to the wonderful hours so many of us can remember. Some may not know about Virginia's first years in show business. She was a fine musician and it recalls our first meeting in 1936. CBS had just bought the station as their flagship and were putting on numerous programs to start their association with the community. One of these programs was The Singing Strings led by Harriet Wilson and her violin. There were six lovely young ladies in this group – all very talented – who made beautiful music each week. I happened to be the lucky fellow assigned to announce and direct their show and there was sweet dear Virginia playing the bass viol. What a pleasure it was to listen but greater pleasure to get to know all the girls in the group. Later in 1937 and 1938 they were the nucleus of a much larger orchestra – some fifty or sixty in all – who were heard coast to coast playing from the Vine Street Theater (where Lux Radio Theater came from and which later became the Huntington Hartford Theater and is now the James Doolittle Theater).

It wasn't too long after those early years that Virginia started her career as an actress . . . first on radio and later in motion pictures and television.

All of us who knew her had the greatest admiration and respect for her professionalism and great talent as an actress. She was called on often because they knew that she would do an outstanding professional job. No one was any better at her craft.

But so many of her admirers never got to know the other side of this great lady. Her generous heart was as big as all outdoors. Whether it was a cat, a dog or a human being, she loved them all and would take them in and love them. She was the kindest, most thoughtful person I know and a part of all of us went with her to her reward with her Creator.

The angels are up there singing, and our dear Virginia is making all of them happier by her presence. – Art Gilmore

Virginia Gregg will always be with us! She lives on through her three fine sons, through the memories of hundreds of friends, through the ideals she set and carried through, through her kindness and love. Because she always gave of herself so freely and so often, we will always be in her debt. She was the consummate actress and in my view, she had no peer. I will never miss her because she will always be with me. – Page Gilman

Virginia Gregg was one of the most beloved actresses ever to grace a Hollywood studio or sound stage. Adored by her three grown sons, who had depended on her to rear them; looked forward to by millions of listeners and viewers, when they learned she was to appear; admired as an actress and treasured friend by other performers who considered it a privilege to work with her – Virginia was a lovely combination of motherhood, professional talent and true friendship.

One of her great loves and an activity to which she was firmly dedicated was Recording for the Blind, to which she gave untold hours of her time and talent. I personally had the great joy of having her as my leading lady on the LET GEORGE DO IT radio series more than thirty years ago. Jack Webb was one of the producers who would not do a radio or TV series or a motion picture without her.

Virginia Gregg's death left personal and professional voids which can never be filled. She was deeply loved. – Olan Soule

Well, first of all, I am not convinced she is gone. The tall golden girl, with the caressing voice. Captain Cat in 'Under Milkwood' said it for me, when one after one, those he cared for most in life speak from the grave But to speak of things that were and are . . . She was an inspiration to work with and to know . . . She was ever loving, sensitive to others, fun and funny, dignified, and then totally human, laughing at her humanness. She was one of our best; ever ready to rise to a challenge. She was brave, romantic, giving and a leader. She was Virginia. Our Virginia. A part of our radio family a very important part that will live on in her work . . . in the love she gave to us all and in her three beautiful sons, now grown, handsome, good, men. They are the living tribute to the exceptional woman, their mother, Virginia Gregg. – Peggy Webber

There isn't much in my positive life lessons that I don't attribute to her. She was funny in the right way, and I appreciated that from an early age. She LOVED animals, and I feel the same. Her empathy for the human condition was a regular topic, and that always impressed me. She valued the many friends in her life, and despite some disappointment, friends were always an important aspect of her personality. The list could go on for a long time. - Jaime del Valle

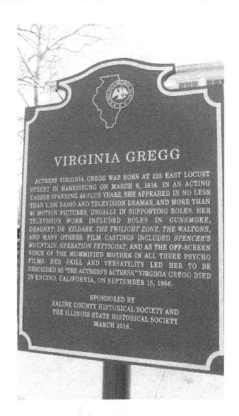

Virginia Gregg Historical Marker, 2020. Photo courtesy Chris Bailey.

Appendix A: Selected Works of Virginia Gregg Listed Chronologically

Radio

<u>Television</u>

Film

The majority of radio show listings include the air date, which is synonymous with the recording date, as most were live. The majority of film and television listings include the United States release date, which most likely means a difference of weeks and months regarding actual recording date.

Lights Out "Come to the Bank" (November 17, 1942)

The Screen Guild Theater "Whistling in Dixie" (May 17, 1943)

Wings to Victory "Story of John 'Rocky' Saunders" (October 7, 1943)

Lux Radio Theatre "Random Harvest" (January 31, 1944)

Lux Radio Theatre "The Phantom Lady" (March 27, 1944)

Cavalcade of America "Mask for Jefferson" (April 17, 1944)

Lux Radio Theatre "Penny Serenade" (May 8, 1944)

Lux Radio Theatre "Naughty Marietta" (June 12, 1944)

Lux Radio Theatre "Only Yesterday" (April 16, 1945)

Lux Radio Theatre "And Now Tomorrow" (May 21, 1945)

The Rudy Vallee Show "The Drene Show: Our First Adventure" (June 13, 1946)

The Count of Monte Cristo "Black Widow" (July 8, 1946)

Play for Tonight "Randy of Coyote Canyon" (August 23, 1946)

The Whistler "Stranger in the House" (September 2, 1946)

Notorious (September 6, 1946)

Cavalcade of America "Danger: Women at Work" (September 9, 1946)

The Whistler "Witness at the Fountain" (September 9, 1946)

The Rudy Vallee Show "The Great Gildersleeve" (September 10, 1946)

The Rudy Vallee Show "Villa Vallee" (October 1, 1946)

Lux Radio Theatre "Together Again" (December 9, 1946)

The Happy Prince: A Radio Play (December 22, 1946)

A Gathering in the Air "A Gathering in the Air" (1946)

A Child's Wish (January 9, 1947)

Marvelous Margie "Marvelous Margie: Episode 1" (February 5, 1947)

The Whistler "Blue Legend" (March 3, 1947)

The Adventures of Ellery Queen "Nikki Porter, Suspect" (March 5, 1947)

Lost Honeymoon (March 29, 1947)

Gentleman's Agreement (March 1947)

Cavalcade of America "School for Men" (May 5, 1947)

Family Theatre "Three Way Love" (May 29, 1947)

Voyage of the Scarlet Queen "The Boston Geisha and Chesapeake Bay" (July 24, 1947)

Dark Venture "Ten Dollar Bill" (August 15, 1947)

Deadline Mystery "Housing Scandal" (August 24, 1947)

The Whistler "Curtain Call" (August 27, 1947)

Voyage of the Scarlet Queen "Grafter's Fort and the Black Pearl of Galayla Bay" (October 23, 1947)

The Whistler "Back Door" (October 29, 1947)

Body and Soul (November 11, 1947)

The Adventures of Ellery Queen "The Saga of Ruffy Rux" (November 27, 1947)

The Adventures of Ellery Queen "Nikki Porter, Bride" (December 11, 1947)

The Adventures of Ellery Queen "The Case of the Melancholy Dane" (December 18, 1947)

Lux Radio Theatre "Miracle on 34th Street" (December 22, 1947)

The Adventures of Ellery Queen "Ellery Queen, Santa Claus" (December 25, 1947)

In Your Name "The Snowman" (February 8, 1948)

The First Nighter Program "Love Stranger than Fiction" (February 12, 1948)

Escape "Misfortune Isle" (March 21, 1948)

Diary of Fate "Edward Matthews" (March 30, 1948)

Family Theatre "Little Boy Blue" (April 1, 1948)

Casbah (April 1948)

All-Star Western Theatre "Ranch for Sale" (May 8, 1948)

Family Theatre "The High Boarded Fence" (June 3, 1948)

Family Theatre "Once upon a Golden Afternoon" (June 10, 1948)

Let George Do It "The Unfit Mother Case/Problem Child" (June 21, 1948)

Let George Do It "Johnathan Thorpe Case/Murder Me Twice" (July 5, 1948)

Command Performance (July 13, 1948)

Let George Do It "Cry Murder" (July 19, 1948)

Diary of Fate "Stanley Becker" (July 27, 1948)

The Amazing Mr. X (July 29, 1948)

Diary of Fate "Darrell James" (August 10, 1948)

Let George Do It "Ghost on Bliss Terrace" (August 16, 1948)

The Gay Intruders (September 2, 1948)

Let George Do It "The Impatient Redhead" (September 6, 1948)

Family Theatre "Once upon a Golden Afternoon" (September 9, 1948)

We Care "The Bimbo from Limbo" (September 26, 1948)

Family Theatre "Gramps" (September 30, 1948)

The Adventures of Philip Marlowe "The Persian Slippers" (October 3, 1948)

The Unexpected "Handle with Care" (November 7, 1948)

The Unexpected "Heard but Not Seen" (December 5, 1948)

Your Movietown Radio Theatre *Title Unknown* (1948)

Let George Do It "Murder and One to Go" (January 3, 1949)

The Adventures of Philip Marlowe "The Restless Day" (January 8, 1949)

The Children's Hour, But Not for Children (January 10, 1949)

Screen Director's Guild Assignment/Playhouse "Let's Live a Little" (January 16, 1949)

Family Theatre "World Without End" (January 19, 1949)

Family Theatre "Melancholy Clown" (January 26, 1949)

Let George Do It "One Against a City" (February 7, 1949)

The Adventures of Philip Marlowe "The Lonesome Reunion" (February 12, 1949)

Let George Do It "Journey into Hate" (February 21, 1949)

Skippy Hollywood Theatre "Schizo-Scherzo" (February 25, 1949)

The Adventures of Philip Marlowe "The Friend from Detroit" (March 5, 1949)

Pat Novak for Hire "Fleet Lady" (March 6, 1949)

Let George Do It "The Roundabout Murder" (March 7, 1949)

Screen Director's Guild Assignment/Playhouse "Suddenly It's Spring" (March 27, 1949)

Family Theatre "Night Elevator" (April 6, 1949)

Lux Radio Theatre "The Song of Bernadette" (April 11, 1949)

Screen Director's Guild Assignment/Playhouse "The Best Years of our Lives" (April 17, 1949)

Richard Diamond, Private Detective "Diamond in the Rough – The Richard Barton Case" (April 24, 1949)

Let George Do It "Lady in Distress" (April 25, 1949)

The Adventures of Philip Marlowe "The Feminine Touch" (May 7, 1949)

Richard Diamond, Private Detective "The Ralph Chase Case" (May 15, 1949)

Family Theatre "The Legacy" (May 18, 1949)

Richard Diamond, Private Detective "The Stolen Purse" (May 22, 1949)

Richard Diamond, Private Detective "The Betty Moran Case" (May 29, 1949)

Richard Diamond, Private Detective "The Bertram Kalmus Case" (June 5, 1949)

The Whistler "Perfect Albi" (June 12, 1949)

The Whistler "That Physical Fact" (June 19, 1949)

Richard Diamond, Private Detective "The Fred Sears Murder Case" (June 19, 1949)

Family Theatre "The Postmistress of Laurel Run" (June 22, 1949)

Richard Diamond, Private Detective "The Tom Waxman Bombing Case" (June 26, 1949)

Richard Diamond, Private Detective "The Bloody Hat Case" (July 2, 1949)

The Adventures of Frank Race "The Juvenile Passenger" (July 3, 1949)

Family Theatre "The Pardoner's Tale" (July 6, 1949)

Richard Diamond, Private Detective "Charles Walsh & Bob Wells" (July 9, 1949)

Richard Diamond, Private Detective "The Man Who Hated Women" (July 16, 1949)

The Whistler "Death in Sixteen Millimeter" (July 17, 1949)

The Adventures of Frank Race "The Silent Heart" (July 17, 1949)

Richard Diamond, Private Detective "The Martin Hyers Case" (July 23, 1949)

The Whistler "Brotherly Hate" (July 31, 1949)

Let George Do It "Perfect Albi" (August 1, 1949)

Family Theatre "The Bishop's Candlesticks" (August 3, 1949)

Richard Diamond, Private Detective "Lynn Knight Wants Protection" (August 6, 1949)

Richard Diamond, Private Detective "The Jean Cooper Murder Case/The Tom Cook Manslaughter Case" (August 20, 1949)

Screen Director's Guild Assignment/Playhouse "Appointment for Love" (August 26, 1949)

Richard Diamond, Private Detective "The Eddie Garrett Case" (August 27, 1949)

Let George Do It "End of Summer" (August 29, 1949)

Richard Diamond, Private Detective "The Harry Baker Case" (September 3, 1949)

Richard Diamond, Private Detective "The Van Dyke Séance" (September 10, 1949)

Family Theatre "Mademoiselle Fifi" (September 14, 1949)

Richard Diamond, Private Detective "Jerome J. Jerome" (September 17, 1949)

Screen Director's Guild Assignment/Playhouse "Don't Trust Your Husband" (September 23, 1949)

Richard Diamond, Private Detective "The Two Thousand Dollar Bundle" (September 24, 1949)

Family Theatre "Evangeline" (September 28, 1949)

California Caravan "The Saga of Charlie Parkhurst" (September 29, 1949)

Richard Diamond, Private Detective "The Gibson Murder Case" (October 8, 1949)

NBC University Theatre "The House of Mirth" (October 9, 1949)

Richard Diamond, Private Detective "Newspaper Boy and Counterfeit Bills" (October 15, 1949)

Screen Director's Guild Assignment/Playhouse "Pitfall" (October 17, 1949)

Richard Diamond, Private Detective "The Rene Benet Protection Case" (October 22, 1949)

Richard Diamond, Private Detective "The Bill Kirby Murder Case" (October 29, 1949)

Let George Do It "Every Shot Counts" (October 31, 1949)

Richard Diamond, Private Detective "Singing Critic/Rival Shamus" (November 5, 1949)

Richard Diamond, Private Detective "$50,000 in Diamonds Stolen" (November 12, 1949)

Guest Star "Fiddle Faddle" (November 12, 1949)

Richard Diamond, Private Detective "The Leon Jacoby Case" (November 19, 1949)

Let George Do It "Sweet Poison" (November 21, 1949)

Family Theatre "The Courtship of Miles Standish" (November 23, 1949)

Richard Diamond, Private Detective "William Carter and Helena Fisher" (November 26, 1949)

The Adventures of Philip Marlowe "The Kid on the Corner" (December 3, 1949)

Richard Diamond, Private Detective "The Ruby Idol Case" (December 3, 1949)

Richard Diamond, Private Detective "The Julia Bates Case: The House of Mystery Case" (December 10, 1949)

Broadway Is My Beat "The Tori Jones Case" (December 10, 1949)

Let George Do It "Partner in Panama" (December 12, 1949)

Richard Diamond, Private Detective "The John Blackwell Case" (December 17, 1949)

The Adventures of Frank Race "Undecided Bride" (December 18, 1949)

Let George Do It "Follow That Train" (December 19, 1949)

Richard Diamond, Private Detective "A Christmas Carol" (December 24, 1949)

Let George Do It "Snow Blind" (December 26, 1949)

Richard Diamond, Private Detective "The Thomas Jason Case" (December 31, 1949)

Let George Do It "Needle in the Haystack" (January 2, 1950)

Family Theatre "Old Judge Priest" (January 4, 1950)

Screen Director's Guild Assignment/Playhouse "Magic Town" (January 6, 1950)

Richard Diamond, Private Detective "Butcher's Protection Racket" (January 7, 1950)

Let George Do It "The Silent Waterfall" (January 9, 1950)

Family Theatre "A Tale of Two Cities" (January 11, 1950)

Night Beat "The Elevator Caper" (January 13, 1950)

Richard Diamond, Private Detective "The Cathy Victor Case" (January 15, 1950)

Let George Do It "Juniper Lane" (January 16, 1950)

Let George Do It "The Floaters" (January 23, 1950)

Let George Do It "The Ugly Duckling" (January 30, 1950)

Let George Do It "The Old Style" (February 6, 1950)

Broadway Is My Beat "The Julie Dixon Case/A Cinderella Girl" (February 10, 1950)

Let George Do It "Go Jump in the Lake" (February 13, 1950)

The Story of Doctor Kildare "Benjamin Barkley" (February 15, 1950)

Broadway Is My Beat "The Dion Hartley Story" (February 17, 1950)

The Whistler "Five Cent Call" (February 19, 1950)

The Story of Doctor Kildare "Rico Marchiano's Dying Wife" (February 22, 1950)

Yours Truly, Johnny Dollar "The Archeologist" (February 24, 1950)

The Adventures of Christopher London "The Price of Sugar" (February 26, 1950)

The Story of Doctor Kildare "Vernon Pendleton Hypochondriac" (March 1, 1950)

The Story of Doctor Kildare "Barbara Lane Dope Addict" (March 8, 1950)

The Whistler "Oriana Affair" (March 19, 1950)

The Story of Doctor Kildare "Jane Dane New Cancer Treatment" (March 22, 1950)

Family Theatre "The Broken Pitcher" (March 22, 1950)

Much Ado About Doolittle (March 25, 1950)

Let George Do It "The Tears of Sorrow" (March 27, 1950)

Let George Do It "The Brothers McIntosh" (April 3, 1950)

The Adventures of Philip Marlowe "The Man on the Roof" (April 4, 1950)

Yours Truly, Johnny Dollar "The Story of the Big Red School" (April 4, 1950)

Let George Do It "Portrait by Pricilla" (April 10, 1950)

Richard Diamond, Private Detective "The Man Who Hated Women" (April 12, 1950)

The Story of Doctor Kildare "Warren Jackson's Allergy" (April 12, 1950)

Let George Do It "Mixup in La Cruza" (April 17, 1950)

Richard Diamond, Private Detective "Messenger Service, Patty Clark" (April 19, 1950)

The Story of Doctor Kildare "Terry Murphy's Hearing Problem" (April 19, 1950)

Let George Do It "Death Begins at 45" (April 24, 1950)

Yours Truly, Johnny Dollar "The Pearl Carrassa Matter" (April 25, 1950)

Richard Diamond, Private Detective "The Ralph Baxter Case" (April 26, 1950)

The Story of Doctor Kildare "Phillip Vancourt's Amnesia" (April 26, 1950)

Let George Do It "The Chair of Humanities" (May 1, 1950)

The Story of Doctor Kildare "Abandoned Baby" (May 3, 1950)

Family Theatre "Sarah Bernhardt" (May 3, 1950)

Let George Do It "Picture with a Black Frame" (May 8, 1950)

Night Beat "The Elevator Caper" (May 8, 1950)

The Adventures of Philip Marlowe "The Hiding Place" (May 9, 1950)

Family Theatre "The Bet" (May 10, 1950)

Let George Do It "The Ant Hill" (May 15, 1950)

The Story of Doctor Kildare "Nurse Parker Resigns" (May 17, 1950)

Let George Do It "Portuguese Cove" (May 22, 1950)

Yours Truly, Johnny Dollar "The Earl Chadwick Matter" (May 23, 1950)

The Story of Doctor Kildare "Dr. Carew's Fat Wife" (May 24, 1950)

One Man's Family "Jack Overwhelms Betty" (May 28, 1950)

Let George Do It "Sudden Storm" (May 29, 1950)

The Story of Doctor Kildare "Dick Brennan Steals Five Thousand Dollars" (May 31, 1950)

The Story of Doctor Kildare "Colonel Beauregard's Paralysis" (June 1, 1950)

Hallmark Playhouse "The Story of Kansas City" (June 1, 1950)

Let George Do It "The Witch of Mill Hollow" (June 5, 1950)

The Story of Doctor Kildare "Gordon Mallory's Lead Poisoning" (June 8, 1950)

Yours Truly, Johnny Dollar "The Caligio Diamond Matter" (June 8, 1950)

Let George Do It "The Iron Cat" (June 12, 1950)

Richard Diamond, Private Detective "The William Carnes Case" (June 14, 1950)

Let George Do It "Solo in Whispers" (Junc 19, 1950)

Richard Diamond, Private Detective "Mrs. X Can't Find Her Husband" (June 21, 1950)

The Halls of Ivy "The Bentheimers and the Census" (June 21, 1950)

Yours Truly, Johnny Dollar "The London Matter" (June 22, 1950)

The Story of Doctor Kildare "Pricilla's Broken Arm" (June 22, 1950)

Let George Do It "Most Likely to Die" (June 26, 1950)

Family Theatre "Sir Lancelot of the Lake" (June 28, 1950)

Richard Diamond, Private Detective "The Mary Bellman Case" (June 28, 1950)

The Story of Doctor Kildare "Dr. Gillespie Almost Gets Engaged" (June 29, 1950)

Let George Do It "The Scream of the Eagle" (July 3, 1950)

Richard Diamond, Private Detective "The Mike Burton Case" (July 5, 1950)

Family Theatre "The Spectre Bridegroom" (July 5, 1950)

The Story of Doctor Kildare "Hunting Trip" (July 6, 1950)

Let George Do It "Island in the Desert" (July 10, 1950)

Richard Diamond, Private Detective "Ice Pick Murder" (July 12, 1950)

Yours Truly, Johnny Dollar "The Calgary Matter" (July 13, 1950)

The Story of Doctor Kildare "Dan Malloy's Peptic Ulcer" (July 13, 1950)

Let George Do It "Eleven O'clock" (July 17, 1950)

Richard Diamond, Private Detective "The William B. Holland Case" (July 19, 1950)

The Story of Doctor Kildare "Mrs. Stanford's Angina Pecturis" (July 20, 1950)

The Line Up "Eddie Gaynor Framed for Murder" (July 20, 1950)

Tales of the Texas Rangers "Apache Peak" (July 22, 1950)

Richard Diamond, Private Detective "Martha Campbell Kidnapped" (July 26, 1950)

T-Man "Big Mexican Dope" (July 29, 1950)

Let George Do It "The Voice of the Giant" (July 31, 1950)

Richard Diamond, Private Detective "The Fixed Fight Case: Max Farmer, Boxer" (August 2, 1950)

Yours Truly, Johnny Dollar "The Blood River Matter" (August 3, 1950)

Let George Do It "Sweet are the Uses of Publicity" (August 7, 1950)

Richard Diamond, Private Detective "The Edna Wolfe Case" (August 9, 1950)

The Story of Doctor Kildare "Buffalo Barnie McClure" (August 10, 1950)

Let George Do It "The High Price of a Penny" (August 14, 1950)

Richard Diamond, Private Detective "The Carnival Case" (August 16, 1950)

The Story of Doctor Kildare "Appendicitis Operation at Sea" (August 17, 1950)

Yours Truly, Johnny Dollar "The Mickey McQueen Matter" (August 17, 1950)

Let George Do It "The Treasure of Millie's Wharf" (August 21, 1950)

Richard Diamond, Private Detective "The Farmer-Evans Murder Case" (August 23, 1950)

Let George Do It "High Card" (August 28, 1950)

Richard Diamond, Private Detective "Big Foot Grafton Case" (August 30, 1950)

Yours Truly, Johnny Dollar "The Virginia Beach Matter" (August 31, 1950)

Let George Do It "Second Degree Affection" (September 4, 1950)

Richard Diamond, Private Detective "The Misplaced Laundry Case" (September 6, 1950)

The Story of Doctor Kildare "Carew Gets Medical Examiner Mixed Up" (September 7, 1950)

Let George Do It "The White Elephant" (September 11, 1950)

Richard Diamond, Private Detective "The George Lexington Case" (September 13, 1950)

The Story of Doctor Kildare "Marion Lewis Teen Age Alcoholic" (September 14, 1950)

Let George Do It "Cover for an Hour" (September 18, 1950)

Richard Diamond, Private Detective "The Bald Head Case" (September 20, 1950)

The Story of Doctor Kildare "Sam Lubinski Has Spinal Paralysis" (September 21, 1950)

The Adventures of Philip Marlowe "The White Carnation" (September 22, 1950)

Let George Do It "Tag! You're It" (September 25, 1950)

Richard Diamond, Private Detective "The Oklahoma Cowboy Murder" (September 27, 1950)

The Story of Doctor Kildare "Willie Mumpkin's First Baby" (September 28, 1950)

Let George Do It "The House that Jack Built" (October 2, 1950)

The Story of Doctor Kildare "Joe Finley's Ulcer" (October 4, 1950)

Richard Diamond, Private Detective "The Pete Rocco Case" (October 4, 1950)

Let George Do It "The Spider and the Fly" (October 9, 1950)

Richard Diamond, Private Detective "The Homing Pigeon Case" (October 11, 1950)

The Story of Doctor Kildare "Oliver Van Meter's Allergy" (October 11, 1950)

One Man's Family "Betty and Her Fifteen Day Diet" (October 12, 1950)

Yours Truly, Johnny Dollar "The Yankee Pride Matter" (October 14, 1950)

One Man's Family "Nicolette Consoles Betty" (October 16, 1950)

Let George Do It "It's a Mystery to me" (October 16, 1950)

One Man's Family "Betty's Long Vigil" (October 17, 1950)

Richard Diamond, Private Detective "Lt. Levinson Kidnapped" (October 18, 1950)

The Story of Doctor Kildare "Anthrax Infection" (October 18, 1950)

The Story of Doctor Kildare "Eddie Jenkins and the Arsonist" (October 20, 1950)

Let George Do It "The Hand in the Coconut" (October 23, 1950)

Richard Diamond, Private Detective "The Rifle Case" (October 25, 1950)

The Story of Doctor Kildare "Ling Co Refuses Leg Surgery" (October 27, 1950)

Yours Truly, Johnny Dollar "The Joan Sebastian Matter" (October 28, 1950)

Tales of the Texas Rangers "Soft Touch" (October 29, 1950)

Let George Do It "Sedan from the City" (October 30, 1950)

Richard Diamond, Private Detective "Traffic Ticket Case" (November 1, 1950)

The Whistler "Just Like a Man" (November 5, 1950)

Richard Diamond, Private Detective "Dead Man's Letter" (November 8, 1950)

Tales of the Texas Rangers "Blood Relative" (November 12, 1950)

Richard Diamond, Private Detective "The Mona Lisa Murder" (November 15, 1950)

The Story of Doctor Kildare "Mr. Bradley's Damaged Heart" (November 17, 1950)

Yours Truly, Johnny Dollar "The Nora Faulkner Matter" (November 18, 1950)

Let George Do It "Cause for Thanksgiving" (November 20, 1950)

Richard Diamond, Private Detective "The Cover-Up Murders: 8 O'clock Killer" (November 22, 1950)

The Story of Doctor Kildare "Mr. Kramer's Chronic Enteritis/Parker Needs a Hobby"

(November 24, 1950)

Let George Do It "Nothing but the Truth" (November 27, 1950)

Richard Diamond, Private Detective "The Calypso" (November 29, 1950)

The Line Up "The Cop-Killer" (November 30, 1950)

The Story of Doctor Kildare "Lady Dunabees Annual Visit" (December 1, 1950)

Escape "This Side of Nowhere" (December 3, 1950)

Let George Do It "And Hope to Die" (December 4, 1950)

Richard Diamond, Private Detective "Missing Night Watchman" (December 6, 1950)

The Line Up "The Jersey Parallel" (December 7, 1950)

The Story of Doctor Kildare "Arthur Morgan Needs Brain Surgery" (December 8, 1950)

Broadway Is My Beat "The Ben Justin Case" (December 8, 1950)

Let George Do It "The Bookworm Turns" (December 11, 1950)

Richard Diamond, Private Detective "The Chapel Hill Case" (December 13, 1950)

Let George Do It "Opportunity Knocks Twice" (December 18, 1950)

Tales of the Texas Rangers "Christmas Present" (December 24, 1950)

Let George Do It "Santa Claus in Glass" (December 25, 1950)

The Line Up "The Elsner Case/Sixty-Year-Old Woman Strangled in the Park" (December 28, 1950)

The Story of Doctor Kildare "David Norton has Pneumonia" (December 29, 1950)

California Caravan "The Poet of Oakland" (1950)

The Line Up "The Case of Frankie and Joyce" (January 4, 1951)

Richard Diamond, Private Detective "Nathan Beeker Case" (January 5, 1951)

The Story of Doctor Kildare "Eddie Lazetti Kidnaps Nurse" (January 5, 1951)

Let George Do It "The Man Behind the Frame" (January 8, 1951)

The Story of Doctor Kildare "Dr. Gillespie's Testimonial Dinner" (January 12, 1951)

Richard Diamond, Private Detective "The Marilyn Conners Case" (January 12, 1951)

Yours Truly, Johnny Dollar "The Port-O-Call Matter" (January 13, 1951)

Let George Do It "Tune on a Triangle" (January 15, 1951)

The Line Up "Yudo in Ypsilanti" (January 18, 1951)

The Story of Doctor Kildare "Dr. Conlon, Quack" (January 19, 1951)

Richard Diamond, Private Detective "The Man with the Scar/Buried Treasure" (January 19, 1951)

Let George Do It "Knock on Wood" (January 22, 1951)

Richard Diamond, Private Detective "The Rawlins Case" (January 26, 1951)

Let George Do It "Christmas in January" (January 29, 1951)

The Line Up "The Grocery Store Murder" (February 1, 1951)

Richard Diamond, Private Detective "The Caspary Case" (February 2, 1951)

Let George Do It "Tongalani" (February 5, 1951)

Screen Director's Guild Assignment/Playhouse "Lucky Jordan" (February 8, 1951)

Richard Diamond, Private Detective "The Blue Serge Suit" (February 9, 1951)

Let George Do It "The Marauder" (February 12, 1951)

The Story of Doctor Kildare "Pete Cosloff is Mentally Ill" (February 16, 1951)

Richard Diamond, Private Detective "The Grey Man" (February 16, 1951)

Let George Do It "How Guilty Can You Get?" (February 19, 1951)

Richard Diamond, Private Detective "The Lady in Distress" (February 23, 1951)

Escape "The Follower" (February 23, 1951)

Let George Do It "See Me Once, You've Seen Me Twice" (February 26, 1951)

Richard Diamond, Private Detective "The Red Rose" (March 2, 1951)

The Story of Doctor Kildare "David Cooper's Burned Face" (March 2, 1951)

Let George Do It "The Public Eye" (March 5, 1951)

Richard Diamond, Private Detective "The Butcher Shop" (March 9, 1951)

Let George Do It "The Prairie Dog" (March 12, 1951)

Richard Diamond, Private Detective "Monsieur Bouchon" (March 16, 1951)

The Story of Doctor Kildare "Amy Dickens Break Her Leg" (March 16, 1951)

Let George Do It "Murder for Two" (March 19, 1951)

The Line Up "The Farmer's Flimsy Fence Case" (March 20, 1951)

The Story of Doctor Kildare "Cathy Morton's Baby" (March 23, 1951)

Richard Diamond, Private Detective "Little Chiva" (March 23, 1951)

The Line Up "The Lapinish Lighter-Upper Case" (March 27, 1951)

Richard Diamond, Private Detective "The Carnival" (March 30, 1951)

The Story of Doctor Kildare "Joan Quinn" (March 30, 1951)

Yours Truly, Johnny Dollar "The Jackie Cleaver Story" (March 31, 1951)

Let George Do It "The Eight Ball" (April 2, 1951)

Richard Diamond, Private Detective "The Dead Heiress" (April 6, 1951)

The Story of Doctor Kildare "Gillespie's New Suit for Henderson Award" (April 6, 1951)

Let George Do It "Uncle Harry's Bones" (April 9, 1951)

The Story of Doctor Kildare "Yukon Joe's Gold Mine" (April 13, 1951)

Richard Diamond, Private Detective "The Right Fix" (April 13, 1951)

Let George Do It "The Noose Hangs High" (April 16, 1951)

Richard Diamond, Private Detective "Tug" (April 20, 1951)

Tales of the Texas Rangers "Canned Death" (April 22, 1951)

Wild Bill Hickok "An Outlaw's Revenge" (April 22, 1951)

Let George Do It "Sabotage" (April 23, 1951)

Yours Truly, Johnny Dollar "The Virginia Towne Matter" (April 25, 1951)

Richard Diamond, Private Detective "The Barrio Case" (April 27, 1951)

Yours Truly, Johnny Dollar "Month-End Raid Matter" (April 28, 1951)

Let George Do It "The Discovery of Ponce the Lion" (April 30, 1951)

Richard Diamond, Private Detective "The Boy Who Made Bad" (May 4, 1951)

Dangerous Assignment "Rotterdam War Criminals" (May 4, 1951)

Broadway Is My Beat "The Harry Foster Case" (May 5, 1951)

Tales of the Texas Rangers "No Living Witnesses" (May 6, 1951)

The Adventures of Maisie "Quakenbush's Universal Elixir" (May 10, 1951)

Richard Diamond, Private Detective "Danny Denver" (May 11, 1951)

Tales of the Texas Rangers "Paid in Full" (May 13, 1951)

The Story of Doctor Kildare "Mysterious Hemophilia Patient" (May 18, 1951)

Richard Diamond, Private Detective "Lonely Hearts" (May 18, 1951)

Let George Do It "Big Brother" (May 21, 1951)

Hallmark Playhouse "Scudda Hoo, Scudda Hay" (May 24, 1951)

The Story of Doctor Kildare "Dr. Gillespie's New Office" (May 25, 1951)

Richard Diamond, Private Detective "Longest Short-Cut in the World" (May 25, 1951)

Wild Bill Hickok "The Road Agents at Red Rock" (May 27, 1951)

Richard Diamond, Private Detective "The Montelli Case" (June 1, 1951)

Night Beat "Will of Mrs. Orloff" (June 1, 1951)

Yours Truly, Johnny Dollar "The Soderberry, Maine Matter" (June 2, 1951)

Night Beat "The Search for Fred" (June 8, 1951)

Richard Diamond, Private Detective "The Darby Affair" (June 8, 1951)

Yours Truly, Johnny Dollar "The George Farmer Matter" (June 9, 1951)

Let George Do It "Sucker Stunt" (June 11, 1951)

Richard Diamond, Private Detective "The Poise Magazine Story" (June 15, 1951)

Yours Truly, Johnny Dollar "The Arthur Boldrick Matter" (June 16, 1951)

Wild Bill Hickok "Press for Justice" (June 17, 1951)

Your Movietown Radio Theatre "Schizo-Scherzo" (June 17, 1951)

The Line Up "Lieutenant Guthrie is Kidnapped" (June 19, 1951)

Yours Truly, Johnny Dollar "The Malcolm Wish, MD Matter" (June 20, 1951)

The Story of Doctor Kildare "Paul Bailey" (June 22, 1951)

Richard Diamond, Private Detective "The Masters Case" (June 22, 1951)

Let George Do It "The Man from French Guiana" (June 25, 1951)

Yours Truly, Johnny Dollar "The Hatchet House Theft Matter" (June 27, 1951)

Richard Diamond, Private Detective "The Monkey Man" (June 29, 1951)

Let George Do It "Is Everybody Happy?" (July 2, 1951)

Yours Truly, Johnny Dollar "The Alonzo Chapman Matter" (July 4, 1951)

The Line Up "The Syncopic Sweazy Sweat-Out Case" (July 5, 1951)

Let George Do It "Lefty's Angel" (July 9, 1951)

Romance "The Sword and the Knitting Needle" (July 9, 1951)

Yours Truly, Johnny Dollar "The Fair-Way Matter" (July 11, 1951)

The Line Up "The Flighty Fulvous Finch Case" (July 12, 1951)

The Story of Doctor Kildare "Valerie and Walter Benton – Murder!" (July 13, 1951)

Wild Bill Hickok "The Trail of Death" (July 15, 1951)

Let George Do It "What Became of Terry Cable?" (July 16, 1951)

The Story of Doctor Kildare "Evelyn Briggs" (July 20, 1951)

The Adventures of Philip Marlowe "Life Can be Murder" (July 21, 1951)

Wild Bill Hickok "The Trail Herd Trouble" (July 22, 1951)

The Whistler "Autumn Song" (July 22, 1951)

O'Hara "The Judas Face" (July 22, 1951)

Let George Do It "Drop Dead?" (July 23, 1951)

The Story of Doctor Kildare "Robert Lane, Intern, Shirks Duties" (July 27, 1951)

Yours Truly, Johnny Dollar "The Horace Lockhart Matter" (August 1, 1951)

The Line Up "The Butane Buttonworth Case" (August 2, 1951)

Screen Director's Guild Assignment/Playhouse "Caged" (August 2, 1951)

The Story of Doctor Kildare "Alice Bradley, Amnesia Victim" (August 3, 1951)

The Whistler "Fateful Reminder" (August 12, 1951)

Let George Do It "The Fearless Clown" (August 13, 1951)

Yours Truly, Johnny Dollar "The Lucky Costa Matter" (August 15, 1951)

Let George Do It "Deal Me Out and I'll Deal You In" (August 20, 1951)

Let George Do It "Murder on Vacation" (August 27, 1951)

The Whistler "Public Hero" (September 2, 1951)

Let George Do It "Blue Plate Special" (September 3, 1951)

The Line Up "The Pointless Pierson Polemic Polarity Case" (September 5, 1951)

Wild Bill Hickok "Logging" (September 9, 1951)

The Line Up "The Senile Slugging Case" (September 12, 1951)

Hallmark Playhouse "Francis Scott Key" (September 13, 1951)

Let George Do It "Framed for Hanging" (September 24, 1951)

The Line Up "The Fur-Flaunting Floozy" (September 26, 1951)

Hallmark Playhouse "Web of Destiny" (September 27, 1951)

Let George Do It "No Way Out" (October 1, 1951)

The Adventures of Maisie "Engaged to Harry Adams" (October 11, 1951)

Richard Diamond, Private Detective "The Lou Turner Case" (October 12, 1951)

The Adventures of Maisie "Jenny Perkins, Author/Spicy Novel" (October 18, 1951)

Richard Diamond, Private Detective "The Jackson Case" (October 19, 1951)

Let George Do It "A Crime Too Simple" (October 22, 1951)

Richard Diamond, Private Detective "Registered Letter" (October 26, 1951)

Yours Truly, Johnny Dollar "The Tolhurst Theft Matter" (October 27, 1951)

Let George Do It "The Woman in Black" (October 29, 1951)

The Line Up "The Jolted Justice Job Case" (November 1, 1951)

Richard Diamond, Private Detective "The Bowery Case" (November 2, 1951)

Yours Truly, Johnny Dollar "The Hannibal Murphy Matter" (November 3, 1951)

The Line Up "The Pixie-Picker Pickle" (November 8, 1951)

Richard Diamond, Private Detective "Buried Treasure" (November 9, 1951)

Yours Truly, Johnny Dollar "The Baskerville Matter" (November 10, 1951)

Richard Diamond, Private Detective "The Hollywood Story" (November 16, 1951)

Let George Do It "Destination: Danger" (November 19, 1951)

Richard Diamond, Private Detective "The Mickey Farmer Case" (November 23, 1951)

Let George Do It "The Meddler" (November 26, 1951)

The Adventures of Maisie "Running for Mayor" (November 29, 1951)

Dragnet "The Big Affair" (November 29, 1951)

Richard Diamond, Private Detective "Goodnight to Nocturne" (November 30, 1951)

Let George Do It "Off the Record" (December 3, 1951)

Richard Diamond, Private Detective "The Brown Envelope Case" (December 7, 1951)

Yours Truly, Johnny Dollar "The Youngstown Credit Group Matter" (December 8, 1951)

Tales of the Texas Rangers "Death Plant" (December 9, 1951)

Let George Do It "The Last Payoff" (December 10, 1951)

Hallmark Playhouse "The Story of John Hancock" (December 13, 1951)

Richard Diamond, Private Detective "The Night Club Case" (December 14, 1951)

The Silent Men "The Bogus G.I." (December 16, 1951)

Let George Do It "Stolen Goods" (December 17, 1951)

Richard Diamond, Private Detective "The Christmas Show" (December 21, 1951)

Wild Bill Hickok "Sir Tommy, the Silver Knight" (December 23, 1951)

Richard Diamond, Private Detective "The Plaid Overcoat Case" (December 28, 1951)

Yours Truly, Johnny Dollar "The Alma Scott Matter" (December 29, 1951)

Tales of the Texas Rangers "Killer's Crop" (December 30, 1951)

Richard Diamond, Private Detective "The Merry-Go-Round Case" (January 4, 1952)

The Whistler "Episode at Thunder Mountain" (January 6, 1952)

Let George Do It "A School of Sharks" (January 7, 1952)

Hollywood Star Playhouse "The Frontier" (January 10, 1952)

Hollywood Sound Stage "Shadow of a Doubt" (January 10, 1952)

Richard Diamond, Private Detective "The White Cow Case" (January 11, 1952)

Tales of the Texas Rangers "Clip Job" (January 13, 1952)

Let George Do It "The Bad Little God" (January 14, 1952)

Hallmark Playhouse "Madame Claire" (January 17, 1952)

Richard Diamond, Private Detective "The Simpson Case" (January 18, 1952)

Let George Do It "A Matter of Honor" (January 21, 1952)

Dragnet "The Big Court" (January 24, 1952)

Richard Diamond, Private Detective "The Al Brenners Case" (January 25, 1952)

Let George Do It "The Common Denominator" (January 28, 1952)

Wild Bill Hickok "The Dark Horse Candidate" (January 30, 1952)

Dragnet "The Big Almost No Show" (January 31, 1952)

Richard Diamond, Private Detective "The Garrabaldi Case" (February 1, 1952)

Let George Do It "Surprise! Surprise!" (February 4, 1952)

The Line Up "The Potting Peter Case" (February 5, 1952)

Dragnet "The Big Honeymoon" (February 7, 1952)

Richard Diamond, Private Detective "The Eddie Burke Case" (February 8, 1952)

Let George Do It "Cortez Island" (February 11, 1952)

Richard Diamond, Private Detective "The Jerry Wilson Incident" (February 15, 1952)

The Silent Men "Stolen Arsenal" (February 17, 1952)

Let George Do It "The Symbol Three" (February 18, 1952)

Dragnet "The Big Producer" (February 21, 1952)

Tarzan, Lord of the Jungle "Demon of Rongu" (February 21, 1952)

Richard Diamond, Private Detective "The Miami Case" (February 22, 1952)

Let George Do It "Starlight Pier" (February 25, 1952)

Dragnet "The Big Speech" S1E6 (February 28, 1952)

Richard Diamond, Private Detective "The Hired Killer Case" (February 29, 1952)

Let George Do It "The Deadly Pines" (March 3, 1952)

Hollywood Sound Stage "Dark Victory" (March 6, 1952)

Richard Diamond, Private Detective "Winthrop and Company" (March 7, 1952)

Broadway Is My Beat "The Eve Hunter Case" (March 8, 1952)

Let George Do It "The Darkest Shadow" (March 10, 1952)

Flesh and Fury (March 12, 1952)

Richard Diamond, Private Detective "The Dixon Case" (March 14, 1952)

Let George Do It "Three Times and Out" (March 17, 1952)

Richard Diamond, Private Detective "The Hank Burton Case" (March 21, 1952)

Let George Do It "The Graystone Ghost" (March 24, 1952)

The Line Up "The Bakery Bandit's Bad Blooper" (March 25, 1952)

Dragnet "The Big Rose" (March 27, 1952)

Richard Diamond, Private Detective "Mr. Walker's Problem" (March 28, 1952)

Richard Diamond, Private Detective "The Enigma of Big Ed" (April 4, 1952)

The Line Up "The Cornered Cop Killer Case" (April 8, 1952)

Wild Bill Hickok "The Monstrous Toothache" (April 9, 1952)

Hallmark Playhouse "Ben Hur" (April 10, 1952)

Dragnet "The Big Show" (April 10, 1952)

Richard Diamond, Private Detective "The Fred Montelli Affair" (April 11, 1952)

Let George Do It "The Forgotten Murder" (April 14, 1952)

Richard Diamond, Private Detective "The Jack Murphy Case" (April 18, 1952)

Let George Do It "War Maneuver" (April 21, 1952)

Hallmark Playhouse "The Professor" (April 24, 1952)

Richard Diamond, Private Detective "The Trixie Hart Case" (April 25, 1952)

The Whistler "Saturday Night" (April 27, 1952)

Let George Do It "Operation Europa" (April 28, 1952)

Hallmark Playhouse "Lorna Doone" (May 1, 1952)

Richard Diamond, Private Detective "The Eddie Ducheck Case" (May 2, 1952)

The Hour of St. Francis "Baa, Baa, Black Sheep" (May 3, 1952)

Tales of the Texas Rangers "Little Sister" (May 4, 1952)

Let George Do It "Come to the Casbah" (May 5, 1952)

Family Theatre "Genius from Hoboken" (May 7, 1952)

Violence "The Case of Arthur Bowman" (May 8, 1952)

Richard Diamond, Private Detective "The Barber Shop Case" (May 9, 1952)

Hollywood Sound Stage "Jezebel" (May 10, 1952)

Let George Do It "The Iron Hat" (May 12, 1952)

Hallmark Playhouse "The Marquis de Lafayette" (May 15, 1952)

Tales of the Texas Rangers "Smart Kill" (May 18, 1952)

Let George Do It "It Happened on Friday" (May 19, 1952)

Family Theatre "World Without End" (May 21, 1952)

Hallmark Playhouse "Marsha Byrnes/Marcia Burns" (May 22, 1952)

Richard Diamond, Private Detective "The George Dale Case" (May 23, 1952)

The Silent Men "The Green Sedan" (May 28, 1952)

Dragnet "The Big Fourth" (May 29, 1952)

Richard Diamond, Private Detective "The Carpenter Case" (May 30, 1952)

Family Theatre "Portrait of Cynthia" (June 4, 1952)

Richard Diamond, Private Detective "The Black Doll Case" (June 6, 1952)

Let George Do It "The Violent Van Pattens" (June 9, 1952)

The Line Up "Lobdell's Poodle-Cut Tomato Case" (June 10, 1952)

Dragnet "The Big Donation" (June 12, 1952)

Richard Diamond, Private Detective "The Frank Taylor Case" (June 13, 1952)

The Whistler "The Last Message" (June 15, 1952)

Let George Do It "The Mystic" (June 16, 1952)

Let George Do It "There Ain't No Justice" (June 17, 1952)

The Line Up "Bentley's Boo-Boo Case/The Liquor Store Robbery" (June 17, 1952)

The Line Up "The Pitiful Patricide Case" (June 17, 1952)

The Halls of Ivy "Math Professor" (June 18, 1952)

Richard Diamond, Private Detective "The Ed Lloyd Case" (June 20, 1952)

Tales of the Texas Rangers "Knockout" (June 22, 1952)

Let George Do It "Portrait of a Suicide" (June 24, 1952)

The Line Up "The Cutie-Calling Culprit Case" (June 24, 1952)

Dragnet "The Big Roll" (June 26, 1952)

Richard Diamond, Private Detective "The Danny Revere Case" (June 27, 1952)

The Line Up "The Guided Gang Case" (July 1, 1952)

Yours Truly, Johnny Dollar "The Amelia Harwell Matter" (July 2, 1952)

The Line Up "The Lugar-Lugging Laddie Case" (July 8, 1952)

Let George Do It "Tonight the Mayhem's Going to be Different" (July 8, 1952)

The Line Up "The Twitching Twist's .22 Tweaking Case" (July 15, 1952)

Family Theatre "Ten O'clock Scholar" (July 16, 1952)

The Line Up "The Drinkler Kidnapping Case" (July 22, 1952)

The Line Up "The Charles Crocked Clobbering Case" (July 29, 1952)

Dragnet "The Big Signet" (July 31, 1952)

Tales of the Texas Rangers "Double Edge" (August 3, 1952)

The Line Up "The Karger Cops a Clinker Case" (August 5, 1952)

Gunsmoke "The Kentucky Tolmans" (August 9, 1952)

Romance "Den of Thieves" (August 11, 1952)

Let George Do It "Seed of Destruction" (August 18, 1952)

Dragnet "The Big Paper" (August 21, 1952)

Tales of the Texas Rangers "Three Victims" (August 24, 1952)

Family Theatre "The People's Choice" (August 27, 1952)

Tales of the Texas Rangers "Misplaced Person" (August 31, 1952)

Dragnet "The Big Ray" (September 4, 1952)

The Whistler "The Secret of Chalk Point" (September 7, 1952)

The Line Up "The Jane Doe Case" (September 10, 1952)

Wild Bill Hickok "The Daring of Digby Dean" (September 10, 1952)

Wild Bill Hickok "Letter of Warning" (September 12, 1952)

Let George Do It "Human Nature" (September 15, 1952)

The Line Up "The Fresno Break Case" (September 17, 1952)

Dragnet "The Big Shot" (September 21, 1952)

Let George Do It "Once a Crook" (September 22, 1952)

Let George Do It "Chance and Probability" (September 29, 1952)

This is O'Shea *Title(s) Unknown* (October 1, 1952)

The Line Up "The Poker-Party Killings (October 1, 1952)

Let George Do It "The Four Seasons" (October 6, 1952)

The Line Up "The Teacher's Pet" (October 8, 1952)

Hallmark Playhouse "Young Mr. Disraeli" (October 12, 1952)

Let George Do It "The Dead of Night" (October 13, 1952)

Confession "The Doris Kane Case" (October 17, 1952)

Dragnet "The Big Pill" (October 19, 1952)

Let George Do It "Calle Reposo" (October 20, 1952)

The Line Up "The Green Cap Case" (October 22, 1952)

The Line Up "The Sobbing Sister Saga" (October 29, 1952)

Let George Do It "Dead on Arrival" (November 10, 1952)

The Line Up "The Buggered Bunco Boys" (November 12, 1952)

Let George Do It "The Stand-In" (November 17, 1952)

The Line Up "The Modern Sounds Case" (November 19, 1952)

Dragnet "The Big Trio" S2E5 (November 20, 1952)

Hallmark Playhouse "The Courtship of Miles Standish" (November 24, 1952)

Let George Do It "Red Spots in the Snow" (November 25, 1952)

The Line Up "The Matthews-Murray Mish-Mosh Case" (November 26, 1952)

Let George Do It "This Ain't No Way to Run a Railroad" (December 2, 1952)

Hallmark Playhouse "A Miracle on the Blotter" (December 7, 1952)

Guest Star "The Blue Amulet" (December 7, 1952)

The Line Up "The Gasoline Bandit Case" (December 12, 1952)

Hallmark Playhouse "A Christmas Carol" (December 21, 1952)

The Survivors "Traffic Safety" (December 21, 1952)

I Was a Communist for the FBI "Hate Song" (December 31, 1952)

The Line Up "Cowardly Castro" (January 2, 1953)

Errand of Mercy "Escape" (January 11, 1953)

Dragnet "The Big String" (January 18, 1953)

Dragnet "The Big Show" S2E11 (January 22, 1953)

Yours Truly, Johnny Dollar "The Marigold Matter" (January 23, 1953)

Dragnet "The Big Layout" (January 25, 1953)

Hallmark Playhouse "Trenton Seventy-Six" (February 1, 1953)

General Electric Theater "Ride the River" S1E2 (February 8, 1953)

Suspense "The Love and Death of Joaquin Murietta" (February 16, 1953)

Yours Truly, Johnny Dollar "The La Tourette Matter" (February 20, 1953)

Dragnet "The Big Smoke" (February 22, 1953)

Wild Bill Hickok "Big Welcome at Shady Rest" (February 27, 1953)

Wild Bill Hickok "The Gun Belt Treasure" (March 2, 1953)

Yours Truly, Johnny Dollar "The Jean Maxwell Matter" (March 6, 1953)

Errand of Mercy "A Living Tribute" (March 8, 1953)

Yours Truly, Johnny Dollar "The Birdy Baskerville Matter" (March 10, 1953)

Yours Truly, Johnny Dollar "The Syndicate Matter" (March 24, 1953)

Yours Truly, Johnny Dollar "The Madison Matter" (April 14, 1953)

Dangerous Assignment "London Passport Forging Racket" (April 22, 1953)

Guest Star "The Headliner" (April 26, 1953)

Yours Truly, Johnny Dollar "The San Antonio Matter" (April 28, 1953)

Dangerous Assignment "Trieste" (May 6, 1953)

Yours Truly, Johnny Dollar "The Rochester Theft Matter" (May 12, 1953)

Dragnet "The Big False Move" (May 17, 1953)

Dragnet "The Big Gun Part I" (May 24, 1953)

Yours Truly, Johnny Dollar "The Brisbane Fraud Matter" (May 26, 1953)

Family Theatre "New Neighbor" (May 27, 1953)

Dragnet "The Big Fourth" S2E29 (May 28, 1953)

Dragnet "The Big Gun Part II" (May 31, 1953)

Rogers of the Gazette *Title Unknown* (June 12, 1953)

Gunsmoke "Wind" (June 20, 1953)

Dragnet "The Big Ham" (June 28, 1953)

Yours Truly, Johnny Dollar "The Jones Matter" (June 30, 1953)

Stars Over Hollywood "To the Bitter End" (July 4, 1953)

Yours Truly, Johnny Dollar "The Shayne Bombing Matter" (July 14, 1953)

Rogers of the Gazette "Dirty Politics" (July 22, 1953)

General Electric Theatre "Penny Serenade" (July 23, 1953)

Guest Star "Fear" (August 2, 1953)

General Electric Theatre "The Virginian" (August 13, 1953)

Dragnet "The Big White Rat" S3E1 (September 3, 1953)

Wild Bill Hickok "The Green Valley Feud" (September 25, 1953)

Wild Bill Hickok "Thundercloud" (October 9, 1953)

Hallmark Hall of Fame "Edwin L. Drake" (October 11, 1953)

Guest Star "Holiday from Crime" (October 11, 1953)

The Freedom Story "To Each According to Need" (October 19, 1953)

Yours Truly, Johnny Dollar "The Allen Saxton Matter" (October 20, 1953)

Family Theatre "A Fine Wedding for Angelita" (October 28, 1953)

Hallmark Hall of Fame "Mary Bickerdyke" (November 1, 1953)

Rogers of the Gazette "Toast of Vienna – Gretchen March" (November 5, 1953)

Yours Truly, Johnny Dollar "The Independent Diamond Traders Matter" (November 24, 1953)

The Six Shooter "A Pressing Engagement" (December 6, 1953)

Rogers of the Gazette "Pastel Christmas Trees" (December 9, 1953)

Hallmark Hall of Fame "Alfred Nobel" (December 13, 1953)

Gunsmoke "Big Girl Lost" (December 19, 1953)

Hallmark Hall of Fame "A Christmas Carol" (December 20, 1953)

Dr. Christian "Tony's Parcel" (December 23, 1953)

The Six Shooter "Cora Plummer Quincy" (December 27, 1953)

Rogers of the Gazette "Eager Twins/Investigative Reporters" (December 30, 1953)

Family Theatre "The Little Prince" (December 30, 1953)

Hallmark Hall of Fame "William Allen White" (January 10, 1954)

Yours Truly, Johnny Dollar "The Celia Woodstock Matter" (January 12, 1954)

Suspense "Want Ad" (January 25, 1954)

Family Theatre "The Cadreman" (January 27, 1954)

Wild Bill Hickok "Eight Hundred Feet Down" (January 27, 1954)

Crime Classics "Boorn/Bourne Brothers & the Hangman: A Study in Nip & Tuck" (January 27, 1954)

Gunsmoke "Big Broad" (February 6, 1954)

Yours Truly, Johnny Dollar "The Harpooned Angler Matter" (February 9, 1954)

Fibber McGee and Molly "Advertising Ingrams Home for Rent" (February 11, 1954)

The Six Shooter "Quiet City" (February 14, 1954)

Yours Truly, Johnny Dollar "The Uncut Canary Matter" (February 16, 1954)

The Six Shooter "Battle at Tower Rock" (February 21, 1954)

NBC Star Playhouse "The Major and the Minor" (February 21, 1954)

Dragnet "The Big Pipe" (February 23, 1954)

Family Theatre "Past Imperfect" (February 24, 1954)

Yours Truly, Johnny Dollar "The Road Test Matter" (March 2, 1954)

The Roy Rogers Show "The Streets of Laredo" (March 4, 1954)

You Were There "All Points Bulletin" (March 7, 1954)

Yours Truly, Johnny Dollar "The Terrified Tuan Matter" (March 9, 1954)

You Were There "Mam-San Frendo" (March 14, 1954)

Yours Truly, Johnny Dollar "The Berlin Matter" (March 16, 1954)

Rocky Fortune "Boarding House Double Cross" (March 30, 1954)

Family Theatre "The Pox" (March 31, 1954)

Crime Classics "Robby-Boy Balfour: How He Wrecked a Big Prison's Reputation" (March 31, 1954)

Hallmark Hall of Fame "Dr. Will Mayo" (April 4, 1954)

Mike Malloy "The Pied Piper of Homicide Alley 1" (April 5, 1954)

Mike Malloy "The Pied Piper of Homicide Alley 2" (April 6, 1954)

Mike Malloy "The Pied Piper of Homicide Alley 3" (April 7, 1954)

The Six Shooter "General Gillford's Widow" (April 8, 1954)

Escape "The Scarlet Plague" (April 8, 1954)

You Were There "Ride it Out" (April 11, 1954)

The Six Shooter "Crisis at Easter Creek" (April 15, 1954)

Yours Truly, Johnny Dollar "The Nathan Swing Matter" (April 20, 1954)

The Six Shooter "Johnny Springer" (April 22, 1954)

The Six Shooter "Revenge at Harness Creek" (April 29, 1954)

Inheritance "In Whatsoever House I Enter" (May 2, 1954)

Dragnet "The Big Look" (May 11, 1954)

Hallmark Hall of Fame "Damon Runyon" (May 16, 1954)

Yours Truly, Johnny Dollar "The Punctilious Firebug Matter" (May 25, 1954)

Gunsmoke "Feud" (May 29, 1954)

Escape "An Ordinary Man" (June 3, 1954)

Romance "Amalfi Summer" (June 12, 1954)

The Six Shooter "Myra Barker" (June 24, 1954)

Yours Truly, Johnny Dollar "The Jan Bruegal Matter" (July 6, 1954)

Escape "The Birds" (July 10, 1954)

You Were There "A Letter to Ann" (July 11, 1954)

Family Theatre "The Strangers" (July 14, 1954)

San Francisco Final "Chinatown" (July 26, 1954)

Suspense "Destruction" (July 27, 1954)

Romance "The Fling" (July 31, 1954)

Suspense "Goodnight Mrs. Russell" (August 3, 1954)

Escape "The Coward" (August 14, 1954)

Gunsmoke "Obie Tater" (August 30, 1954)

Romance "The Postmistress of Laurel" (September 4, 1954)

Dragnet (September 4, 1954)

Barrie Craig, Confidential Investigator "Ghosts Don't Die in Bed" (September 7, 1954)

Romance "The Return of Maria Sanchez" (September 11, 1954)

Dragnet "The Big Pair" S4E4 (September 16, 1954)

Lux Radio Theatre "David and Bathsheba" (October 19, 1954)

Family Theatre "Stay Up for the Sunrise" (October 20, 1954)

Gunsmoke "Ma Tennis" (October 23, 1954)

Wild Bill Hickok "The Bellson Boys" (October 29, 1954)

Suspense "The Last Letter of Dr. Bronson" (November 4, 1954)

Dragnet "The Big Gangster: Part 2" S4E11 (November 4, 1954)

Dragnet "The Big Coin" (November 9, 1954)

Dragnet "The Big Want Ad" S4E13 (November 18, 1954)

You Were There "Down to the Sea" (November 21, 1954)

Romance "Point of View" (December 4, 1954)

Guest Star "End of the Line" (December 5, 1954)

Suspense "On a Country Road" (December 9, 1954)

Romance "The Third Swan from the Left" (December 11, 1954)

Hallmark Hall of Fame "A Christmas Carol" (December 19, 1954)

Wild Bill Hickok "A Shiny Silver Star" (December 24, 1954)

Hallmark Hall of Fame "J. Edgar Hoover" (December 26, 1954)

Family Theatre "The Little Prince" (December 29, 1954)

Family Theatre "Stranger in Town" (January 12, 1955)

Lux Radio Theatre "Awful Truth" (January 18, 1955)

Public Defender "Your Witness" S2E22 (January 27, 1955)

Hallmark Hall of Fame "Sigmund Freud" (February 6, 1955)

Romance "Zeea's Dream/Zia's Dream" (February 19, 1955)

Dragnet "The Big Key" S4E26 (February 24, 1955)

Barrie Craig, Confidential Investigator "Corpse on the Town" (March 9, 1955)

Hallmark Hall of Fame "Dr. Lev Kowarski" (March 20, 1955)

The Lineup "The Ann Brennizer Case" S1E27 (April 1, 1955)

Family Theatre "Act of Contrition" (April 20, 1955)

Gunsmoke "Potato Road" (May 7, 1955)

The Whistler "Night Melody" (May 12, 1955)

Romance "You Really Ought to Get away for a While" (May 21, 1955)

Gunsmoke "Jealousy" (June 4, 1955)

Romance "Transport to Terror" (July 16, 1955)

You Were There "On Our Way" (July 17, 1955)

Gunsmoke "Tap Day for Kitty" (July 30, 1955)

Romance "Such a Wonderful Team" (July 30, 1955)

Gunsmoke "Johnny Red" (August 13, 1955)

Love is a Many-Splendored Thing (August 18, 1955)

Romance "The Vortegs" (August 20, 1955)

Dragnet "The Big Fellow" (August 30, 1955)

Suspense "The Lady in the Red Hat" (August 30, 1955)

Dragnet "The Big Pipe" S5E1 (September 1, 1955)

Suspense "A Story of Poison" (September 13, 1955)

Dragnet "The Big Daughter" (September 13, 1955)

Gunsmoke "Indian White" (September 24, 1955)

Romance "The Winds of June" (September 24, 1955)

Yours Truly, Johnny Dollar "The McCormack Matter 1" (October 3, 1955)

Suspense "Goodbye, Miss Lizzie Borden" (October 4, 1955)

Yours Truly, Johnny Dollar "The McCormack Matter 2" (October 4, 1955)

The Danny Thomas Show/Make Room for Daddy "Love Thy Neighbor" S3E4 (October 4, 1955)

Yours Truly, Johnny Dollar "The McCormack Matter 3" (October 5, 1955)

Yours Truly, Johnny Dollar "The McCormack Matter 4" (October 6, 1955)

Yours Truly, Johnny Dollar "The McCormack Matter 5" (October 7, 1955)

Yours Truly, Johnny Dollar "The Molly K Matter 1" (October 10, 1955)

Yours Truly, Johnny Dollar "The Molly K Matter 2" (October 11, 1955)

Yours Truly, Johnny Dollar "The Molly K Matter 3" (October 12, 1955)

Yours Truly, Johnny Dollar "The Molly K Matter 4" (October 13, 1955)

Yours Truly, Johnny Dollar "The Molly K Matter 5" (October 14, 1955)

Romance "The Mission" (October 22, 1955)

Alfred Hitchcock Presents "Don't Come Back Alive" S1E4 (October 23, 1955)

Yours Truly, Johnny Dollar "The Alvin Summers Matter 1" (October 24, 1955)

Yours Truly, Johnny Dollar "The Alvin Summers Matter 2" (October 25, 1955)

Yours Truly, Johnny Dollar "The Alvin Summers Matter 3" (October 26, 1955)

Yours Truly, Johnny Dollar "The Alvin Summers Matter 4" (October 27, 1955)

Yours Truly, Johnny Dollar "The Alvin Summers Matter 5" (October 28, 1955)

Romance "The Bear" (November 5, 1955)

Yours Truly, Johnny Dollar "The Broderick Matter 1" (November 14, 1955)

Yours Truly, Johnny Dollar "The Broderick Matter 2" (November 15, 1955)

Yours Truly, Johnny Dollar "The Broderick Matter 3" (November 16, 1955)

Yours Truly, Johnny Dollar "The Broderick Matter 4" (November 17, 1955)

Yours Truly, Johnny Dollar "The Broderick Matter 5" (November 18, 1955)

Alfred Hitchcock Presents "Santa Claus and the Tenth Avenue Kid" S1E12 (December 18, 1955)

Yours Truly, Johnny Dollar "The Amy Bradshaw Matter 1" (November 21, 1955)

Yours Truly, Johnny Dollar "The Amy Bradshaw Matter 2" (November 22, 1955)

Yours Truly, Johnny Dollar "The Amy Bradshaw Matter 3" (November 23, 1955)

Yours Truly, Johnny Dollar "The Amy Bradshaw Matter 4" (November 24, 1955)

Yours Truly, Johnny Dollar "The Amy Bradshaw Matter 5" (November 25, 1955)

Gunsmoke "Amy's Good Deed" (November 27, 1955)

Yours Truly, Johnny Dollar "The Cronin Matter 1" (December 5, 1955)

Yours Truly, Johnny Dollar "The Cronin Matter 2" (December 6, 1955)

Suspense "When the Bough Breaks" (December 6, 1955)

Yours Truly, Johnny Dollar "The Cronin Matter 3" (December 7, 1955)

Yours Truly, Johnny Dollar "The Cronin Matter 4" (December 8, 1955)

Yours Truly, Johnny Dollar "The Cronin Matter 5" (December 9, 1955)

Yours Truly, Johnny Dollar "The Nick Shurn Matter 1" (December 19, 1955)

Yours Truly, Johnny Dollar "The Nick Shurn Matter 2" (December 20, 1955)

Yours Truly, Johnny Dollar "The Nick Shurn Matter 3" (December 21, 1955)

Yours Truly, Johnny Dollar "The Nick Shurn Matter 4" (December 22, 1955)

Yours Truly, Johnny Dollar "The Nick Shurn Matter 5" (December 23, 1955)

Romance "Richer by One Christmas" (December 24, 1955)

I'll Cry Tomorrow (December 25, 1955)

Jane Wyman Presents the Fireside Theatre "Big Joe's Comin' Home" S1E18 (December 27, 1955)

Yours Truly, Johnny Dollar "The Caylin Matter 1" (January 2, 1956)

Yours Truly, Johnny Dollar "The Caylin Matter 2" (January 3, 1956)

Yours Truly, Johnny Dollar "The Caylin Matter 3" (January 4, 1956

Yours Truly, Johnny Dollar "The Caylin Matter 4" (January 5, 1956)

Yours Truly, Johnny Dollar "The Caylin Matter 5" (January 6, 1956)

Yours Truly, Johnny Dollar "The Flight Six Matter 1" (January 30, 1956)

Yours Truly, Johnny Dollar "The Flight Six Matter 2" (January 31, 1956)

Yours Truly, Johnny Dollar "The Flight Six Matter 3" (February 1, 1956)

Yours Truly, Johnny Dollar "The Flight Six Matter 4" (February 2, 1956)

Yours Truly, Johnny Dollar "The Flight Six Matter 5" (February 3, 1956)

Alfred Hitchcock Presents "And So Died Riabouchinska" S1E20 (February 12, 1956)

CBS Radio Workshop "Season of Disbelief/Hail & Farewell" (February 17, 1956)

Romance "Jackhammer Leg" (February 25, 1956)

Fort Laramie "Captain's Widow" (February 26, 1956)

The Star and the Story "They" S2E17 (March 3, 1956)

Fort Laramie "Hattie Pelfrey" (March 11, 1956)

Romance "Point of View" (March 17, 1956)

Yours Truly, Johnny Dollar "The Jolly Roger Fraud 1" (March 19, 1956)

Suspense "Gallardo" (March 20, 1956)

Yours Truly, Johnny Dollar "The Jolly Roger Fraud 4" (March 22, 1956)

Yours Truly, Johnny Dollar "The Jolly Roger Fraud 5" (March 23, 1956)

Gunsmoke "Hanging Man" (March 25, 1956)

Yours Truly, Johnny Dollar "The La Marr Matter 1" (March 26, 1956)

Yours Truly, Johnny Dollar "The La Marr Matter 2" (March 27, 1956)

Yours Truly, Johnny Dollar "The La Marr Matter 3" (March 28, 1956)

Yours Truly, Johnny Dollar "The La Marr Matter 4" (March 29, 1956)

Yours Truly, Johnny Dollar "The La Marr Matter 5" (March 30, 1956)

CBS Radio Workshop "Speaking of Cinderella – If the Shoe Fits" (April 6, 1956)

CBS Radio Workshop "Jacob's Hands" (April 13, 1956)

Yours Truly, Johnny Dollar "The Shepherd Matter 1" (April 16, 1956)

Yours Truly, Johnny Dollar "The Shepherd Matter 2" (April 17, 1956)

Yours Truly, Johnny Dollar "The Shepherd Matter 3" (April 18, 1956)

Yours Truly, Johnny Dollar "The Shepherd Matter 4" (April 19, 1956)

Yours Truly, Johnny Dollar "The Shepherd Matter 5" (April 20, 1956)

Yours Truly, Johnny Dollar "The Lonely Hearts Matter 1" (April 23, 1956)

Yours Truly, Johnny Dollar "The Lonely Hearts Matter 2" (April 24, 1956)

Yours Truly, Johnny Dollar "The Lonely Hearts Matter 3" (April 25, 1956)

Yours Truly, Johnny Dollar "The Lonely Hearts Matter 4" (April 26, 1956)

Yours Truly, Johnny Dollar "The Lonely Hearts Matter 5" (April 27, 1956)

Terror at Midnight (April 27, 1956)

Romance "Roman Afternoon" (April 28, 1956)

Yours Truly, Johnny Dollar "The Callicles Matter 1" (April 30, 1956)

Yours Truly, Johnny Dollar "The Callicles Matter 2" (May 1, 1956)

Yours Truly, Johnny Dollar "The Callicles Matter 3" (May 2, 1956)

Yours Truly, Johnny Dollar "The Callicles Matter 4" (May 3, 1956)

Yours Truly, Johnny Dollar "The Callicles Matter 5" (May 4, 1956)

CBS Radio Workshop "The Enormous Radio" (May 11, 1956)

Romance "The Lady and the Tiger" (May 12, 1956)

Yours Truly, Johnny Dollar "The Matter of the Medium: Well-Done 1" (May 14, 1956)

Yours Truly, Johnny Dollar "The Matter of the Medium: Well-Done 2" (May 15, 1956)

Yours Truly, Johnny Dollar "The Matter of the Medium: Well-Done 3" (May 16, 1956)

Yours Truly, Johnny Dollar "The Matter of the Medium: Well-Done 4" (May 17, 1956)

Yours Truly, Johnny Dollar "The Matter of the Medium: Well-Done 5" (May 18, 1956)

Fort Laramie "Gold/Black Hills Gold" (May 20, 1956)

Yours Truly, Johnny Dollar "The Tears of Night Matter 1" (May 21, 1956)

Yours Truly, Johnny Dollar "The Tears of Night Matter 2" (May 22, 1956)

Yours Truly, Johnny Dollar "The Tears of Night Matter 3" (May 23, 1956)

Yours Truly, Johnny Dollar "The Tears of Night Matter 4" (May 24, 1956)

Yours Truly, Johnny Dollar "The Tears of Night Matter 5" (May 25, 1956)

Fort Laramie "Sergeant's Baby" (May 27, 1956)

Cavalcade of America "The Boy Nobody Wanted" S4E24 (May 29, 1956)

Fort Laramie "Don't Kick my Horse" (June 3, 1956)

Suspense "The Twelfth Rose" (June 5, 1956)

Romance "The Bachelor" (June 9, 1956)

Crime in the Streets (June 10, 1956)

Yours Truly, Johnny Dollar "The Laughing Matter 1" (June 11, 1956)

Suspense "A Matter of Timing" (June 12, 1956)

Yours Truly, Johnny Dollar "The Laughing Matter 2" (June 12, 1956)

Yours Truly, Johnny Dollar "The Laughing Matter 3" (June 13, 1956)

Yours Truly, Johnny Dollar "The Laughing Matter 4" (June 14, 1956)

Yours Truly, Johnny Dollar "The Laughing Matter 5" (June 15, 1956)

Yours Truly, Johnny Dollar "The Long Shot Matter 1" (June 25, 1956)

Yours Truly, Johnny Dollar "The Long Shot Matter 2" (June 26, 1956)

Yours Truly, Johnny Dollar "The Long Shot Matter 3" (June 27, 1956)

Yours Truly, Johnny Dollar "The Long Shot Matter 4" (June 28, 1956)

Yours Truly, Johnny Dollar "The Long Shot Matter 5" (June 29, 1956)

Yours Truly, Johnny Dollar "The Midas Touch Matter 1" (July 2, 1956)

Yours Truly, Johnny Dollar "The Midas Touch Matter 2" (July 3, 1956)

Yours Truly, Johnny Dollar "The Midas Touch Matter 3" (July 4, 1956)

Yours Truly, Johnny Dollar "The Midas Touch Matter 4" (July 5, 1956)

Yours Truly, Johnny Dollar "The Midas Touch Matter 5" (July 6, 1956)

The Fastest Gun Alive (July 6, 1956)

Suspense "Want Ad" (July 11, 1956)

Romance "Ragged Individualist" (July 14, 1956)

Four Star Playhouse "Success Story" S4E41 (July 26, 1956)

Fort Laramie "Nature Boy" (July 29, 1956)

Yours Truly, Johnny Dollar "The Sea Legs Matter 1" (July 30, 1956)

Yours Truly, Johnny Dollar "The Sea Legs Matter 2" (July 31, 1956)

Yours Truly, Johnny Dollar "The Sea Legs Matter 3" (August 1, 1956)

Yours Truly, Johnny Dollar "The Sea Legs Matter 4" (August 2, 1956)

Yours Truly, Johnny Dollar "The Sea Legs Matter 5" (August 3, 1956)

Yours Truly, Johnny Dollar "The Alder Matter 1" (August 6, 1956)

Yours Truly, Johnny Dollar "The Alder Matter 2" (August 7, 1956)

Yours Truly, Johnny Dollar "The Alder Matter 3" (August 8, 1956)

Yours Truly, Johnny Dollar "The Alder Matter 4" (August 9, 1956)

Yours Truly, Johnny Dollar "The Alder Matter 5" (August 10, 1956)

Fort Laramie "Goodbye Willa" (August 19, 1956)

Yours Truly, Johnny Dollar "The Kranesburg Matter 1" (August 24, 1956)

Fort Laramie "The Chaplain" (August 26, 1956)

Yours Truly, Johnny Dollar "The Kranesburg Matter 2" (August 27, 1956)

Yours Truly, Johnny Dollar "The Kranesburg Matter 3" (August 28, 1956)

Yours Truly, Johnny Dollar "The Kranesburg Matter 4" (August 29, 1956

Yours Truly, Johnny Dollar "The Kranesburg Matter 5" (August 30, 1956)

Yours Truly, Johnny Dollar "The Kranesburg Matter 6" (August 31, 1956)

Fort Laramie "The Return of Hattie Pelfrey" (September 2, 1956)

Yours Truly, Johnny Dollar "The Confidential Matter 1" (September 10, 1956)

Yours Truly, Johnny Dollar "The Confidential Matter 2" (September 11, 1956

Yours Truly, Johnny Dollar "The Confidential Matter 3" (September 12, 1956)

Yours Truly, Johnny Dollar "The Confidential Matter 4" (September 13, 1956)

Yours Truly, Johnny Dollar "The Confidential Matter 5" (September 14, 1956)

Romance "The Man from Venus" (September 15, 1956)

Yours Truly, Johnny Dollar "The Imperfect Alibi Matter 1" (September 17, 1956)

Yours Truly, Johnny Dollar "The Imperfect Alibi Matter 2" (September 18, 1956)

Yours Truly, Johnny Dollar "The Imperfect Alibi Matter 3" (September 19, 1956)

Yours Truly, Johnny Dollar "The Imperfect Alibi Matter 4" (September 20, 1956)

Yours Truly, Johnny Dollar "The Imperfect Alibi Matter 5" (September 21, 1956)

Yours Truly, Johnny Dollar "The Meg's Place Matter 1" (September 24, 1956)

Yours Truly, Johnny Dollar "The Meg's Place Matter 2" (September 25, 1956)

Yours Truly, Johnny Dollar "The Meg's Place Matter 3" (September 26, 1956)

Yours Truly, Johnny Dollar "The Meg's Place Matter 4" (September 27, 1956)

Yours Truly, Johnny Dollar "The Meg's Place Matter 5" (September 28, 1956)

Romance "Earthquake" (October 6, 1956)

The Danny Thomas Show/Make Room for Daddy "Boarding School" S4E1 (October 1, 1956)

Yours Truly, Johnny Dollar "The Phantom Chase Matter 1" (October 15, 1956)

Yours Truly, Johnny Dollar "The Phantom Chase Matter 2" (October 16, 1956)

Yours Truly, Johnny Dollar "The Phantom Chase Matter 3" (October 17, 1956)

Yours Truly, Johnny Dollar "The Phantom Chase Matter 4" (October 18, 1956)

Yours Truly, Johnny Dollar "The Phantom Chase Matter 5" (October 19, 1956)

Gunsmoke "Till Death Do Us Part" (October 21, 1956)

Yours Truly, Johnny Dollar "The Phantom Chase Matter 6" (October 22, 1956)

Yours Truly, Johnny Dollar "The Phantom Chase Matter 7" (October 23, 1956)

Yours Truly, Johnny Dollar "The Phantom Chase Matter 8" (October 24, 1956)

Yours Truly, Johnny Dollar "The Phantom Chase Matter 9" (October 25, 1956)

Romance "Lovely Dead Letter" (October 27, 1956)

Fort Laramie "Army Wife" (October 28, 1956)

Yours Truly, Johnny Dollar "The Silent Queen Matter 1" (October 29, 1956)

O'Hara "The Lost Boy" (October 29, 1956)

Yours Truly, Johnny Dollar "The Silent Queen Matter 2" (October 30, 1956)

Yours Truly, Johnny Dollar "The Silent Queen Matter 3" (October 31, 1956)

Lux Video Theatre "You Can't Escape Forever" S7E7 (November 1, 1956)

Yours Truly, Johnny Dollar "The Silent Queen Matter 4" (November 1, 1956)

Wire Service "The Night of August 7th" S1E5 (November 1, 1956)

Yours Truly, Johnny Dollar "The Silent Queen Matter 5" (November 2, 1956)

CBS Radio Workshop "Colloquy Four: The Joe Miller Joke Book" (November 4, 1956)

Studio 57 "The Charlatan" S3E8 (November 7, 1956)

General Electric Theater "The Charlatan" S5E9 (November 7, 1956)

Gunsmoke "Crowbait Bob" (November 10, 1956)

Yours Truly, Johnny Dollar "The Big Scoop Matter" (November 11, 1956)

Yours Truly, Johnny Dollar "The Markham Matter" (November 18, 1956)

The Joseph Cotten Show: On Trial "The Trial of Mary Surratt" S1E8 (November 23, 1956)

Romance "London Interlude – 1940" (November 24, 1956)

Yours Truly, Johnny Dollar "The Royal Street Matter" (November 25, 1956)

Yours Truly, Johnny Dollar "The Burning Car Matter" (December 9, 1956)

Romance "The Indian Sign" (December 15, 1956)

Yours Truly, Johnny Dollar "The Rasmussen Matter" (December 16, 1956)

Jane Wyman Presents the Fireside Theatre "A Point of Law" S2E16 (December 18, 1956)

Cavalcade of America "The Blessed Midnight" S5E12 (December 18, 1956)

Gunsmoke "Beeker's Barn" (December 23, 1956)

Romance "A Quiet Little Party" (December 29, 1956)

Yours Truly, Johnny Dollar "The Ellen Dear Matter" (January 6, 1957)

Wire Service "World of the Lonely" S1E14 (January 10, 1957)

Matinee Theatre "If This Be Error" S2E83 (January 11, 1957)

Yours Truly, Johnny Dollar "The De Salle Matter" (January 13, 1957)

Alfred Hitchcock Presents "Nightmare in 4-D" S2E16 (January 13, 1957)

Gunsmoke "Woman Called Mary" (January 27, 1957)

Yours Truly, Johnny Dollar "The Kirby Will Matter" (February 3, 1957)

The Lineup "The Robert Ericson Case" S3E20 (February 15, 1957)

Gunsmoke "Impact" (February 24, 1957)

CBS Radio Workshop "Air Raid (Prevarications of Mr. Peeps)" (March 10, 1957)

Studio 57 "Big Joe's Coming Home" S3E22 (March 13, 1957)

The Joseph Cotten Show: On Trial "The Freeman Case" S1E20 (March 15, 1957)

Yours Truly, Johnny Dollar "The Clever Chemist Matter" (March 17, 1957)

Gunsmoke "Saddle Sore Sal" (March 24, 1957)

Yours Truly, Johnny Dollar "The Moonshine Murder Matter" (March 31, 1957)

Suspense "A Good Neighbor" (March 31, 1957)

CBS Radio Workshop "No Plays of Japan" (April 7, 1957)

Lassie "The Snob" S3E31 (April 7, 1957)

Suspense "The Vanishing Lady" (April 7, 1957)

Crossroads "Big Sombrero" S2E28 (April 12, 1957)

Yours Truly, Johnny Dollar "The Ming Toy Murphy Matter" (April 14, 1957)

Yours Truly, Johnny Dollar "The Melancholy Memory Matter" (April 28, 1957)

Gunsmoke "Medicine Man" (April 28, 1957)

Yours Truly, Johnny Dollar "The Peerless Fire Matter" (May 5, 1957)

Yours Truly, Johnny Dollar "The Michael Meany Mirage Matter" (May 19, 1957)

The D.I. (May 30, 1957)

CBS Radio Workshop "Epitaphs - Spoon River Anthology" (June 2, 1957)

Yours Truly, Johnny Dollar "The Mason-Dixon Mismatch Matter" (June 9, 1957)

Yours Truly, Johnny Dollar "The Funny Money Matter" (June 30, 1957)

Yours Truly, Johnny Dollar "The Heatherstone Players Matter" (July 14, 1957)

Yours Truly, Johnny Dollar "The Wayward Widow Matter" (August 4, 1957)

The New Adventures of Charlie Chan "Your Money or Your Wife" S1E1 (August 9, 1957)

CBS Radio Workshop "Malihini Magic Vacations" (August 11, 1957)

Portland Expose (August 11, 1957)

Yours Truly, Johnny Dollar "The Poor Little Rich Girl Matter" (September 1, 1957)

Gunsmoke "Looney McCluny" (September 8, 1957)

Yours Truly, Johnny Dollar "The Bum Steer Matter" (October 6, 1957)

Yours Truly, Johnny Dollar "The Silver Belle Matter" (October 13, 1957)

Suspense "Sorry, Wrong Number" (October 20, 1957)

Yours Truly, Johnny Dollar "The Model Picture Matter" (November 3, 1957)

Colt .45 "Gallows at Granite Gap" S1E4 (November 8, 1957)

The Danny Thomas Show/Make Room for Daddy "Two Sleepy People" S5E6 (November

11, 1957)

Goodyear Theatre "Hurricane" S1E5 (November 25, 1957)

Suspense "Jet Stream" (December 1, 1957)

Gunsmoke "Where'd They Go?" (December 29, 1957)

Perry Mason "The Case of the Cautious Coquette" S1E18 (January 18, 1958)

Mr. Adams and Eve "Me, the Jury" S2E18 (January 24, 1958)

Yours Truly, Johnny Dollar "The Price of Fame Matter" (February 2, 1958)

Frontier Gentleman "The Shelton Brothers/South Sunday" (February 2, 1958)

Maverick "Day of Reckoning" S1E19 (February 2, 1958)

Tombstone Territory "Postmarked for Death" S1E18 (February 12, 1958)

Trackdown "The Wedding" S1E19 (February 14, 1958)

Yours Truly, Johnny Dollar "The Time and Tide Matter" (February 16, 1958)

State Trooper "Full Circle" S2E14 (February 16, 1958)

Frontier Gentleman "The Honkytonkers" (February 16, 1958)

Yours Truly, Johnny Dollar "The Durango Laramie Matter" (February 23, 1958)

Frontier Gentleman "The Lost Mine" (March 2, 1958)

Richard Diamond, Private Detective "The George Dale Case" S2E10 (March 6, 1958)

Frontier Gentleman "The Claim Jumpers" (March 9, 1958)

Gunsmoke "Joke's on Us" S3E27 (March 15, 1958)

Goodyear Theatre "Seventh Letter" S1E12 (March 17, 1958)

Yours Truly, Johnny Dollar "The Denver Dispersal Matter" (March 23, 1958)

Frontier Gentleman "Gentle Virtue" (March 30, 1958)

Yours Truly, Johnny Dollar "The Eastern-Western Matter" (April 6, 1958)

Panic! "Emergency" S2E1 (April 6, 1958)

The Court of Last Resort "The Allen Cutler Case" S1E26 (April 11, 1958)

State Trooper "Crisis at Comstock" S2E18 (April 13, 1958)

Yours Truly, Johnny Dollar "The Wayward Money Matter" (April 13, 1958)

Frontier Gentleman "Some Random Notes from a Stagecoach" (April 27, 1958)

Sugarfoot "Price on His Head" S1E17 (April 29, 1958)

Frontier Gentleman "Daddy Bucks' Bucks/The Richest Man in the West" (May 4, 1958)

Hi, Grandma (May 7, 1958)

Suspense "Subway Stop" (May 11, 1958)

Frontier Gentleman "Advice to the Lovelorn" (May 18, 1958)

Yours Truly, Johnny Dollar "The Ghost to Ghost Matter" (May 18, 1958)

Frontier Gentleman "School Days/Duel for a School Marm" (June 1, 1958)

Frontier Gentleman "The Bellboy's Prisoner" (June 8, 1958)

Yours Truly, Johnny Dollar "The Delectable Damsel Matter" (June 15, 1958)

Frontier Gentleman "The Well" (June 15, 1958)

Yours Truly, Johnny Dollar "The Ugly Pattern Matter" (June 29, 1958)

Mike Hammer "My Son and Heir" S1E25 (July 5, 1958)

Yours Truly, Johnny Dollar "The Mojave Red Matter 2" (July 20, 1958)

Jefferson Drum "The Hanging of Joe Lavett" S1E14 (August 1, 1958)

Frontier Gentleman "Nebraska Jack" (August 3, 1958)

Twilight for the Gods (August 6, 1958)

Frontier Gentleman "Wonder Boy/The Fastest Gun That Never Was" (August 17, 1958)

Suspense "The Bridge" (August 17, 1958)

Yours Truly, Johnny Dollar "The Noxious Needle Matter" (August 24, 1958)

Yours Truly, Johnny Dollar "The Johnson Payroll Matter" (September 21, 1958)

Yours Truly, Johnny Dollar "The Gruesome Spectacle Matter" (September 28, 1958)

Frontier Gentleman "The Golddigger" (September 28, 1958)

Frontier Gentleman "The Librarian" (October 5, 1958)

Zane Grey Theater "Homecoming" S3E3 (October 23, 1958)

M Squad "The Trap" S2E5 (October 24, 1958)

Frontier Gentleman "The Rainmaker" (October 26, 1958)

Have Gun Will Travel "A Sense of Justice" S2E8 (November 1, 1958)

Frontier Gentleman "Nasty People/The Deadly Grover Family" (November 2, 1958)

The Jack Benny Program "Stars' Wives Show" S9E4 (November 2, 1958)

Frontier Gentleman "Holiday" (November 9, 1958)

Frontier Gentleman "Some Random Notes from a Train" (November 16, 1958)

Yours Truly, Johnny Dollar "The Double Trouble Matter" (November 16, 1958)

Yours Truly, Johnny Dollar "The Hair Raising Matter" (November 30, 1958)

Schlitz Playhouse "Third Son" S8E6 (December 5, 1958)

Have Gun, Will Travel "Ella West" (December 7, 1958)

Suspense "For Old Time's Sake" (December 14, 1958)

Wanted: Dead or Alive "Eight Cent Reward" S1E16 (December 20, 1958)

Gunsmoke "Where'd They Go?" (December 21, 1958)

Have Gun, Will Travel "No Visitors" (December 28, 1958)

Whispering Streets "Daryl Madison & Lynn Russell (1958)

Whispering Streets "Dana Russell & the Puppy" (1958)

Yours Truly, Johnny Dollar "The Hollywood Mystery Matter" (January 4, 1959)

Yours Truly, Johnny Dollar "The Deadly Doubt Matter" (January 11, 1959)

MacKenzie's Raiders "Blood on the Rio" S1E15 (January 17, 1959)

Have Gun, Will Travel "The Teacher" (January 25, 1959)

Yours Truly, Johnny Dollar "The Doting Dowager Matter" (January 25, 1959)

Whirlybirds "Rest in Peace" S2E39 (January 26, 1959)

Have Gun, Will Travel "A Matter of Ethics" (February 1, 1959)

The Hanging Tree (February 11, 1959)

Have Gun, Will Travel "Return of Dr. Thackery" (February 15, 1959)

Goodyear Theatre "Success Story" S2E10 (February 16, 1959)

Have Gun, Will Travel "Winchester Quarantine" (February 22, 1959)

Have Gun, Will Travel "Hey Boy's Revenge" (March 1, 1959)

Behind Closed Doors "The Meeting" S1E21 (March 5, 1959)

Have Gun, Will Travel "Death of a Young Gunfighter" (March 15, 1959)

Yours Truly, Johnny Dollar "The Baldero Matter" (March 15, 1959)

One Man's Family "Betty Drops a Bombshell" (March 26, 1959)

Yours Truly, Johnny Dollar "The Jimmy Carter Matter" (March 29, 1959)

Have Gun, Will Travel "A Sense of Justice" (March 29, 1959)

Have Gun, Will Travel "Maggie O'Bannion" (April 5, 1959)

Yours Truly, Johnny Dollar "The Frisco Fire Matter" (April 5, 1959)

One Man's Family "Betty Salvages a Lesson from Disaster" (April 8, 1959)

Have Gun, Will Travel "The Colonel and the Lady" (April 12, 1959)

Yours Truly, Johnny Dollar "The Fair Weather Friend Matter" (April 12, 1959)

Yours Truly, Johnny Dollar "The Cautious Celibate Matter" (April 19, 1959)

Have Gun, Will Travel "Birds of a Feather" (April 19, 1959)

One Man's Family "Betty Lowers the Boom" (April 22, 1959)

Yours Truly, Johnny Dollar "The Winsome Widow Matter" (April 26, 1959)

Have Gun, Will Travel "The Gunsmith" (April 26, 1959)

Rawhide "Incident of the Misplaced Indians" S1E16 (May 1, 1959)

Have Gun, Will Travel "Gunshy" (May 3, 1959)

Have Gun, Will Travel "The Statue of San Sebastian" (May 10, 1959)

Yours Truly, Johnny Dollar "The Fatal Fillet Matter" (May 10, 1959)

Have Gun, Will Travel "The Silver Queen" (May 17, 1959)

Mike Hammer "Curtains for an Angel" S2E21 (May 22, 1959)

Yours Truly, Johnny Dollar "The Big H Matter" (May 31, 1959)

Have Gun, Will Travel "Roped" (June 7, 1959)

Yours Truly, Johnny Dollar "The Wayward Heiress Matter" (June 7, 1959)

Sugarfoot "Wolf" S2E20 (June 9, 1959)

Have Gun, Will Travel "Bitter Wine" (June 14, 1959)

Have Gun, Will Travel "Trouble in North Fork" (June 21, 1959)

Gunsmoke "Carmen" (June 21, 1959)

Yours Truly, Johnny Dollar "The Life at Stake Matter" (June 21, 1959)

Have Gun, Will Travel "Homecoming" (June 28, 1959)

Yours Truly, Johnny Dollar "The Mei-Ling Buddha Matter" (June 28, 1959)

Yours Truly, Johnny Dollar "The Only One Butt Matter" (July 5, 1959)

Have Gun, Will Travel "Comanche" (July 5, 1959)

Have Gun, Will Travel "Young Gun" (July 12, 1959)

Yours Truly, Johnny Dollar "The Will and a Way Matter" (July 19, 1959)

Have Gun, Will Travel "Deliver the Body" (July 19, 1959)

Yours Truly, Johnny Dollar "The Bolt out of the Blue Matter" (July 26, 1959)

Have Gun, Will Travel "The Wager" (July 26, 1959)

Have Gun, Will Travel "High Wire" (August 2, 1959)

Yours Truly, Johnny Dollar "The Deadly Chain Matter" (August 2, 1959)

State Trooper "The Woman Who Cried Wolf" S2E30 (August 6, 1959)

Have Gun, Will Travel "Finn Alley" (August 9, 1959)

Suspense "Everything Will be Different" (August 9, 1959)

Yours Truly, Johnny Dollar "The Night in Paris Matter" (August 16, 1959)

Have Gun, Will Travel "The Lady" (August 16, 1959)

Have Gun, Will Travel "Bonanza" (August 23, 1959)

Have Gun, Will Travel "Love Birds" (August 30, 1959)

Yours Truly, Johnny Dollar "The Really Gone Matter" (August 30, 1959)

Have Gun, Will Travel "All That Glitters" (September 6, 1959)

Yours Truly, Johnny Dollar "The Backfire that Backfired Matter" (September 6, 1959)

Wanted: Dead or Alive "The Healing Woman" S2E2 (September 12, 1959)

Have Gun, Will Travel "Treasure Hunt" (September 13, 1959)

Maverick "Pappy" S3E1 (September 13, 1959)

Have Gun, Will Travel "Stardust" (September 20, 1959)

Yours Truly, Johnny Dollar "The Little Man Who Was There Matter" (September 20, 1959)

Have Gun, Will Travel "Like Father" (September 27, 1959)

Have Gun, Will Travel "Contessa Marie Desmoulins" (October 4, 1959)

Philip Marlowe "The Ugly Duckling" S1E1 (October 6, 1959)

Have Gun, Will Travel "Stopover in Tombstone" (October 11, 1959)

Captain David Grief "The Return of Blackbeard" S2E5 (October 18, 1959)

Have Gun, Will Travel "When in Rome" (October 25, 1959)

Yours Truly, Johnny Dollar "The Missing Missile Matter" (October 25, 1959)

The Detectives "The Hiding Place" S1E3 (October 30, 1959)

Yours Truly, Johnny Dollar "The Hand of Providential Matter" (November 1, 1959)

Wichita Town "Man on the Hill" S1E6 (November 4, 1959)

Yours Truly, Johnny Dollar "The Larson Arson Matter" (November 8, 1959)

Have Gun, Will Travel "Hired Gun/Assignment in Stone's Crossing" (November 8, 1959)

Have Gun, Will Travel "Landfall" (November 15, 1959)

Yours Truly, Johnny Dollar "The Bayou Body Matter" (November 15, 1959)

Yours Truly, Johnny Dollar "The Fancy Bridgework Matter" (November 22, 1959)

Have Gun, Will Travel "Fair Fugitive" (November 22, 1959)

Have Gun, Will Travel "Bitter Vengeance" (November 29, 1959)

Yours Truly, Johnny Dollar "The Wrong Man Matter" (November 29, 1959)

Hound-Dog Man (November 1959)

Have Gun, Will Travel "Out of Evil" (December 13, 1959)

Have Gun, Will Travel "Ranch Carnival/Ranse Carnival" (December 20, 1959)

Gunsmoke "Beeker's Barn" (December 20, 1959)

Operation Petticoat (December 24, 1959)

Have Gun, Will Travel "About Face/The Marriage" (December 27, 1959)

Yours Truly, Johnny Dollar "The Burning Desire Matter" (December 27, 1959)

The Witness "Parents and the Rigors of the Teens" (1959)

The Witness "The Abused Child" (1959)

The Witness "Kindness and Understanding" (1959)

The Witness "Parents and Juvenile Delinquency" (1959)

The Witness "Who is a Friend Indeed?" (1959)

The Witness "Blending Ethnic Backgrounds" (1959)

The Witness "A Boy's Mother Dies" (1959)

The Witness "A Farm Couple Adopts" (1959)

The Witness "The Good Samaritan of the Highway" (1959)

The Witness "Love Children" (1959)

The Witness "Mixed Races" (1959)

The Witness "Who is my Neighbor?" (1959)

The Witness "An Atmosphere of Love and Trust" (1959)

The Witness *Title Unknown* (1959)

Have Gun, Will Travel "Return Engagement" (January 3, 1960)

Yours Truly, Johnny Dollar "The Hapless Ham Matter" (January 3, 1960)

Have Gun, Will Travel "The Lonely One" (January 10, 1960)

Yours Truly, Johnny Dollar "The Unholy Two Matter" (January 10, 1960)

General Electric Theater "R.S.V.P." S8E17 (January 10, 1960)

Bourbon Street Beat "Inside Man" S1E15 (January 11, 1960)

Have Gun, Will Travel "French Leave" (January 17, 1960)

Have Gun, Will Travel "Nataemhon" (January 24, 1960)

Yours Truly, Johnny Dollar "The Nuclear Goof Matter" (January 24, 1960)

Have Gun, Will Travel "Bad Bert" (January 31, 1960)

Have Gun, Will Travel "The Boss" (February 7, 1960)

Have Gun, Will Travel "Bring Him Back Alive" (February 14, 1960)

Suspense "Sorry, Wrong Number" (February 14, 1960)

Yours Truly, Johnny Dollar "The Alvin's Alfred Matter" (February 21, 1960)

Gunsmoke "Mr. and Mrs. Amber" (February 21, 1960)

Have Gun, Will Travel "That Was No Lady" (February 21, 1960)

Yours Truly, Johnny Dollar "The Look Before the Leap Matter" (February 28, 1960)

Have Gun, Will Travel "The Dollhouse in Diamond Springs" (February 28, 1960)

Have Gun, Will Travel "Somebody Out There Hates Me" (March 6, 1960)

Yours Truly, Johnny Dollar "The Moonshine Matter" (March 6, 1960)

Yours Truly, Johnny Dollar "The Deep Down Matter" (March 13, 1960)

Have Gun, Will Travel "Montana Vendetta" (March 13, 1960)

Have Gun, Will Travel "Caesar's Wife" (March 20, 1960)

Johnny Midnight "An Old-Fashioned Frame" S1E13 (March 25, 1960)

Have Gun, Will Travel "They Told Me You Were Dead" (March 27, 1960)

Yours Truly, Johnny Dollar "The False Alarm Matter" (March 27, 1960)

The Man from Blackhawk "The Last Days of Jessie Turnbull" S1E25 (April 1, 1960)

Have Gun, Will Travel "Shanghai is a Verb" (April 3, 1960)

Gunsmoke "Greater Love" (April 3, 1960)

Have Gun, Will Travel "So True, Mr. Barnum" (April 10, 1960)

Have Gun, Will Travel "Prunella's Fella" (April 17, 1960)

The DuPont Show with June Allyson "Surprise Party" S1E28 (April 18, 1960)

Have Gun, Will Travel "Irish Luck" (April 24, 1960)

Yours Truly, Johnny Dollar "The Silver Queen Matter" (April 24, 1960)

Have Gun, Will Travel "Dressed to Kill" (May 1, 1960)

Yours Truly, Johnny Dollar "The Fatal Switch Matter" (May 1, 1960)

Gunsmoke "Nettie Sitton" (May 1, 1960)

Yours Truly, Johnny Dollar "The Phony Phone Matter" (May 8, 1960)

Have Gun, Will Travel "Pat Murphy" (May 8, 1960)

Have Gun, Will Travel "Lena Countryman" (May 15, 1960)

Yours Truly, Johnny Dollar "The Mystery Gal Matter" (May 15, 1960)

Gunsmoke "Marryin' Bertha" (May 22, 1960)

Have Gun, Will Travel "Dusty" (May 22, 1960)

Have Gun, Will Travel "Lucky Penny" (May 29, 1960)

Yours Truly, Johnny Dollar "The Red Rock Matter" (May 29, 1960)

Bronco "Winter Kill" S2E19 (May 31, 1960)

Have Gun, Will Travel "Apache Concerto" (June 5, 1960)

Yours Truly, Johnny Dollar "The Canned Canary Matter" (June 5, 1960)

Yours Truly, Johnny Dollar "The Harried Heiress Matter" (June 12, 1960)

Have Gun, Will Travel "Search for Wylie Dawson" (June 12, 1960)

Have Gun, Will Travel "Doctor from Vienna" (June 26, 1960)

Yours Truly, Johnny Dollar "The Wholly Unexpected Matter" (June 26, 1960)

Have Gun, Will Travel "Dad-Blamed Luck" (July 3, 1960)

Yours Truly, Johnny Dollar "The Collectors Matter" (July 3, 1960)

Have Gun, Will Travel "Five Days to Yuma" (July 10, 1960)

Have Gun, Will Travel "Little Guns" (July 17, 1960)

Yours Truly, Johnny Dollar "The Back to the Back Matter" (July 17, 1960)

Have Gun, Will Travel "My Son Must Die" (July 31, 1960)

Have Gun, Will Travel "Viva/Father O'Toole's Organ Part 1" (August 7, 1960)

Gunsmoke "Old Fool" (August 7, 1960)

Have Gun, Will Travel "Viva Extended/Father O'Toole's Organ Part 2" (August 14, 1960)

Yours Truly, Johnny Dollar "The Paradise Lost Matter" (August 14, 1960)

Yours Truly, Johnny Dollar "The Deadly Debt Matter" (August 28, 1960)

Have Gun, Will Travel "For the Birds" (August 28, 1960)

Have Gun, Will Travel "Eat Crow" (September 4, 1960)

Psycho (September 8, 1960)

Have Gun, Will Travel "Deadline" (September 11, 1960)

Have Gun, Will Travel "Nellie Watson's Boy" (September 18, 1960)

All the Fine Young Cannibals (September 22, 1960)

Have Gun, Will Travel "Bringing Up Ollie" (September 25, 1960)

Yours Truly, Johnny Dollar "The Five Down Matter" (September 25, 1960)

Have Gun, Will Travel "Talika/The Snoop" (October 2, 1960)

Have Gun, Will Travel "Sam Crow/Skeeter Hickshaw" (October 9, 1960)

The Barbara Stanwyck Show "Discreet Deception" S1E3 (October 10, 1960)

Have Gun, Will Travel "Stardust" (October 16, 1960)

Yours Truly, Johnny Dollar "The Twins of Tahoe Matter" (October 16, 1960)

Have Gun, Will Travel "Hell Knows No Fury/Billy Boggs" (October 23, 1960)

Yours Truly, Johnny Dollar "The Unworthy Kin Matter" (October 23, 1960)

Yours Truly, Johnny Dollar "The What Goes Matter" (October 30, 1960)

Have Gun, Will Travel "Oil" (October 30, 1960)

Klondike "Saints and Stickups" S1E3 (October 31, 1960)

The Deputy "Bitter Root" S2E6 (November 5, 1960)

Have Gun, Will Travel "The Odds" (November 6, 1960)

Have Gun, Will Travel "The Map" (November 13, 1960)

Have Gun, Will Travel "Martha Nell" (November 20, 1960)

Yours Truly, Johnny Dollar "The Double Deal Matter" (November 20, 1960)

Yours Truly, Johnny Dollar "The Empty Threat Matter" (November 27, 1960)

Have Gun, Will Travel "From Here to Boston" (November 27, 1960)

The Westerner "Going Home" S1E11 (December 16, 1960)

The Search *Title Unknown* (Cop's son gets involved with a gang) (1960)

The Search *Title Unknown* (Couple planning to divorce spend the weekend together) (1960)

The Search *Title Unknown* (Young boy meet Scrooge after running away from home during a snowstorm) (1960)

The Search *Title Unknown* (Wealthy man and lawyer force sister to sell stock) (1960)

The Search *Title Unknown* (Neighbors quarrel over a backyard tree) (1960)

The Search *Title Unknown* (A couple from the big city tries to adjust to suburb living) (1960)

Gunsmoke "The Wake" (January 15, 1961)

Checkmate "Hour of Execution" S1E16 (January 21, 1961)

The Americans "Harper's Ferry" S1E1 (January 23, 1961)

The Rebel "Paperback Hero" S2E20 (January 26, 1961)

Maverick "The Ice Man" E4S20 (January 29, 1961)

Bat Masterson "A Lesson in Violence" E3S20 (February 23, 1961)

Zane Grey Theater "The Atoner" S5E25 (April 6, 1961)

Gunsmoke "Minnie" S6E30 (April 15, 1961)

Thriller "Mr. George" S1E32 (May 9, 1961)

Gunsmoke "The Imposter" S6E34 (May 13, 1961)

Man-Trap (September 20, 1961)

77 Sunset Strip "The Rival Eye Caper" S4E1 (September 22, 1961)

Hawaiian Eye "Satan City" S3E1 (September 27, 1961)

Calvin and the Colonel "The Television Job" S1E1 (October 3, 1961)

Calvin and the Colonel "The Polka Dot Bandit" S1E2 (October 10, 1961)

Calvin and the Colonel "Thanksgiving Dinner" S1E3 (October 17, 1961)

Calvin and the Colonel "The Costume Ball" S1E4 (October 24, 1961)

Perry Mason "The Case of the Pathetic Patient" S5E7 (October 28, 1961)

Calvin and the Colonel "Sycamore Lodge" S1E5 (October 31, 1961)

Calvin and the Colonel "Money in the Closet" S1E6 (November 7, 1961)

Adventures in Paradise "The Pretender" S3E7 (November 12, 1961)

Dr. Kiladare "Johnny Temple" S1E14 (December 28, 1961)

The New Breed "The All-American Boy" S1E14 (January 2, 1962)

Calvin and the Colonel "Calvin Gets Psychoanalyzed" S1E7 (January 27, 1962)

Calvin and the Colonel "Wheeling and Dealing" S1E8 (February 3, 1962)

Calvin and the Colonel "The Wrecking Crew" S1E9 (February 10, 1962)

Calvin and the Colonel "The Colonel's Old Flame" S1E10 (February 17, 1962)

Calvin and the Colonel "Sister Sue and the Police Captain" S1E11 (February 24, 1962)

Calvin and the Colonel "Jim Dandy Cleaners" S1E12 (March 3, 1962)

Have Gun Will Travel "Don't Shoot the Piano Player" S5E26 (March 10, 1962)

Calvin and the Colonel "Jealousy" S1E13 (March 10, 1962)

Lawman "Clootey Hutter" S4E26 (March 11, 1962)

Calvin and the Colonel "Cloakroom" S1E14 (March 17, 1962)

General Electric Theater "My Dark Days: Part 1" S10E25 (March 18, 1962)

Calvin and the Colonel "Sister Sue's Sweetheart" S1E15 (March 24, 1962)

General Electric Theater "My Dark Days: Part 2" S10E26 (March 25, 1962)

Calvin and the Colonel "The Winning Number" S1E16 (March 31, 1962)

Calvin and the Colonel "Calvin's Glamour Girl" S1E17 (April 7, 1962)

House of Women (April 11, 1962)

Calvin and the Colonel "Colonel Out-Foxes Himself" S1E18 (April 14, 1962)

Calvin and the Colonel "Nephew Newton's Fortune" S1E19 (April 21, 1962)

Calvin and the Colonel "Calvin's Tax Problem" S1E20 (April 28, 1962)

The Real McCoys "Don't Judge a Book" S5E28 (May 3, 1962)

Calvin and the Colonel "Women's Club Picnic" S1E21 (May 5, 1962)

Ben Casey "An Uncommonly Innocent Killing" S1E30 (May 7, 1962)

Calvin and the Colonel "Magazine Romance" S1E22 (May 12, 1962)

Calvin and the Colonel "Ring Reward" S1E23 (May 19, 1962)

Hazel "Heat Wave" S1E33 (May 24, 1962)

Calvin and the Colonel "The Carnappers" S1E24 (May 26, 1962)

Shootout at Big Sag (June 1, 1962)

Calvin and the Colonel "Colonel Traps a Thief" S1E25 (June 2, 1962)

Calvin and the Colonel "Back to Nashville" S1E26 (June 9, 1962)

Hawaiian Eye "Koko Kate" S3E38 (June 13, 1962)

Gunsmoke "The Search" S8E1 (September 15, 1962)

Sam Benedict "Tears for a Nobody Doll" S1E5 (October 13, 1962)

77 Sunset Strip "The Raiders" S5E4 (November 2, 1962)

Gunsmoke "Phoebe Strunk" S8E9 (November 10, 1962)

Going My Way "A Matter of Principle" S1E8 (November 21, 1962)

Hazel "Genie with the Light Brown Lamp" S2E10 (November 22, 1962)

The Danny Thomas Show/Make Room for Daddy "Jose, the Scholar" S10E9 (November 26, 1962)

Hawaiian Eye "Shannon Malloy" S4E11 (December 18, 1962)

The Eleventh Hour "Which Man Will Die?" S1E13 (January 2, 1963)

Wide Country "Whose Hand at My Throat?" S1E20 (February 14, 1963)

The Twilight Zone "Jess-Belle" S4E7 (February 14, 1963)

Empire "A House in Order" S1E23 (March 5, 1963)

Perry Mason "The Case of the Velvet Claws" S6E22 (March 21, 1963)

Rawhide "Incident of the Comanchero" S5E23 (March 22, 1963)

The Eleventh Hour "A Medicine Man in This Day and Age?" S1E29 (May 1, 1963)

Hazel "Maid of the Month" S2E31 (May 2, 1963)

Spencer's Mountain (May 16, 1963)

The Third Man "Who Killed Harry Lime?" S4E17 (August 24, 1963)

The Kiss of the Vampire (September 11, 1963)

Hazel "Potluck a la Mode" S3E1 (September 19, 1963)

Hootenanny "Boston University #1" S2E1 (September 21, 1963)

The Alfred Hitchcock Hour "A Home Away from Home" S2E1 (September 27, 1963)

Breaking Point "There Are the Hip, and There Are the Square" S1E5 (October 14, 1963)

Temple Houston "Jubilee" S1E8 (November 14, 1963)

77 Sunset Strip "Deposit with Caution" S6E10 (November 29, 1963)

Wagon Train "The Fenton Canaby Story" S7E15 (December 30, 1963)

77 Sunset Strip "Queen of the Cats" S6E20 (February 7, 1964)

Arrest and Trial "A Roll of the Dice" S1E22 (February 23, 1964)

The Twilight Zone "The Masks" S5E25 (March 20, 1964)

The Virginian "The Secret of Brynmar Hall" S2E26 (April 1, 1964)

Rawhide "Incident of the Banker" S6E25 (April 2, 1964)

Breaking Point "Confounding Her Astronomers" S1E28 (April 6, 1964)

Ben Casey "For a Just Man Falleth Seven Times" S3E32 (April 15, 1964)

Gorath (May 15, 1964)

Kraft Suspense Theatre "The Robrioz Ring" S1E27 (May 28, 1964)

This is the Life "Out of Bondage" (September 20, 1964)

Wagon Train "The John Gillman Story" S8E3 (October 4, 1964)

Bonanza "Logan's Treasure" S6E5 (October 18, 1964)

Arch Oboler's Plays "Come to the Bank" (October 31, 1964)

Arch Oboler's Plays "Big Ben" (November 14, 1964)

Arch Oboler's Plays "Mirage" (December 19, 1964)

The Farmer's Daughter "Like Father, Like Son" S2E15 (December 25, 1964)

The Alfred Hitchcock Hour "Consider Her Ways" S3E11 (December 28, 1964)

My Favorite Martian "How Are Things in Glocca, Martin?" S2E16 (January 10, 1965)

Two on a Guillotine (January 13, 1965)

Hazel "Love 'em and Leave 'em" S4E18 (January 21, 1965)

Wendy and Me "Jeff Takes a Turn for the Nurse" S1E23 (February 22, 1965)

The Alfred Hitchcock Hour "Thou Still Unravished Bride" S3E22 (March 22, 1965)

The Fugitive "A.P.B." S2E28 (April 6, 1965)

Joy in the Morning (May 5, 1965)

The Legend of Jesse James "Three Men from Now" S1E1 (September 13, 1965)

My Three Sons "Red Tape Romance" S6E2 (September 23, 1965)

My Three Sons "Brother, Ernie" S6E3 (September 30, 1965)

Camp Runamuck "Today is Parent's Day" S1E9 (November 12, 1965)

Perry Mason "The Case of the Silent Six" S9E11 (November 21, 1965)

The Addams Family "Feud in the Addams Family" S2E11 (November 26, 1965)

Ben Casey "In Case of Emergency, Cry Havoc" S5E16 (January 3, 1966)

Ben Casey "Meantime, We Shall Express Our Darker Purpose" S5E17 (January 10, 1966)

Ben Casey "For San Diego, You Need a Different Bus" S5E18 (January 17, 1966)

Ben Casey "Smile, Baby, Smile, It's Only Twenty Dols of Pain" S5E19 (January 24, 1966)

Dragnet (January 27, 1966)

Ben Casey "Fun and Games and Other Tragic Things" S5E20 (January 31, 1966)

Gunsmoke "Sanctuary" S11E23 (February 26, 1966)

Dr. Kiladare "Travel a Crooked Road" S5E54 (March 22, 1966)

A Big Hand for the Little Lady (May 31, 1966)

The Girl from U.N.C.L.E. "The Danish Blue Affair" S1E7 (October 25, 1966)

The Bubble (December 21, 1966)

The Big Valley "The Stallion" S2E20 (January 30, 1967)

Dragnet "The Candy Store Robberies" S1E8 (March 9, 1967)

Dragnet "The Jade Story" S1E10 (March 23, 1967)

The Road West "The Agreement" S1E28 (April 24, 1967)

The Guns of Will Sonnett "A Son for a Son" S1E7 (October 20, 1967)

The Herculoids "Mekkano, the Machine Master/Tiny World of Terror" S1E7 (October 21, 1967)

The Herculoids "The Beaked People/The Raider" S1E3 (September 23, 1967)

The Herculoids "The Gladiators of Kyanite/Temple of Trax S1E8 (October 28, 1967)

The Virginian "Bitter Autumn" S6E8 (November 1, 1967)

Run for Your Life "Cry Hard, Cry Fast: Part 1" S3E11 (November 22, 1967)

Dragnet "The Pyramid Swindle" S2E12 (November 30, 1967)

Daniel Boone "The Witness" S4E17 (January 25, 1968)

Dragnet "The Big Clan" S2E21 (February 8, 1968)

Prescription: Murder (February 20, 1968)

Dragnet "The Big Gambler" S2E27 (March 21, 1968)

Madigan (March 29, 1968)

Insight "The Ghetto Trap" S1E203 (May 26, 1968)

The Outcasts "Take Your Lover in the Ring" S1E5 (October 28, 1968)

The Virginian "Ride to Misadventure" S7E8 (November 6, 1968)

Dragnet "Training: DR-18" S3E9 (November 21, 1968)

Dragnet "Public Affairs: DR-14" S3E10 (November 28, 1968)

Mod Squad "Twinkle, Twinkle Little Starlet" S1E11 (December 17, 1968)

The Night Before Christmas (December 1968)

Bewitched "Samantha's Super Maid" S5E14 (January 2, 1969)

Gunsmoke "The Twisted Heritage" S14E15 (January 6, 1969)

Mod Squad "A Hint of Darkness, a Hint of Light" S1E18 (February 11, 1969)

Dragnet "Juvenile: DR-32" S3E24 (March 27, 1969)

The Big Valley "Point and Counterpoint" S4E26 (May 19, 1969)

Heaven with a Gun (June 13, 1969)

The Great Bank Robbery (September 10, 1969)

The Bold Ones: The New Doctors "To Save a Life" S1E1 (September 14, 1969)

Dragnet "Personnel: The Shooting" S4E1 (September 18, 1969)

Dragnet "Homicide: The Student" S4E2 (September 25, 1969)

Mannix "Color Her Missing" S3E2 (October 4, 1969)

Ironside "Eye of the Hurricane" S3E4 (October 9, 1969)

Along Came a Spider (February 3, 1970)

Adam-12 "Log 54: Impersonation" S2E16 (February 7, 1970)

The Virginian "A Time of Terror" S8E19 (February 11, 1970)

Quarantined (February 24, 1970)

Dragnet "Missing Persons: The Body" S4E20 (March 5, 1970)

Dragnet "I.A.D.: The Receipt" S4E23 (March 26, 1970)

Dragnet "Burglary: Baseball" S4E25 (April 9, 1970)

A Walk in the Spring Rain (April 9, 1970)

Ironside "A Killing Will Occur" S4E1 (September 17, 1970)

The Bold Ones: The New Doctors "Killer on the Loose" S2E2 (October 11, 1970)

The Other Man (October 19, 1970)

Adam-12 "Log 75: Have a Nice Weekend" S3E7 (November 7, 1970)

Crowhaven Farm (November 24, 1970)

The Bold Ones: The Lawyers "The People Against Doctor Chapman" S2E4 (December 6, 1970)

Bracken's World "Will Freddy's Real Father Please Stand Up?" S2E13 (December 11, 1970)

D.A.: Conspiracy to Kill (January 11, 1971)

Mannix "The Color Murder" S4E22 (February 27, 1971)

Mod Squad "Welcome to Our City" S3E21 (March 2, 1971)

The Interns "The Choice" S1E24 (March 26, 1971)

Insight "The Immigrant" (June 26, 1971)

O'Hara, U.S. Treasury "Operation: Time Fuse" S1E5 (October 15, 1971)

Mission: Impossible "Encounter" S6E7 (October 30, 1971)

The D.A. "The People vs. Lindsey" S1E7 (November 5, 1971)

O'Hara, U.S. Treasury "Operation: Crystal Springs" S1E11 (December 3, 1971)

Owen Marshall, Counselor at Law "The Triangle" S1E14 (December 30, 1971)

The Night Stalker (January 11, 1972)

Emergency! "The Wedsworth-Townsend Act" S1E1 (January 15, 1972)

Ironside "And Then There Was One" S5E19 (January 20, 1972)

Emergency! "Botulism" S1E2 (January 29, 1972)

Marcus Welby, M.D. "I'm Really Trying" S3E19 (February 1, 1972)

Alias Smith and Jones "Which Way to the O.K. Corral?" S2E20 (February 10, 1972)

Emergency! "Cook's Tour" S1E3 (February 12, 1972)

Love, American Style "Love and the Happy Days/Love and the Newscasters" S3E22 (February 25, 1972)

Same Time, Same Station "Oboler Omnibus I" (April 16, 1972)

Adam-12 "Dirt Duel" S5E1 (September 13, 1972)

The ABC Saturday Superstar Movie "Gidget Makes the Wrong Connection" S1E11 (November 18, 1972)

All My Darling Daughters (November 22, 1972)

Emergency! "Musical Mania" S2E11 (December 9, 1972)

The Sixth Sense "Gallows in the Wind" S2E11 (December 16, 1972)

Hec Ramsey "Mystery of the Yellow Rose" S1E4 (January 28, 1973)

The Stranger (February 26, 1973)

Chase "Pilot" S1E1 (March 24, 1973)

Kung Fu "The Third Man" S1E14 (April 26, 1973)

Butch Cassidy "The Scientist" S1E1 (September 8, 1973)

Yogi's Gang "Dr. Bigot" S1E1 (September 8, 1973)

Cannon "He Who Digs a Grave" S3E1 (September 12, 1973)

Emergency! "Alley Cat" S3E3 (October 6, 1973)

Adam-12 "Capture" S6E9 (November 14, 1973)

Yogi's Gang "Lotta Litter" S1E12 (November 24, 1973)

Yogi's Gang "Mr. Hothead" S1E15 (December 15, 1973)

Chase "Right to an Attorney" S1E13 (January 8, 1974)

The Six Million Dollar Man "Population: Zero" S1E1 (January 18, 1974)

Police Story "The Ripper" S1E15 (February 12, 1974)

Cannon "Bobby Loved Me" S3E22 (February 27, 1974)

Adam-12 "A Clinic on 18th Street" S6E24 (March 13, 1974)

Apple's Way "The Accident" S1E11 (May 5, 1974)

These are the Days "Sensible Ben" S1E1 (September 7, 1974)

Police Woman "The Beautiful Die Young" S1E2 (September 20, 1974)

Happy Days "Who's Sorry Now?" S2E3 (September 24, 1974)

Cannon "Voice from the Grave" S4E3 (September 25, 1974)

The Six Million Dollar Man "The Pal-Mir Escort" S2E4 (October 4, 1974)

CBS Radio Mystery Theater "The Doll" (October 10, 1974)

Ironside "The Last Cotillion" S8E7 (October 31, 1974)

Marcus Welby, M.D. "The Last Rip-Off" S6E11 (November 26, 1974)

Kolchak: The Night Stalker "The Spanish Moss Murders" S1E9 (December 6, 1974)

The Ray Bradbury Theatre "The Great Conflagration up at the Place" (1974)

The Ray Bradbury Theatre "Forever and the Earth" (1974)

The Streets of San Francisco "Letters from the Grave" S3E16 (January 16, 1975)

Attack on Terror: The FBI vs. the Ku Klux Klan (February 20, 1975)

You Lie So Deep, My Love (February 25, 1975)

Emergency! "905-Wild" S4E22 (March 1, 1975)

The Rockford Files "Roundabout" S1E22 (March 7, 1975)

Adam-12 "Something Worth Dying For: Part 1" S7E23 (May 13, 1975)

Mobile Two (September 2, 1975)

CBS Radio Mystery Theater "The Ghost Plane" (September 12, 1975)

The Six Million Dollar Man "The Return of the Bionic Woman: Part 2" S3E2 (September 21, 1975)

Airport 1975 (October 18, 1975)

Run, Joe, Run "The Hitchhiker" S2E8 (October 25, 1975)

Bronk "Deception" S1E12 (December 7, 1975)

Threads of Glory (1975)

The Streets of San Francisco "The Honorable Profession" S4E16 (January 15, 1976)

The Waltons "The Fledgling" S4E23 (February 26, 1976)

S.W.A.T. "Dragons and Owls" S2E21 (March 6, 1976)

No Way Back (April 23, 1976)

State Fair (May 14, 1976)

Clue Club "The Paper Shaper Caper" S1E1 (August 14, 1976)

Clue Club "The Case of the Lighthouse Mouse" S1E2 (August 21, 1976)

Rich Man, Poor Man – Book II "Chapter I" S1E1 (September 21, 1976)

Police Woman "The Lifeline Agency" S3E7 (November 23, 1976)

The Streets of San Francisco "Hang Tough" S5E16 (February 17, 1977)

Man from Atlantis "Man from Atlantis" S1E1 (March 4, 1977)

A Flintstone Christmas (December 7, 1977)

Police Woman "The Buttercup Killer" S4E6 (December 13, 1977)

Captain Caveman and the Teen Angels "The Mystery Mansion Mix-Up" S1E15 (December 17, 1977)

The Waltons "The Ordeal" S6E19 (February 16, 1978)

Sam "Episode #1.1" (March 14, 1978)

Project U.F.O. "Sighting 4004: The Howard Crossing Incident" S1E4 (March 19, 1978)

Richie Brockelman, Private Eye "A Title on the Door and a Carpet on the Floor" S1E3 (March 31, 1978)

Goodbye, Franklin High (April 1978)

Project U.F.O. "Sighting 4013: The St. Hilary Incident" S1E13 (June 4, 1978)

Little Women "Part I" S1E1 (October 2, 1978)

Little Women "Part II" S1E2 (October 3, 1978)

Yogi's Space Race "The Saturn 500" S1E1 (September 9, 1978)

Yogi's Space Race "The Neptune 9000" S1E2 (September 16, 1978)

Yogi's Space Race "The Pongo Tongo Classic" S1E3 (September 30, 1978)

Yogi's Space Race "Nebuloc-The Prehistoric Planet" S1E4 (September 30, 1978)

Yogi's Space Race "The Spartikan Spectacular" S1E5 (October 7, 1978)

Yogi's Space Race "The Mizar Marathon" S1E6 (October 14, 1978)

Yogi's Space Race "The Lost Planet of Atlantis" S1E7 (October 21, 1978)

The Scooby-Doo/Dynomutt Hour "The Creepy Case of Old Iron Face" S3E7 (October 21, 1978)

Yogi's Space Race "Race Through Oz" S1E8 (October 28, 1978)

Yogi's Space Race "Race Through Wet Galoshes" S1E9 (November 4, 1978)

Yogi's Space Race "The Borealis Triangle" S1E10 (November 11, 1978)

Yogi's Space Race "Race to the Center of the Universe" S1E11 (November 18, 1978)

Yogi's Space Race "Race Through the Planet of the Monsters" S1E12 (November 25, 1978)

Sears Radio Theatre "Hostages" (February 7, 1979)

Sears Radio Theatre "This Home is Dissolved" (February 15, 1979)

Sears Radio Theatre "The Lady and the Outlaw" (March 5, 1979)

Lou Grant "Skids" S2E23 (April 2, 1979)

Sears Radio Theatre "A Matter of Priorities" (April 5, 1979)

Sears Radio Theatre "The Duke of Nevers" (April 16, 1979)

Sears Radio Theatre "The Old Boy" (April 18, 1979)

Sears Radio Theatre "Bruja/Brew-Ha" (April 20, 1979)

Sears Radio Theatre "The Other Grandmother" (May 3, 1979)

Sears Radio Theatre "Here's Morgan Again" (May 8, 1979)

Sears Radio Theatre "Country of Fear" (May 18, 1979)

Sears Radio Theatre "Here's Morgan Once More" (May 22, 1979)

Sears Radio Theatre "The Perfect Hostess" (June 13, 1979)

Sears Radio Theatre "Old Bones" (June 25, 1979)

Sears Radio Theatre "Katie Macbeth" (July 9, 1979)

Sears Radio Theatre "Spring Cleaning" (July 12, 1979)

Sears Radio Theatre "Uncle Zora Comes to the Pig Festival" (July 23, 1979)

Sears Radio Theatre "Reunion" (July 26, 1979)

Charlie's Angels "Of Ghosts and Angels" S4E13 (January 2, 1980)

Captain Caveman and the Teen Angels "Cavey and the Volcanic Villain" S3E3 (March 22, 1980)

Evita Peron (February 23, 1981)

242 • Lona Bailey

Concrete Cowboys/Ramblin' Man "A Token for Winnie" S1E7 (March 21, 1981)

S.O.B. (July 1, 1981)

Space Stars "Attack of the Space Sharks (Space Ghost)" S1E1 (September 12, 1981)

Space Stars "The Sorceress (Space Ghost)" S1E2 (September 19, 1981)

Space Stars "The Antimatter Man (Space Ghost)" S1E3 (September 26, 1981)

Space Stars "The Starfly (Space Ghost)" S1E4 (October 3, 1981)

Space Stars "Space Spectre (Space Ghost)" S1E5 (October 10, 1981)

Space Stars "The Toymaker (Space Ghost)" S1E6 (October 17, 1981)

Space Stars "The Shadow People (Space Ghost)" S1E7 (October 24, 1981)

Space Stars "Time Chase (Space Ghost)" S1E8 (October 31, 1981)

Space Stars "City in Space (Space Ghost)" S1E9 (November 7, 1981)

Space Stars "Eclipse Woman (Space Ghost)" S1E10 (November 14, 1981)

Space Stars "The Haunted Space Station (Space Ghost)" S1E11 (November 21, 1981)

Forbidden Love (October 18, 1982)

Heidi's Song (November 19, 1982)

The 25th Man (1982)

Trapper John, M.D. "Baby on the Line" (January 9, 1983)

Psycho II (June 3, 1983)

Dynasty "The Arrest" S4E1 (September 28, 1983)

Hanna-Barbera's The Greatest Adventure: Stories from the Bible S1E6 December 15, 1985)

Hanna-Barbera's The Greatest Adventure: Stories from the Bible: Samson and Delilah (April 25, 1986)

Psycho III (July 2, 1986)

Appendix B: Selected Radio Performances of Virginia Gregg with Show Description

No exhaustive radiography or filmography of Virginia Gregg exists. The following is the closest to complete chronical of her work. My independent research has been informed by the radio logs of John Dunning's *Tune in Yesterday: The Ultimate Encyclopedia of Old Time Radio 1925-1976,* J. David Goldin's RadioGOLDINdex, Old-TimeRadioDownloads.com, Jerry Haendiges' Vintage Radio Logs, RUSC Old Time Radio, and The Digital Deli. Disputed dates and network details are noted, but in cases where there are multiple possible dates for episode recordings, I have documented the most widely accepted date among parent sources. Due to the passage of time, not all show descriptions and details are available. Entries are in chronological order according to the date of the first episode in a show's total run.

The dates listed have been cross referenced among the logs of many different radio researchers and are the closest original broadcast dates. Not all rebroadcast dates are included. In multiple part episodes, Virginia may not have performed in every individual sub-episode (For example, in a multiple part episode, she may have performed in parts 1, 3, and 4, but not in part 2, though the entire episode is listed below). Certain spellings may differ among records. The rounded general duration of shows is included. All shows listed are American old-time radio shows.

1. **Title:** *Lights Out* (January 3, 1934 – August 6, 1947) was a 1930s-1940s horror series known for its especially frightening sound

patterns and dramatic narration, beginning each episode with the eerie introduction: "It is later than you think," along with fair warning to turn the dial if faint of heart. The series was created by Wyllis Cooper and eventually taken over by Arch Oboler. Virginia is credited in only one episode of *Lights Out*, though she likely performed in additional episodes either uncredited or undocumented.

Genre: Horror/Suspense

General Duration: 30mins

Network(s): WENR Chicago, NBC's Red Network, CBS, & ABC

Episode(s): "Come to the Bank" (November 17, 1942)

2. Title: *The Screen Guild Theater* (January 8, 1939 – June 29, 1952) was a CBS anthology series that adapted popular films of the day to radio. It was broadcast under different names throughout its running including *The Gulf Screen Guild Show/Theatre*, *The Lady Esther Screen Guild Theatre*, and *The Camel Screen Guild Players*. The show was in partnership with the charitable organization The Motion Picture & Television Fund (MPTF). The Screen Guild Theatre ran for 14 seasons and included many of the greats such as Joan Crawford, Gary Cooper, Clark Gable, Gene Kelly, Shirley Temple, and Humphrey Bogart. The featured actors would donate their fees to the MPTF in support of the Motion Picture Country House. Sometimes *The Screen Guild Theater* is confused with *Screen Director's Guild Assignment* and *Hollywood Sound Stage*. Virginia is credited with only one performance in *The Screen Guild Theater*, but she likely performed in additional episodes over the 527-show run.

Genre: Dramatic Anthology

General Duration: 30mins

Network(s): CBS, NBC, & ABC

Episode(s): "Whistling in Dixie" (May 17, 1943)

3. Title: *Wings to Victory* (1940 – October 7, 1943) was a war drama broadcast over the Armed Forces Radio Station (AFRS) based on front line combat reports of WWII. Each episode follows "Lt. Roddy Johns" portrayed by Howard Duff in his Air Force adventures. The show was created in great patriotic effort to simultaneously to boost morale back home, while also encouraging Air Force enlistment. Virginia is credited in only one episode of *Wings to Victory*, though likely performed in additional episodes either uncredited or undocumented.

Genre: War Drama
General Duration: 30mins
Network(s): NBC's Blue Network's KECA & AFRS
Episode(s): "Story of John 'Rocky' Saunders" (October 7, 1943)

4. Title: *Lux Radio Theatre* (October 14, 1934 – June 7, 1955) began as a serial adaption of the plays of Broadway, and later in its run transitioned from Broadway to Hollywood – literally and contextually. The show moved from New York to Hollywood in 1936 and added Cecil B. DeMille as its host. With the geographical move, writers shifted their airwave deliverables from Broadway adaptations to Hollywood film adaptations. *Lux Radio Theatre* is considered one of the longest running shows in radio history. It regularly featured stars of the Hollywood glory days such as Joan Crawford, Clark Gable, Van Johnson, Maureen O'Hara, Lana Turner, Shirley Temple, and Barbara Stanwyck. Virginia performed in several episodes of *Lux Radio Theatre* after its move to Hollywood.

Genre: Dramatic Anthology
General Duration: 60mins
Network(s): CBS
Episode(s): "Random Harvest" (January 31, 1944)
"The Phantom Lady" (March 27, 1944)
"Penny Serenade" (May 8, 1944)
"Naughty Marietta" (June 12, 1944)
"Only Yesterday" (April 16, 1945)

"And Now Tomorrow" (May 21, 1945)
"Together Again" (December 9, 1946)
"Miracle on 34th Street" (December 22, 1947)
"The Song of Bernadette" (April 11, 1949)
"David and Bathsheba" (October 19, 1954)
"Awful Truth" (January 18, 1955)

5. Title: *Cavalcade of America* (October 9, 1935 – March 31, 1953) was a historical anthology with dramatizations of events in American history. The show was created in part by the DuPont Company in a brand-saving effort after controversy surrounded their name upon accusations of their profiting through their gunpowder sales during WWI. Throughout its eighteen-year run, the *Cavalcade of America* featured such stars as Bob Hope, Gregory Peck, Franchot Tone, Ronald Regan, Alan Ladd, John Garfield, Agnes Moorehead etc. Virginia is credited in three episodes of *Cavalcade of America*, though given its long run, she likely performed in additional episodes.
Genre: Historical Anthology
General Duration: 30mins
Network(s): CBS & NBC
Episode(s): "Mask for Jefferson" (April 17, 1944)
"Danger: Women at Work" (September 9, 1946)
"School for Men" (May 5, 1947)

6. Title: *A Gathering in the Air* (1946) (AFRS)
Genre: War Drama
General Duration: 15mins
Network(s): AFRS
Episode(s): "A Gathering in the Air" (1946)

7. Title: *Play for Tonight*
Genre: Drama

General Duration: 15mins
Network(s): NBC
Episode(s): "Randy of Coyote Canyon" (audition) (August 23, 1946)

8. Title: *The Rudy Vallee Show/The Fleischmann's Yeast Hour* (October 24, 1929 – May 23, 1939) was a musical variety show considered the first of its kind in many ways. Singer and musician Rudy Vallee hosted the show that featured such talents as Alice Faye, Red Skelton, and Milton Berle from 1929 to 1936 under its alternate name *The Fleischmann's Yeast Hour* and ran from 1936 to May 23, 1939, as *The Royal Gelatin Hour*. Vallee remained on the air waves for many subsequent years in a variety of capacities. Virginia was acquainted with him from her days as a musician, as was her first husband, Lou Butterman, who was a regular in Vallee's studio orchestra as bass player. Virginia performed in three episodes credited, but may have performed in additional shows uncredited or undocumented.
Genre: Variety
General Duration: 30mins
Network(s): NBC
Episode(s): "The Drene Show: Our First Adventure" (June 13, 1946)
"The Great Gildersleeve" (September 10, 1946)
"Villa Vallee" (October 1, 1946)

9. Title: *The Whistler* (May 16, 1942 – September 22, 1955) was a mystery drama that ran for thirteen years with great reception, originally written and produced by J. Donald Wilson. The show details various mysteries in a sinister commentary by "The Whistler" himself. "The Whistler" was played most often by Bill Forman, but also by a few other greats such as Marvin Miller, Bill Johnstone, Everett Clarke, Joseph Kearns, and Gale Gordon. The actual "whistle" was contributed by Dorothy Roberts. With a knack for suspenseful scripts, Virginia performed in many episodes of *The Whistler*.
Genre: Mystery Drama/Crime

General Duration: 30mins
Network(s): CBS, AFRS
Episode(s): "Stranger in the House" (September 2, 1946)
"Witness at the Fountain" (September 9, 1946)
"Blue Legend" (March 3, 1947)
"Curtain Call" (August 27, 1947)
"Back Door" (October 29, 1947)
"Perfect Albi" (June 12, 1949)
"That Physical Fact" (June 19, 1949)
"Death in Sixteen Millimeter" (July 17, 1949)
"Brotherly Hate" (July 31, 1949)
"Five Cent Call" (February 19, 1950)
"Oriana Affair" (March 19, 1950)
"Just Like a Man" (November 5, 1950)
"Autumn Song" (July 22, 1951)
"Fateful Reminder" (August 12, 1951)
"Public Hero" (September 2, 1951)
"Episode at Thunder Mountain" (January 6, 1952)
"Saturday Night" (April 27, 1952)
"The Last Message" (June 15, 1952)
"The Secret of Chalk Point" (September 7, 1952)
"Night Melody" (May 12, 1955)

10. Title: *The Happy Prince: A Radio Play* (1946) was a radio adaption of Oscar Wilde's short story "The Happy Prince." A few different versions of this piece exist that aired or were recorded in the 1940s. The recording featuring Virginia's performance also includes June Foray, Lou Crosby, and Jay Novello.
Genre: Fairy Tale
General Duration: 30mins
Network(s): NBC's Blue Network, syndicated
Episode(s): "The Happy Prince" (December 22, 1946)

11. Title: *A Child's Wish* (1947) (AFRS)
Genre: Drama
General Duration: 15mins
Network(s): AFRS
Episode(s): "A Child's Wish" (January 9, 1947)

12. Title: *Marvelous Margie*
Genre: Comedy
General Duration: 30mins
Network(s): *Unavailable
Episode(s): "Marvelous Margie: Episode 1" (audition) (February 5, 1947)

13. Title: *The Adventures of Ellery Queen* (June 18, 1939 – May 27, 1948) was a detective series created and produced by George Zachary. It was based on character "Hugh Marlowe" created by cousins Frederic Dannay and Manfred Lee and renamed "Ellery Queen" for radio. The airwaves were engorged with detective shows and mysteries in the 1940s and 1950s, but the novelty of *The Adventures of Ellery Queen* was in how the mysteries were solved. "Ellery" narrated various mysteries only to have a panel of "armchair detectives" (usually well-knowns in the entertainment industry) solve them upon the show's conclusion. Virginia performed credited in five episodes of *The Adventures of Ellery Queen*, in a variety of supporting roles, though she may have performed in additional episodes.
Genre: Crime/Mystery
General Duration: 30mins
Network(s): CBS, NBC, & ABC
Episode(s): "Nikki Porter, Suspect" (March 5, 1947)
"The Saga of Ruffy Rux" (November 27, 1947)
"Nikki Porter, Bride" (December 11, 1947)
"The Case of the Melancholy Dane" (December 18, 1947)
"Ellery Queen, Santa Claus" (December 25, 1947)

14. Title: *Family Theatre* (February 13, 1947 – September 11, 1957) was a dramatic anthology that told stories of family life very relatable to audiences in the 1940s and 1950s. The show delivered a variety of genres in its ten-year run including comedies, science fictions, westerns, mysteries, and romances. Its famous slogan, "The family that prays together, stays together" was coined by the Holy Cross Family Ministries, the show's associate producing organization, to encourage American families to pray together. *Family Theatre* was a personal favorite of Virginia's and she played myriad roles throughout its run.

Genre: Dramatic Anthology

General Duration: 30mins

Network(s): Mutual Broadcasting Network, Don Lee

Episode(s): "Three Way Love" (May 29, 1947)

"Little Boy Blue" (April 1, 1948)

"The High Boarded Fence" (June 3, 1948)

"Once upon a Golden Afternoon" (June 10, 1948 & September 9, 1948)

"Gramps" (September 30, 1948)

"World Without End" (January 19, 1949)

"Melancholy Clown" (January 26, 1949)

"Night Elevator" (April 6, 1949)

"The Legacy" (May 18, 1949)

"The Postmistress of Laurel Run" (June 22, 1949)

"The Pardoner's Tale" (July 6, 1949)

"The Bishop's Candlesticks" (August 3, 1949)

"Mademoiselle Fifi" (September 14, 1949)

"Evangeline" (September 28, 1949)

"The Courtship of Miles Standish" (November 23, 1949)

"Old Judge Priest" (January 4, 1950)

"A Tale of Two Cities" (January 11, 1950)

"The Broken Pitcher" (March 22, 1950)

"Sarah Bernhardt" (May 3, 1950)

"The Bet" (May 10, 1950)
"Sir Lancelot of the Lake" (June 28, 1950)
"The Spectre Bridegroom" (July 5, 1950)
"Genius from Hoboken" (May 7, 1952)
"World Without End" (May 21, 1952)
"Portrait of Cynthia" (June 4, 1952)
"Ten O'clock Scholar" (July 16, 1952)
"The People's Choice" (August 27, 1952)
"New Neighbor" (May 27, 1953)
"A Fine Wedding for Angelita" (October 28, 1953)
"The Little Prince" (December 30, 1953)
"The Cadreman" (January 27, 1954)
"Past Imperfect" (February 24, 1954)
"The Pox" (March 31, 1954)
"The Strangers" (July 14, 1954)
"Stay Up for the Sunrise" (October 20, 1954)
"The Little Prince" (December 29, 1954)
"Stranger in Town" (January 12, 1955)
"Act of Contrition" (April 20, 1955)

15. Title: *Voyage of the Scarlet Queen* (July 3, 1947 – February 14, 1948) was an adventure series that follows seaman "Philip Carney" (played by Elliott Lewis) as master of his "ketch" *Scarlet Queen*. The show was produced by James Burton with scripts written by Robert Tallman and Gil Doud. "Philip Carney" was originally played by Howard Duff in the pilot with Elliott Lewis in the role of "First Officer Red Gallagher." For subsequent episodes, Lewis moved into the main role, and Ed Max played the first officer. Virginia is credited with two performances in this series, though she may have given additional performances uncredited or undocumented.
Genre: Adventure
General Duration: 30mins
Network(s): Mutual Broadcasting Network, Don Lee, AFRS

Episode(s): "The Boston Geisha and Chesapeake Bay" (July 24, 1947) "Grafter's Fort and the Black Pearl of Galayla Bay" (October 23, 1947)

16. Title: *Dark Venture* (June 6, 1945 – February 24, 1947) was a thriller anthology created by Leonard Reeg and J. Donald Wilson. Episodes are narrated by John Lake. The show ran for fifty-two episodes from 1945 to 1947. Virginia is credited with only one episode of *Dark Venture*, though she may have performed in additional episodes uncredited or undocumented.
Genre: Horror/Mystery Anthology
General Duration: 30mins
Network(s): KGO, ABC, KECA
Episode(s): "Ten Dollar Bill" (August 15, 1947)

17. Title: *Deadline Mystery* (April 20, 1947 – August 24, 1947) was a crime drama directed by Dave Titus. The show follows newspaper man "Lucky Larson" (played by Steve Dunn) in his mystery capers. Sam Edwards, Jack Kruschen, and June Whildey were a few cast regulars. Virginia is credited with only one episode of *Deadline Mystery*, though she may have performed in additional episodes uncredited or undocumented.
Genre: Mystery/Crime Drama
General Duration: 30mins
Network(s): ABC
Episode(s): "Housing Scandal" (August 24, 1947)

18. Title: *In Your Name*
Genre: Drama
General Duration: 15mins
Network(s): Syndicated, American Red Cross
Episode(s): "The Snowman" (February 8, 1948)

19. Title: *The First Nighter Program* (November 27, 1930 – September 27, 1953) was a popular playhouse series that ran for more two decades. The show was hosted by "Mr. First Nighter" played by a number of greats, though Charles P. Hughes was the first, with Don Ameche perhaps the most memorable as "radio's first sex symbol."[109] The show provided audiences of the 1930s, 40s, and 50s a peek into Broadway's opening nightlife in a dramatic (and sometimes comedic) playhouse format. The show was produced and directed by Joseph Ainley, the first husband of Virginia's friend and colleague, Betty Lou Gerson. Virginia is credited with only one episode of *The First Nighter*, though she may have performed in additional episodes uncredited or undocumented.
Genre: Drama/Comedy
General Duration: 30mins
Network(s): CBS
Episode(s): "Love Stranger than Fiction" (February 12, 1948)

20. Title: *Escape* (July 7, 1947 – September 25, 1954) was an adventure series produced by Norman MacDonnell and narrated by Paul Frees and William Conrad with the famous line, "Tired of the everyday grind? Ever dream of a life of romantic adventure? Want to get away from it all? We offer you . . . *escape!*" Virginia performed in several episodes of *Escape*, throughout its seven-year run, though she may have performed in more episodes than credited or documented.
Genre: Adventure
General Duration: 30mins
Network(s): CBS
Episode(s): "Misfortune Isle" (March 21, 1948)
"This Side of Nowhere" (December 3, 1950)
"The Follower" (February 23, 1951)
"The Scarlet Plague" (April 8, 1954)
"An Ordinary Man" (June 3, 1954)

"The Birds" (July 10, 1954)
"The Coward" (August 14, 1954)

21. Title: *Diary of Fate* (December 15, 1947 – August 10, 1948) was a mystery/thriller series narrated by "Fate" (played by Herb Lytton) with the famous opening line, "Heed well you who listen, and remember, there is a page for you in . . . *The Diary of Fate!*" The shows take listeners through the sagas of unfortunate souls who, usually faced with some life-altering decision, discover much to their dismay that "Fate" *always* wins. Virginia is credited with three performances of *Diary of Fate*, though she may have performed in more episodes than credited or documented.
Genre: Mystery/Thriller
General Duration: 30mins
Network(s): CBS, ABC's KECA, syndicated
Episode(s): "Edward Matthews" (March 30, 1948)
"Stanley Becker" (July 27, 1948)
"Darrell James" (August 10, 1948)

22. Title: *All-Star Western Theatre* (August 11, 1946 – January 28, 1949) was a western variety show that combines compelling stories of the Wild West, with country western music by Foy Willing and The Riders of the Purple Sage. Some of the most well-known guests of *All-Sar Western Theatre* were Johnny Mack Brown, Tex Ritter, Hank Williams, and Eddy Arnold. Virginia is credited in only one episode of *All-Star Western Theatre*, though she may have performed in additional episodes either uncredited or undocumented.
Genre: Variety/Western
General Duration: 30mins
Network(s): CBS's KNX, Mutual, syndicated
Episode(s): "Ranch for Sale" (May 8, 1948)

23. Title: *Let George Do It* (October 18, 1946 – September 27, 1954) was a detective drama that follows "George Valentine" in his investigations with the famous opening line, "Personal notice: Danger's my stock in trade. If the job's too tough for you to handle, you've got a job for me, George Valentine." In this series, Virginia most often played "Valentine's" secretary "Claire Brooks" or "Brooksie," though she also voiced several other characters (often in the same script). Fellow actress Frances Robinson first voiced "Brooksie" but was replaced by Virginia after seventy-nine shows. Turnabout is fair play, as Frances briefly replaced Virginia in the role of "Helen Asher" in *Richard Diamond, Private Detective* in 1950.

Genre: Detective Drama

General Duration: 30mins

Network(s): Mutual Broadcasting Network (Don Lee)

Episode(s): "The Unfit Mother Case/Problem Child" (June 21, 1948)

"Johnathan Thorpe Case/Murder Me Twice" (July 5, 1948)

"Cry Murder" (July 19, 1948)

"Ghost on Bliss Terrace" (August 16, 1948)

"The Impatient Redhead" (September 6, 1948)

"Murder and One to Go" (January 3, 1949)

"One Against a City" (February 7, 1949)

"Journey into Hate" (February 21, 1949)

"The Roundabout Murder" (March 7, 1949)

"Lady in Distress" (April 25, 1949)

"Perfect Albi" (August 1, 1949)

"End of Summer" (August 29, 1949)

"Every Shot Counts" (October 31, 1949)

"Sweet Poison" (November 21,1949)

"Partner in Panama" (December 12, 1949)

"Follow That Train" (December 19, 1949)

"Snow Blind" (December 26, 1949)

"Needle in the Haystack" (January 2, 1950)

"The Silent Waterfall" (January 9, 1950)

"Juniper Lane" (January 16, 1950)

"The Floaters" (January 23, 1950)

"The Ugly Duckling" (January 30, 1950)

"The Old Style" (February 6, 1950)

"Go Jump in the Lake" (February 13, 1950)

"The Tears of Sorrow" (March 27, 1950)

"The Brothers McIntosh" (April 3, 1950)

"Portrait by Pricilla" (April 10, 1950)

"Mixup in La Cruza" (April 17, 1950)

"Death Begins at 45" (April 24, 1950)

"The Chair of Humanities" (May 1, 1950)

"Picture with a Black Frame" (May 8, 1950)

"The Ant Hill" (May 15, 1950)

"Portuguese Cove" (May 22, 1950)

"Sudden Storm" (May 29, 1950)

"The Witch of Mill Hollow" (June 5, 1950)

"The Iron Cat" (June 12, 1950)

"Solo in Whispers" (June 19, 1950)

"Most Likely to Die" (June 26, 1950)

"The Scream of the Eagle" (July 3, 1950)

"Island in the Desert" (July 10, 1950)

"Eleven O'clock" (July 17, 1950)

"The Voice of the Giant" (July 31, 1950)

"Sweet are the Uses of Publicity" (August 7, 1950)

"The High Price of a Penny" (August 14, 1950)

"The Treasure of Millie's Wharf" (August 21, 1950)

"High Card" (August 28, 1950)

"Second Degree Affection" (September 4, 1950)

"The White Elephant" (September 11, 1950)

"Cover for an Hour" (September 18, 1950)

"Tag! You're It" (September 25, 1950)

"The House that Jack Built" (October 2, 1950)

"The Spider and the Fly" (October 9, 1950)
"It's a Mystery to me" (October 16, 1950)
"The Hand in the Coconut" (October 23, 1950)
"Sedan from the City" (October 30, 1950)
"Cause for Thanksgiving" (November 20, 1950)
"Nothing but the Truth" (November 27, 1950)
"And Hope to Die" (December 4, 1950)
"The Bookworm Turns" (December 11, 1950)
"Opportunity Knocks Twice" (December 18, 1950)
"Santa Claus in Glass" (December 25, 1950)
"The Man Behind the Frame" (January 8, 1951)
"Tune on a Triangle" (January 15, 1951)
"Knock on Wood" (January 22, 1951)
"Christmas in January" (January 29, 1951)
"Tongalani" (February 5, 1951)
"The Marauder" (February 12, 1951)
"How Guilty Can You Get?" (February 19, 1951)
"See Me Once, You've Seen Me Twice" (February 26, 1951)
"The Public Eye" (March 5, 1951)
"The Prairie Dog" (March 12, 1951)
"Murder for Two" (March 19, 1951)
"The Eight Ball" (April 2, 1951)
"Uncle Harry's Bones" (April 9, 1951)
"The Noose Hangs High" (April 16, 1951)
"Sabotage" (April 23, 1951)
"The Discovery of Ponce the Lion" (April 30, 1951)
"Big Brother" (May 21, 1951)
"Sucker Stunt" (June 11, 1951)
"The Man from French Guiana" (June 25, 1951)
"Is Everybody Happy?" (July 2, 1951)
"Lefty's Angel" (July 9, 1951)
"What Became of Terry Cable?" (July 16, 1951)
"Drop Dead?" (July 23, 1951)

"The Fearless Clown" (August 13, 1951)

"Deal Me Out and I'll Deal You In" (August 20, 1951)

"Murder on Vacation" (August 27, 1951)

"Blue Plate Special" (September 3, 1951)

"Framed for Hanging" (September 24, 1951)

"No Way Out" (October 1, 1951)

"A Crime Too Simple" (October 22, 1951)

"The Woman in Black" (October 29, 1951)

"Destination: Danger" (November 19, 1951)

"The Meddler" (November 26, 1951)

"Off the Record" (December 3, 1951)

"The Last Payoff" (December 10, 1951)

"Stolen Goods" (December 17, 1951)

"A School of Sharks" (January 7, 1952)

"The Bad Little God" (January 14, 1952)

"A Matter of Honor" (January 21, 1952)

"The Common Denominator" (January 28, 1952)

"Surprise! Surprise!" (February 4, 1952)

"Cortez Island" (February 11, 1952)

"The Symbol Three" (February 18, 1952)

"Starlight Pier" (February 25, 1952)

"The Deadly Pines" (March 3, 1952)

"The Darkest Shadow" (March 10, 1952)

"Three Times and Out" (March 17, 1952)

"The Graystone Ghost" (March 24, 1952)

"The Forgotten Murder" (April 14, 1952)

"War Maneuver" (April 21, 1952)

"Operation Europa" (April 28, 1952)

"Come to the Casbah" (May 5, 1952)

"The Iron Hat" (May 12, 1952)

"It Happened on Friday" (May 19, 1952)

"The Violent Van Pattens" (June 9, 1952)

"The Mystic" (June 16, 1952)

"There Ain't No Justice" (June 17, 1952)
"Portrait of a Suicide" (June 24, 1952)
"Tonight the Mayhem's Going to be Different" (July 8, 1952)
"Seed of Destruction" (August 18, 1952)
"Human Nature" (September 15, 1952)
"Once a Crook" (September 22, 1952)
"Chance and Probability" (September 29, 1952)
"The Four Seasons" (October 6, 1952)
"The Dead of Night" (October 13, 1952)
"Calle Reposo" (October 20, 1952)
"Dead on Arrival" (November 10, 1952)
"The Stand-In" (November 17, 1952)
"Red Spots in the Snow" (November 25, 1952)
"This Ain't No Way to Run a Railroad" (December 2, 1952)

24. Title: *Command Performance* (July 13, 1948)
Genre: Comedy
General Duration: 30mins
Network(s): AFRS

25. Title: *We Care* (1948) was a fifteen-minute drama sponsored by the nonprofit food agency CARE. The show's host was Douglas Fairbanks, Jr., who at the time was chair of the Share Through Care Committee. Scripts were delivered around solicitation of aid for those left hungry by the war. The show was written by Milton Geiger, directed by William P. Rousseau, and produced by Don Sharp. Virginia is credited with one performance in *We Care*.
Genre: Drama
General Duration: 15mins
Network(s): ABC
Episode(s): "The Bimbo from Limbo" (September 26, 1948)

26. Title: *The New Adventures of Philip Marlowe/The Adventures of Philip Marlowe* (June 17, 1947 – September 15, 1951) was a detective drama created by Raymond Chandler. Initially starring Van Heflin as the tough, street-smart "Philip Marlowe," in 1948, the role was taken over by Gerald Mohr (except in one episode in which William Conrad voiced "Marlowe" in "The Anniversary Gift" in 1950) under Norman MacDonnell as director and producer. Virginia performed in several episodes of *The Adventures of Philip Marlowe* in various roles.

Genre: Detective Drama

General Duration: 30mins

Network(s): NBC & CBS

Episode(s): "The Persian Slippers" (October 3, 1948)

"The Restless Day" (January 8, 1949)

"The Lonesome Reunion" (February 12, 1949)

"The Friend from Detroit" (March 5, 1949)

"The Feminine Touch" (May 7, 1949)

"The Kid on the Corner" (December 3, 1949)

"The Man on the Roof" (April 4, 1950)

"The Hiding Place" (May 9, 1950)

"The White Carnation" (September 22, 1950)

"Life Can be Murder" (July 21, 1951)

27. Title: *The Unexpected* (April 11, 1948 – December 26, 1948) was a thriller series, albeit short-lived while on air, that delivers dark, dramatic tales full of suspense until their shocking and *unexpected* conclusions – all in fifteen minutes! Written by Frank Burt and directed by Frank K. Danzig, the show's infamous slogan was, "A secret future, a hidden destiny, waiting for you . . . perhaps in just a moment you too will meet the unexpected!"[110] Virginia is credited with two performances in *The Unexpected*, though she may have performed in additional episodes uncredited or undocumented.

Genre: Thriller

General Duration: 15mins
Network(s): Mutual Broadcasting Network, Don Lee, syndicated
Episode(s): "Handle with Care" (November 7, 1948)
"Heard but Not Seen" (December 5, 1948)

28. **Title:** *Your Movietown Radio Theatre* (August 29, 1947 – 1951) was a series hosted by Les Mitchell and introduced by a different star each episode. After the comedy or drama presented, the guest star was briefly interviewed by Mitchell at the conclusion. Most scripts were of dramatic or comedic nature featuring many "it people" of the day including Eddie Albert, Cathy Lewis, Kirk Douglas, Jane Wyatt, and of course Virginia Gregg.
Genre: Anthology
General Duration: 30mins
Network(s): Syndicated, ZIV Productions
Episode(s): *Title Unknown* (1948)
"Schizo-Scherzo" (June 17, 1951)

29. **Title:** *The Children's Hour, But Not for Children* (1949) was a docudrama produced in tandem with the Los Angeles Tenth District Parent-Teacher Association to herald the need for higher quality media options for children in 1940s. The presentation serves as a critique of the popular children's media at that time in terms of quality, educational value, and age-appropriateness.[111]
Genre: Docudrama
General Duration: 30mins
Network(s): KFI, syndicated
Episode(s): "The Children's Hour, but not for Children" (January 10, 1949)

30. **Title:** *Screen Director's Guild Assignment/Playhouse* (January 9, 1949 – September 28, 1951) was an anthology series that adapted films to radio with the original film directors often introducing

the adaptation. Many of the original stars such as Bette Davis, John Wayne, Lucille Ball, Joseph Cotten, and Alfred Hitchcock performed in the radio adaptations of their popular films of the 1940s and 1950s in the *Screen Director's Guild Assignment*, later known as the *Screen Director's Playhouse*. Virginia had a number of supporting roles in this series, playing a variety of characters.

Genre: Anthology

General Duration: 30mins/60mins

Network(s): NBC

Episode(s): "Let's Live a Little" (January 16, 1949)

"Suddenly It's Spring" (March 27, 1949)

"The Best Years of our Lives" (April 17, 1949)

"Appointment for Love" (August 26, 1949)

"Don't Trust Your Husband" (September 23, 1949)

"Pitfall" (October 17, 1949)

"Magic Town" (January 6, 1950)

"Lucky Jordan" (February 8, 1951)

"Caged" (August 2, 1951)

31. Title: *Skippy Hollywood Theatre* (1941 – 1950) was one of the few pre-recorded shows in the 1940s. It was produced by Les Mitchell and C.P. "Chick" MacGregor and directed by Madeline Mitchell. In prerecording, the show avoided the potential flaws of live performances in its syndication of dramatic, comedic, and romantic scripts with MacGregor interviewing the featured stars of each episode much like Cecil B. DeMille did on *Lux Radio Theatre* after its New York to Hollywood move in 1936. The show's sponsor was "Skippy Peanut Butter," giving it its name for the fifty-two-show run. Virginia is credited in only one episode of *Skippy Hollywood Theatre*, though she may have performed in additional episodes either uncredited or undocumented.

Genre: Anthology

General Duration: 30mins

Network(s): ABC, CBS, NBC, The Blue Network
Episode(s): "Schizo-Scherzo" (February 25, 1949)

32. Title: *Pat Novak for Hire* (August 1946 – November 30, 1947 & February 13, 1949 – June 25, 1949) began as *The Gallenkamp Shoe Show* at KGO and ran for two different stretches as a crime drama set in San Francisco. Jack Webb originally played the street-savvy "Pat Novak" who is always on a caper for a dollar. Ben Morris replaced Webb in the role in 1947, though Webb reprised the role for a few episodes in 1949 before *Dragnet's* boom. Virginia is credited in only one episode of *Pat Novak for Hire*, though she likely performed in additional episodes either uncredited or undocumented.
Genre: Crime Drama
General Duration: 30mins
Network(s): KGO & ABC
Episode(s): "Fleet Lady" (March 6, 1949)

33. Title: *Richard Diamond, Private Detective* (April 24, 1949 – September 20, 1953) was a detective drama like no other heard on the air waves in the 1940s and 1950s, starring Dick Powell as "Richard Diamond," the charming, quick-witted singing gumshoe. "Diamond" solves all types of cases with great cunning and levity on the half hour show, and even has time enough to sing a number around the piano at the end of most episodes. Virginia plays the recurring role of Diamond's ever-understanding Park Avenue girl-friend, "Helen Asher" for the majority of the show's run along with various supporting roles often within the same script. Fellow actress Frances Robinson took over the role of "Helen Asher" during a brief absence of Virginia's in 1950. Frances was a fine actress in her own right, but the on-air chemistry between Virginia and Dick simply couldn't be replicated. Virginia was absent from *Diamond* from January 1950 until April 1950, and upon her return in "The Man Who Hated Women" recorded on April 12, 1950, she was credited as "Virginia del Valle" – her legal, married name at the time. She resumed her stage name "Gregg" after only a couple of episodes ("Mrs. X Can't Find her Husband" recorded on June 14, 1950) Virginia's second husband Jaime del Valle directed several *Diamond* episodes.

Genre: Detective drama

General Duration: 30mins

Network(s): NBC, ABC, & CBS

Episode(s): "Diamond in the Rough – The Richard Barton Case" (April 24, 1949 or May 1, 1949)

"The Ralph Chase Case" (May 15, 1949)

"The Stolen Purse" (May 22, 1949)

"The Betty Moran Case" (May 29, 1949)

"The Bertram Kalmus Case" (June 5, 1949)

"The Fred Sears Murder Case" (June 19, 1949)

"The Tom Waxman Bombing Case" (June 26, 1949)

"The Bloody Hat Case" (July 2, 1949)

"Charles Walsh & Bob Wells" (July 9, 1949)

"The Man Who Hated Women" (July 16, 1949)

"The Martin Hyers Case" (July 23, 1949)

"Lynn Knight Wants Protection" (August 6, 1949)

"The Jean Cooper Murder Case/The Tom Cook Manslaughter Case" (August 20, 1949)

"The Eddie Garrett Case" (August 27, 1949)

"The Harry Baker Case" (September 3, 1949)

"The Van Dyke Séance" (September 10, 1949)

"Jerome J. Jerome" (September 17, 1949)

"The Two Thousand Dollar Bundle" (September 24, 1949)

"The Gibson Murder Case" (October 8, 1949)

"Newspaper Boy and Counterfeit Bills" (October 15, 1949)

"The Rene Benet Protection Case" (October 22, 1949)

"The Bill Kirby Murder Case" (October 29, 1949)

"Singing Critic/Rival Shamus" (November 5, 1949)

"$50,000 in Diamonds Stolen" (November 12, 1949)

"The Leon Jacoby Case" (November 19, 1949)

"William Carter and Helena Fisher" (November 26, 1949)

"The Ruby Idol Case" (December 3, 1949)

"The Julia Bates Case: The House of Mystery Case" (December 10, 1949)

"The John Blackwell Case" (December 17, 1949)

"A Christmas Carol" (December 24, 1949)

"The Thomas Jason Case" (December 31, 1949)

"Butcher's Protection Racket" (January 7, 1950)

"The Cathy Victor Case" (January 15, 1950)

"The Man Who Hated Women" (April 12, 1950)

"Messenger Service, Patty Clark" (April 19, 1950)

"The Ralph Baxter Case" (April 26, 1950)

"The William Carnes Case" (June 14, 1950)

"Mrs. X Can't Find Her Husband" (June 21, 1950)

"The Mary Bellman Case" (June 28, 1950)

"The Mike Burton Case" (July 5, 1950)

"Ice Pick Murder" (July 12, 1950)

"The William B. Holland Case" (July 19, 1950)

"Martha Campbell Kidnapped" (July 26, 1950)

"The Fixed Fight Case: Max Farmer, Boxer" (August 2, 1950)

"The Edna Wolfe Case" (August 9, 1950)

"The Carnival Case" (August 16, 1950)

"The Farmer-Evans Murder Case" (August 23, 1950)

"Big Foot Grafton Case" (August 30, 1950)

"The Misplaced Laundry Case" (September 6, 1950)

"The George Lexington Case" (September 13, 1950)

"The Bald Head Case" (September 20, 1950)

"The Oklahoma Cowboy Murder" (September 27, 1950)

"The Pete Rocco Case" (October 4, 1950)

"The Homing Pigeon Case" (October 11, 1950)

"Lt. Levinson Kidnapped" (October 18, 1950)

"The Rifle Case" (October 25, 1950)

"Traffic Ticket Case" (November 1, 1950)

"Dead Man's Letter" (November 8, 1950)

"The Mona Lisa Murder" (November 15, 1950)

"The Cover-Up Murders: 8 O'clock Killer" (November 22, 1950)

"The Calypso" (November 29, 1950)

"Missing Night Watchman" (December 6, 1950)

"The Chapel Hill Case" (December 13, 1950)

"Nathan Beeker Case" (January 5, 1951)

"The Marilyn Conners Case" (January 12, 1951)

"The Man with the Scar/Buried Treasure" (January 19, 1951)

"The Rawlins Case" (January 26, 1951)

"The Caspary Case" (February 2, 1951)

"The Blue Serge Suit" (February 9, 1951)

"The Grey Man" (February 16, 1951)

"The Lady in Distress" (February 23, 1951)

"The Red Rose" (March 2, 1951)

"The Butcher Shop" (March 9, 1951)

"Monsieur Bouchon" (March 16, 1951)

"Little Chiva" (March 23, 1951)

"The Carnival" (March 30, 1951)

"The Dead Heiress" (April 6, 1951)

"The Right Fix" (April 13, 1951)

"Tug" (April 20, 1951)

"The Barrio Case" (April 27, 1951)

"The Boy Who Made Bad" (May 4, 1951)

"Danny Denver" (May 11, 1951)

"Lonely Hearts" (May 18, 1951)

"Longest Short-Cut in the World" (May 25, 1951)

"The Montelli Case" (June 1, 1951)

"The Darby Affair" (June 8, 1951)

"The Poise Magazine Story" (June 15, 1951)

"The Masters Case" (June 22, 1951)

"The Monkey Man" (June 29, 1951)
"The Lou Turner Case" (October 12, 1951)
"The Jackson Case" (October 19, 1951)
"Registered Letter" (October 26, 1951)
"The Bowery Case" (November 2, 1951)
"Buried Treasure" (November 9, 1951)
"The Hollywood Story" (November 16, 1951)
"The Mickey Farmer Case" (November 23, 1951)
"Goodnight to Nocturne" (November 30, 1951)
"The Brown Envelope Case" (December 7, 1951)
"The Night Club Case" (December 14, 1951)
"The Christmas Show" (December 21, 1951)
"The Plaid Overcoat Case" (December 28, 1951)
"The Merry-Go-Round Case" (January 4, 1952)
"The White Cow Case" (January 11, 1952)
"The Simpson Case" (January 18, 1952)
"The Al Brenners Case" (January 25, 1952)
"The Garrabaldi Case" (February 1, 1952)
"The Eddie Burke Case" (February 8, 1952)
"The Jerry Wilson Incident" (February 15, 1952)
"The Miami Case" (February 22, 1952)
"The Hired Killer Case" (February 29, 1952)
"Winthrop and Company" (March 7, 1952)
"The Dixon Case" (March 14, 1952)
"The Hank Burton Case" (March 21, 1952)
"Mr. Walker's Problem" (March 28, 1952)
"The Enigma of Big Ed" (April 4, 1952)
"The Fred Montelli Affair" (April 11, 1952)
"The Jack Murphy Case" (April 18, 1952)
"The Trixie Hart Case" (April 25, 1952)
"The Eddie Ducheck Case" (May 2, 1952)
"The Barber Shop Case" (May 9, 1952)
"The George Dale Case" (May 23, 1952)

"The Carpenter Case" (May 30, 1952)
"The Black Doll Case" (June 6, 1952)
"The Frank Taylor Case" (June 13, 1952)
"The Ed Lloyd Case" (June 20, 1952)
"The Danny Revere Case" (June 27, 1952)

34. Title: *The Adventures of Frank Race* (May 1, 1949 – February 19, 1950) tells stories of insurance investigator "Frank Race" (first played by Tom Collins, then Paul Debrov) and his partner "Marc Donovan" (played by Tony Barrett) who find themselves mixed up in the thrills of investigating colorful criminals in underworld operations. Virginia is credited in three episodes of *Frank Race*, though she may have performed in additional episodes uncredited or undocumented.
Genre: Adventure
General Duration: 30mins
Network(s): WINS, syndicated by Bruce Eells Productions
Episode(s): "The Juvenile Passenger" (July 3, 1949)
"The Silent Heart" (July 17, 1949)
"Undecided Bride" (December 18, 1949)

35. Title: *California Caravan* (1947 – 1949) was a documentary series about California's history told through dramatic scripts by many favorites of the day like Virginia Gregg, Paul Frees, Jerry Farber, Lou Holtz, and Herb Vigran.
Genre: Documentary Series
General Duration: 30mins
Network(s): Mutual Broadcasting Network, Don Lee
Episode(s): "The Saga of Charlie Parkhurst" (September 29, 1949)
"The Poet of Oakland" (1950)

36. Title: *NBC University Theatre* (July 30, 1948 – February 14, 1951) was a radio anthology that presents adaptations of classic novels by such greats as Ernest Hemingway, John Steinbeck, and Sinclair Lewis. While the show was generally well received initially, later in 1949, producers realized the word "university" in the show's title might have been a bit intimidating to some listeners, so the title was changed to *NBC Theatre*. Virginia is only credited in one episode of *NBC University Theatre*, though she may have performed in additional episodes either uncredited or undocumented.

Genre: Anthology

General Duration: 30mins/60mins

Network(s): WMAQ & NBC

Episode(s): "The House of Mirth" (October 9, 1949)

37. Title: *The Count of Monte Cristo* (1944 – 1952) was an adventure series based on a novel by the same name written by Alexandre Dumas and adapted to radio by Anthony Ellis. Set in France in the 1830s, Carlton Young stars as "Edmond Dantes," who becomes Count after escaping a falsely handed-down prison sentence. Anne Stone plays Dantes' love interest, "Marie Duchene." Virginia played a number of supporting roles in this adventure favorite, and her second husband Jaime del Valle directed the series after its move to Mutual in 1949. Virginia is credited with one performance below, though she most likely performed in many additional episodes either uncredited or undocumented.

Genre: Adventure/Drama

General Duration: 60mins

Network(s): Don Lee, Mutual, Syndicated

Episode(s): "Black Widow" (July 8, 1946)

38. Title: *Broadway Is My Beat* (February 27, 1949 – August 1, 1954) was a 1940s- 1950s series of New York police detective "Danny Clover's" adventures. It was written by Morton Fine and David Friedkin and produced and directed by Elliot Lewis. Larry Thor plays "Danny Clover" and Charles Calvert plays "Detective Tartaglia."

Virginia performed in several supporting roles during the show's five-year run.

Genre: Detective Drama

General Duration: 30mins

Network(s): CBS

Episode(s): "The Tori Jones Case" (December 10, 1949)

"The Julie Dixon Case/A Cinderella Girl" (February 10, 1950)

"The Dion Hartley Story" (February 17, 1950)

"The Ben Justin Case" (December 8, 1950)

"The Harry Foster Case" (May 5, 1951)

"The Eve Hunter Case" (March 8, 1952)

39. Title: *Night Beat* (February 6, 1950 – September 25, 1952) was a crime drama that shared the exciting encounters of veteran *Chicago Star* reporter "Randy Stone" (Frank Lovejoy). Produced and directed by Warren Lewis, the show may be best remembered by its famous line, "Sometimes the best stories a reporter gets are the ones he can't print." Virginia plays various supporting roles in this series, perhaps more than credited or documented.

Genre: Crime Drama

General Duration: 30mins

Network(s): NBC

Episode(s): "The Elevator Caper" (audition) (January 13, 1950)

"The Elevator Caper" (May 8, 1950)

"Will of Mrs. Orloff" (June 1, 1951)

"The Search for Fred" (June 8, 1951)

40. Title: *Yours Truly, Johnny Dollar* (February 11, 1949 – September 30, 1962) was an immensely popular crime show in the 1940s-1960s about the expense account escapades of insurance investigator "Johnny Dollar." "Dollar" took on the usual cases of the average detective show: murders, jewel robberies, blackmail, but his approach was a novelty among the other shows of the day. He was a heroic playing it cagey until justice was served – to the penny – signing off at the end of every episode with, "End of report. Yours truly, Johnny Dollar." The role of "Dollar" was assumed by a number of well-knowns including Dick Powell, Charles Russell, Edmond O'Brien, John Lund, Bob Bailey, Robert Readick, and Mandel Kramer, though Bob Bailey's artistic interpretation of "Dollar" might be the most memorable. *Yours Truly, Johnny Dollar* was a flagship show for both Virginia and her second husband Jaime del Valle. Virginia played *Johnny Dollar* weekly during the 1950s in the regular role of "Dollar's" girlfriend "Betty Lewis," as well as in various supporting roles. del Valle produced and directed *Johnny Dollar* for quite a stretch throughout its thirteen-year run.

Genre: Crime

General Duration: 30mins

Network(s): CBS

Episode(s): "The Archeologist" (February 24, 1950)
"The Story of the Big Red School" (April 4, 1950)
"The Pearl Carrassa Matter" (April 25, 1950)
"The Earl Chadwick Matter" (May 23, 1950)
"The Caligio Diamond Matter" (June 8, 1950)
"The London Matter" (June 22, 1950)
"The Calgary Matter" (July 13, 1950)
"The Blood River Matter" (August 3, 1950)
"The Mickey McQueen Matter" (August 17, 1950)
"The Virginia Beach Matter" (August 31, 1950)
"The Yankee Pride Matter" (October 14, 1950)
"The Joan Sebastian Matter" (October 28, 1950)
"The Nora Faulkner Matter" (November 18, 1950)
"The Port-O-Call Matter" (January 13, 1951)
"The Jackie Cleaver Story" (March 31, 1951)
"The Virginia Towne Matter" (April 25, 1951)
"Month-End Raid Matter" (April 28, 1951)
"The Soderberry, Maine Matter" (June 2, 1951)

"The George Farmer Matter" (June 9, 1951)

"The Arthur Boldrick Matter" (June 16, 1951)

"The Malcolm Wish, MD Matter" (June 20, 1951)

"The Hatchet House Theft Matter" (June 27, 1951)

"The Alonzo Chapman Matter" (July 4, 1951)

"The Fair-Way Matter" (July 11, 1951)

"The Horace Lockhart Matter" (August 1, 1951)

"The Lucky Costa Matter" (August 15, 1951)

"The Tolhurst Theft Matter" (October 27, 1951)

"The Hannibal Murphy Matter" (November 3, 1951)

"The Baskerville Matter" (November 10, 1951)

"The Youngstown Credit Group Matter" (December 8, 1951)

"The Alma Scott Matter" (December 29, 1951)

"The Amelia Harwell Matter" (July 2, 1952)

"The Marigold Matter" (January 23, 1953)

"The La Tourette Matter" (February 20, 1953)

"The Jean Maxwell Matter" (March 6, 1953)

"The Birdy Baskerville Matter" (March 10, 1953)

"The Syndicate Matter" (March 24, 1953)

"The Madison Matter" (April 14, 1953)

"The San Antonio Matter" (April 28, 1953)

"The Rochester Theft Matter" (May 12, 1953)

"The Brisbane Fraud Matter" (May 26, 1953)

"The Jones Matter" (June 30, 1953)

"The Shayne Bombing Matter" (July 14, 1953)

"The Allen Saxton Matter" (October 20, 1953)

"The Independent Diamond Traders Matter" (November 24, 1953)

"The Celia Woodstock Matter" (January 12, 1954)

"The Harpooned Angler Matter" (February 9, 1954)

"The Uncut Canary Matter" (February 16, 1954)

"The Road Test Matter" (March 2, 1954)

"The Terrified Tuan Matter" (March 9, 1954)

"The Berlin Matter" (March 16, 1954)

"The Nathan Swing Matter" (April 20, 1954)
"The Punctilious Firebug Matter" (May 25, 1954)
"The Jan Bruegal Matter" (July 6, 1954)
"The McCormack Matter 1" (October 3, 1955)
"The McCormack Matter 2" (October 4, 1955)
"The McCormack Matter 3" (October 5, 1955)
"The McCormack Matter 4" (October 6, 1955)
"The McCormack Matter 5" (October 7, 1955)
"The Molly K Matter 1" (October 10, 1955)
"The Molly K Matter 2" (October 11, 1955)
"The Molly K Matter 3" (October 12, 1955)
"The Molly K Matter 4" (October 13, 1955)
"The Molly K Matter 5" (October 14, 1955)
"The Alvin Summers Matter 1" (October 24, 1955)
"The Alvin Summers Matter 2" (October 25, 1955)
"The Alvin Summers Matter 3" (October 26, 1955)
"The Alvin Summers Matter 4" (October 27, 1955)
"The Alvin Summers Matter 5" (October 28, 1955)
"The Broderick Matter 1" (November 14, 1955)
"The Broderick Matter 2" (November 15, 1955)
"The Broderick Matter 3" (November 16, 1955)
"The Broderick Matter 4" (November 17, 1955)
"The Broderick Matter 5" (November 18, 1955)
"The Amy Bradshaw Matter 1" (November 21, 1955)
"The Amy Bradshaw Matter 2" (November 22, 1955)
"The Amy Bradshaw Matter 3" (November 23, 1955)
"The Amy Bradshaw Matter 4" (November 24, 1955)
"The Amy Bradshaw Matter 5" (November 25, 1955)
"The Cronin Matter 1" (December 5, 1955)
"The Cronin Matter 2" (December 6, 1955)
"The Cronin Matter 3" (December 7, 1955)
"The Cronin Matter 4" (December 8, 1955)
"The Cronin Matter 5" (December 9, 1955)

"The Nick Shurn Matter 1" (December 19, 1955)
"The Nick Shurn Matter 2" (December 20, 1955)
"The Nick Shurn Matter 3" (December 21, 1955)
"The Nick Shurn Matter 4" (December 22, 1955)
"The Nick Shurn Matter 5" (December 23, 1955)
"The Caylin Matter 1" (January 2, 1956)
"The Caylin Matter 2" (January 3, 1956)
"The Caylin Matter 3" (January 4, 1956)
"The Caylin Matter 4" (January 5, 1956)
"The Caylin Matter 5" (January 6, 1956)
"The Flight Six Matter 1" (January 30, 1956)
"The Flight Six Matter 2" (January 31, 1956)
"The Flight Six Matter 3" (February 1, 1956)
"The Flight Six Matter 4" (February 2, 1956)
"The Flight Six Matter 5" (February 3, 1956)
"The Jolly Roger Fraud 1" (March 19, 1956)
"The Jolly Roger Fraud 4" (March 22, 1956)
"The Jolly Roger Fraud 5" (March 23, 1956)
"The La Marr Matter 1" (March 26, 1956)
"The La Marr Matter 2" (March 27, 1956)
"The La Marr Matter 3" (March 28, 1956)
"The La Marr Matter 4" (March 29, 1956)
"The La Marr Matter 5" (March 30, 1956)
"The Shepherd Matter 1" (April 16, 1956)
"The Shepherd Matter 2" (April 17, 1956)
"The Shepherd Matter 3" (April 18, 1956)
"The Shepherd Matter 4" (April 19, 1956)
"The Shepherd Matter 5" (April 20, 1956)
"The Lonely Hearts Matter 1" (April 23, 1956)
"The Lonely Hearts Matter 2" (April 24, 1956)
"The Lonely Hearts Matter 3" (April 25, 1956)
"The Lonely Hearts Matter 4" (April 26, 1956)
"The Lonely Hearts Matter 5" (April 27, 1956)

"The Callicles Matter 1" (April 30, 1956)
"The Callicles Matter 2" (May 1, 1956)
"The Callicles Matter 3" (May 2, 1956)
"The Callicles Matter 4" (May 3, 1956)
"The Callicles Matter 5" (May 4, 1956)
"The Matter of the Medium: Well-Done 1" (May 14, 1956)
"The Matter of the Medium: Well-Done 2" (May 15, 1956)
"The Matter of the Medium: Well-Done 3" (May 16, 1956)
"The Matter of the Medium: Well-Done 4" (May 17, 1956)
"The Matter of the Medium: Well-Done 5" (May 18, 1956)
"The Tears of Night Matter 1" (May 21, 1956)
"The Tears of Night Matter 2" (May 22, 1956)
"The Tears of Night Matter 3" (May 23, 1956)
"The Tears of Night Matter 4" (May 24, 1956)
"The Tears of Night Matter 5" (May 25, 1956)
"The Laughing Matter 1" (June 11, 1956)
"The Laughing Matter 2" (June 12, 1956)
"The Laughing Matter 3" (June 13, 1956)
"The Laughing Matter 4" (June 14, 1956)
"The Laughing Matter 5" (June 15, 1956)
"The Long Shot Matter 1" (June 25, 1956)
"The Long Shot Matter 2" (June 26, 1956)
"The Long Shot Matter 3" (June 27, 1956)
"The Long Shot Matter 4" (June 28, 1956)
"The Long Shot Matter 5" (June 29, 1956)
"The Midas Touch Matter 1" (July 2, 1956)
"The Midas Touch Matter 2" (July 3, 1956)
"The Midas Touch Matter 3" (July 4, 1956)
"The Midas Touch Matter 4" (July 5, 1956)
"The Midas Touch Matter 5" (July 6, 1956)
"The Sea Legs Matter 1" (July 30, 1956)
"The Sea Legs Matter 2" (July 31, 1956)
"The Sea Legs Matter 3" (August 1, 1956)

"The Sea Legs Matter 4" (August 2, 1956)
"The Sea Legs Matter 5" (August 3, 1956)
"The Alder Matter 1" (August 6, 1956)
"The Alder Matter 2" (August 7, 1956)
"The Alder Matter 3" (August 8, 1956)
"The Alder Matter 4" (August 9, 1956)
"The Alder Matter 5" (August 10, 1956)
"The Kranesburg Matter 1" (August 24, 1956)
"The Kranesburg Matter 2" (August 27, 1956)
"The Kranesburg Matter 3" (August 28, 1956)
"The Kranesburg Matter 4" (August 29, 1956)
"The Kranesburg Matter 5" (August 30, 1956)
"The Kranesburg Matter 6" (August 31, 1956)
"The Confidential Matter 1" (September 10, 1956)
"The Confidential Matter 2" (September 11, 1956)
"The Confidential Matter 3" (September 12, 1956)
"The Confidential Matter 4" (September 13, 1956)
"The Confidential Matter 5" (September 14, 1956)
"The Imperfect Alibi Matter 1" (September 17, 1956)
"The Imperfect Alibi Matter 2" (September 18, 1956)
"The Imperfect Alibi Matter 3" (September 19, 1956)
"The Imperfect Alibi Matter 4" (September 20, 1956)
"The Imperfect Alibi Matter 5" (September 21, 1956)
"The Meg's Place Matter 1" (September 24, 1956)
"The Meg's Place Matter 2" (September 25, 1956)
"The Meg's Place Matter 3" (September 26, 1956)
"The Meg's Place Matter 4" (September 27, 1956)
"The Meg's Place Matter 5" (September 28, 1956)
"The Phantom Chase Matter 1" (October 15, 1956)
"The Phantom Chase Matter 2" (October 16, 1956)
"The Phantom Chase Matter 3" (October 17, 1956)
"The Phantom Chase Matter 4" (October 18, 1956)
"The Phantom Chase Matter 5" (October 19, 1956)

"The Phantom Chase Matter 6" (October 22, 1956)
"The Phantom Chase Matter 7" (October 23, 1956)
"The Phantom Chase Matter 8" (October 24, 1956)
"The Phantom Chase Matter 9" (October 25, 1956)
"The Silent Queen Matter 1" (October 29, 1956)
"The Silent Queen Matter 2" (October 30, 1956)
"The Silent Queen Matter 3" (October 31, 1956)
"The Silent Queen Matter 4" (November 1, 1956)
"The Silent Queen Matter 5" (November 2, 1956)
"The Big Scoop Matter" (November 11, 1956)
"The Markham Matter" (November 18, 1956)
"The Royal Street Matter" (November 25, 1956)
"The Burning Car Matter" (December 9, 1956)
"The Rasmussen Matter" (December 16, 1956)
"The Ellen Dear Matter" (January 6, 1957)
"The De Salle Matter" (January 13, 1957)
"The Kirby Will Matter" (February 3, 1957)
"The Clever Chemist Matter" (March 17, 1957)
"The Moonshine Murder Matter" (March 31, 1957)
"The Ming Toy Murphy Matter" (April 14, 1957)
"The Melancholy Memory Matter" (April 28, 1957)
"The Peerless Fire Matter" (May 5, 1957)
"The Michael Meany Mirage Matter" (May 19, 1957)
"The Mason-Dixon Mismatch Matter" (June 9, 1957)
"The Funny Money Matter" (June 30, 1957)
"The Heatherstone Players Matter" (July 14, 1957)
"The Wayward Widow Matter" (August 4, 1957)
"The Poor Little Rich Girl Matter" (September 1, 1957)
"The Bum Steer Matter" (October 6, 1957)
"The Silver Belle Matter" (October 13, 1957)
"The Model Picture Matter" (November 3, 1957)
"The Price of Fame Matter" (February 2, 1958)
"The Time and Tide Matter" (February 16, 1958)

"The Durango Laramie Matter" (February 23, 1958)
"The Denver Dispersal Matter" (March 23, 1958)
"The Eastern-Western Matter" (April 6, 1958)
"The Wayward Money Matter" (April 13, 1958)
"The Ghost to Ghost Matter" (May 18, 1958)
"The Delectable Damsel Matter" (June 15, 1958)
"The Ugly Pattern Matter" (June 29, 1958)
"The Mojave Red Matter 2" (July 20, 1958)
"The Noxious Needle Matter" (August 24, 1958)
"The Johnson Payroll Matter" (September 21, 1958)
"The Gruesome Spectacle Matter" (September 28, 1958)
"The Double Trouble Matter" (November 16, 1958)
"The Hair Raising Matter" (November 30, 1958)
"The Hollywood Mystery Matter" (January 4, 1959)
"The Deadly Doubt Matter" (January 11, 1959)
"The Doting Dowager Matter" (January 25, 1959)
"The Baldero Matter" (March 15, 1959)
"The Jimmy Carter Matter" (March 29, 1959)
"The Frisco Fire Matter" (April 5, 1959)
"The Fair Weather Friend Matter" (April 12, 1959)
"The Cautious Celibate Matter" (April 19, 1959)
"The Winsome Widow Matter" (April 26, 1959)
"The Fatal Fillet Matter" (May 10, 1959)
"The Big H Matter" (May 31, 1959)
"The Wayward Heiress Matter" (June 7, 1959)
"The Life at Stake Matter" (June 21, 1959)
"The Mei-Ling Buddha Matter" (June 28, 1959)
"The Only One Butt Matter" (July 5, 1959)
"The Will and a Way Matter" (July 19, 1959)
"The Bolt out of the Blue Matter" (July 26, 1959)
"The Deadly Chain Matter" (August 2, 1959)
"The Night in Paris Matter" (August 16, 1959)
"The Really Gone Matter" (August 30, 1959)

"The Backfire that Backfired Matter" (September 6, 1959)
"The Little Man who was There Matter" (September 20, 1959)
"The Missing Missile Matter" (October 25, 1959)
"The Hand of Providential Matter" (November 1, 1959)
"The Larson Arson Matter" (November 8, 1959)
"The Bayou Body Matter" (November 15, 1959)
"The Fancy Bridgework Matter" (November 22, 1959)
"The Wrong Man Matter" (November 29, 1959)
"The Burning Desire Matter" (December 27, 1959)
"The Hapless Ham Matter" (January 3, 1960)
"The Unholy Two Matter" (January 10, 1960)
"The Nuclear Goof Matter" (January 24, 1960)
"The Alvin's Alfred Matter" (February 21, 1960)
"The Look Before the Leap Matter" (February 28, 1960)
"The Moonshine Matter" (March 6, 1960)
"The Deep Down Matter" (March 13, 1960)
"The False Alarm Matter" (March 27, 1960)
"The Silver Queen Matter" (April 24, 1960)
"The Fatal Switch Matter" (May 1, 1960)
"The Phony Phone Matter" (May 8, 1960)
"The Mystery Gal Matter" (May 15, 1960)
"The Red Rock Matter" (May 29, 1960)
"The Canned Canary Matter" (June 5, 1960)
"The Harried Heiress Matter" (June 12, 1960)
"The Wholly Unexpected Matter" (June 26, 1960)
"The Collectors Matter" (July 3, 1960)
"The Back to the Back Matter" (July 17, 1960)
"The Paradise Lost Matter" (August 14, 1960)
"The Deadly Debt Matter" (August 28, 1960)
"The Five Down Matter" (September 25, 1960)
"The Twins of Tahoe Matter" (October 16, 1960)
"The Unworthy Kin Matter" (October 23, 1960)
"The What Goes Matter" (October 30, 1960)

"The Double Deal Matter" (November 20, 1960)
"The Empty Threat Matter" (November 27, 1960)

41. Title: *The Adventures of Christopher London* (February 5, 1950 – May 29, 1950) was a short detective serial featuring "Christopher London" in his investigative adventures. Glenn Ford portrays the rough and tough "London," but despite Ford's popularity, the show never gained momentum. Initially it received favorable reception but ran for only three episodes. Virginia performs in the second episode of the series.
Genre: Detective Drama
General Duration: 30mins
Network(s): NBC
Episode(s): "The Price of Sugar" (February 26, 1950)

42. Title: *The Story of Doctor Kildare* (February 1, 1950 – August 3, 1951) was a radio medical drama developed from the 1938 film of the same name in part by Les Crutchfield. The radio serial stars Lew Ayres in his intrigues as "Dr. James Kildare," the earnest, young doctor interning under the veteran curmudgeon "Dr. Leonard Gillespie" portrayed by Lionel Barrymore. Virginia portrays fussy, old Nurse "Nosy" Parker who stays in a constant tizzy with the cantankerous "Dr. Gillespie." I'm sure audiences would have been astounded to know that the show's beloved "old maid Parker," was actually only in her early 30s and pregnant during her performances in many episodes!
Genre: Medical Drama
General Duration: 30mins
Network(s): WMGM, syndicated
Episode(s): "Benjamin Barkley" (February 15, 1950)
"Rico Marchiano's Dying Wife" (February 22, 1950)
"Vernon Pendleton Hypochondriac" (March 1, 1950)
"Barbara Lane Dope Addict" (March 8, 1950)

"Jane Dane New Cancer Treatment" (March 22, 1950)
"Warren Jackson's Allergy" (April 12, 1950)
"Terry Murphy's Hearing Problem" (April 19, 1950)
"Phillip Vancourt's Amnesia" (April 26, 1950)
"Abandoned Baby" (May 3, 1950)
"Nurse Parker Resigns" (May 17, 1950)
"Dr. Carew's Fat Wife" (May 24, 1950)
"Dick Brennan Steals Five Thousand Dollars" (May 31, 1950)
"Colonel Beauregard's Paralysis" (June 1, 1950)
"Gordon Mallory's Lead Poisoning" (June 8, 1950)
"Pricilla's Broken Arm" (June 22, 1950)
"Dr. Gillespie Almost Gets Engaged" (June 29, 1950)
"Hunting Trip" (July 6, 1950)
"Dan Malloy's Peptic Ulcer" (July 13, 1950)
"Mrs. Stanford's Angina Pecturis" (July 20, 1950)
"Buffalo Barnie McClure" (August 10, 1950)
"Appendicitis Operation at Sea" (August 17, 1950)
"Carew Gets Medical Examiner Mixed Up" (September 7, 1950)
"Marion Lewis Teen Age Alcoholic" (September 14, 1950)
"Sam Lubinski Has Spinal Paralysis" (September 21, 1950)
"Willie Mumpkin's First Baby" (September 28, 1950)
"Joe Finley's Ulcer" (October 4, 1950)
"Oliver Van Meter's Allergy" (October 11, 1950)
"Anthrax Infection" (October 18, 1950)
"Eddie Jenkins and the Arsonist" (October 20, 1950)
"Ling Co Refuses Leg Surgery" (October 27, 1950)
"Mr. Bradley's Damaged Heart" (November 17, 1950)
"Mr. Kramer's Chronic Enteritis/Parker Needs a Hobby" (November 24, 1950)
"Lady Dunabees Annual Visit" (December 1, 1950)
"Arthur Morgan Needs Brain Surgery" (December 8, 1950)
"David Norton has Pneumonia" (December 29, 1950)
"Eddie Lazetti Kidnaps Nurse" (January 5, 1951)

"Dr. Gillespie's Testimonial Dinner" (January 12, 1951)
"Dr. Conlon, Quack" (January 19, 1951)
"Pete Cosloff is Mentally Ill" (February 16, 1951)
"David Cooper's Burned Face" (March 2, 1951)
"Amy Dickens Break Her Leg" (March 16, 1951)
"Cathy Morton's Baby" (March 23, 1951)
"Joan Quinn" (March 30, 1951)
"Gillespie's New Suit for Henderson Award" (April 6, 1951)
"Yukon Joe's Gold Mine" (April 13, 1951)
"Mysterious Hemophilia Patient" (May 18, 1951)
"Dr. Gillespie's New Office" (May 25, 1951)
"Paul Bailey" (June 22, 1951)
"Valerie and Walter Benton – Murder!" (July 13, 1951)
"Evelyn Briggs" (July 20, 1951)
"Robert Lane, Intern, Shirks Duties" (July 27, 1951)
"Alice Bradley, Amnesia Victim" (August 3, 1951)

43. Title: *Much Ado About Doolittle* (1950)
Genre: Unavailable
General Duration: 30mins
Network(s): ABC
Title(s): "Much Ado About Doolittle" (audition) (March 25, 1950)

44. Title: *One Man's Family* (April 29, 1932 – May 8, 1959) is known as "the longest-running uninterrupted dramatic serial in the history of American radio."[112] The series was created by Carlton E. Morse in the 1930s about the San Francisco family, the "Barbours," whose typical American family sagas amid the fast-changing nation in the early 20th century were cathartic to many listeners. The weekly stories of the "Barbours" are told through life chapters, making it an airwave novelty at the time. This serial formula was one of the archetypes for the modern American television soap opera. It aired April 29th, 1932, and ran for an astonishing twenty-seven years on radio, eventually moving to television. It survived the Great Depression, WWII, and even the radio-to- television transition with Morse at the helm. Virginia plays "Betty Barbour," the daughter-in-law of main characters "Henry and Fanny Barbour." The episode logs are far too vast to determine exactly which episodes Virginia appears in beyond the obvious listed below, but her character first joined in the cast in 1950 and remained throughout its radio run. She played "Jack Barbour's" wife "Betty" whenever the script called for her character. This series has a complex and fascinating history of its own beyond the scope of this book. It was a favorite of Virginia's.

Genre: Drama
General Duration: 30mins
Network(s): NBC
Episode(s): "Jack Overwhelms Betty" (May 28, 1950)
"Betty and Her Fifteen Day Diet" (October 12, 1950)
"Nicolette Consoles Betty" (October 16, 1950)
"Betty's Long Vigil" (October 17, 1950)
"Betty Drops a Bombshell" (March 26, 1959)
"Betty Salvages a Lesson from Disaster" (April 8, 1959)
"Betty Lowers the Boom" (April 22, 1959)

45. Title: *Hallmark Playhouse* (June 10, 1948 – February 1, 1953) was created by and for the Hallmark Cards company in 1948, also known as *The Hallmark Hall of Fame* later in its run. In the initial playhouse format, modern and classic literature was adapted to radio, in part by the efforts of writer James Hilton. Hilton also hosted the show the first several years. *Hallmark Playhouse* was a popular series of the day that served as an entertaining ballyhoo of the Hallmark brand that incidentally is still thriving after more than 100 years since its founding. Virginia performed in many episodes of *Playhouse* as well as in those later episodes under *Hallmark Hall of Fame.*

Genre: Literary Anthology

General Duration: 30mins
Network(s): CBS
Episode(s): "The Story of Kansas City" (June 1, 1950)
"Scudda Hoo, Scudda Hay" (May 24, 1951)
"Francis Scott Key" (September 13, 1951)
"Web of Destiny" (September 27, 1951)
"The Story of John Hancock" (December 13, 1951)
"Madame Claire" (January 17, 1952)
"Ben Hur" (April 10, 1952)
"The Professor" (April 24, 1952)
"Lorna Doone" (May 1, 1952)
"The Marquis de Lafayette" (May 15, 1952)
"Marsha Byrnes/Marcia Burns" (May 22, 1952)
"Young Mr. Disraeli" (October 12, 1952)
"The Courtship of Miles Standish" (November 24, 1952)
"A Miracle on the Blotter" (December 7, 1952)
"A Christmas Carol" (December 21, 1952)
"Trenton Seventy-Six" (February 1, 1953)

46. Title: *The Halls of Ivy* (January 6, 1950 – June 25, 1952) was a Don Quinn creation heard on NBC for its two-year run. Much like *Fibber McGee & Molly*, another creation of Quinn's, *The Halls of Ivy* was a popular situation comedy. The show stars real-life husband and wife team Ronald Colman and Benita Hume together, with Colman as "William Todhunter Hall," the president of Midwestern Ivy College, and Hume as his wife "Victoria" in their amusing campus adventures. *The Halls of Ivy* eventually moved to television on CBS, with Colman and Hume maintaining their lead roles. Virginia performed in two episodes of *The Halls of Ivy* during its two-year radio run.
Genre: Situation Comedy
General Duration: 30mins
Network(s): NBC

Episode(s): "The Bentheimers and the Census" (June 21, 1950)
"Math Professor" (June 18, 1952)

47. Title: *The Lineup* (July 6, 1950 – February 20, 1953) was a
crime series that showcases the plight of the San Francisco cop
in tracking down perpetrators using the "line up" method of
identification in all types of crimes from petty theft to heinous,
cold-blooded murders. *The Line Up* is similar to *Dragnet*, often
featuring the same talents, though *The Lineup* was not based on
actual police files like its counterpart. Elliot Lewis initially directed
and produced the show, but Jaime del Valle (Virginia's second husband) took Lewis' place soon after the show's takeoff. del Valle
also produced the film *The Line Up* in 1958 and was instrumental
in the series' transition from radio to television in 1954. Virginia
performed in a number of episodes of *The Line Up* in supporting
roles, though the running joke was that she preferred to work for
Jack Webb in *Dragnet* compared to her then husband del Valle in
The Line Up.
Genre: Crime Drama
General Duration: 30mins
Network(s): CBS
Episode(s): "Eddie Gaynor Framed for Murder" (July 20, 1950)
"The Cop-Killer" (November 30, 1950)
"The Jersey Parallel" (December 7, 1950)
"The Elsner Case/Sixty-Year-Old Woman Strangled in the Park"
(December 28, 1950)
"The Case of Frankie and Joyce" (January 4, 1951)
"Yudo in Ypsilanti" (January 18, 1951)
"The Grocery Store Murder" (February 1, 1951)
"The Farmer's Flimsy Fence Case" (March 20, 1951)
"The Lapinish Lighter-Upper Case" (March 27, 1951)
"Lieutenant Guthrie is Kidnapped" (June 19, 1951)
"The Syncopic Sweazy Sweat-Out Case" (July 5, 1951)

"The Flighty Fulvous Finch Case" (July 12, 1951)

"The Butane Buttonworth Case" (August 2, 1951)

"The Pointless Pierson Polemic Polarity Case" (September 5, 1951)

"The Senile Slugging Case" (September 12, 1951)

"The Fur-Flaunting Floozy" (September 26, 1951)

"The Jolted Justice Job Case" (November 1, 1951)

"The Pixie-Picker Pickle" (November 8, 1951)

"The Potting Peter Case" (February 5, 1952)

"The Bakery Bandit's Bad Blooper" (March 25, 1952)

"The Cornered Cop Killer Case" (April 8, 1952)

"Lobdell's Poodle-Cut Tomato Case" (June 10, 1952)

"Bentley's Boo-Boo Case/The Liquor Store Robbery" (June 17, 1952)

"The Pitiful Patricide Case" (June 17, 1952)

"The Cutie-Calling Culprit Case" (June 24, 1952)

"The Guided Gang Case" (July 1, 1952)

"The Lugar-Lugging Laddie Case" (July 8, 1952)

"The Twitching Twist's .22 Tweaking Case" (July 15, 1952)

"The Drinkler Kidnapping Case" (July 22, 1952)

"The Charles Crocked Clobbering Case" (July 29, 1952)

"The Karger Cops a Clinker Case" (August 5, 1952)

"The Jane Doe Case" (September 10, 1952)

"The Fresno Break Case" (September 17, 1952)

"The Poker-Party Killings (October 1, 1952)

"The Teacher's Pet" (October 8, 1952)

"The Green Cap Case" (October 22, 1952)

"The Sobbing Sister Saga" (October 29, 1952)

"The Buggered Bunco Boys" (November 12, 1952)

"The Modern Sounds Case" (November 19, 1952)

"The Matthews-Murray Mish-Mosh Case" (November 26, 1952)

"The Gasoline Bandit Case" (December 12, 1952)

"Cowardly Castro" (January 2, 1953)

48. Title: *Tales of the Texas Rangers* (July 8, 1950 – September 14, 1952) was a Texan adventure series that, much like *Dragnet*, used the files of actual Texas ranger cases to develop storylines. Produced and directed by Stacy Keach Sr., the show features Joel McCrea as "Texas Ranger Jayce Pearson" with "Charcoal" his trusty horse. Virginia performed in several episodes of *Tales of the Texas Rangers* in a variety of supporting roles during its two-year run.

Genre: Crime Drama

General Duration: 30mins

Network(s): NBC

Episode(s): "Apache Peak" (July 22, 1950)

"Soft Touch" (October 29, 1950)

"Blood Relative" (November 12, 1950)

"Christmas Present" (December 24, 1950)

"Canned Death" (April 22, 1951)

"No Living Witnesses" (May 6, 1951)

"Paid in Full" (May 13, 1951)

"Death Plant" (December 9, 1951)

"Killer's Crop" (December 30, 1951)

"Clip Job" (January 13, 1952)

"Little Sister" (May 4, 1952)

"Smart Kill" (May 18, 1952)

"Knockout" (June 22, 1952)

"Double Edge" (August 3, 1952)

"Three Victims" (August 24, 1952)

"Misplaced Person" (August 31, 1952)

49. Title: *T-Man* (April 29, 1949 – 1950; 1956) was a dramatic series that spotlights the plight of the United States Treasury Agents in their investigations of counterfeiters. In its first run, Dennis O'Keefe starred as a different treasury agent in each storyline who investigates various crooks (or would-be crooks) with a brawny approach to justice. Later in 1956, *T-Man* reprised with Gordon Glenwright starring as "Tax Agent Jack Ketch" who tackles similar cases. Virginia performed in at least one episode of *T-Man* during its initial run, though she may have performed in additional episodes uncredited or undocumented.

Genre: Crime
General Duration: 30mins
Network(s): CBS, Syndicated
Episode(s): "Big Mexican Dope" (July 29, 1950)

50. Title: *Dangerous Assignment* (July 9, 1949 – July 1, 1953) was a crime series starring Brian Donlevy as "Steve Mitchell" the operative who received "dangerous assignments" from the operation's chief known only as "The Commissioner." With the intrigue of spies and espionage of the 1940s and 1950s, this show blended in with the others, and had a relatively short run. Virginia performed in at least three episodes of *Dangerous Assignment*.

Genre: Crime
General Duration: 30mins
Network(s): NBC
Episode(s): "Rotterdam War Criminals" (May 4, 1951)
"London Passport Forging Racket" (April 22, 1953)
"Trieste" (May 6, 1953)

51. Title: *The Adventures of Maisie* (November 24, 1949 – December 13, 1951) stars Ann Sothern as sassy secretary "Maisie Ravier" based on Sothern's on-screen portrayal of the same character in the late 1930s and 1940s film series of the same name. The situation comedy details the adventures of Brooklyn-born entertainer/secretary "Maisie" who is always finding herself in jams of the liberated, single working-girl. Virginia performed in at least four episodes of *The Adventures of Maisie* during its two-year run.

Genre: Situation Comedy
General Duration: 30mins

Network(s): CBS, Mutual, syndicated
Episode(s): "Quakenbush's Universal Elixir" (May 10, 1951)
"Engaged to Harry Adams" (October 11, 1951)
"Jenny Perkins, Author/Spicy Novel" (October 18, 1951)
"Running for Mayor" (November 29, 1951)

52. Title: *Wild Bill Hickok* (April 1, 1951 – 1956) was a western series starring Guy Madison as famed frontier lawman "Will Bill Hickok" in his adventure effort of taming the Wild West along with his sidekick "Jingles" played by Andy Devine. This is a lovable show that ran over the airwaves alongside its television version for several seasons. Both versions were adored by fans of all ages. Virginia performed in many episodes of the radio series throughout its run.
Genre: Western
General Duration: 30mins
Network(s): Mutual Broadcasting Network (Don Lee)
Episode(s): "An Outlaw's Revenge" (April 22, 1951)
"The Road Agents at Red Rock" (May 27, 1951)
"Press for Justice" (June 17, 1951)
"The Trail of Death" (July 15, 1951)
"The Trail Herd Trouble" (July 22, 1951)
"Logging" (September 9, 1951)
"Sir Tommy, the Silver Knight" (December 23, 1951)
"The Dark Horse Candidate" (January 30, 1952)
"The Monstrous Toothache" (April 9, 1952)
"The Daring of Digby Dean" (September 10, 1952)
"Letter of Warning" (September 12, 1952)
"Big Welcome at Shady Rest" (February 27, 1953)
"The Gun Belt Treasure" (March 2, 1953)
"The Green Valley Feud" (September 25, 1953)
"Thundercloud" (October 9, 1953)
"Eight Hundred Feet Down" (January 27, 1954)
"The Bellson Boys" (October 29, 1954)

"A Shiny Silver Star" (December 24, 1954)

53. Title: *Romance* (April 19, 1943 – January 5, 1957) was an anthology series that delivers romantic stories of the humanities with twists of drama, mystery, and even science fiction on occasion. Initially it was written by Charles S. Monroe and directed by Albert Ward. Virginia performed in many episodes of *Romance*, along with many of her close colleagues who were also A-lister character players among various series of the 1940s and 1950s like John Dehner, Ben Wright, Harry Bartell, Lawrence Dobkin, and Jack Moyles.

Genre: Romantic Anthology

General Duration: 30mins

Network(s): CBS

Episode(s): "The Sword and the Knitting Needle" (July 9, 1951)
"Den of Thieves" (August 11, 1952)
"Amalfi Summer" (June 12, 1954)
"The Fling" (July 31, 1954)
"The Postmistress of Laurel" (September 4, 1954)
"The Return of Maria Sanchez" (September 11, 1954)
"Point of View" (December 4, 1954)
"The Third Swan from the Left" (December 11, 1954)
"Zeea's Dream/Zia's Dream" (February 19, 1955)
"You Really Ought to Get away for a While" (May 21, 1955)
"Transport to Terror" (July 16, 1955)
"Such a Wonderful Team" (July 30, 1955)
"The Vortegs" (August 20, 1955)
"The Winds of June" (September 24, 1955)
"The Mission" (October 22, 1955)
"The Bear" (November 5, 1955)
"Richer by One Christmas" (December 24, 1955)
"Jackhammer Leg" (February 25, 1956)
"Point of View" (March 17, 1956)
"Roman Afternoon" (April 28, 1956)

"The Lady and the Tiger" (May 12, 1956)
"The Bachelor" (June 9, 1956)
"Ragged Individualist" (July 14, 1956)
"The Man from Venus" (September 15, 1956)
"Earthquake" (October 6, 1956)
"Lovely Dead Letter" (October 27, 1956)
"London Interlude – 1940" (November 24, 1956)
"The Indian Sign" (December 15, 1956)
"A Quiet Little Party" (December 29, 1956)

54. Title: *Dragnet* (June 3, 1949 – February 26, 1957) was a sensational crime drama created, produced, and directed by industry kingpin Jack Webb. Webb fashioned episodes out of true crimes detailed in the records of the Los Angeles Police Department. The series starred Webb himself as "Sgt. Joe Friday" – the hardboiled detective who, with his partner "Officer Frank Smith" (Ben Alexander) fought every type of crime the streets of LA had to offer. *Dragnet* ran on radio for nearly eight years while overlapping on television for another eight. The show was immensely successful on both media and had a later reprisal in 1967, with Harry Morgan as Friday's partner "Officer Bill Gannon." Feature films also developed from the series' success through Webb's production company Mark VII Limited. Webb's stock company included Virginia's name at the top of its list, so there was hardly an episode on radio and the first air on television in which she did not perform. She also appeared frequently in the later *Dragnet* television series. In addition to Virginia, Webb's stock company was comprised of other favorites like Olan Soule, Art Gilmore, Barney Phillips, Herb Vigran, Peggy Webber, Harry Bartell, Jack Kruschen, Stacy Harris, and Vic Perrin. Not all episodes in which Virginia performed are listed.
Genre: Crime Drama
General Duration: 30mins
Network(s): NBC

Episode(s): "The Big Affair" (November 29, 1951)
"The Big Court" (January 24, 1952)
"The Big Almost No Show" (January 31, 1952)
"The Big Honeymoon" (February 7, 1952)
"The Big Producer" (February 21, 1952)
"The Big Rose" (March 27, 1952)
"The Big Show" (April 10, 1952)
"The Big Fourth" (May 29, 1952)
"The Big Donation" (June 12, 1952)
"The Big Roll" (June 26, 1952)
"The Big Signet" (July 31, 1952)
"The Big Paper" (August 21, 1952)
"The Big Ray" (September 4, 1952)
"The Big Shot" (September 21, 1952)
"The Big Pill" (October 19, 1952)
"The Big String" (January 18, 1953)
"The Big Layout" (January 25, 1953)
"The Big Smoke" (February 22, 1953)
"The Big False Move" (May 17, 1953)
"The Big Gun Part I" (May 24, 1953)
"The Big Gun Part II" (May 31, 1953)
"The Big Ham" (June 28, 1953)
"The Big Pipe" (February 23, 1954)
"The Big Look" (May 11, 1954)
"The Big Coin" (November 9, 1954)
"The Big Fellow" (August 30, 1955)
"The Big Daughter" (September 13, 1955)

55. Title: *The Silent Men* (October 14, 1951 – May 28, 1952) stars Douglas Fairbanks Jr. in the adventures of undercover agents working in all things espionage. The series is an adventure drama relaying the stories of the special operations world through the eyes of a different agent each episode. Fairbanks portrayed the various agents week-to-week, which was an artistic echo of his real-life experience with special operations in WWII. Virginia performed in at least three episodes of *The Silent Men* during its nearly one-year run.

Genre: Crime Drama

General Duration: 30mins

Network(s): NBC

Episode(s): "The Bogus G.I." (December 16, 1951)

"Stolen Arsenal" (February 17, 1952)

"The Green Sedan" (May 28, 1952)

56. Title: *Hollywood Star Playhouse* (April 24, 1950 – February 15, 1953), produced and directed by Jack Johnstone, was an anthology with original scripts of various genres. It ran for three years and featured some of the greatest talents of Hollywood like Jimmy Stewart, Deborah Kerr, Vincent Price, Dick Powell, and Rex Harrison. Virginia performed in at least one episode of *Hollywood Star Playhouse*.

Genre: Dramatic Anthology

General Duration: 30mins

Network(s): CBS, ABC, & NBC

Episode(s): "The Frontier" (January 10, 1952)

57. Title: *Hollywood Sound Stage/Stars in the Air* (December 13, 1951 – March 27, 1952) was an anthology series produced by The Screen Actor's Guild (SAG). It is known for its radio adaptations of popular Hollywood films of the day with some of the biggest name stars such as Dana Andrews, Tyrone Power, Claudette Colbert, Douglas Fairbanks Jr., and Barbara Stanwyck. Virginia performed in at least three episodes of *Hollywood Sound Stage* during its relatively short run.

Genre: Anthology

General Duration: 30mins

Network(s): CBS, Syndicated

Episode(s): "Shadow of a Doubt" (January 10, 1952)

"Dark Victory" (March 6, 1952)
"Jezebel" (May 10, 1952)

58. Title: *Tarzan, Lord of the Jungle* (January 11, 1951 – May 9, 1953) was a radio adventure series based on Edgar Rice Burroughs' 1912 novel *Tarzan of the Apes*. There were at least two other *Tarzan* radio series based on the same literary work, each with different slants, though all generally telling the famed story of "Tarzan," the untamed man living in the African jungles among animals who raised him from an abandoned boy. Virginia performed in at least one episode of *Tarzan, Lord of the Jungle* during its 1950s run.
Genre: Adventure
General Duration: 30mins
Network(s): Mutual, Don-Lee, CBS, syndicated by Commodore Productions
Episode(s): "Demon of Rongu" (February 21, 1952)

59. Title: *The Hour of St. Francis* (December 1946 – 1953) was a dramatic anthology created by Fr. Hugh Noonan of St. Joseph's Church in Los Angeles. Each episode delivers inspirational, parable-like dramas of modern dynamics. Rosalind Russell, Ward Bond, and Ann Blyth are among the notable performers heard on *The Hour of St. Francis* in leading roles. Virginia performed in at least one episode of the show during its nearly seven-year run.
Genre: Dramatic Anthology
General Duration: 15mins
Network(s): Syndicated, Third Order of St. Francis
Episode(s): "Baa, Baa, Black Sheep" (May 3, 1952)

60. Title: *Violence* (May 8, 1952) was a one-episode radio show produced and directed by Norman MacDonnell. The audition script features fictious murderer "Arthur Bowman" who recounts the grisly details of his crime during an interview with a psychiatrist.

The cast includes Harry Bartell, Ted Osborne, Dick Beals, and of course Virginia Gregg.

Genre: Crime
General Duration: 30mins
Network(s): CBS
Episode(s): "The Case of Arthur Bowman" (audition) (May 8, 1952)

61. Title: *Gunsmoke* (April 26, 1952 – June 11, 1961) the American Western series is considered one of the greatest radio shows of all time across all genres. John Metson and Norman MacDonnell first brought *Gunsmoke* to the air waves in 1952. It features the adventures of the ever-stoic "Marshall Matt Dillon" of Dodge City, Kansas just after the Civil War, in his efforts to bring law and order to the Wild West. William Conrad plays "Matt Dillon," and Georgia Ellis plays saloon owner "Miss Kitty," who is also Marshall Dillon's subtle love interest. Parley Baer plays the Marshall's simple-minded, but earnest deputy "Chester," and Howard McNear Dodge's kindly old physician "Doc Adams." Virginia performed in many of radio's *Gunsmoke* episodes, as well as television's after it was picked up by the small screen in 1955. After screenwriter Charles Marquis Warren adapted *Gunsmoke* to television, it became the longest running series in history (before *Law & Order: SVU*) running twenty consecutive seasons.

Genre: Western
General Duration: 30mins
Network(s): CBS
Episode(s): "The Kentucky Tolmans" (August 9, 1952)
"Wind" (June 20, 1953)
"Big Girl Lost" (December 19, 1953)
"Big Broad" (February 6, 1954)
"Feud" (May 29, 1954)
"Obie Tater" (August 30, 1954)
"Ma Tennis" (October 23, 1954)

"Potato Road" (May 7, 1955)

"Jealousy" (June 4, 1955)

"Tap Day for Kitty" (July 30, 1955)

"Johnny Red" (August 13, 1955)

"Indian White" (September 24, 1955)

"Amy's Good Deed" (November 27, 1955)

"Hanging Man" (March 25, 1956)

"Till Death Do Us Part" (October 21, 1956)

"Crowbait Bob" (November 10, 1956)

"Beeker's Barn" (December 23, 1956)

"Woman Called Mary" (January 27, 1957)

"Impact" (February 24, 1957)

"Saddle Sore Sal" (March 24, 1957)

"Medicine Man" (April 28, 1957)

"Looney McCluny" (September 8, 1957)

"Where'd They Go?" (December 29, 1957)

"Where'd They Go?" (December 21, 1958)

"Carmen" (June 21, 1959)

"Beeker's Barn" (December 20, 1959)

"Mr. and Mrs. Amber" (February 21, 1960)

"Greater Love" (April 3, 1960)

"Nettie Sitton" (May 1, 1960)

"Marryin' Bertha" (May 22, 1960)

"Old Fool" (August 7, 1960)

"The Wake" (January 15, 1961)

62. Title: *This is O'Shea* (1952) was a short-lived series about the oversea adventures of journalist "O'Shea" who gets into a variety of scrapes with danger in his work. This show was directed by Albert Capstaff and produced by Joseph C. Donohue. Virginia performed in the audition episode of *This is O'Shea*, along with Herb Butterfield, Jerry Hausner, and Hy Averback as announcer.

Genre: Drama

General Duration: 30mins
Network(s): Unavailable
Episode(s): *Title(s) Unknown* Audition (October 1, 1952)

63. Title: *Guest Star* (March 27, 1947 – 1950s) was a public service program produced by the U.S. Treasury Department. This anthology series featured notable celebrities each week in encouraging listeners to buy savings bonds. Virginia performed in six known episodes of *Guest Star* during its run.
Genre: Anthology
General Duration: 15mins
Network(s): Syndicated
Episode(s): "Fiddle Faddle" (November 12, 1949)
"The Blue Amulet" (December 7, 1952)
"The Headliner" (April 26, 1953)
"Fear" (August 2, 1953)
"Holiday from Crime" (October 11, 1953)
"End of the Line" (December 5, 1954)

64. Title: *I Was a Communist for the FBI* (April 23, 1952 – October 14, 1953) was a compelling series that aired just after the first wave of the Red Scare of the 1940s. Audiences were intrigued and horrified by the mysteries of communism and the FBI's role to fight it. *I Was a Communist for the FBI* is based on the true accounts of undercover FBI agent Matt Cvetic who assimilated into Communist party leadership to aid the bureau. Cvetic's stories were published in popular media and eventually made it to syndicated radio for a brief run on-air. Despite the show's name, the FBI declined to have any part of the production. Dana Andrews stars as undercover FBI agent Cvetic, with his famous concluding line, "I was a Communist for the FBI. I walk alone." Virginia performed in at least one episode of *I Was a Communist for the FBI*.
Genre: Crime

General Duration: 30mins
Network(s): Syndicated, ZIV Productions
Episode(s): "Hate Song" (December 31, 1952)

65. Title: *The Survivors* (December 21, 1952) was a single episode radio drama produced in conjunction with the National Safety Council in a creative public service announcement (PSA) on the far-reaching consequences traffic accidents can have on families and communities. J.C. Furnace authored the show, with Harry Bubeck as producer, and John Robinson as director. Virginia performed in *The Survivors* with some of her favorite fellow actors and actresses like Lawrence Dobkin, Gilbert Fry, and June Whitley.
Genre: PSA drama
General Duration: 30mins
Network(s): NBC
Episode(s): "Traffic Safety" (December 21, 1952)

66. Title: *Errand of Mercy* (February 13, 1949 – May 14, 1950) was a short docudrama series syndicated by The American Red Cross. Not many details on this show's life and death are in circulation, but the general thrust of the show seems to be the creative delivery of public service announcements produced by The American Red Cross. Virginia is credited with two performances in *Errand of Mercy*, though she may have performed in additional episodes either uncredited or undocumented.
Genre: Docudrama
General Duration: 15mins
Network(s): Syndicated, American Red Cross
Episode(s): "Escape" (January 11, 1953)
"A Living Tribute" (March 8, 1953)

67. Title: *Suspense* (June 17, 1942 – September 30, 1962) was a thriller series that ran for a grand twenty years on air. Known as "radio's outstanding theatre of thrills," *Suspense* was produced by a variety of greats over the years including Norman MacDonnell, William N. Robson, William Spier, Bruno Zirato Jr., and Elliot Lewis. *Suspense* is a psychologically thrilling anthology with haunting scripts delivered by some of Hollywood's best like Agnes Moorehead, Orson Welles, Henry Fonda, Olivia De Havilland, and Gregory Peck. Virginia gave listeners many thrills in several episodes of *Suspense* during its long run.

Genre: Thriller

General Duration: 30mins

Network(s): CBS

Episode(s): "The Love and Death of Joaquin Murietta" (February 16, 1953)

"Want Ad" (January 25, 1954)

"Destruction" (July 27, 1954)

"Goodnight Mrs. Russell" (August 3, 1954)

"The Last Letter of Dr. Bronson" (November 4, 1954)

"On a Country Road" (December 9, 1954)

"The Lady in the Red Hat" (August 30, 1955)

"A Story of Poison" (September 13, 1955)

"Goodbye, Miss Lizzie Borden" (October 4, 1955)

"When the Bough Breaks" (December 6, 1955)

"Gallardo" (March 20, 1956)

"The Twelfth Rose" (June 5, 1956)

"A Matter of Timing" (June 12, 1956)

"Want Ad" (July 11, 1956)

"A Good Neighbor" (March 31, 1957)

"The Vanishing Lady" (April 7, 1957)

"Sorry, Wrong Number" (October 20, 1957 & February 14, 1960)

"Jet Stream" (December 1, 1957)

"Subway Stop" (May 11, 1958)

"The Bridge" (August 17, 1958)

"For Old Time's Sake" (December 14, 1958)

"Everything Will be Different" (August 9, 1959)

68. Title: *Rogers of the Gazette* (June 10, 1953 – January 20, 1954) was a situation comedy revolving around newspaperman "Rogers" (played by Will Rogers Jr.) in his adventures of small-town reporting in a community of busybodies. Virginia plays various supporting roles in this lovable, but short-lived series.
Genre: Situation Comedy
General Duration: 30mins
Network(s): CBS
Episode(s): *Title Unknown* (rehearsal) (June 12, 1953)
"Dirty Politics" (July 22, 1953)
"Toast of Vienna – Gretchen March" (November 5, 1953)
"Pastel Christmas Trees" (December 9, 1953)
"Eager Twins/Investigative Reporters" (December 30, 1953)

69. Title: *Confession* (July 5, 1953 – September 13, 1953) was a short crime series that features the criminal confessions taken from case files of true crimes. In *Dragnet* form, the names and certain details were changed for radio adaptation. The novelty of *Confession* is that crimes are detailed in the criminal's own person. Virginia is credited with the audition performance of this series.
Genre: Crime
General Duration: 30mins
Network(s): NBC & CBS
Episode(s): "The Doris Kane Case" (audition) (October 17, 1952)

70. Title: *Stars Over Hollywood* (May 31, 1941 – September 25, 1954) was an original anthology series produced and directed by Paul Pierce, Les Mitchel, and Don Clark. It had a long radio run with scripts in almost every genre and leads by such talents as Mary Astor, Phil Harris, Alan Ladd, and Joan Crawford. Virginia is credited in only one episode of *Stars Over Hollywood*, though she may have performed in additional episodes either uncredited or undocumented.

Genre: Anthology
General Duration: 30mins
Network(s): CBS
Episode(s): "To the Bitter End" (July 4, 1953)

71. Title: *General Electric Theatre* (July 9, 1953 – October 1, 1953) was a short-lived series on radio, though its move to television was wildly successful with a ten-season run. Jaime del Valle, Virginia's second husband, directed the radio series with Ronald Reagan as host on both the radio and television series. *General Electric Theatre* is an anthology that features some of the biggest stars in Hollywood in the 1950s, such as Cary Grant, Joan Fontaine, William Holden, Jane Wyman, and Van Johnson. Virginia is credited with two performances in the show's four-month radio run.
Genre: Anthology
General Duration: 30mins
Network(s): CBS
Episode(s): "Penny Serenade" (July 23, 1953)
"The Virginian" (August 13, 1953)

72. Title: *Hallmark Hall of Fame* (February 8, 1953 – March 27, 1955) is considered the later version of *Hallmark Playhouse*. Hallmark broke away from the playhouse format for this later series and produced dramatic stories of world history. After the transition into the new format and title, James Hilton was replaced as host by the legendary Lionel Barrymore. This later version did well on air and eventually moved to television. Virginia performed in a number of radio episodes in *Hallmark Playhouse* and *Hallmark Hall of Fame*.
Genre: Dramatic/Historic Anthology
General Duration: 30mins
Network(s): CBS
Episode(s): "Edwin L. Drake" (October 11, 1953)
"Mary Bickerdyke" (November 1, 1953)

"Alfred Nobel" (December 13, 1953)
"A Christmas Carol" (December 20, 1953)
"William Allen White" (January 10, 1954)
"Dr. Will Mayo" (April 4, 1954)
"Damon Runyon" (May 16, 1954)
"A Christmas Carol" (December 19, 1954)
"J. Edgar Hoover" (December 26, 1954)
"Sigmund Freud" (February 6, 1955)
"Dr. Lev Kowarski" (March 20, 1955)

73. Title: *The Freedom Story* (1953)
Genre: *Unavailable
General Duration: 15mins
Network(s): *Unavailable
Episode(s): "To Each According to Need" (October 19, 1953)

74. Title: *The Six Shooter* (September 20, 1953 – June 24, 1954) was a western drama that was fairly short-lived on air. Famed actor Jimmy Stewart stars as "Britt Ponset" the wandering, mild-mannered frontier hero. The show was written by Frank Burt and directed by Jack Johnstone. A number of supporting radio regulars are featured on the show like Harry Bartell, Parley Baer, Sam Edwards, and of course Virginia Gregg.
Genre: Western Drama
General Duration: 30mins
Network(s): NBC
Episode(s): "A Pressing Engagement" (December 6, 1953)
"Cora Plummer Quincy" (December 27, 1953)
"Quiet City" (February 14, 1954)
"Battle at Tower Rock" (February 21, 1954)
"General Gillford's Widow" (April 8, 1954)
"Crisis at Easter Creek" (April 15, 1954)
"Johnny Springer" (April 22, 1954)

"Revenge at Harness Creek" (April 29, 1954)
"Myra Barker" (June 24, 1954)

75. Title: *Dr. Christian* (November 7, 1937 – January 6, 1954) was an incredibly popular medical drama, initially premiering as *Dr. Christian of River's End*, that ran for an extraordinary seventeen years on air. Jean Hersholt played the kindly, small-town "Dr. Christian" who encounters aliments and dramas of all kinds in his practice, with Rosemary DeCamp as his steadfast nurse, "Judy." Hersholt was apparently so convincing as the good doctor, that he actually received fan mail soliciting medical advice throughout the run of the show. Virginia is credited in the archives with one performance on *Dr. Christian*, but she certainly performed in additional episodes, though the titles and air dates are difficult to individually track down due to the show's extensive run.
Genre: Medical Drama
General Duration: 30mins
Network(s): CBS
Episode(s): "Tony's Parcel" (December 23, 1953)

76. Title: *Crime Classics* (June 15, 1953 – June 30, 1954) was a crime series produced by Elliot Lewis with the essence of a historical anthology. Following the formula of *Calling All Cars* and later *Dragnet,* the show tells true crime stories with narration by Lou Merrill in the role of "Thomas Hyland" who, on the show, is described as "a connoisseur of crime, a student of violence, and a teller of murders." Virginia performed in at least two *Crime Classics* episodes.
Genre: Crime
General Duration: 30mins
Network(s): CBS
Episode(s): "Boorn/Bourne Brothers & the Hangman: A Study in Nip & Tuck" (January 27, 1954)
"Robby-Boy Balfour: How He Wrecked a Big Prison's Reputation" (March 31, 1954)

77. Title: *Fibber McGee and Molly* (April 16, 1935 – October 2, 1959) was a wildly popular long-running situation comedy created by Don Quinn and the stars of the show, real-life married couple, Jim and Marian Jordan. With hints of vaudeville, the show features antics of the typical American couple, endearingly known to the nation as "Fibber and Molly." *Fibber McGee and Molly* was a radio staple that made its way into the Radio Hall of Fame in 1989. Virginia is credited with one performance in this series.
Genre: Situation Comedy
General Duration: 15mins
Network(s): WMAQ, NBC, & Blue Network
Episode(s): "Advertising Ingrams Home for Rent" (February 11, 1954)

78. Title: *NBC Star Playhouse* (October 4, 1953 – April 11, 1954) was a radio anthology that delivers radio adaptations of classic literature and films usually with a well-known star as host and/or narrator each episode. Some of the most memorable stars that performed on *NBC Star Playhouse* during its short run were Glenn Ford, June Allyson, Marlene Dietrich, Helen Hayes, and Rex Harrison. Virginia is credited with one performance in this series.
Genre: Anthology
General Duration: 60mins
Network(s): NBC
Episode(s): "The Major and the Minor" (February 21, 1954)

79. Title: *The Roy Rogers Show* (November 21, 1944 – 1955) was a western variety show starring "King of the Cowboys" Roy Rogers and his wife Dale Evans. Also featured in the cast are Rogers' trusty horse, "Trigger," and dog, "Bullet," who like Rogers, became household names in the 1940s and 1950s. The show's signature closing song is "Happy Trails," written by Dale Evans and performed by the starring duo. The show and theme song are still used as a pop culture reference on occasion even today. Virginia is credited in one episode of *The Roy Rogers Show*, though given its long run, she may have performed in additional episodes either uncredited or undocumented.

Genre: Western Variety
General Duration: 30mins
Network(s): Mutual, NBC
Episode(s): "The Streets of Laredo" (March 4, 1954)

80. Title: *You Were There* (1953 – 1956) was a drama syndicated by the Red Cross in the 1950s. It is not to be confused with the similarly titled CBS show, *You Are There*, a long-running historical anthology. There is not much detailed information about *You Were There* in circulation, though Virginia is credited in six episodes.

Genre: Drama
General Duration: 15mins
Network(s): Red Cross Syndication
Episode(s): "All Points Bulletin" (March 7, 1954)
"Mam-San Frendo" (March 14, 1954)
"Ride it Out" (April 11, 1954)
"A Letter to Ann" (July 11, 1954)
"Down to the Sea" (November 21, 1954)
"On Our Way" (July 17, 1955)

81. Title: *Rocky Fortune* (October 6, 1953 – March 30, 1954) was created by George Lefferts and produced by Andrew Love. It only ran for a little over a year but was an audience favorite for a time with acclaimed singer Frank Sinatra as renaissance man and detective "Rocky Fortune." Occasionally Sinatra would even gift listeners with a song in "Fortune's" character if it could be worked into the script in between his scrapes with danger. Virginia performed in the final episode of *Rocky Fortune*.

Genre: Drama
General Duration: 30mins

Network(s): NBC
Episode(s): "Boarding House Double Cross" (March 30, 1954)

82. Title: *Mike Malloy*
Genre: Crime Drama
General Duration: 15mins
Network(s): ABC
Episode(s): "The Pied Piper of Homicide Alley 1" (April 5, 1954)
"The Pied Piper of Homicide Alley 2" (April 6, 1954)
"The Pied Piper of Homicide Alley 3" (April 7, 1954)

83. Title: *Inheritance* (April 4, 1954 – May 1, 1955) was a historical anthology produced by NBC in partnership with The American Legion in the 1950s. Its creation was in response, in part, to the Red Scare era of the 1940s-1950s. Episodes showcased notable individuals and events in American history to educate and entertain, but to also cultivate a sense of patriotism in audiences during a very difficult time in the nation. Virginia is credited with one performance in this series though she may have performed in additional episodes uncredited or undocumented.
Genre: Historical Anthology
General Duration: 30mins
Network(s): NBC
Episode(s): "In Whatsoever House I Enter" (May 2, 1954)

84. Title: *San Francisco Final* (1954) was a short series, consisting by most accounts of only one episode, starring Jeff Chandler with supporting roles by Harry Bartell, Tony Barrett, Herb Butterfield, Jerry Housner, Lillian Biaff, Barney Phllips, Vic Perren, Olan Soule, and of course Virginia Gregg.
Genre: *Unavailable
General Duration: 30mins
Network(s): NBC, syndicated

Episode(s): "Chinatown" (July 26, 1954)

85. Title: *Barrie Craig, Confidential Investigator* (October 3, 1951 – June 30, 1955) was a detective drama starring William Gargan as Madison Avenue private eye "Barry Craig" and Ralph Bell as "Craig's" associate "Lt. Rogers." "Craig" is the antithesis of the typical hard-nosed detective in his laid-back approach to his investigations. The show primarily aired from New York until the last year of its run when it moved to Hollywood in 1954. Virginia is credited with performances in two episodes after the transition from its New York broadcast to Hollywood.
Genre: Detective Drama
General Duration: 30mins
Network(s): NBC
Episode(s): "Ghosts Don't Die in Bed" (September 7, 1954)
"Corpse on the Town" (March 9, 1955)

86. Title: *CBS Radio Workshop* (January 27, 1956 – September 22, 1957) was fairly short-lived anthology heard on CBS in the 1950s that delivered shows through experimental means in "workshop" fashion. Its creation was an attempt to revive a previous workshop series on the same network that began in the 1930s and ended in the 1940s. During its almost two-year run, various genres were heard on *CBS Radio Workshop* with many of the most well-known radio actors of the day including William Conrad, Parley Baer, Herb Butterfield, Vic Perrin, Lurene Tuttle, and of course, Virginia Gregg.
Genre: Anthology
General Duration: 30mins
Network(s): CBS
Episode(s): "Season of Disbelief/Hail & Farewell" (February 17, 1956)
"Speaking of Cinderella – If the Shoe Fits" (April 6, 1956)
"Jacob's Hands" (April 13, 1956)

"The Enormous Radio" (May 11, 1956)
"Colloquy Four: The Joe Miller Joke Book" (November 4, 1956)
"Air Raid (Prevarications of Mr. Peeps)" (March 10, 1957)
"No Plays of Japan" (April 7, 1957)
"Epitaphs - Spoon River Anthology" (June 2, 1957)
"Malihini Magic Vacations" (August 11, 1957)

87. Title: *Fort Laramie* (January 22, 1956 – October 28, 1956) was a western drama produced and directed by Norman MacDonnell in 1956. The relatively short-lived show takes listeners back to the 19th century Wild West to Wyoming's famous Fort Laramie. Raymond Burr stars as the show's protagonist, "Captain Lee Quince," while other radio moguls are among the recurring supporting cast including Vic Perrin, Harry Bartell, and Jack Moyles. Virginia performed in several of *Fort Laramie*'s 40 episodes.
Genre: Western Drama
General Duration: 30mins
Network(s): CBS
Episode(s): "Captain's Widow" (February 26, 1956)
"Hattie Pelfrey" (March 11, 1956)
"Gold/Black Hills Gold" (May 20, 1956)
"Sergeant's Baby" (May 27, 1956)
"Don't Kick my Horse" (June 3, 1956)
"Nature Boy" (July 29, 1956)
"Goodbye Willa" (August 19, 1956)
"The Chaplain" (August 26, 1956)
"The Return of Hattie Pelfrey" (September 2, 1956)
"Army Wife" (October 28, 1956)

88. Title: *O'Hara* (April 7, 1951 – September 30, 1951; May 14, 1958 – October 29, 1956) was a crime drama with two short-lived runs on air. Jack Moyles first stars as "O'Hara," the Hong Kong reporter who gets mixed up in a variety of adventures his investigative journalism. After Moyles, Stacy Harris plays "O'Hara" in the later run. Virginia is credited with two episodes of *O'Hara*, though it is likely she performed in additional episodes. Many recordings for this show are not in circulation, and it is difficult to determine her total log on *O'Hara*.

Genre: Crime Drama
General Duration: 30mins
Network(s): CBS
Episode(s): "The Judas Face" (July 22, 1951)
"The Lost Boy" (October 29, 1956)

89. Title: *Whispering Streets* (March 3, 1952 – November 25, 1960) was a dramatic series that used the "soap opera" formula through which stories were delivered each week leaving audiences hanging until the next for the story's continuance. Major and minor characters within the scripts narrate, and the novelty of the show, aside from its overall formula, was leaving audiences to wonder week-to-week which character would narrate next. Bette Davis was a favorite narrator on *Whispering Streets*, in addition to Cathy Lewis, Gertrude Warner, and Anne Seymour. Virginia performed in at least two episodes *Whispering Streets*.

Genre: Drama/Soap Opera
General Duration: 30mins
Network(s): ABC & CBS
Episode(s): "Daryl Madison & Lynn Russell (1958)
"Dana Russell & the Puppy" (1958)

90. Title: *Frontier Gentleman* (February 2, 1958 – November 16, 1958) was a western drama created, written, and produced by Anthony Ellis. John Dehner plays the starring role of "Kendall" the refined British journalist upon his tour of the American frontier. The show follows "Kendall's" adventures in encountering his next "story," which usually includes a mix of fictional and non-fictional characters of the Wild West. Virginia plays many supporting roles in this short-lived series with her fondness for the western genre, and her great comradery with Ellis and Dehner.

Genre: Western Drama

General Duration: 30mins

Network(s): KNX, CBS

Episode(s): "The Shelton Brothers/South Sunday" (February 2, 1958)

"The Honkytonkers" (February 16, 1958)

"The Lost Mine" (March 2, 1958)

"The Claim Jumpers" (March 9, 1958)

"Gentle Virtue" (March 30, 1958)

"Some Random Notes from a Stagecoach" (April 27, 1958)

"Daddy Bucks' Bucks/The Richest Man in the West" (May 4, 1958)

"Advice to the Lovelorn" (May 18, 1958)

"School Days/Duel for a School Marm" (June 1, 1958)

"The Bellboy's Prisoner" (June 8, 1958)

"The Well" (June 15, 1958)

"Nebraska Jack" (August 3, 1958)

"Wonder Boy/The Fastest Gun That Never Was" (August 17, 1958)

"The Golddigger" (September 28, 1958)

"The Librarian" (October 5, 1958)

"The Rainmaker" (October 26, 1958)

"Nasty People/The Deadly Grover Family" (November 2, 1958)

"Holiday" (November 9, 1958)

"Some Random Notes from a Train" (November 16, 1958)

91. Title: *Have Gun, Will Travel* (November 23, 1958 – November 1960) was a western series set in San Francisco that follows frontier hero "Paladin" (played by John Dehner) who, for a price, will enact justice into any western calamity that requires it – either by his calm sense of negotiation or his fast draw. Ben Wright plays the role of "Hey Boy," "Paladin's" Asian friend who works at the hotel "Paladin" calls home. Virginia plays the recurring role of "Hey Boy's" girlfriend "Miss Wong" along with various supporting roles throughout the series. The most unusual aspect of this production is that it ran on television before radio and was fairly successful on both media.

Genre: Western Drama

General Duration: 30mins

Network(s): ABC, CBS, syndicated

Episode(s): "Ella West" (December 7, 1958)

"No Visitors" (December 28, 1958)

"The Teacher" (January 25, 1959)

"A Matter of Ethics" (February 1, 1959)

"Return of Dr. Thackery" (February 15, 1959)

"Winchester Quarantine" (February 22, 1959)

"Hey Boy's Revenge" (March 1, 1959)

"Death of a Young Gunfighter" (March 15, 1959)

"A Sense of Justice" (March 29, 1959)

"Maggie O'Bannion" (April 5, 1959)

"The Colonel and the Lady" (April 12, 1959)

"Birds of a Feather" (April 19, 1959)

"The Gunsmith" (April 26, 1959)

"Gunshy" (May 3, 1959)

"The Statue of San Sebastian" (May 10, 1959)

"The Silver Queen" (May 17, 1959)

"Roped" (June 7, 1959)

"Bitter Wine" (June 14, 1959)

"Trouble in North Fork" (June 21, 1959)

"Homecoming" (June 28, 1959)

"Comanche" (July 5, 1959)

"Young Gun" (July 12, 1959)

"Deliver the Body" (July 19, 1959)

"The Wager" (July 26, 1959)

"High Wire" (August 2, 1959)

"Finn Alley" (August 9, 1959)

"The Lady" (August 16, 1959)

"Bonanza" (August 23, 1959)

"Love Birds" (August 30, 1959)

"All That Glitters" (September 6, 1959)

"Treasure Hunt" (September 13, 1959)

"Stardust" (September 20, 1959)

"Like Father" (September 27, 1959)

"Contessa Marie Desmoulins" (October 4, 1959)

"Stopover in Tombstone" (October 11, 1959)

"When in Rome" (October 25, 1959)

"Hired Gun/Assignment in Stone's Crossing" (November 8, 1959))

"Landfall" (November 15, 1959)

"Fair Fugitive" (November 22, 1959)

"Bitter Vengeance" (November 29, 1959)

"Out of Evil" (December 13, 1959)

"Ranch Carnival/Ranse Carnival" (December 20, 1959)

"About Face/The Marriage" (December 27, 1959)

"Return Engagement" (January 3, 1960)

"The Lonely One" (January 10, 1960)

"French Leave" (January 17, 1960)

"Nataemhon" (January 24, 1960)

"Bad Bert" (January 31, 1960)

"The Boss" (February 7, 1960)

"Bring Him Back Alive" (February 14, 1960)

"That Was No Lady" (February 21, 1960)

"The Dollhouse in Diamond Springs" (February 28, 1960)

"Somebody Out There Hates Me" (March 6, 1960)

"Montana Vendetta" (March 13, 1960)

"Caesar's Wife" (March 20, 1960)

"They Told Me You Were Dead" (March 27, 1960)

"Shanghai is a Verb" (April 3, 1960)

"So True, Mr. Barnum" (April 10, 1960)

"Prunella's Fella" (April 17, 1960)
"Irish Luck" (April 24, 1960)
"Dressed to Kill" (May 1, 1960)
"Pat Murphy" (May 8, 1960)
"Lena Countryman" (May 15, 1960)
"Dusty" (May 22, 1960)
"Lucky Penny" (May 29, 1960)
"Apache Concerto" (June 5, 1960)
"Search for Wylie Dawson" (June 12, 1960)
"Doctor from Vienna" (June 26, 1960)
"Dad-Blamed Luck" (July 3, 1960)
"Five Days to Yuma" (July 10, 1960)
"Little Guns" (July 17, 1960)
"My Son Must Die" (July 31, 1960)
"Viva/Father O'Toole's Organ Part 1" (August 7, 1960)
"Viva Extended/Father O'Toole's Organ Part 2" (August 14, 1960)
"For the Birds" (August 28, 1960)
"Eat Crow" (September 4, 1960)
"Deadline" (September 11, 1960)
"Nellie Watson's Boy" (September 18, 1960)
"Bringing Up Ollie" (September 25, 1960)
"Talika/The Snoop" (October 2, 1960)
"Sam Crow/Skeeter Hickshaw" (October 9, 1960)
"Stardust" (October 16, 1960)
"Hell Knows No Fury/Billy Boggs" (October 23, 1960)
"Oil" (October 30, 1960)
"The Odds" (November 6, 1960)
"The Map" (November 13, 1960)
"Martha Nell" (November 20, 1960)
"From Here to Boston" (November 27, 1960)

92. Title: *The Witness* (1959) was a dramatic anthology similar to the 1960 show *The Search*. *The Witness* tells the stories of average people being put to the test upon witnessing unusual scenarios that interrupt their everyday lives. Much like *The Search, The Witness* was also hosted by Robert Young, and syndicated through The Episcopal Church. Virginia performed in many episodes of both series.

Genre: Dramatic Anthology

General Duration: 15mins

Network(s): Syndicated, The Episcopal Church

Episode(s): "Parents and the Rigors of the Teens" (1959)

"The Abused Child" (1959)

"Kindness and Understanding" (1959)

"Parents and Juvenile Delinquency" (1959)

"Who is a Friend Indeed?" (1959)

"Blending Ethnic Backgrounds" (1959)

"A Boy's Mother Dies" (1959)

"A Farm Couple Adopts" (1959)

"The Good Samaritan of the Highway" (1959)

"Love Children" (1959)

"Mixed Races" (1959)

"Who is my Neighbor?" (1959)

"An Atmosphere of Love and Trust" (1959)

Title Unknown (1959)

93. Title: *The Search* (1960) was an anthology created and produced in association with The Episcopal Church in the telling of inspirational and cautionary tales of the humanities. The show's hosts, Robert Young and Art Gilmore, were involved in the show's creation, and while it is similar to *The Witness*, *The Search* is a bit heavier on religious ideology. Virginia appeared in a number of episodes in both series, though the exact titles are unclear for her performances on *The Search*. Descriptions, in lieu of titles, are listed below.

Genre: Dramatic/Inspirational Anthology

General Duration: 15mins

Network(s): Syndicated, The Episcopal Church, AFRTS

Episode(s): *Title Unknown* (Cop's son gets involved with a gang) (1960)
Title Unknown (Couple planning to divorce spend the weekend together) (1960)
Title Unknown (Young boy meets Scrooge after running away from home during a snowstorm) (1960)
Title Unknown (Wealthy man and lawyer force sister to sell stock) (1960)
Title Unknown (Neighbors quarrel over a backyard tree) (1960)
Title Unknown (A couple from the big city tries to adjust to suburb living) (1960)

94. Title: *Arch Oboler's Plays* (March 25, 1939 – October 11, 1945; October 3, 1964 – December 26, 1964) was an anthology series created, produced, and directed by radio kingpin Arch Oboler himself. Technically considered a dramatic anthology, *Plays* is mostly made up of thrills and mysteries similar to Oboler's work on *Lights Out* a few years prior. Oboler himself carried a great intensity that bled over into all his productions. Virginia was a favorite of his, appearing in many of his brainchildren. Part of her artistic appeal to Oboler probably lies in her fabulous ability to maintain and deliver the proper tension of a thriller or mystery script. She is credited with three *Plays* performances though she may have performed in additional episodes either uncredited or undocumented.
Genre: Anthology
General Duration: 30mins
Network(s): NBC and Mutual, Don Lee
Episode(s): "Come to the Bank" (October 31, 1964)
"Big Ben" (November 14, 1964)
"Mirage" (December 19, 1964)

95. Title: *Same Time, Same Station* was a rebroadcast of many of Arch Oboler's classics originally heard in the 1930s-1950s. Virginia is credited with one performance in this series.
Genre: Anthology
General Duration: 60mins
Network(s): KRLA, Pasadena
Episode(s): "Oboler Omnibus I" (April 16, 1972)

96. Title: *CBS Radio Mystery Theater* (1974 – 1982) was a popular radio show in the 1970s-1980s produced by Himan Brown, several years after the Golden Age of radio. Brown created this anthology packed full of thrills across all genres through CBS until its on-air end in 1982. Virginia is credited in two episodes of *CBS Radio Mystery Theater,* though she may have performed in additional episodes either uncredited or undocumented.
Genre: Anthology
General Duration: 60mins
Network(s): CBS, syndicated
Episode(s): "The Doll" (October 10, 1974)
"The Ghost Plane" (September 12, 1975)

97. Title: *The Ray Bradbury Theatre*
Genre: Anthology
General Duration: 30mins
Network(s): *Unavailable
Episode(s): "The Great Conflagration up at the Place" (1974)
"Forever and the Earth" (1974)

98. Title: *Threads of Glory* (1975)
Genre: Docudrama/Historical
General Duration: 60mins
Network(s): London Records (commercial release)

99. Title: *Sears Radio Theatre* (February 5, 1979 – August 2, 1979) was a dramatic anthology that ran in 1979, well after the end of the Golden Age of radio. Backed by Sears, it ran nightly on CBS and eventually on Mutual. It is an interesting series with scripts on a variety of subjects that never would have been mentioned on air during the Golden Age. Stories are told through themes respective to each weeknight during its run. Westerns were presented on Mondays with Lorne Green hosting, comedies on Tuesdays with Andy Griffith hosting, mysteries on Wednesdays with Vincent Price hosting, Thursdays were "Love and Hate Nights" with Cicely Tyson hosting, and adventures on Fridays with Richard Widmark (later Howard Duff) hosting. Virginia performed in episodes across all five genres of *Sears*, but mystery Wednesdays seemed to especially showcase her talent.

Genre: Dramatic Anthology

General Duration: 60mins

Network(s): CBS, Mutual

Episode(s): "Hostages" (February 7, 1979)

"This Home is Dissolved" (February 15, 1979)

"The Lady and the Outlaw" (March 5, 1979)

"A Matter of Priorities" (April 5, 1979)

"The Duke of Nevers" (April 16, 1979)

"The Old Boy" (April 18, 1979)

"Bruja/Brew-Ha" (April 20, 1979)

"The Other Grandmother" (May 3, 1979)

"Here's Morgan Again" (May 8, 1979)

"Country of Fear" (May 18, 1979)

"Here's Morgan Once More" (May 22, 1979)

"The Perfect Hostess" (June 13, 1979)

"Old Bones" (June 25, 1979)

"Katie Macbeth" (July 9, 1979)

"Spring Cleaning" (July 12, 1979)

"Uncle Zora Comes to the Pig Festival" (July 23, 1979)

"Reunion" (July 26, 1979)

Additional Radio Shows, Exact Dates of Performances Unknown

100. Title: *Calling All Cars* (November 1933 – September 1939) is considered one of the first true-crime police dramas on radio. It was written by William N. Robson, Mel Williamson, and Sam Pierce. It was produced by William N. Robson and directed by Robert Hixon. Chief James E. Davis of the Los Angeles Police Department hosted the show, and much like *Dragnet*, true-crime stories are told in intriguing dramatizations. Virginia cited *Calling All Cars* as her first official radio debut, but this show was not in the habit of crediting its players, so it is difficult to determine precisely in which shows she performed.
Genre: Crime/Drama
General Duration: 30mins
Network(s): CBS, Mutual, Don-Lee, & syndicated
Episode(s): *Title(s) & Air Dates Unknown

101. Title: *Romance of the Ranchos* (September 7, 1941 – May 10, 1942 and May 16, 1948 – May 23, 1948) was a historical anthology that tells dramatic stories of Long Beach, California's rich history. John Dunkel and Les Farber wrote many of the scripts for the thirty-five-episode run, based on E. Palmer Conner's historical text, *Romance of the Ranchos*. The episode entitled "The Story of the Carrillo Family" that first aired in 1942 tells the true story of Virginia's second husband, Jaime del Valle's family who had deep roots in California's founding.
Genre: Historical Anthology
General Duration: 30mins
Network(s): CBS, KNX
Episode(s): *Title(s) & Air Dates Unknown

102. Title: *Red Ryder* (February 3, 1942 – 1951) was a western series based off a popular comic strip by the same name created by Stephen Slesinger and Fred Harman. The series features western hero "Red Ryder" (first played by Reed Hadley) on his frontier adventures with his pals "Buckskin," (Horace Murphy) "Little Beaver," (first played by Tommy Cook) and trusty horse "Thunder." Virginia plays in various supporting roles throughout this series, though the titles and air dates are unknown.

Genre: Western
General Duration: 30mins
Network(s): NBC Blue Network
Episode(s): *Titles & Air Dates Unknown

103. Title: *Mayor of the Town* (September 6, 1942 – July 3, 1949) was a dramatic comedy featuring the talents of the legendary Lionel Barrymore as a cantankerous, albeit endearing hometown Mayor (a similar character perhaps to his "Dr. Gillespie" on *The Story of Doctor Kildare*). Agnes Moorehead plays "Marilly," the mayor's devoted housekeeper. A host of other characters appear on the show in the small-town dramas, and Virginia plays in various supporting roles throughout this series, though the titles and air dates are unknown.

Genre: Drama/Comedy
General Duration: 30mins
Network(s): CBS, NBC, ABC
Episode(s): *Titles & Air Dates Unknown

104. Title: *The Cisco Kid* (October 2, 1942 - 1959) was a popular western series in the 1940s-1950s based on O. Henry's 1907 short story "The Caballero's Way." The heroic lead, "The Cisco Kid" himself, was first played by Jackson Beck and later Jack Mather, with his trusty sidekick "Pancho" first played by Louis Sorin, then Harry Lang, and later Mel Blanc. Virginia plays in various supporting roles in this series, though the titles and air dates are unknown.

Genre: Western/Adventure
General Duration: 30mins

Network(s): WOR-Mutual & CBS
Episode(s): *Titles & Air Dates Unknown

105. Title: *The Casebook of Gregory Hood* (June 3, 1946 – 1950) was a detective series starring Gale Gordon as "Gregory Hood." The series was written by Denis Green and Anthony Boucher who also wrote Mutual's *Sherlock Holmes*. Hood is featured in his adventures as an importer out of San Francisco whose charming persona gets him into a variety of scrapes with sticky cases. "Hood's" loyal attorney "Sanderson Taylor" (first played by Art Gilmore) was always ready to help his friend out of his jams. Virginia plays in various supporting roles in this series, though the titles and air dates are unknown.
Genre: Crime
General Duration: 30mins
Network(s): Mutual, ABC, syndicated, Don Lee
Episode(s): *Titles & Air Dates Unknown

106. Title: *Favorite Story* (1946 – 1949) was an anthology series hosted by Ronald Colman that was very popular in the late 1940s. The series brings literary classics to life through some of the most talented voices in radio. Virginia plays in various supporting roles in this series, though the titles and air dates are unknown.
Genre: Anthology
General Duration: 30mins
Network(s): NBC, ZIV syndicated
Episode(s): *Titles & Air Dates Unknown

107. Title: *I Deal in Crime* (January 21, 1946 – September 4, 1948) was written by Ted Hediger and directed by Leonard Reeg. The show features "Ross Dolan" (William Gargan) as Navy veteran turned private detective in his adventures in solving a variety of cases. Supporting players on the show include Hans Conreid, Betty

Lou Gerson, Joseph Kearns, and Lurene Tuttle. Virginia play in various supporting roles in this series, though the titles and air dates are unknown.

Genre: Crime
General Duration: 30mins
Network(s): ABC, Mutual
Episode(s): *Titles & Air Dates Unknown

108. Title: *The Private Practice of Dr. Dana* (1947 – 1948)
Genre: Medical Drama
General Duration: 15mins
Network(s): CBS
Episode(s): "Dr. Dana Meets a Lady Doctor" (Air date unknown) "Dr. Carol Tracey's Secret" (Air date unknown)

109. Title: *Straight Arrow* (1948 – 1951) was a western adventure series that primarily appealed to younger audiences during its original broadcast. The series tells the story of a man in the Wild West who leads a fascinating double life as the Comanche Indian known as "Straight Arrow," and ordinary rancher known as "Steve Adams." Howard Culver stars in the dual role. Virginia plays in various supporting roles in this series, though the titles and air dates are unknown.

Genre: Western
General Duration: 30mins
Network(s): Don Lee, Mutual
Episode(s): *Titles & Air Dates Unknown

110. Title: *Life with Luigi* (September 21, 1948 – March 3, 1953) was a situation comedy about the loveable Italian immigrant "Luigi Basco" in his adventures of coming to America and assimilating into Chicago life just after WWII. "Luigi" is played by J. Carroll Naish, and others in the cast include Hans Conried, Alan Reed,

Jody Gilbert, Mary Shipp, Joe Forte, and Ken Peters. Virginia plays in various supporting roles in this series, though exact episodes and air dates of her performances are unknown.

Genre: Situation Comedy
General Duration: 15mins
Network(s): CBS
Episode(s): *Title(s) & Air Dates Unknown

111. Title: *Operation Little Vittles*
Genre: Drama
General Duration: *Unknown
Network(s): AFRS

112. Title: *The Heartbeat Theatre* (1956 – 1985) was considered the last live radio show to be regularly scheduled in radio history. It is a dramatic anthology that was sponsored by The Salvation Army and ran from 1956 until 1985, well beyond the Golden Age of radio, making it a favorite for Golden Age players like Virginia. She enjoyed performing in this series in her later life, though the titles and air dates of her performances are unknown.

Genre: Dramatic Anthology
General Duration: 30mins
Network(s): Syndicated, Salvation Army
*Title(s) & Air Dates Unknown
(And this is probably just the tip of the iceberg of Virginia's *truly complete* radiography.)

Appendix C: Selected Television Performances of Virginia Gregg with Description

1. **Title:** *Dragnet*; "The Big Speech" S1E6
Air Date: February 28, 1952
Genre: Crime
Duration: 30mins
VG's Role: Iris
Director(s): Jack Webb
Producer(s): Jack Webb
Production Company: Mark VII Ltd.
Distributor(s): NBC
Writer(s): Jack Webb & Kitty Buhler
Starring: Jack Webb, Barney Phillips, & Virginia Gregg
Episode Description: "Sgt. Friday" (Jack Webb) gives a speech at his former high school during an investigation of a student narcotic addict accused of attacking and robbing a local druggist.

2. **Title:** *Dragnet*; "The Big Trio" S2E5
Air Date: November 20, 1952
Genre: Crime
Duration: 30mins
VG's Role: Evelyn Monroe
Director(s): Jack Webb
Producer(s): Jack Webb
Production Company: Mark VII Ltd.
Distributor(s): NBC

Writer(s): Jack Webb
Starring: Jack Webb, Herbert Ellis, & Cliff Arquette
Episode Description: Over the holiday weekend, three traffic accidents require criminal investigation.

3. Title: *Dragnet*; "The Big Show" S2E11
Air Date: January 22, 1953
Genre: Crime
Duration: 30mins
VG's Role: Marjorie Lewis
Director(s): Jack Webb
Producer(s): Jack Webb
Production Company: Mark VII Ltd.
Distributor(s): NBC
Writer(s): James E. Moser & Jack Webb
Starring: Jack Webb, Ben Alexander, & Virginia Gregg
Episode Description: A baby is reported abandoned at a bus depot, but "Sgt. Friday" (Jack Webb) soon learns there is much more to the story.

4. Title: *General Electric Theater*; "Ride the River" S1E2
Air Date: February 8, 1953
Genre: Dramatic comedy
Duration: 30mins
VG's Role: May
Director(s): Sheldon Leonard
Producer(s): Gilbert Ralston & Arthur Ripley
Production Company: Revue Productions
Distributor(s): CBS
Writer(s): Douglas Heyes
Starring: Neville Brand, Bob Crane, & Broderick Crawford
Episode Description: A young outlaw joins forces with law enforcement to bring down a mutual enemy.

5. Title: *Dragnet*; "The Big Fourth" S2E29
Air Date: May 28, 1953
Genre: Crime
Duration: 30mins
VG's Role: Mrs. Doris Roth
Director(s): Jack Webb
Producer(s): Jack Webb
Production Company: Mark VII Ltd.
Distributor(s): NBC
Writer(s): Jack Webb & James E. Moser
Starring: Jack Webb, Ben Alexander, & Harry Bartell
Episode Description: "Sgt. Friday" (Jack Webb) is on the trail of a baby snatcher who kidnaps babies, then leaves them to be discovered soon after, unharmed.

6. Title: *Dragnet*; "The Big White Rat" S3E1
Air Date: September 3, 1953
Genre: Crime
Duration: 30mins
VG's Role: Voice
Director(s): Jack Webb
Producer(s): Michael Meshekoff
Production Company: Mark VII Ltd.
Distributor(s): NBC
Writer(s): Jack Webb, Ben Alexander, & John Robinson
Starring: Jack Webb, Dorothy Abbott, & Billy Chapin
Episode Description: A drug ring is investigated after reports of their activity.

7. Title: *Dragnet*; "The Big Pair" S4E4
Air Date: September 16, 1954
Genre: Crime
Duration: 30mins

VG's Role: Millie (voice, uncredited)
Director(s): Jack Webb
Producer(s): Michael Meshekoff
Production Company: Mark VII Ltd.
Distributor(s): NBC
Writer(s): Jack Webb
Starring: Jack Webb, Ben Alexander, & Beverly Washburn
Episode Description: Thieves pose as husband and wife in burglarizing the home of an old man and his granddaughter.

8. Title: *Dragnet*; "The Big Gangster: Part 2" S4E11
Air Date: November 4, 1954
Genre: Crime
Duration: 30mins
VG's Role: Audrey Thompson
Director(s): Jack Webb
Producer(s): Jack Webb
Production Company: Mark VII Ltd.
Distributor(s): NBC
Writer(s): Jack Webb & James E. Moser
Starring: Jack Webb, Michael Barrett, & Virginia Gregg
Episode Description: The death of a notorious gangster is investigated in the midst of an impending gang war.

9. Title: *Dragnet*; "The Big Want Ad" S4E13
Air Date: November 18, 1954
Genre: Crime
Duration: 30mins
VG's Role: Viola Palmer
Director(s): Jack Webb
Producer(s): Jack Webb
Production Company: Mark VII Ltd.
Distributor(s): NBC

Writer(s): Jack Webb
Starring: Jack Webb, Helen Andrews, & Virginia Gregg
Episode Description: "Sgt. Friday" (Jack Webb) goes undercover as an ex-con when a classified ad is answered by someone looking to hire a hit man.

10. Title: *Public Defender*; "Your Witness" S2E22
Air Date: January 27, 1955
Genre: Crime
Duration: 30mins
VG's Role: Judge Knox
Director(s): Harve Foster
Producer(s): Hal Roach Jr.
Production Company: Hal Roach Studios
Distributor(s): CBS
Writer(s): William P. Rousseau, Mort R. Lewis, & Sam Shayon
Starring: Reed Hadley, Walter Coy, & Virginia Gregg
Episode Description: Public defender "Bart Matthews" (Reed Hadley) defends accused killer "Karl Novak" (Walter Coy) after a shopkeeper is brutally murdered.

11. Title: *Dragnet*; "The Big Key" (1955) S4E26
Air Date: February 24, 1955
Genre: Crime
Duration: 30mins
VG's Role: Voice
Director(s): Jack Webb
Producer(s): Jack Webb
Production Company: Mark VII Ltd.
Distributor(s): NBC
Writer(s): Jack Webb
Starring: Jack Webb, William Boyett, & Virginia Gregg

Episode Description: When a woman is murdered, the LAPD has only a key to go on in tracking down her killer.

12. Title: *The Lineup;* "The Ann Brennizer Case" S1E27
Air Date: April 1, 1955
Genre: Crime
Duration: 30mins
VG's Role: Ann Brennizer
Director(s): Hollingsworth Morse
Producer(s): *Unavailable
Production Company: CBS Television Network
Distributor(s): CBS
Writer(s): *Unavailable
Starring: Warner Anderson, Tom Tully, & Marshall Reed
Episode Description: A strange case of robbery is investigated when only accounting records are stolen from a produce company.

13. Title: *Dragnet;* "The Big Pipe" (1955) S5E1
Air Date: September 1, 1955
Genre: Crime
Duration: 30mins
VG's Role: Minna Joyce
Director(s): Jack Webb
Producer(s): Jack Webb
Production Company: Mark VII Ltd.
Distributor(s): NBC
Writing: Jack Webb, John Robinson, & Frank Burt
Starring: Jack Webb, Ben Alexander, & Dan Barton
Episode Description: A woman is found beaten to death with a lead pipe, and it is up to the LAPD to catch her killer.

14. Title: *The Danny Thomas Show/Make Room for Daddy;* "Love Thy Neighbor" S3E4

Air Date: October 4, 1955
Genre: Comedy
Duration: 30mins
VG's Role: "Actress"
Director(s): Sheldon Leonard
Producer(s): Sheldon Leonard
Production Company: Marterto Productions
Distributor(s): ABC
Writer(s): Henry Garson
Starring: Danny Thomas, Frank Faylen, & Virginia Gregg
Episode Description: "Terry" (Sherry Jackson) plays referee when Danny and a new neighbor find themselves at odds.

15. Title: *Alfred Hitchcock Presents*; "Don't Come Back Alive" S1E4
Air Date: October 23, 1955
Genre: Thriller
Duration: 30mins
VG's Role: Mildred Partridge
Director(s): Robert Stevenson
Producer(s): Joan Harrison
Production Company: Shamley Productions
Distributor(s): CBS
Writer(s): Robert C. Dennis
Starring: Alfred Hitchcock, Sidney Blackmer, & Virginia Gregg
Episode Description: A husband and wife (Sidney Blackmer & Virginia Gregg) believe they have developed the perfect insurance scheme to come into a large sum of money, but their plan backfires.

16. Title: *Alfred Hitchcock Presents*; "Santa Claus and the Tenth Avenue Kid" S1E12
Air Date: December 18, 1955
Genre: Thriller
Duration: 30mins

VG's Role: Miss Clementine Webster
Director(s): Don Weis
Producer(s): Joan Harrison
Production Company: Shamley Productions
Distributor(s): CBS
Writer(s): Marian B. Cockrell & Margaret Cousins
Starring: Alfred Hitchcock, Barry Fitzgerald, & Virginia Gregg
Episode Description: A department store Santa with a past comes to the aid of a young boy.

17. **Title:** *Jane Wyman Presents the Fireside Theatre*; "Big Joe's Comin' Home" S1E18
Air Date: December 27, 1955
Genre: Drama
Duration: 30mins
VG's Role: Rosa
Director(s): Blake Edwards
Producer(s): William Asher
Production Company: Lewman Productions
Distributor(s): NBC
Writer(s): David P. Harmon
Starring: Jane Wyman, Tol Avery, & Jackie Blanchard
Episode Description: A gangster kingpin is released from prison after a twenty-five-year sentence and comes home surprised things are not the same.

18. **Title:** *Alfred Hitchcock Presents*; "And So Died Riabouchinska" S1E20
Air Date: February 12, 1956
Genre: Thriller
Duration: 30mins
VG's Role: Riabouchinska (voice)
Director(s): Robert Stevenson

Producer(s): Joan Harrison
Production Company: Shamley Productions
Distributor(s): CBS
Writer(s): Mel Dinelli & Ray Bradbury
Starring: Alfred Hitchcock, Claude Rains, & Charles Bronson
Episode Description: A detective gets a peculiar tip from a puppet during his investigation of a murder at an old vaudevillian theatre.

19. Title: *The Star and the Story;* "They" S2E17
Air Date: March 3, 1956
Genre: Drama
Duration: 30mins
VG's Role: *Unavailable
Director(s): Robert Stevenson
Producer(s): Warren Lewis
Production Company: Four Star Productions
Distributor(s): *Unavailable
Writer(s): Lawrence B. Marcus
Starring: Henry Fonda, Marjorie Bennett, & Chuck Connors
Episode Description: *Unavailable

20. Title: *Cavalcade of America;* "The Boy Nobody Wanted" S4E24
Air Date: May 29, 1956
Genre: Drama
Duration: 30mins
VG's Role: Mrs. Sherman
Director(s): Richard Kinon
Producer(s): Warren Lewis
Production Company: Four Star Productions
Distributor(s): ABC
Writer(s): László Görög, Winfred Van Atta, & Gwendolen Sherman
Starring: Virginia Gregg, Jean Inness, & Roy Barcroft

Episode Description: A young boy is implicated in the death of a playmate.

21. Title: *Four Star Playhouse*; "Success Story" S4E41
Air Date: July 26, 1956
Genre: Drama
Duration: 30mins
VG's Role: "Actress"
Director(s): Anton Leader
Producer(s): Dick Powell
Production Company: Four Star Productions
Distributor(s): CBS
Writer(s): James Bloodworth
Starring: Dick Powell, Robert Burton, & Peggie Castle
Episode Description: An ambitious businessman is hospitalized, and rethinks his life after meeting a certain young woman during his stay.

22. Title: *The Danny Thomas Show/ Make Room for Daddy*; "Boarding School" S4E1
Air Date: October 1, 1956
Genre: Comedy
Duration: 30mins
VG's Role: Dr. Paris
Director(s): Sheldon Leonard
Producer(s): Sheldon Leonard
Production Company: Marterto Productions
Distributor(s): ABC
Writer(s): Bill Manhoff
Starring: Danny Thomas, Sherry Jackson, & Rusty Hamer
Episode Description: Danny sends his children away to boarding school after losing his wife.

23. Title: *Lux Video Theatre;* "You Can't Escape Forever" S7E7
Air Date: November 1, 1956
Genre: Comedy
Duration: 60mins
VG's Role: Gerry Krale
Director(s): Norman Morgan
Producer(s): Earl Eby
Production Company: J. Walter Thompson Agency
Distributor(s): NBC
Writer(s): Roy Chanslor, Hector Chevigny, Ed James, & Fred Niblo Jr.
Starring: Leon Askin, Robert Burton, & Ken Carpenter
Episode Description: A newspaperman is assigned with writing a love advice column. He is initially disappointed in his assignment, but soon gets a lead on a big story.

24. Title: *Wire Service;* "The Night of August 7th" S1E5
Air Date: November 1, 1956
Genre: Drama
Duration: 60mins
VG's Role: Marie
Director(s): Alvin Ganzer
Producer(s): *Unavailable
Production Company: Desilu Productions
Distributor(s): ABC
Writer(s): Al C. Ward
Starring: George Brent, Malcolm Atterbury, & Virginia Gregg
Episode Description: State prisoners request a reporter be their witness in a cell block takeover.

25. Title: *General Electric Theater;* "The Charlatan" S5E9
Air Date: November 7, 1956
Genre: Drama

Duration: 30mins
VG's Role: Mamie
Director(s): John Brahm
Producer(s): William Frye
Production Company: Revue Productions
Distributor(s): CBS
Writer(s): Wells Root
Starring: Ronald Reagan, Bart Burns, & Virginia Gregg
Episode Description: *Unavailable

26. **Title:** *Studio 57*; "The Charlatan" S3E8
Air Date: November 7, 1956
Genre: Drama
Duration: 30mins
VG's Role: Mamie
Director(s): John Brahm
Producer(s): *Unavailable
Production Company: *Unavailable
Distributor(s): *Unavailable
Writer(s): Wells Root
Starring: Bart Burns, Virginia Gregg, & Jeff Morrow
Episode Description: *Unavailable

27. **Title:** *The Joseph Cotten Show: On Trial*; "The Trial of Mary Surratt" S1E8
Air Date: November 23, 1956
Genre: Crime
Duration: 30mins
VG's Role: Mary Surratt
Director(s): Ida Lupino
Producer(s): *Unavailable
Production Company: Fordyce Enterprises Productions
Distributor(s): NBC

Writer(s): *Unavailable
Starring: Ray Collins, Joseph Cotten, & Virginia Gregg
Episode Description: *Unavailable

28. Title: *Cavalcade of America*; "The Blessed Midnight" S5E12
Air Date: December 18, 1956
Genre: Drama
Duration: 30mins
VG's Role: Aunt Agnes
Director(s): Laslo Benedek
Producer(s): Warren Lewis & Don Sharpe
Production Company: Desilu Studios
Distributor(s): ABC
Writer(s): William Fay
Starring: Maureen O'Sullivan, Danny Richards Jr., & David Saber
Episode Description: On Christmas Eve, a young boy steals a cake for his aunt, and a friend tries to make up for his transgression.

29. Title: *Jane Wyman Presents the Fireside Theatre*; "A Point of Law" S2E16
Air Date: December 18, 1956
Genre: Drama
Duration: 30mins
VG's Role: Judge Swanson
Director(s): *Unavailable
Producer(s): *Unavailable
Production Company: Lewman Productions
Distributor(s): NBC
Writer(s): Hewitt Leonard Ballowe
Starring: Anthony Eustrel, Virginia Gregg, & Virginia Grey
Episode Description: *Unavailable

30. Title: *Wire Service;* "World of the Lonely" S1E14
Air Date: January 10, 1957
Genre: Drama
Duration: 60mins
VG's Role: Nora
Director(s): Anton Leader
Producer(s): *Unavailable
Production Company: Desilu Productions
Distributor(s): ABC
Writer(s): Gabrielle Upton
Starring: Mercedes McCambridge, Robert Cornthwaite, & Virginia Gregg
Episode Description: *Unavailable

31. Title: *Matinee Theatre;* "If This Be Error" S2E83
Air Date: January 11, 1957
Genre: Drama
Duration: 30mins
VG's Role: *Unavailable
Director(s): *Unavailable
Producer(s): *Unavailable
Production Company: NBC
Distributor(s): NBC
Writer(s): William Kendall Clark & Rachel Grieve
Starring: John Conte, John Dehner, & Virginia Gregg
Episode Description: A woman with a past meets the family of her new husband.

32. Title: *Alfred Hitchcock Presents;* "Nightmare in 4-D" S2E16
Air Date: January 13, 1957
Genre: Thriller
Duration: 30mins
VG's Role: Norma Parker

Director(s): Justus Addiss
Producer(s): Joan Harrison
Production Company: Shamley Productions
Distributor(s): CBS
Writer(s): Robert C. Dennis & Stuart Jerome
Starring: Alfred Hitchcock, Henry Jones, & Barbara Baxley
Episode Description: A man finds himself inside a nightmare that results in murder.

33. **Title:** *The Lineup;* "The Robert Ericson Case" S3E20
Air Date: February 15, 1957
Genre: Crime
Duration: 30mins
VG's Role: *Unavailable
Director(s): *Unavailable
Producer(s): *Unavailable
Production Company: CBS Television Network
Distributor(s): CBS
Writer(s): *Unavailable
Starring: Warner Anderson, Tom Tully, & Marshall Reed
Episode Description: *Unavailable

34. **Title:** *Studio 57;* "Big Joe's Coming Home" S3E22
Air Date: March 13, 1957
Genre: Drama
Duration: 30mins
VG's Role: Rosa
Director(s): Blake Edwards
Producer(s): William Asher
Production Company: Revue Productions
Distributor(s): *Unavailable
Writer(s): David P. Harmon
Starring: Tol Avery, Jackie Blanchard, & Douglass Dumbrille

Episode Description: A gangster kingpin is released from prison after a twenty-five-year sentence and comes home surprised things are not the same.

35. **Title:** *The Joseph Cotten Show: On Trial;* "The Freeman Case" S1E20
Air Date: March 15, 1957
Genre: Crime
Duration: 30mins
VG's Role: Fanny Seward
Director(s): *Unavailable
Producer(s): *Unavailable
Production Company: Fordyce Enterprises Productions
Distributor(s): NBC
Writer(s): *Unavailable
Starring: Joseph Cotten, Henry Daniell, & Virginia Gregg
Episode Description: *Unavailable

36. **Title:** *Lassie;* "The Snob" S3E31
Air Date: April 7, 1957
Genre: Drama
Duration: 30mins
VG's Role: Mrs. Powell
Director(s): Lesley Selander
Producer(s): Dusty Bruce & Robert Maxwell
Production Company: Robert Maxwell Associates
Distributor(s): CBS
Writer(s): Miriam Geiger, Eric Knight, & Joel Rapp
Starring: Jan Clayton, Tommy Rettig, & George Cleveland
Episode Description: "Jeff's" (Tommy Rettig) new neighbors are wealthy, and he becomes embarrassed of his family's lifestyle compared to theirs.

37. Title: *Crossroads*; "Big Sombrero" S2E28
Air Date: April 12, 1957
Genre: Drama
Duration: 30mins
VG's Role: Miss Dody
Director(s): *Unavailable
Producer(s): *Unavailable
Production Company: Federal Telefilms
Distributor(s): ABC
Writer(s): *Unavailable
Starring: John Alderson, Douglass Dumbrille, & Virginia Gregg
Episode Description: *Unavailable

38. Title: *The New Adventures of Charlie Chan*; "Your Money or Your Wife" S1E1
Air Date: August 9, 1957
Genre: Mystery
Duration: 30mins
VG's Role: Ms. Parsons
Director(s): Charles F. Haas
Producer(s): Sidney Marshall
Production Company: Television Programs of America (TPA)
Distributor(s): King Bee Video
Writer(s): Earl Derr Biggers, Richard Grey, & Brock Williams
Starring: J. Carrol Nash, Lowell Gilmore, & Virginia Gregg
Episode Description: "Charlie" (J. Carrol Nash) investigates what starts out as a murder plot, but when his client's wife is kidnapped and found murdered during the investigation, a new suspect is fingered.

39. Title: *Colt .45*; "Gallows at Granite Gap" S1E4
Air Date: November 8, 1957
Genre: Western

Duration: 30mins
VG's Role: Martha Naylor
Director(s): Franklin Adreon
Producer(s): Joseph Hoffman
Production Company: Warner Brothers Television
Distributor(s): ABC
Writer(s): Joseph Chadwick & William F. Leicester
Starring: Wayde Preston, John Smith, & Virginia Gregg
Episode Description: An infamous outlaw is captured, but a woman (Virginia Gregg) claiming to be his mother comes to town and complicates matters.

40. **Title:** *The Danny Thomas Show/Make Room for Daddy*; "Two Sleepy People" S5E6
Air Date: November 11, 1957
Genre: Comedy
Duration: 30mins
VG's Role: Sue ver Hagen
Director(s): Sheldon Leonard
Producer(s): Sheldon Leonard
Production Company: Marterto Productions
Distributor(s): CBS
Writer(s): Robert O'Brien & Irving Elinson
Starring: Danny Thomas, Marjorie Lord, & Rusty Hamer
Episode Description: After Danny and Kathy are told they have a humdrum lifestyle they decide to liven things up in competition with other active people their age.

41. **Title:** *Goodyear Theatre*; "Hurricane" S1E5
Air Date: November 25, 1957
Genre: Drama
Duration: 30mins
VG's Role: Judith Kennedy

Director(s): Tay Garnett
Producer(s): Robert Fellows
Production Company: Four Star Films
Distributor(s): NBC
Writer(s): Harold Swanton
Starring: Jane Powell, Douglas Dick, & Virginia Gregg
Episode Description: Two men bicker over inheritance, and one ends up dead during a hurricane.

42. **Title:** *Perry Mason*; "The Case of the Cautious Coquette" S1E18
Air Date: January 18, 1958
Genre: Crime
Duration: 60mins
VG's Role: Sheila Cromwell
Director(s): Laslo Benedek
Producer(s): Ben Brady
Production Company: CBS Television Network
Distributor(s): CBS
Writer(s): Erle Stanley Gardner, Leo Townsend, & Gene Wang
Starring: Raymond Burr, Barbara Hale, & William Hopper
Episode Description: "Perry" (Raymond Burr) investigates the claims of a woman who says she is being threatened and blackmailed by her husband. The case takes on a number of twists and turns when the husband ends up dead during the investigation.

43. **Title:** *Mr. Adams and Eve*; "Me, the Jury" S2E18
Air Date: January 24, 1958
Genre: Comedy
Duration: 30mins
VG's Role: Judge Banks
Director(s): *Unavailable
Producer(s): *Unavailable
Production Company: Four Star Productions

Distributor(s): CBS
Writer(s): Collier Young
Starring: Howard Duff, Ida Lupino, & Olive Carey
Episode Description: During production on a new movie, "Eve" (Ida Lupino) is called for jury duty. She is eager to serve, but her fame becomes a distraction for others.

44. Title: *Maverick*; "Day of Reckoning" S1E19
Air Date: February 2, 1958
Genre: Western
Duration: 60mins
VG's Role: Amy Hardie
Director(s): Leslie H. Martinson
Producer(s): Roy Huggins
Production Company: Warner Brothers Television
Distributor(s): ABC
Writer(s): Carey Wilber
Starring: James Garner, Jean Willes, & Mort Mills
Episode Description: Chaos ensues in town when a cowhand accuses "Maverick" (James Garner) of cheating during a card game and the Marshall must get involved.

45. Title: *Tombstone Territory*; "Postmarked for Death" S1E18
Air Date: February 12, 1958
Genre: Western
Duration: 30mins
VG's Role: Ella Hawley
Director(s): Ted Post
Producer(s): *Unavailable
Production Company: ZIV Television Programs
Distributor(s): ABC
Writer(s): Martin Berkeley & Clarke Reynolds
Starring: Pat Conway, Richard Eastham, & Virginia Gregg

Episode Description: A postmaster is gunned down on his route. "Clay" (Pat Conway) and his deputy soon learn the postmaster's death is related to a robbery in Tombstone committed by locals.

46. Title: *Trackdown*; "The Wedding" S1E19
Air Date: February 14, 1958
Genre: Western
Duration: 30mins
VG's Role: Matilda Parsons
Director(s): Don McDougall
Producer(s): Vincent M. Fennelly
Production Company: Four Star Productions
Distributor(s): CBS
Writer(s): Sidney Marshall
Starring: Robert Culp, Virginia Gregg, & Robert Burton
Episode Description: "Hoby Gilman" (Robert Culp) investigates when a wealthy man is killed on his wedding day.

47. Title: *State Trooper*; "Full Circle" S2E14
Air Date: February 16, 1958
Genre: Crime
Duration: 30mins
VG's Role: Laura Marco
Director(s): Tom Gries
Producer(s): *Unavailable
Production Company: Revue Productions
Distributor(s): MCA-TV
Writer(s): John Draft & Fenton Earnshaw
Starring: Rod Cameron, Virginia Gregg, & Bartlett Robinson
Episode Description: "Lt. Rod Blake" (Rod Cameron) investigates when a man is found murdered in his car.

48. Title: *Richard Diamond, Private Detective*; "The George Dale Case" S2E10
Air Date: March 6, 1958
Genre: Crime
Duration: 30mins
VG's Role: Vivian (voice)
Director(s): Richard Whorf
Producer(s): Mark Sandrich Jr.
Production Company: Four Star Productions
Distributor(s): CBS
Writer(s): Richard Carr, Sidney Michaels, & Blake Edwards
Starring: David Janssen, Regis Toomey, & Jean Willes
Episode Description: "Richard Diamond's" (David Janssen) newest client turns out to be a fraud who uses him as a fall guy.

49. Title: *Gunsmoke*; "Joke's on Us" S3E27
Air Date: March 15, 1958
Genre: Western
Duration: 30mins
VG's Role: Mrs. Tilman
Director(s): Ted Post
Producer(s): Norman MacDonnell
Production Company: CBS Television Network
Distributor(s): CBS
Writer(s): John Meston, Norman MacDonnell, & Charles Marquis Warren
Starring: James Arness, Dennis Weaver, & Milburn Stone
Episode Description: A man suspected of stealing a horse is lynched by his so-called friends. After his death, they learn he was in fact innocent, but now someone is killing off each person involved in his lynching.

50. Title: *Goodyear Theatre*; "Seventh Letter" S1E12
Air Date: March 17, 1958
Genre: Drama
Duration: 30mins
VG's Role: Louise Carter
Director(s): Robert Florey
Producer(s): Vincent M. Fennelly
Production Company: Four Star Films
Distributor(s): NBC
Writer(s): Charles Smith
Starring: Robert Ryan, Virginia Gregg, & Willard Sage
Episode Description: A policeman, overly dedicated to his work, is suspicious of his own wife as a possible murderess.

51. Title: *Panic!;* "Emergency" S2E1
Air Date: April 6, 1958
Genre: Drama
Duration: 30mins
VG's Role: Nurse Supervisor
Director(s): Fletcher Markle
Producer(s): Al Simon
Production Company: Al Simon Productions Inc.
Distributor(s): NBC
Writer(s): Charles Smith & Harold Swanton
Starring: Elisha Cook Jr., Peggy Webber, & Paul Harber
Episode Description: In order to save a boy's life, a man must lie about being his father.

52. Title: *The Court of Last Resort*; "The Allen Cutler Case" S1E26
Air Date: April 11, 1958
Genre: Crime
Duration: 30mins
VG's Role: Edith Cutler

Director(s): *Unavailable
Producer(s): *Unavailable
Production Company: Paisano Productions
Distributor(s): NBC
Writer(s): Erle Stanley Gardner & Harry Steeger
Starring: Robert H. Harris, Carleton Young, & S. John Launer
Episode Description: *Unavailable

53. Title: *State Trooper*; "Crisis at Comstock" S2E18
Air Date: April 13, 1958
Genre: Crime
Duration: 30mins
VG's Role: Helen Domby
Director(s): John English
Producer(s): *Unavailable
Production Company: Revue Productions
Distributor(s): Timeless Media
Writer(s): Barry Shipman
Starring: Rod Cameron, Douglas Kennedy, & Virginia Gregg
Episode Description: A spinster (Virginia Gregg) finds herself involved in criminal dealings after falling for the wrong man.

54. Title: *Sugarfoot*; "Price on His Head" S1E17
Air Date: April 29, 1958
Genre: Western
Duration: 60mins
VG's Role: Jane Lansing
Director(s): Richard L. Bare
Producer(s): Harry Tatelman
Production Company: Warner Brothers Television
Distributor(s): ABC
Writer(s): Henry Kuttner, C.L. Moore, Pamela Chais, & Leo Guild
Starring: Will Hutchins, Patrick McVey, & Venetia Stevenson

Episode Description: "Tom Brewster's" (Will Hutchins) stagecoach is hijacked and he along with the other passengers are taken hostage by three hooded outlaws until ransom is paid.

55. Title: *Mike Hammer;* "My Son and Heir" S1E25
Air Date: July 5, 1958
Genre: Crime
Duration: 30mins
VG's Role: Mrs. Oland
Director(s): Sherman Marks
Producer(s): *Unavailable
Production Company: Revue Productions
Distributor(s): MCA-TV
Writer(s): Mickey Spillane, Lawrence Kimble, & Stephen Marlowe
Starring: Darren McGavin, Robert F. Simon, & Douglas Dick
Episode Description: A wealthy businessman wants someone to rough up his son (and heir) because of his displeasing choice in a wife. The businessman hires "Mike" (Darren McGavin) for the job, and though he refuses, he soon learns the bride-to-be is dead.

56. Title: *Jefferson Drum;* "The Hanging of Joe Lavett" S1E14
Air Date: August 1, 1958
Genre: Western
Duration: 30mins
VG's Role: Louise Hammond
Director(s): *Unavailable
Producer(s): Mark Goodson, Matthew Rapf, & Bill Todman
Production Company: Mark Goodson-Bill Todman Productions
Distributor(s): NBC
Writer(s): *Unavailable
Starring: Jeff Richards, Eugene Mazzola, Cyril Delevanti
Episode Description: A woman comes to Jubilee to marry the man she has been engaged to, only to learn he has been hanged.

57. Title: *Zane Grey Theater*; "Homecoming" S3E3
Air Date: October 23, 1958
Genre: Western
Duration: 30mins
VG's Role: Hannah Benton
Director(s): John English
Producer(s): Hal Hudson
Production Company: Four Star Productions
Distributor(s): CBS
Writer(s): Bob Eisenbach, Nina Laemmle, & Ted Sherdeman
Starring: Lloyd Nolan, Rachel Ames, & Dennis Patrick
Episode Description: After a man robs a bank, his wife persuades him to return the money, but two outlaws stand in the way.

58. Title: *M Squad*; "The Trap" S2E5
Air Date: October 24, 1958
Genre: Crime
Duration: 30mins
VG's Role: Mrs. Mitchell
Director(s): Don Medford
Producer(s): John Francis Larkin
Production Company: Latimer Productions
Distributor(s): NBC
Writer(s): Donald S. Sanford
Starring: Lee Marvin, Paul Newlan, & Betty Lynn
Episode Description: A man is mistaken for a thief when he is shopping for an engagement ring. When the store owner accuses the man of stealing, a fight breaks out and the owner is accidently killed.

59. Title: *Have Gun Will Travel*; "A Sense of Justice" S2E8
Air Date: November 1, 1958
Genre: Western

Duration: 30mins
VG's Role: Widow Briggs
Director(s): Lamont Johnson
Producer(s): Sam Rolfe
Production Company: CBS Television Network
Distributor(s): CBS
Writer(s): John Kneubuhl, Herb Meadow, & Sam Rolfe
Starring: Richard Boone, Karl Swenson, & Virginia Gregg
Episode Description: "Paladin" (Richard Boone) intervenes when a mob goes after a man accused of murdering a notorious womanizer.

60. **Title:** *The Jack Benny Program*; "Stars' Wives Show" S9E4
Air Date: November 2, 1958
Genre: Comedy
Duration: 30mins
VG's Role: Secretary
Director(s): Seymour Berns
Producer(s): *Unavailable
Production Company: J&M Productions
Distributor(s): CBS
Writer(s): Sam Perrin, George Balzer, Al Gordon, & Hal Goldman
Starring: Jack Benny, Eddie "Rochester" Anderson, & Dennis Day
Episode Description: Jack hires a painter (Mel Blanc) who he rushes to save money. The Committee for the Improvement of Beverly Hills is made up of movie stars' wives, and they call a meeting with the mayor.

61. **Title:** *Schlitz Playhouse*; "Third Son" S8E6
Air Date: December 5, 1958
Genre: Drama
Duration: 30mins
VG's Role: Lissie Harpenning
Director(s): *Unavailable

Producer(s): *Unavailable
Production Company: Revue Studios
Distributor(s): CBS
Writer(s): Ernest Haycox & Tom Seller
Starring: Phil Chambers, Steve Forrest, & Virginia Gregg
Episode Description: The youngest of the three Harpenning brothers tries to decide what life path he should take.

62. Title: *Wanted: Dead or Alive;* "Eight Cent Reward" S1E16
Air Date: December 20, 1958
Genre: Western
Duration: 30mins
VG's Role: Hilda Stone
Director(s): Thomas Carr
Producer(s): John Robinson
Production Company: Four Star Productions
Distributor(s): CBS
Writer(s): John Robinson & Christopher Knopf
Starring: Steve McQueen, Mort Mills, & Virginia Gregg
Episode Description: A young boy offers "Josh Randall" (Steve McQueen) eight cents to bring Santa Claus in.

63. Title: *MacKenzie's Raiders;* "Blood on the Rio" S1E15
Air Date: January 17, 1959
Genre: Western
Duration: 30mins
VG's Role: Jenny Henderson
Director(s): Lew Landers
Producer(s): Elliott Lewis & Stephen Alexander
Production Company: ZIV Television Programs
Distributor(s): Timeless Media
Writer(s): Jim Thompson & Russell P. Reeder
Starring: Richard Carlson, Virginia Gregg, & Robert Anderson

Episode Description: A ranch owner ignores a warning to vacate during flooding, but an outlaw gang raids the ranch before rescue.

64. Title: *Whirlybirds;* "Rest in Peace" S2E39
Air Date: January 26, 1959
Genre: Adventure
Duration: 30mins
VG's Role: Mrs. Weldon
Director(s): Robert Altman
Producer(s): John H. Auer
Production Company: Desilu Productions
Distributor(s): CBS
Writer(s): Jerry Adelman, Jo Napoleon, & Art Napoleon
Starring: Kenneth Tobey, Craig Hill, & Bruce Bennett
Episode Description: A savvy businessman has a sneaky way of determining the true feelings of his potential clients.

65. Title: *Goodyear Theatre;* "Success Story" S2E10
Air Date: February 16, 1959
Genre: Drama
Duration: 30mins
VG's Role: Fay Lantry
Director(s): Walter Grauman
Producer(s): William Froug
Production Company: Briskin Productions
Distributor(s): NBC
Writer(s): Harold Jack Bloom, William Cowley, & Helen Spencer
Starring: Jim Backus, Virginia Gregg, & Carolyn Kearney
Episode Description: A smooth-talking relative (Jim Backus) comes home to visit with his usual wild tales of success, but his family soon learns he hasn't been quite as successful as he says.

66. Title: *Behind Closed Doors*; "The Meeting" S1E21
Air Date: March 5, 1959
Genre: Drama
Duration: 30mins
VG's Role: Zina
Director(s): John Peyser
Producer(s): Sidney Marshall
Production Company: Jane Gallu Productions Inc.
Distributor(s): NBC
Writer(s): Robert C. Dennis
Starring: Bruce Gordon, Wolfe Barzell, & Judith Braun
Episode Description: *Unavailable

67. Title: *Rawhide*; "Incident of the Misplaced Indians" S1E16
Air Date: May 1, 1959
Genre: Western
Duration: 60mins
VG's Role: Clarissa Gray
Director(s): Jesse Hibbs
Producer(s): Charles Marquis Warren
Production Company: CBS Television Network
Distributor(s): CBS
Writer(s): David Victor, Herbert Little Jr., & Charles Marquis Warren
Starring: Eric Fleming, Clint Eastwood, & Sheb Wooley
Episode Description: Indians are found dead near a woman's home, and she is so traumatized she can't speak.

68. Title: *Mike Hammer*; "Curtains for an Angel" S2E21
Air Date: May 22, 1959
Genre: Crime
Duration: 30mins
VG's Role: Elsa Hurlbert

Director(s): William Witney
Producer(s): *Unavailable
Production Company: Revue Productions
Distributor(s): *Unavailable
Writer(s): Mickey Spillane
Starring: Darren McGavin, Richard Crane, & Abby Dalton
Episode Description: The wife of an affluent professor runs a theatre. "Hammer" (Darren McGavin) gets called in to investigate when an actor is accused of murdering her.

69. Title: *Sugarfoot*; "Wolf" S2E20
Air Date: June 9, 1959
Genre: Western
Duration: 60mins
VG's Role: Belle Kellogg
Director(s): Joseph Lejtes
Producer(s): Harry Tatelman
Production Company: Warner Brothers Television
Distributor(s): ABC
Writer(s): Milton S. Gelman & Robert Moore Williams
Starring: Will Hutchins, Judy Nugent, & William Fawcett
Episode Description: The town is divided when a homesteader is accused of cattle rustling, and his son, a gunslinger, returns home.

70. Title: *State Trooper*; "The Woman Who Cried Wolf" S2E30
Air Date: August 6, 1959
Genre: Crime
Duration: 30mins
VG's Role: Clara Lacey
Director(s): John English
Producer(s): Richard Irving
Production Company: Revue Productions
Distributor(s): MCA-TV

Writer(s): Barry Shipman
Starring: Rod Cameron, Richard H. Cutting, & Virginia Gregg
Episode Description: "Lt. Rod Blake" (Rod Cameron) investigates when a woman (Virginia Gregg) claims she is being harassed after her husband (Billy Snyder) replaces her in his vaudeville show.

71. Title: *Wanted Dead or Alive*; "The Healing Woman" S2E2
Air Date: September 12, 1959
Genre: Western
Duration: 30mins
VG's Role: Amanda Summers
Director(s): Don McDougall
Producer(s): John Robinson
Production Company: Four Star Productions
Distributor(s): CBS
Writer(s): Charles Beaumont & Richard Matheson
Starring: Steve McQueen, Mort Mills, & Virginia Gregg
Episode Description: "Josh Randall" (Steve McQueen) tries to persuade a couple (Mort Mills & Virginia Gregg) to get their son proper medical treatment instead of witch healing when he is diagnosed with appendicitis.

72. Title: *Maverick*; "Pappy" S3E1
Air Date: September 13, 1959
Genre: Western
Duration: 60mins
VG's Role: Gida Jamison
Director(s): Montgomery Pittman
Producer(s): Coles Trapnell
Production Company: Warner Brothers Television
Distributor(s): ABC
Writer(s): Montgomery Pittman
Starring: James Garner, Jack Kelly, & Adam West

Episode Description: Brothers "Bret" (James Garner) and "Bart" (Jack Kelly) find out their Pappy is engaged to a much younger woman whose father wants Pappy dead.

73. Title: *Philip Marlowe*; "The Ugly Duckling" S1E1
Air Date: October 6, 1959
Genre: Crime
Duration: 30mins
VG's Role: Luceille Jordan
Director(s): Robert Ellis Miller
Producer(s): Gene Wang
Production Company: Bilmar Productions
Distributor(s): ABC
Writer(s): Raymond Chandler & Gene Wang
Starring: Philip Carey, Virginia Gregg, & Rhys Williams
Episode Description: "Philip Marlowe" (Philip Carey) investigates when a woman believes her husband and his mistress wish her dead.

74. Title: *Captain David Grief*; "The Return of Blackbeard" S2E5
Air Date: October 18, 1959
Genre: Adventure
Duration: 30mins
VG's Role: China Mary
Director(s): Stuart Heisler
Producer(s): Sidney T. Bruckner & Duke Goldstone
Production Company: Guild Films
Distributor(s): *Unavailable
Writer(s): Jack London
Starring: Maxwell Reed, George Wallace, & Arthur Shields
Episode Description: *Unavailable

75. Title: *The Detectives*; "The Hiding Place" S1E3
Air Date: October 30, 1959

Genre: Crime
Duration: 30mins
VG's Role: Mrs. Cooper
Director(s): Joseph H. Lewis
Producer(s): Arthur Gardner, Arnold Laven, & Jules V. Levy
Production Company: Four Star Productions
Distributor(s): ABC
Writer(s): Donald S. Sanford
Starring: Robert Taylor, Tige Andrews, & Lee Farr
Episode Description: *Unavailable

76. **Title:** *Wichita Town*; "Man on the Hill" S1E6
Air Date: November 4, 1959
Genre: Western
Duration: 30mins
VG's Role: Mal Slocum
Director(s): *Unavailable
Producer(s): *Unavailable
Production Company: Four Star Productions
Distributor(s): NBC
Writer(s): *Unavailable
Starring: Don Grady, Virginia Gregg, & Jennifer Lea
Episode Description: *Unavailable

77. **Title:** *General Electric Theater;* "R.S.V.P." S8E17
Air Date: January 10, 1960
Genre: Drama
Duration: 30mins
VG's Role: Sybil
Director(s): Richard Irving
Producer(s): Joseph T. Naar
Production Company: Revue Studios
Distributor(s): CBS

Writer(s): Jameson Brewer & Al Hine
Starring: Ronald Reagan, Joe Cranston, & Ralph Dumke
Episode Description: Theatrical diva, "Antonia Stuart" (Greer Garson), accepts an invitation to visit a former schoolmate at her home in the country. As the visit progresses, it becomes clear that the hostess's real reason for inviting "Antonia" is revenge.

78. Title: *Bourbon Street Beat*; "Inside Man" S1E15
Air Date: January 11, 1960
Genre: Crime
Duration: 60mins
VG's Role: Ma Ballard
Director(s): Leslie H. Martinson
Producer(s): Charles Hoffman & Harry Tatelman
Production Company: Warner Brothers Television
Distributor(s): ABC
Writer(s): Howard Browne, Ivan Goff, & Ben Roberts
Starring: Richard Long, Andrew Duggan, & Van Williams
Episode Description: When "Rex's" friend is found dead, he goes undercover to find the murderers.

79. Title: *Johnny Midnight*; "An Old-Fashioned Frame" S1E13
Air Date: March 25, 1960
Genre: Crime
Duration: 30mins
VG's Role: Mona Kent
Director(s): John English
Producer(s): Jack Chertok
Production Company: Midnight Productions
Distributor(s): *Unavailable
Writer(s): László Görög & Liam O'Brien
Starring: Edmond O'Brien, Yuki Shimoda, & Virginia Gregg

Episode Description: A woman is found dead in an apparent suicide, but "Johnny Midnight" (Edmond O'Brien) suspects foul play and investigates.

80. Title: *The Man from Blackhawk*; "The Last Days of Jessie Turnbull" S1E25
Air Date: April 1, 1960
Genre: Western
Duration: 30mins
VG's Role: Julie Turnbull
Director(s): *Unavailable
Producer(s): Herb Meadow
Production Company: Stuart-Oliver Inc.
Distributor(s): ABC
Writer(s): Frank Baron
Starring: Robert Rockwell, Virginia Gregg, & Chubby Johnson
Episode Description: *Unavailable

81. Title: *The DuPont Show with June Allyson*; "Surprise Party" S1E28
Air Date: April 18, 1960
Genre: Drama
Duration: 30mins
VG's Role: Dorothy
Director(s): David Lowell Rich
Producer(s): Alvin Cooperman & Shelley Hull
Production Company: Four Star Television
Distributor(s): CBS
Writer(s): David P. Harmon
Starring: Myrna Loy, Shepperd Strudwick, & Gerald Mohr
Episode Description: "Mary Sidney" (Myrna Loy) is on her way home where her family and friends have planned a surprise party for her. She is delayed when she runs into an old flame.

82. Title: *Bronco*; "Winter Kill" S2E19
Air Date: May 31, 1960
Genre: Western
Duration: 60mins
VG's Role: Kate Crowley
Director(s): Jesse Hibbs
Producer(s): Arthur W. Silver
Production Company: Warner Brothers Television
Distributor(s): ABC
Writer(s): Walter Doniger & Kenneth Higgins
Starring: Ty Hardin, Edgar Buchanan, & Virginia Gregg
Episode Description: "Marshal Sample" (John Litel) and "Bronco" (Ty Hardin) save a prisoner from hanging, but an embittered mother who has sworn revenge on the prisoner interferes with his escort.

83. Title: *The Barbara Stanwyck Show*; "Discreet Deception" S1E3
Air Date: October 10, 1960
Genre: Drama
Duration: 30mins
VG's Role: Vivian Lambert
Director(s): *Unavailable
Producer(s): William H. Wright & Louis F. Edelman
Production Company: ESW Productions
Distributor(s): Entertainment One
Writer(s): *Unavailable
Starring: Barbara Stanwyck, Virginia Gregg, & Patric Knowles
Episode Description: Theatre producer "Amelia Lambert" (Barbara Stanwyck) falls for her late husband's brother (Patric Knowles) who is already married.

84. Title: *Klondike*; "Saints and Stickups" S1E3
Air Date: October 31, 1960
Genre: Western

Duration: 30mins
VG's Role: Harmony Hariess
Director(s): William Conrad
Producer(s): *Unavailable
Production Company: ZIV Television Programs
Distributor(s): NBC
Writer(s): Richard Donovan & Fritz Goodwin
Starring: Ralph Taeger, James Coburn, & Whit Bissell
Episode Description: *Unavailable

85. Title: *The Deputy*; "Bitter Root" S2E6
Air Date: November 5, 1960
Genre: Western
Duration: 30mins
VG's Role: Hester Macklin
Director(s): Louis King
Producer(s): Michael Kraike
Production Company: Top Gun Productions
Distributor(s): NBC
Writer(s): Kay Lenard, Jess Carneol, & Roland Kibbee
Starring: Henry Fonda, Allen Case, & Read Morgan
Episode Description: A lonely, irascible woman, "Hester Macklin" (Virginia Gregg), owns the only good water hole in the area and harbors a wounded fugitive (Don Megowan) from "Deputy Clay McCord" (Allen Case) and "Sgt. Hapgood Tasker" (Read Morgan).

86. Title: *The Westerner*; "Going Home" S1E11
Air Date: December 16, 1960
Genre: Western
Duration: 30mins
VG's Role: Sabetha
Director(s): Elliot Silverstein
Producer(s): Sam Peckinpah

Production Company: Four Star Productions
Distributor(s): NBC
Writer(s): Jack Curtis & Sam Peckinpah
Starring: Brian Keith, Virginia Gregg, & Jack Kruschen
Episode Description: "Dave" (Brian Keith) helps protect two women and an injured man who are dodging a bounty hunter.

87. **Title:** *Checkmate*; "Hour of Execution" S1E16
Air Date: January 21, 1961
Genre: Crime
Duration: 60mins
VG's Role: Ethyl Addison
Director(s): John English
Producer(s): Jon Kubichan & Herbert Coleman
Production Company: Jamco Productions
Distributor(s): CBS
Writer(s): Eric Ambler, Robert Libott, & Helen Nielsen
Starring: Anthony George, Doug McClure, & Sebastian Cabot
Episode Description: "Checkmate" investigates when a friend of "Dr. Hyatt's" who is a judge (James Gregory) is being threatened if a man he sent to prison is executed.

88. **Title:** *The Americans*; Harper's Ferry S1E1
Air Date: January 23, 1961
Genre: Action
Duration: 60mins
VG's Role: *Unavailable
Director(s): Douglas Heyes
Producer(s): Gordon Kay & Frank Telford
Production Company: NBC
Distributor(s): NBC
Writer(s): James Warner Bellah & John Gay
Starring: Darryl Hickman, Richard Davalos, & John McIntire

Episode Description: The Canfield family is torn when the Civil War begins.

89. Title: *The Rebel*; "Paperback Hero" S2E20
Air Date: January 26, 1961
Genre: Western
Duration: 30mins
VG's Role: Emily Stevens
Director(s): Bernard L. Kowalski
Producer(s): Andrew J. Fenady
Production Company: Mark Goodson-Bill Todman Productions
Distributor(s): ABC
Writer(s): Nick Adams, Andrew J. Fenady, & Frederick Louis Fox
Starring: Nick Adams, Bobby Diamond, & Virginia Gregg
Episode Description: A female reporter (Virginia Gregg) turns "Yuma" (Nick Adams) into a frontier hero after seeing him defend a young boy against a bully.

90. Title: *Maverick*; "The Ice Man" E4S20
Air Date: January 29, 1961
Genre: Western
Duration: 60mins
VG's Role: Abbey
Director(s): Charles F. Haas
Producer(s): William T. Orr
Production Company: Warner Brothers Television
Distributor(s): ABC
Writer(s): Peter Germano & Palmer Thompson
Starring: Jack Kelly, Andrew Duggan, & Shirley Knight
Episode Description: "Maverick" (Jack Kelly) finds a body in ice, but his investigation into how the body got there gets complicated.

91. Title: *Bat Masterson*; "A Lesson in Violence" E3S20
Air Date: February 23, 1961
Genre: Western
Duration: 30mins
VG's Role: Nora Grant
Director(s): Franklin Adreon
Producer(s): Frank Pittman & Andy White
Production Company: ZIV Television Programs
Distributor(s): NBC
Writer(s): Richard O'Connor & Frank Grenville
Starring: Gene Barry, Richard Eastham, & Allen Jaffe
Episode Description: "Bat" (Gene Barry) travels to a Texas ranch after receiving a telegram to drive cattle to Abilene. When he arrives at the ranch, the owners, the Grants, think he is a hired gunman.

92. Title: *Zane Grey Theater*; "The Atoner" S5E25
Air Date: April 6, 1961
Genre: Western
Duration: 30mins
VG's Role: Sarah Tompkins
Director(s): Laslo Benedek
Producer(s): Aaron Spelling
Production Company: Four Star Productions
Distributor(s): CBS
Writer(s): Howard Dimsdale
Starring: Herbert Marshall, Edward Binns, & Britt Lomond
Episode Description: A town's religious leader outlaws saloons and gambling halls and will stop at nothing to maintain his iron first over the town.

93. Title: *Gunsmoke*; "Minnie" S6E30
Air Date: April 15, 1961
Genre: Western

Duration: 30mins
VG's Role: Minnie
Director(s): Harry Harris
Producer(s): Norman MacDonnell
Production Company: Arness and Co.
Distributor(s): CBS
Writer(s): John Meston, Norman MacDonnell, & Charles Marquis Warren
Starring: James Arness, Dennis Weaver, & Milburn Stone
Episode Description: "Minnie" (Virginia Gregg), the rugged woman of a skinner, comes to Dodge in need of medical attention. She falls in love with Doc Adams after he treats her injuries much to the chagrin of her husband who comes to town looking for her.

94. Title: *Thriller*; "Mr. George" S1E32
Air Date: May 9, 1961
Genre: Crime
Duration: 60mins
VG's Role: Edna Leggett
Director(s): Ida Lupino
Producer(s): William Frye
Production Company: Hubbell Robinson Productions
Distributor(s): Image Entertainment
Writer(s): August Derleth & Donald S. Sanford
Starring: Boris Karloff, Virginia Gregg, & Howard Freeman
Episode Description: A young girl named "Priscilla" (Gina Gillespie) who lives with greedy relatives is protected by a ghostly presence named "Mr. George."

95. Title: *Gunsmoke*; "The Imposter" S6E34
Air Date: May 13, 1961
Genre: Western
Duration: 30mins

VG's Role: Mrs. Clara Curtin
Director(s): Byron Paul
Producer(s): Norman MacDonnell
Production Company: Arness and Co.
Distributor(s): CBS
Writer(s): John Meston, Kathleen Hite, & Norman MacDonnell
Starring: James Arness, Dennis Weaver, & Milburn Stone
Episode Description: A sheriff comes to Dodge with a secret that is soon revealed by an old enemy.

96. Title: *77 Sunset Strip*; "The Rival Eye Caper" S4E1
Air Date: September 22, 1961
Genre: Drama
Duration: 60mins
VG's Role: Nola Chase
Director(s): Jeffrey Hayden
Producer(s): Fenton Earnshaw
Production Company: Warner Brothers Television
Distributor(s): ABC
Writer(s): Sonya Roberts & William Pugsley
Starring: Efrem Zimbalist Jr., Roger Smith, & Edd Byrnes
Episode Description: "Stuart Bailey" (Efrem Zimbalist Jr.) and "Jeff Spencer" (Roger Smith) become suspicious when they encounter a private eye business that seems to solve all their crimes instantly.

97. Title: *Hawaiian Eye*; "Satan City" S3E1
Air Date: September 27, 1961
Genre: Crime
VG's Role: Hilda Barton
Director(s): Paul Landres
Producer(s): Ed Jurist
Production Company: Warner Brothers Television
Distributor(s): ABC

Writer(s): Ed Jurist, Gibson Fox, & Darryl Hickman
Starring: Grant Williams, Connie Stevens, & Poncie Ponce
Episode Description: "Greg" (Grant Williams) investigates when a writer's latest manuscript comes up missing shortly after she arrives in Hawaii.

98. Title: *Perry Mason*; "The Case of the Pathetic Patient" S5E7
Air Date: October 28, 1961
Genre: Crime
Duration: 60mins
VG's Role: Mrs. Osborn
Director(s): Bernard L. Kowalski
Producer(s): Arthur Marks
Production Company: CBS Television Network
Distributor(s): CBS
Writer(s): Erle Stanley Gardner & Maurice Zimm
Starring: Raymond Burr, Barbara Hale, & William Hopper
Episode Description: "Perry" (Raymond Burr) gets involved when a doctor is accused of malpractice and a murder occurs during the investigation.

99. Title: *Adventures in Paradise*; "The Pretender" S3E7
Air Date: November 12, 1961
Genre: Adventure
Duration: 60mins
VG's Role: Kate Anthony
Director(s): Robert Florey
Producer(s): Martin Manulis & Art Wallace
Production Company: Martin Manulis Productions
Distributor(s): ABC
Writer(s): George Bellak, James A. Michener, & Louis Vittes
Starring: Gardner McKay, Guy Stockwell, & James Holden

Episode Description: "Adam" (Gardner McKay) helps a young girl find her missing uncle.

100. Title: *Dr. Kildare*; "Johnny Temple" S1E14
Air Date: December 28, 1961
Genre: Drama
Duration: 60mins
VG's Role: Grace Temple
Director(s): Ralph Senensky
Producer(s): Herbert Hirschman
Production Company: Arena Productions
Distributor(s): NBC
Writer(s): Archie L. Tegland & David P. Harmon
Starring: Richard Chamberlain, Raymond Massey, & Peter Whitney
Episode Description: A teenager is stabbed in a street fight and starts behaving strangely after he recovers, though his parents are not cooperative with treatment recommendations.

101. Title: *The New Breed*; "The All-American Boy" S1E14
Air Date: January 2, 1962
Genre: Drama
Duration: 60mins
VG's Role: Georgine
Director(s): *Unavailable
Producer(s): Arthur Fellows & Quinn Martin
Production Company: Quinn Martin Productions
Distributor(s): ABC
Writer(s): Hank Searls
Starring: Leslie Nielsen, John Beradino, & Edward Binns
Episode Description: "Lt. Price Adams" (Leslie Nielsen) faces criticism after wounding a popular high school student.

102. Title: *Have Gun Will Travel*; "Don't Shoot the Piano Player" S5E26
Air Date: March 10, 1962
Genre: Western
Duration: 30mins
VG's Role: Big Nellie
Director(s): William Conrad
Producer(s): Frank Pierson
Production Company: CBS Television Network
Distributor(s): CBS
Writer(s): Shimon Wincelberg, Herb Meadow, & Sam Rolfe
Starring: Richard Boone, Fintan Meyler, & George Kennedy
Episode Description: "Paladin" (Richard Boone) is hired to find a girl's lover. "Paladin" finds him working as a piano player in a saloon and must win a bet to set him free from his position.

103. Title: *Lawman*; "Clootey Hutter" S4E26
Air Date: March 11, 1962
Genre: Western
Duration: 30mins
VG's Role: Clootey Hutter
Director(s): Richard C. Sarafian
Producer(s): Jules Schermer
Production Company: Warner Brothers Television
Distributor(s): ABC
Writer(s): Robert Vincent Wright
Starring: John Russell, Peter Brown, & Peggie Castle
Episode Description: Gunslinging "Clootey Hutter" (Virginia Gregg) comes into town and has a run in with two rowdy brothers, and one challenges her to a gunfight.

104. Title: *General Electric Theater*; "My Dark Days: Part 1" S10E25
Air Date: March 18, 1962

Genre: Drama
Duration: 30mins
VG's Role: Helen
Director(s): Charles F. Haas
Producer(s): *Unavailable
Production Company: Revue Studios
Distributor(s): CBS
Writer(s): Marion Miller
Starring: Gail Bonney, Jeanne Crain, & Robert Emhardt
Episode Description: *Unavailable

105. **Title:** *General Electric Theater;* "My Dark Days: Part 2" S10E26
Air Date: March 25, 1962
Genre: Drama
Duration: 30mins
VG's Role: Helen
Director(s): Charles F. Haas
Producer(s): *Unavailable
Production Company: Revue Studios
Distributor(s): CBS
Writer(s): Marion Miller
Starring: Gail Bonney, Jeanne Crain, & Robert Emhardt
Episode Description: *Unavailable

106. **Title:** *The Real McCoys;* "Don't Judge a Book" S5E28
Air Date: May 3, 1962
Genre: Family
Duration: 30mins
VG's Role: Sarah
Director(s): David Alexander
Producer(s): Danny Arnold
Production Company: Brennan-Westgate
Distributor(s): ABC

Writer(s): Irving Elinson, Fred S. Fox, & Irving Pincus
Starring: Walter Brennan, Richard Crenna, & Kathleen Nolan
Episode Description: When relatives "Harry" (Edward Andrews) and "Sarah" (Virginia Gregg) come to visit the McCoys, "Grandpa" (Walter Brennan) tries to help their marriage.

107. **Title:** *Ben Casey*; "An Uncommonly Innocent Killing" S1E30
Air Date: May 7, 1962
Genre: Drama
Duration: 60mins
VG's Role: Mrs. Billstrom
Director(s): Alex March
Producer(s): *Unavailable
Production Company: Bing Crosby Productions
Distributor(s): ABC
Writer(s): James E. Moser, Don Brinkley, & Lester Pine
Starring: Vince Edwards, Sam Jaffe, & Philip Abbott
Episode Description: "Gene Billstrom" (Eddie Albert) and his family are well-known in the community. He must struggle with the stigma of mental illness when admitted to the hospital for an evaluation.

108. **Title:** *Hazel*; "Heat Wave" S1E33
Air Date: May 24, 1962
Genre: Comedy
Duration: 30mins
VG's Role: Mrs. Merryweather
Director(s): William D. Russell
Producer(s): James Fonda
Production Company: Screen Gems
Distributor(s): NBC
Writer(s): Ted Key & Louella MacFarlene
Starring: Shirley Booth, Don DeFore, & Whitney Blake

Episode Description: "Hazel" (Shirley Booth) tries to convince "Mr. Baxter" (Don DeFore) to install an air conditioning in the home after a neighbor gets a new air conditioning system their maid brags about.

109. Title: *Calvin and the Colonel*; "The Television Job" S1E1
Air Date: October 3, 1961
Genre: Animation
Duration: 30mins
VG's Role: Maggie Belle Klaxon (voice)
Director(s): Charles McKimson
Producer(s): Joe Connelly, Bob Ganon, Bob Mosher, Sam Nicholson, & Gerald Ray
Production Company: Kayro Productions
Distributor(s): ABC
Writer(s): Freeman F. Godsen, Charles J. Correll, Joe Connelly, & Bob Mosher
Starring: Freeman F. Godsen, Charles J. Correll, & Beatrice Kay
Episode Description: "Calvin" and "the Colonel" (Charles J. Correll & Freeman F. Gosden) get a job picking up and delivering television sets. The job gets complicated when there's a mix up.

110. Title: *Calvin and the Colonel*; "The Polka Dot Bandit" S1E2
Air Date: October 10, 1961
Genre: Animation
Duration: 30mins
VG's Role: Maggie Belle Klaxon (voice)
Director(s): Charles McKimson
Producer(s): Joe Connelly, Bob Ganon, Bob Mosher, Sam Nicholson, & Gerald Ray
Production Company: Kayro Productions
Distributor(s): ABC

Writer(s): Freeman F. Godsen, Charles J. Correll, Joe Connelly, & Bob Mosher
Starring: Freeman F. Godsen, Charles J. Correll, & Beatrice Kay
Episode Description: "The Colonel" (Freeman F. Gosden) becomes suspicious of his sister-in-law.

111. Title: *Calvin and the Colonel*; "Thanksgiving Dinner" S1E3
Air Date: October 17, 1961
Genre: Animation
Duration: 30mins
VG's Role: Maggie Belle Klaxon (voice)
Director(s): Charles McKimson
Producer(s): Joe Connelly, Bob Ganon, Bob Mosher, Sam Nicholson, & Gerald Ray
Production Company: Kayro Productions
Distributor(s): ABC
Writer(s): Freeman F. Godsen, Charles J. Correll, Joe Connelly, & Bob Mosher
Starring: Freeman F. Godsen, Charles J. Correll, & Beatrice Kay
Episode Description: "The Colonel" (Freeman F. Gosden) scrambles to get Thanksgiving dinner ready for his family he forgot he invited.

112. Title: *Calvin and the Colonel*; "The Costume Ball" S1E4
Air Date: October 24, 1961
Genre: Animation
Duration: 30mins
VG's Role: Maggie Belle Klaxon (voice)
Director(s): Charles McKimson
Producer(s): Joe Connelly, Bob Ganon, Bob Mosher, Sam Nicholson, & Gerald Ray
Production Company: Kayro Productions
Distributor(s): ABC

Writer(s): Freeman F. Godsen, Charles J. Correll, Joe Connelly, & Bob Mosher
Starring: Freeman F. Godsen, Charles J. Correll, & Beatrice Kay
Episode Description: "Maggie Belle" (Virginia Gregg) kicks "the Colonel" (Freeman F. Gosden) out, but then they run into each other at a costume ball.

113. Title: *Calvin and the Colonel*; "Sycamore Lodge" S1E5
Air Date: October 31, 1961
Genre: Animation
Duration: 30mins
VG's Role: Maggie Belle Klaxon (voice)
Director(s): Charles McKimson
Producer(s): Joe Connelly, Bob Ganon, Bob Mosher, Sam Nicholson, & Gerald Ray
Production Company: Kayro Productions
Distributor(s): ABC
Writer(s): Freeman F. Godsen, Charles J. Correll, Joe Connelly, & Bob Mosher
Starring: Freeman F. Godsen, Charles J. Correll, & Beatrice Kay
Episode Description: "The Colonel" (Freeman F. Gosden) rents a cabin in the mountains that ends up flooding. He sticks "Calvin" (Charles J. Correll) with the cabin after he can't get his money refunded.

114. Title: *Calvin and the Colonel*; "Money in the Closet" S1E6
Air Date: November 7, 1961
Genre: Animation
Duration: 30mins
VG's Role: Maggie Belle Klaxon (voice)
Director(s): Charles McKimson
Producer(s): Joe Connelly, Bob Ganon, Bob Mosher, Sam Nicholson, & Gerald Ray

Production Company: Kayro Productions
Distributor(s): ABC
Writer(s): Freeman F. Godsen, Charles J. Correll, Joe Connelly, & Bob Mosher
Starring: Freeman F. Godsen, Charles J. Correll, & Virginia Gregg
Episode Description: After overspending, "the Colonel" (Freeman F. Gosden) tries to convince "Calvin" (Charles J. Correll) he is a potential movie star.

115. **Title:** *Calvin and the Colonel*; "Calvin Gets Psychoanalyzed" S1E7
Air Date: January 27, 1962
Genre: Animation
Duration: 30mins
VG's Role: Maggie Belle Klaxon (voice)
Director(s): Charles McKimson
Producer(s): Joe Connelly, Bob Ganon, Bob Mosher, Sam Nicholson, & Gerald Ray
Production Company: Kayro Productions
Distributor(s): ABC
Writer(s): Freeman F. Godsen & Charles J. Correll
Starring: Freeman F. Godsen, Charles J. Correll, & Virginia Gregg
Episode Description: "Calvin" (Charles J. Correll) goes to a psychiatrist after his girlfriend, "Georgianna," dumps him.

116. **Title:** *Calvin and the Colonel*; "Wheeling and Dealing" S1E8
Air Date: February 3, 1962
Genre: Animation
Duration: 30mins
VG's Role: Maggie Belle Klaxon (voice)
Director(s): Charles McKimson
Producer(s): Joe Connelly, Bob Ganon, Bob Mosher, Sam Nicholson, & Gerald Ray

Production Company: Kayro Productions
Distributor(s): ABC
Writer(s): Freeman F. Godsen, Charles J. Correll, & T. Hee
Starring: Freeman F. Godsen, Charles J. Correll, & Virginia Gregg
Episode Description: "The Colonel" (Freeman F. Godsen) tries to get insurance after he damages his nephew's vehicle.

117. **Title:** *Calvin and the Colonel;* "The Wrecking Crew" S1E9
Air Date: February 10, 1962
Genre: Animation
Duration: 30mins
VG's Role: Maggie Belle Klaxon (voice)
Director(s): Charles McKimson
Producer(s): Joe Connelly, Bob Ganon, Bob Mosher, Sam Nicholson, & Gerald Ray
Production Company: Kayro Productions
Distributor(s): ABC
Writer(s): Freeman F. Godsen, Charles J. Correll, & Bob Ross
Starring: Freeman F. Godsen, Charles J. Correll, & Virginia Gregg
Episode Description: "The Colonel" (Freeman F. Godsen) gets construction work and decides he can make even more money if he gets injured on the job.

118. **Title:** *Calvin and the Colonel;* "The Colonel's Old Flame" S1E10
Air Date: February 17, 1962
Genre: Animation
Duration: 30mins
VG's Role: Maggie Belle Klaxon (voice)
Director(s): Charles McKimson
Producer(s): Joe Connelly, Bob Ganon, Bob Mosher, Sam Nicholson, & Gerald Ray
Production Company: Kayro Productions
Distributor(s): ABC

Writer(s): Freeman F. Godsen & Charles J. Correll
Starring: Freeman F. Godsen, Charles J. Correll, & Virginia Gregg
Episode Description: An old flame of "the Colonel's" (Freeman F. Godsen), "Boo Boo Winters," pays him a visit.

119. **Title:** *Calvin and the Colonel*; "Sister Sue and the Police Captain" S1E11
Air Date: February 24, 1962
Genre: Animation
Duration: 30mins
VG's Role: Maggie Belle Klaxon (voice)
Director(s): Charles McKimson
Producer(s): Joe Connelly, Bob Ganon, Bob Mosher, Sam Nicholson, & Gerald Ray
Production Company: Kayro Productions
Distributor(s): ABC
Writer(s): Freeman F. Godsen & Charles J. Correll
Starring: Freeman F. Godsen, Charles J. Correll, & Virginia Gregg
Episode Description: *Unavailable

120. **Title:** *Calvin and the Colonel*; "Jim Dandy Cleaners" S1E12
Air Date: March 3, 1962
Genre: Animation
Duration: 30mins
VG's Role: Maggie Belle Klaxon (voice)
Director(s): Charles McKimson
Producer(s): Joe Connelly, Bob Ganon, Bob Mosher, Sam Nicholson, & Gerald Ray
Production Company: Kayro Productions
Distributor(s): ABC
Writer(s): Freeman F. Godsen & Charles J. Correll
Starring: Freeman F. Godsen, Charles J. Correll, & Virginia Gregg

Episode Description: "Maggie Belle" (Virginia Gregg) has to have "the Colonel's" (Freeman F. Godsen) help at her workplace when she gets sick.

121. Title: *Calvin and the Colonel*; "Jealousy" S1E13
Air Date: March 10, 1962
Genre: Animation
Duration: 30mins
VG's Role: Maggie Belle Klaxon (voice)
Director(s): Charles McKimson
Producer(s): Joe Connelly, Bob Ganon, Bob Mosher, Sam Nicholson, & Gerald Ray
Production Company: Kayro Productions
Distributor(s): ABC
Writer(s): Freeman F. Godsen & Charles J. Correll
Starring: Freeman F. Godsen, Charles J. Correll, & Virginia Gregg
Episode Description: *Unavailable

122. Title: *Calvin and the Colonel*; "Cloakroom" S1E14
Air Date: March 17, 1962
Genre: Animation
Duration: 30mins
VG's Role: Maggie Belle Klaxon (voice)
Director(s): Charles McKimson
Producer(s): Joe Connelly, Bob Ganon, Bob Mosher, Sam Nicholson, & Gerald Ray
Production Company: Kayro Productions
Distributor(s): ABC
Writer(s): Freeman F. Godsen, Charles J. Correll, Joe Connelly, & Bob Mosher
Starring: Freeman F. Godsen, Charles J. Correll, & Virginia Gregg

Episode Description: "Calvin" (Charles J. Correll) and "the Colonel" (Freeman F. Godsen) pick up a cloakroom operation at a nightclub, but after a mix-up, they reconsider their business venture.

123. Title: *Calvin and the Colonel*; "Sister Sue's Sweetheart" S1E15
Air Date: March 24, 1962
Genre: Animation
Duration: 30mins
VG's Role: Maggie Belle Klaxon (voice)
Director(s): Charles McKimson
Producer(s): Joe Connelly, Bob Ganon, Bob Mosher, Sam Nicholson, & Gerald Ray
Production Company: Kayro Productions
Distributor(s): ABC
Writer(s): Freeman F. Godsen, Charles J. Correll, Joe Connelly, & Bob Mosher
Starring: Freeman F. Godsen, Charles J. Correll, & Beatrice Kay
Episode Description: *Unavailable

124. Title: *Calvin and the Colonel*; "The Winning Number" S1E16
Air Date: March 31, 1962
Genre: Animation
Duration: 30mins
VG's Role: Maggie Belle Klaxon (voice)
Director(s): Charles McKimson
Producer(s): Joe Connelly, Bob Ganon, Bob Mosher, Sam Nicholson, & Gerald Ray
Production Company: Kayro Productions
Distributor(s): ABC
Writer(s): Freeman F. Godsen & Charles J. Correll
Starring: Freeman F. Godsen, Charles J. Correll, & Virginia Gregg
Episode Description: *Unavailable

125. Title: *Calvin and the Colonel*; "Calvin's Glamour Girl" S1E17
Air Date: April 7, 1962
Genre: Animation
Duration: 30mins
VG's Role: Maggie Belle Klaxon (voice)
Director(s): Charles McKimson
Producer(s): Joe Connelly, Bob Ganon, Bob Mosher, Sam Nicholson, & Gerald Ray
Production Company: Kayro Productions
Distributor(s): ABC
Writer(s): Freeman F. Godsen & Charles J. Correll
Starring: Freeman F. Godsen, Charles J. Correll, & Virginia Gregg
Episode Description: *Unavailable

126. Title: *Calvin and the Colonel*; "Colonel Out-Foxes Himself" S1E18
Air Date: April 14, 1962
Genre: Animation
Duration: 30mins
VG's Role: Maggie Belle Klaxon (voice)
Director(s): Charles McKimson
Producer(s): Joe Connelly, Bob Ganon, Bob Mosher, Sam Nicholson, & Gerald Ray
Production Company: Kayro Productions
Distributor(s): ABC
Writer(s): Freeman F. Godsen & Charles J. Correll
Starring: Freeman F. Godsen, Charles J. Correll, & Virginia Gregg
Episode Description: *Unavailable

127. Title: *Calvin and the Colonel*; "Nephew Newton's Fortune" S1E19
Air Date: April 21, 1962
Genre: Animation

Duration: 30mins
VG's Role: Maggie Belle Klaxon (voice)
Director(s): Charles McKimson
Producer(s): Joe Connelly, Bob Ganon, Bob Mosher, Sam Nicholson, & Gerald Ray
Production Company: Kayro Productions
Distributor(s): ABC
Writer(s): Freeman F. Godsen, Charles J. Correll, & Bob Ross
Starring: Freeman F. Godsen, Charles J. Correll, & Beatrice Kay
Episode Description: "The Colonel" (Freeman F. Godsen) learns his nephew "Newton" owns stock worth thousands.

128. **Title:** *Calvin and the Colonel*; "Calvin's Tax Problem" S1E20
Air Date: April 28, 1962
Genre: Animation
Duration: 30mins
VG's Role: Maggie Belle Klaxon (voice)
Director(s): Charles McKimson
Producer(s): Joe Connelly, Bob Ganon, Bob Mosher, Sam Nicholson, & Gerald Ray
Production Company: Kayro Productions
Distributor(s): ABC
Writer(s): Freeman F. Godsen, Charles J. Correll, Joe Connelly, & Bob Mosher
Starring: Freeman F. Godsen, Charles J. Correll, & Virginia Gregg
Episode Description: *Unavailable

129. **Title:** *Calvin and the Colonel;* "Women's Club Picnic" S1E21
Air Date: May 5, 1962
Genre: Animated
Duration: 30mins
VG's Role: Maggie Belle Klaxon (voice)
Director(s): Charles McKimson

Producer(s): Joe Connelly, Bob Ganon, Bob Mosher, Sam Nicholson, & Gerald Ray
Production Company: Kayro Productions
Distributor(s): ABC
Writer(s): Freeman F. Gosden & Charles J. Correll
Starring: Freeman F. Gosden, Charles J. Correll, & Virginia Gregg
Episode Description: *Unavailable

130. **Title:** *Calvin and the Colonel*; "Magazine Romance" S1E22
Air Date: May 12, 1962
Genre: Animation
Duration: 30mins
VG's Role: Maggie Belle Klaxon (voice)
Director(s): Charles McKimson
Producer(s): Joe Connelly, Bob Ganon, Bob Mosher, Sam Nicholson, & Gerald Ray
Production Company: Kayro Productions
Distributor(s): ABC
Writer(s): Freeman F. Gosden & Charles J. Correll
Starring: Freeman F. Gosden, Charles J. Correll, & Virginia Gregg
Episode Description: *Unavailable

131. **Title:** *Calvin and the Colonel*; "Ring Reward" S1E23
Air Date: May 19, 1962
Genre: Animation
Duration: 30mins
VG's Role: Maggie Belle Klaxon (voice)
Director(s): Charles McKimson
Producer(s): Joe Connelly, Bob Ganon, Bob Mosher, Sam Nicholson, & Gerald Ray
Production Company: Kayro Productions
Distributor(s): ABC
Writer(s): Freeman F. Gosden & Charles J. Correll

Starring: Freeman F. Gosden, Charles J. Correll, & Virginia Gregg
Episode Description: *Unavailable

132. **Title:** *Calvin and the Colonel*; "The Carnappers" S1E24
Air Date: May 26, 1962
Genre: Animation
Duration: 30mins
VG's Role: Maggie Belle Klaxon (voice)
Director(s): Charles McKimson
Producer(s): Joe Connelly, Bob Ganon, Bob Mosher, Sam Nicholson, & Gerald Ray
Production Company: Kayro Productions
Distributor(s): ABC
Writer(s): Freeman F. Gosden & Charles J. Correll
Starring: Freeman F. Gosden, Charles J. Correll, & Virginia Gregg
Episode Description: *Unavailable

133. **Title:** *Calvin and the Colonel*; "Colonel Traps a Thief" S1E25
Air Date: June 2, 1962
Genre: Animation
Duration: 30mins
VG's Role: Maggie Belle Klaxon (voice)
Director(s): Charles McKimson
Producer(s): Joe Connelly, Bob Ganon, Bob Mosher, Sam Nicholson, & Gerald Ray
Production Company: Kayro Productions
Distributor(s): ABC
Writer(s): Freeman F. Gosden & Charles J. Correll
Starring: Freeman F. Gosden, Charles J. Correll, & Virginia Gregg
Episode Description: *Unavailable

134. **Title:** *Calvin and the Colonel*; "Back to Nashville" S1E26
Air Date: June 9, 1962

Genre: Animation
Duration: 30mins
VG's Role: Maggie Belle Klaxon (voice)
Director(s): Charles McKimson
Producer(s): Joe Connelly, Bob Ganon, Bob Mosher, Sam Nicholson, & Gerald Ray
Production Company: Kayro Productions
Distributor(s): ABC
Writer(s): Freeman F. Gosden & Charles J. Correll
Starring: Freeman F. Gosden, Charles J. Correll, & Virginia Gregg
Episode Description: *Unavailable

135.**Title:** *Hawaiian Eye*; "Koko Kate" S3E38
Air Date: June 13, 1962
Genre: Crime
Duration: 30mins
VG's Role: Koko Kate
Director(s): Otto Lang
Producer(s): Charles Hoffman
Production Company: Warner Brothers Television
Distributor(s): ABC
Writer(s): Robert J. Shaw
Starring: Robert Conrad, Anthony Eisley, & Grant Williams
Episode Description: After several reports of robberies aboard ships in Honolulu Harbor, "Tom Lopaka" (Robert Conrad) investigates.

136. **Title:** *Gunsmoke*; "The Search" S8E1
Air Date: September 15, 1962
Genre: Western
Duration: 60mins
VG's Role: Ess Cutler
Director(s): Harry Harris
Producer(s): Norman MacDonnell

Production Company: Arness Production Company
Distributor(s): CBS
Writer(s): Kathleen Hite, Norman MacDonnell, & John Meston
Starring: James Arness, Dennis Weaver, & Milburn Stone
Episode Description: "Marshall Dillon" (James Arness) must go for help when his friend "Cale" (Carl Reindel) is thrown from a horse and paralyzed.

137. Title: *Sam Benedict*; "Tears for a Nobody Doll" S1E5
Air Date: October 13, 1962
Genre: Drama
Duration: 60mins
VG's Role: Judge Semmler
Director(s): Roger Kay
Producer(s): William Froug
Production Company: MGM Television
Distributor(s): NBC
Writer(s): Ellis Marcus & E. Jack Neuman
Starring: Edmond O'Brien, Richard Rust, & Miyoshi Umeki
Episode Description: "Sam Benedict" (Edmond O'Brien) represents a pregnant woman whose in-laws are trying to gain custody of the unborn child.

138. Title: *77 Sunset Strip*; "The Raiders" S5E4
Air Date: November 2, 1962
Genre: Crime
Duration: 60mins
VG's Role: Fran Duncan
Director(s): Robert Sparr
Producer(s): Fenton Earnshaw
Production Company: Warner Brothers Television
Distributor(s): ABC
Writer(s): Lawrence Kimble & Fred Schiller

Starring: Efrem Zimbalist Jr., Roger Smith, & Virginia Gregg
Episode Description: "Stuart Bailey" (Efrem Zimbalist Jr.) helps a small-town official by going undercover to bust a gambling ring.

139. Title: *Gunsmoke*; "Phoebe Strunk" S8E9
Air Date: November 10, 1962
Genre: Western drama
Duration: 60mins
VG's Role: Phoebe Strunk
Director(s): Andrew V. McLaglen
Producer(s): Norman MacDonnell
Production Company: Arness Production Company
Distributor(s): CBS
Writer(s): John Meston, Norman MacDonnell, & Charles Marquis Warren
Starring: James Arness, Milburn Stone, & Burt Reynolds
Episode Description: "Phoebe Strunk" (Virginia Gregg) and her boorish sons kill and steal at will on their travels. When the family terrorizes a young woman named "Annie" (Joan Freeman), "Marshall Dillion" becomes involved to try and stop their brutality once and for all.

140. Title: *Going My Way*; "A Matter of Principle" S1E8
Air Date: November 21, 1962
Genre: Drama
Duration: 60mins
VG's Role: Margaret Murphy
Director(s): Fielder Cook
Producer(s): Joe Connelly
Production Company: Kerry
Distributor(s): ABC
Writer(s): Richard Baer

Starring: Gene Kelly, Dick York, & Leo G. Carroll
Episode Description: *Unavailable

141. **Title:** *Hazel*; "Genie with the Light Brown Lamp" S2E10
Air Date: November 22, 1962
Genre: Comedy
Duration: 30mins
VG's Role: Miss Tilcy
Director(s): William D. Russell
Producer(s): James Fonda
Production Company: Screen Gems
Distributor(s): NBC
Writer(s): Robert Riley Crutcher & Ted Key
Starring: Shirley Booth, Don DeFore, & Whitney Blake
Episode Description: After "Hazel" (Shirley Booth) reads "Harold" (Bobby Buntrock) a story about Aladdin, he becomes convinced that a gravy boat in the window of a local store is a magic lamp.

142. **Title:** *The Danny Thomas Show/Make Room for Daddy*; "Jose, the Scholar" S10E9
Air Date: November 26, 1962
Genre: Comedy
Duration: 30mins
VG's Role: Miss Brown
Director(s): Coby Ruskin
Producer(s): Jack Elinson & Charles Stewart
Production Company: T&L Productions
Distributor(s): CBS
Writer(s): Charles Stewart & Jack Elinson
Starring: Danny Thomas, Marjorie Lord, & Rusty Hamer
Episode Description: Danny and Kathy's (Danny Thomas & Marjorie Lord) friend, "Jose" (Bill Dana), attends night school, but struggles with his American history class.

143. Title: *Hawaiian Eye*; "Shannon Malloy" S4E11
Air Date: December 18, 1962
Genre: Crime
Duration: 60mins
VG's Role: Mavis Sloan
Director(s): Irving J. Moore
Producer(s): Charles Hoffman
Production Company: Warner Brothers Television
Distributor(s): ABC
Writer(s): Robert Hamner & Phillip Sanford
Starring: Connie Stevens, Troy Donahue, & Robert Conrad
Episode Description: "Shannon Malloy" (Susan Silo), a young artist who works as a cocktail waitress, mysteriously inherits a fortune.

144. Title: *The Eleventh Hour*; "Which Man Will Die?" S1E13
Air Date: January 2, 1963
Genre: Drama
Duration: 60mins
VG's Role: Arlene Montebello
Director(s): *Unavailable
Producer(s): Norman Felton & Sam Rolfe
Production Company: Arena Productions
Distributor(s): NBC
Writer(s): *Unavailable
Starring: Wendell Corey, Harry Guardino, & Carolyn Kearney
Episode Description: The governor hopes a killer who is scheduled for execution has experienced remorse since his sentencing and asks "Dr. Bassett" (Wendell Corey) to find out if he has.

145. Title: *The Twilight Zone*; "Jess-Belle" S4E7
Air Date: February 14, 1963
Genre: Drama
Duration: 60mins

VG's Role: Ossie Stone
Director(s): Buzz Kulik
Producer(s): Herbert Hirschman
Production Company: Cayuga Productions
Distributor(s): CBS
Writer(s): Earl Hamner Jr. & Rod Serling
Starring: Anne Francis, James Best, & Laura Devon
Episode Description: Desperate to win the love of "Billy Ben" (James Best), "Jess-Belle" (Anne Francis) goes to the local witch (Jeanette Nolan) for help, but the price she pays has eternal consequences.

146. Title: *Wide Country*; "Whose Hand at My Throat?" S1E20
Air Date: February 14, 1963
Genre: Western
Duration: 60mins
VG's Role: Alice Bearing
Director(s): John Brahm
Producer(s): Frank Telford
Production Company: Ralph Edwards Productions
Distributor(s): NBC
Writer(s): Gustave Field
Starring: Earl Holliman, Andrew Prine, & Eduard Franz
Episode Description: Friction arises when a surgeon from Hungary comes to town as a practicing veterinarian because he still gives medical advice to humans much to the chagrin of the local physician.

147. Title: *Empire*; "A House in Order" S1E23
Air Date: March 5, 1963
Genre: Western
Duration: 60mins
VG's Role: Mrs. Austin
Director(s): Byron Paul

Producer(s): *Unavailable
Production Company: Wilrich Productions
Distributor(s): NBC
Writer(s): Kathleen Hite, Cyril Hume, & Preston Wood
Starring: Richard Egan, Anne Seymour, & Ryan O'Neal
Episode Description: A fatal diagnosis encourages "Lucia Garrett" (Anne Seymour) to improve her relationships with family and friends.

148. Title: *Perry Mason*; "The Case of the Velvet Claws" S6E22
Air Date: March 21, 1963
Genre: Crime
Duration: 60mins
VG's Role: Mrs. Vickers
Director(s): Harmon Jones
Producer(s): Arthur Marks
Production Company: CBS Television Network
Distributor(s): CBS Media Ventures
Writer(s): Erle Stanley Gardner & Jackson Gillis
Starring: Raymond Burr, Barbara Hale, & William Hopper
Episode Description: "Perry" (Raymond Burr) gets involved in a messy case of blackmail and illegal gambling when "Eva Belter" (Patricia Barry) asks for his help. The investigation takes a number of twists and turns with the final being murder.

149. Title: *Rawhide*; "Incident of the Comanchero" S5E23
Air Date: March 22, 1963
Genre: Western
Duration: 60mins
VG's Role: Sister Margaret
Director(s): Thomas Carr
Producer(s): Vincent M. Fennelly
Production Company: CBS Television Network

Distributor(s): CBS
Writer(s): Al C. Ward & Charles Marquis Warren
Starring: Eric Fleming, Clint Eastwood, & Paul Brinegar
Episode Description: A pair of stranded nuns (Virginia Gregg & Nina Shipman) save an outlaw's life, but his captors pursue after they find he has been rescued.

150. **Title:** *The Eleventh Hour*; "A Medicine Man in This Day and Age?" S1E29
Air Date: May 1, 1963
Genre: Drama
Duration: 60mins
VG's Role: Aunt Tabitha
Director(s): John Peyser
Producer(s): Sam Rolfe
Production Company: Arena Productions
Distributor(s): NBC
Writer(s): Harry Julian Fink & S.S. Schweitzer
Starring: Wendell Corey, Jack Ging, & Don Gordon
Episode Description: An Indian healer is arrested when he tries to help an injured boy using his tribal methods. He is released on the condition that he attend college, but he struggles with the decision to remain loyal to his tribe as their healer or accept college training.

151. **Title:** *Hazel*; "Maid of the Month" S2E31
Air Date: May 2, 1963
Genre: Comedy
Duration: 30mins
VG's Role: Secretary
Director(s): William D. Russell
Producer(s): James Fonda
Production Company: Screen Gems
Distributor(s): NBC

Writer(s): Robert Riley Crutcher & Ted Key
Starring: Shirley Booth, Don DeFore, & Whitney Blake
Episode Description: "Hazel" (Shirley Booth) is interviewed by a reporter after winning the maid of the month magazine contest.

152. **Title:** *The Third Man*; "Who Killed Harry Lime?" S4E17
Air Date: August 24, 1963
Genre: Crime
Duration: 30mins
VG's Role: Nina Taggert
Director(s): Robert M. Leeds
Producer(s): Irving Asher & Vernon Burns
Production Company: British Broadcasting Company
Distributor(s): *Unavailable
Writer(s): Graham Greene & Philip Saltzman
Starring: Michael Rennie, Jonathan Harris, & Ann Atmar
Episode Description: *Unavailable

153. **Title:** *Hazel*; "Potluck a la Mode" S3E1
Air Date: September 19, 1963
Genre: Comedy
Duration: 30mins
VG's Role: Mrs. Lydia Sudley
Director(s): William D. Russell
Producer(s): James Fonda
Production Company: Screen Gems
Distributor(s): NBC
Writer(s): Jane Klove & Ted Sherdeman
Starring: Shirley Booth, Don DeFore, & Whitney Blake
Episode Description: After a scheduling mix up, "Hazel" (Shirley Booth) must singlehandedly entertain "the Baxter's" dinner guests (Virginia Gregg & Philip Ober)

154.**Title:** *Hootenanny*; "Boston University #1" S2E1
Air Date: September 21, 1963
Genre: Music
Duration: *Unavailable
VG's Role: *Unavailable
Director(s): Garth Dietrick
Producer(s): Richard Lewine
Production Company: *Unavailable
Distributor(s): ABC
Writer(s): David Greggory
Starring: The Chad Mitchell Trio, The Rooftop Singers, & Nancy Ames
Episode Description: *Unavailable

155. **Title:** *The Alfred Hitchcock Hour*; "A Home Away from Home" S2E1
Air Date: September 27, 1963
Genre: Horror
Duration: 60mins
VG's Role: Miss Gibson
Director(s): Herschel Daugherty
Producer(s): David Lowell Rich
Production Company: Shamley Productions
Distributor(s): CBS
Writer(s): Robert Bloch
Starring: Alfred Hitchcock, Ray Milland, & Claire Griswold
Episode Description: A patient in a mental institution takes over after killing the doctor and replacing staff members with other patients. When the doctor's niece comes for a visit, she must determine the difference between the real doctors and real patients.

156. **Title:** *Breaking Point*; "There Are the Hip, and There Are the Square" S1E5
Air Date: October 14, 1963

Genre: Drama
Duration: 60mins
VG's Role: Mrs. Price
Director(s): Don Siegel
Producer(s): George Lefferts
Production Company: Bing Crosby Productions
Distributor(s): ABC
Writer(s): Meta Rosenberg & Mark Rodgers
Starring: Paul Richards, Eduard Franz, & John Cassavetes
Episode Description: Circumstances surrounding the death of one of "Dr. Thompson's" (Paul Richards) patients make it difficult to determine if it was accidental or intentional.

157. **Title:** *Temple Houston*; "Jubilee" S1E8
Air Date: November 14, 1963
Genre: Western
Duration: 60mins
VG's Role: Elizabeth Clendennon
Director(s): Robert Totten
Producer(s): Joseph Dackow
Production Company: Apollo Productions
Distributor(s): NBC
Writer(s): John Robinson & Paul Savage
Starring: Jeffrey Hunter, Jack Elam, & Paul Birch
Episode Description: *Unavailable

158. **Title:** *77 Sunset Strip*; "Deposit with Caution" S6E10
Air Date: November 29, 1963
Genre: Crime
Duration: 60mins
VG's Role: Trudie
Director(s): Byron Paul
Producer(s): William Conrad

Production Company: Warner Brothers Television
Distributor(s): ABC
Writer(s): Robert Leslie Bellem
Starring: Efrem Zimbalist Jr., Harold J. Stone, & Nancy Malone
Episode Description: After a NYC police officer is framed, "Stuart Bailey" (Efrem Zimbalist Jr.) is hired to investigate.

159. Title: *Wagon Train*; "The Fenton Canaby Story" S7E15
Air Date: December 30, 1963
Genre: Western
Duration: 60mins
VG's Role: Grace Lowe
Director(s): Joseph Pevney
Producer(s): Howard Christie
Production Company: Revue Studios
Distributor(s): ABC
Writer(s): Thomas Thompson
Starring: Robert Fuller, John McIntire, & Frank McGrath
Episode Description: "Fenton Canaby" (Jack Kelly) is rumored to have led a wagon train into peril and becomes the object of scorn when he joins "Hale's" (John McIntire) wagon train, on which a vengeful widow (Virginia Gregg) is also travelling.

160. Title: *77 Sunset Strip*; "Queen of the Cats" S6E20
Air Date: February 7, 1964
Genre: Crime
Duration: 60mins
VG's Role: Helen Johnson
Director(s): Lawrence Dobkin
Producer(s): William Conrad
Production Company: Warner Brothers Television
Distributor(s): ABC
Writer(s): Louis Vittes

Starring: Efrem Zimbalist Jr., Virginia Gregg, & Joan Staley
Episode Description: A wealthy heiress hires "Stuart Bailey" (Efrem Zimbalist Jr.) to track down her mother.

161. Title: *Arrest and Trial*; "A Roll of the Dice" S1E22
Air Date: February 23, 1964
Genre: Crime
Duration: 60mins
VG's Role: Mrs. Blake
Director(s): David Lowell Rich
Producer(s): Arthur H. Nadel
Production Company: Revue Studios
Distributor(s): ABC
Writer(s): Aben Kandel & Herb Meadow
Starring: Chuck Connors, Ben Gazzara, & John Larch
Episode Description: A young gambler finances his addiction by embezzling.

162. Title: *The Twilight Zone*; "The Masks" S5E25
Air Date: March 20, 1964
Genre: Horror
Duration: 30mins
VG's Role: Emily Harper
Director(s): Ida Lupino
Producer(s): Bert Granet
Production Company: Caygua Productions
Distributor(s): CBS
Writer(s): Rod Serling
Starring: Robert Keith, Milton Selzer, & Virginia Gregg
Episode Description: A greedy family visits their dying, wealthy patriarch and gets more than they bargained for in Mardi Gras-style.

163. Title: *The Virginian*; "The Secret of Brynmar Hall" S2E26
Air Date: April 1, 1964
Genre: Western
Duration: 60mins
VG's Role: Mrs. Tyson
Director(s): Robert Totten
Producer(s): Don Ingalls
Production Company: Revue Studios
Distributor(s): NBC
Writer(s): Herman Groves, Charles Marquis Warren, & Owen Wister
Starring: Lee J. Cobb, Doug McClure, & Gary Clarke
Episode Description: "Randy" (Randy Boone), "Betsy" (Roberta Shore), and friends visit an old mansion they remember fondly from their youth. When a storm prevents them from leaving, they relive tragic memories of their hostess's daughter's death, and strange things begin to happen.

164. Title: *Rawhide*; "Incident of the Banker" S6E25
Air Date: April 2, 1964
Genre: Western
Duration: 60mins
VG's Role: Sarah Goodley
Director(s): Christian Nyby
Producer(s): Vincent M. Fennelly
Production Company: CBS Television Network
Distributor(s): CBS
Writer(s): Chris Miller & Charles Marquis Warren
Starring: Eric Fleming, Clint Eastwood, & Paul Brinegar
Episode Description: "Gil Favor" (Eric Fleming) goes into town to visit the bank and general store after the weather interrupts his wagon train. While in town, the banker convinces him to switch places to prove something to his wife.

165. Title: *Breaking Point*; "Confounding Her Astronomers" S1E28
Air Date: April 6, 1964
Genre: Drama
Duration: 60mins
VG's Role: Mrs. Bronson
Director(s): Paul Wendkos
Producer(s): Morton S. Fine, David Friedkin, & George Lefferts
Production Company: Bing Crosby Productions
Distributor(s): ABC
Writer(s): Meta Rosenberg & Scott Morgan
Starring: Paul Richards, Eduard Franz, & Kathleen Nolan
Episode Description: A gifted young girl has difficulty getting adopted because she is viewed as eccentric.

166. Title: *Ben Casey*; "For a Just Man Falleth Seven Times" S3E32
Air Date: April 15, 1964
Genre: Drama
Duration: 60mins
VG's Role: Elizabeth Hardin
Director(s): Vince Edwards
Producer(s): Fred Freiberger
Production Company: Bing Crosby Productions
Distributor(s): ABC
Writer(s): James E. Moser, Gilbert Ralston, & Harry Rellis
Starring: Vince Edwards, Sam Jaffe, & Michael Abelar
Episode Description: A man with a doomed fate decides to have one last hoorah.

167. Title: *Kraft Suspense Theatre*; "The Robrioz Ring" S1E27
Air Date: May 28, 1964
Genre: Crime
Duration: 60mins
VG's Role: Kate Taylor

Director(s): David Lowell Rich
Producer(s): David Lowell Rich
Production Company: Roncom Films
Distributor(s): NBC
Writer(s): James Gunn & Hugh Wheeler
Starring: Julie Harris, Robert Loggia, & Julie Adams
Episode Description: After a woman sells a family ring, her son (Robert Loggia) romances the new buyer in order to get it back. Things get complicated when the two being to get serious about each other.

168. Title: *This is the Life*; "Out of Bondage"
Air Date: September 20, 1964
Genre: Drama
Duration: *Unavailable
VG's Role: Judge Steele
Director(s): *Unavailable
Producer(s): *Unavailable
Production Company: *Unavailable
Distributor(s): *Unavailable
Writer(s): *Unavailable
Starring: John Archer, Dorothy Green, & Virginia Gregg
Episode Description: *Unavailable

169. Title: *Wagon Train*; "The John Gillman Story" S8E3
Air Date: October 4, 1964
Genre: Western
Duration: 60mins
VG's Role: Miss Roberts
Director(s): Joseph Pevney
Producer(s): Frederick Shorr
Production Company: Revue Studios
Distributor(s): ABC

Writer(s): Calvin Clements Sr.
Starring: John McIntire, Robert Fuller, & Frank McGrath
Episode Description: A hardboiled outlaw (Bobby Darin) finds himself stuck with a little orphaned girl (Betsy Hale) while running from a posse.

170. **Title:** *Bonanza*; "Logan's Treasure" S6E5
Air Date: October 18, 1964
Genre: Western
Duration: 60mins
VG's Role: Angie Malone
Director(s): Don McDougall
Producer(s): David Dortort
Production Company: NBC
Distributor(s): NBC
Writer(s): Ken Pettus, Robert Sabaroff, & David Dortort
Starring: Lorne Greene, Pernell Roberts, & Dan Blocker
Episode Description: After "Sam Logan" (Dan Duryear) gets out of prison, he stays with "the Cartwrights" because others are after him and his knowledge of where a gold stash is hidden.

171. **Title:** *The Farmer's Daughter*; "Like Father, Like Son" S2E15
Air Date: December 25, 1964
Genre: Comedy
Duration: 30mins
VG's Role: Elizabeth Chase
Director(s): Bob Claver
Producer(s): Bob Claver
Production Company: Associated Arts N.V.
Distributor(s): ABC
Writer(s): Peggy Chantler Dick & Hella Wuolijoki
Starring: Inger Stevens, William Windom, & Cathleen Nesbitt

Episode Description: A savvy politician cons "Congressman Glen" (William Windom) out of a favor, which frustrates things between "Glen" and "Steve" (Mickey Sholdar).

172. Title: *The Alfred Hitchcock Hour*; "Consider Her Ways" S3E11
Air Date: December 28, 1964
Genre: Horror
Duration: 60mins
VG's Role: The 3rd Doctor
Director(s): Robert Stevens
Producer(s): Joan Harrison
Production Company: Alfred J. Hitchcock Productions
Distributor(s): NBC
Writer(s): Oscar Millard & John Wyndham
Starring: Alfred Hitchcock, Barbara Barrie, & Gladys Cooper
Episode Description: A woman (Barbara Barrie) with amnesia awakens in a strange society with no men in which all women are categorized according to their fertility capabilities.

173. Title: *My Favorite Martian*; "How Are Things in Glocca, Martin?" S2E16
Air Date: January 10, 1965
Genre: Comedy
Duration: 30mins
VG's Role: Eileen McGinty
Director(s): Byron Paul
Producer(s): Jack Chertok
Production Company: Jack Chertok Television Productions
Distributor(s): CBS
Writer(s): Albert E. Lewin, Burt Styler, & John L. Greene
Starring: Ray Walston, Bill Bixby, & Sean McClory
Episode Description: "Tim's" wealthy "Uncle Seamus" (Sean McClory), known for his frugality, visits. "Seamus" becomes

suspicious of "Martin" (Ray Walston) after he sees a bit of his Martianisms. "Seamus" thinks "Martin" is a leprechaun and tries to take advantage of his magic, but "Martin" finds "Seamus"' long-lost love, "Eileen" (Virginia Gregg), and the two rekindle their romance.

174. Title: *Hazel*; "Love 'em and Leave 'em" S4E18
Air Date: January 21, 1965
Genre: Comedy
Duration: 30mins
VG's Role: Miss Tilcy
Director(s): William D. Russell
Producer(s): James Fonda
Production Company: Screen Gems
Distributor(s): NBC
Writer(s): Robert Riley Crutcher & Ted Key
Starring: Shirley Booth, Don DeFore, & Whitney Blake
Episode Description: "Harold" (Bobby Buntrock) trades a prized possession in order to take a date to his school dance.

175. Title: *Wendy and Me*; "Jeff Takes a Turn for the Nurse" S1E23
Air Date: February 22, 1965
Genre: Comedy
Duration: 30mins
VG's Role: *Unavailable
Director(s): Gene Reynolds
Producer(s): George Burns
Production Company: Natwill Productions
Distributor(s): ABC
Writer(s): William Burns, Elon Packard, & Norman Paul
Starring: Connie Stevens, Ron Harper, & James T. Callahan
Episode Description: Nurse aide "Wendy" (Connie Stevens) sees her very first patient: "Jeff" (Ron Harper).

176. Title: *The Alfred Hitchcock Hour*; "Thou Still Unravished Bride"
S3E22
Air Date: March 22, 1965
Genre: Horror
Duration: 60mins
VG's Role: Mrs. Essie Setlin
Director(s): David Friedkin
Producer(s): Morton S. Fine, & David Friedkin
Production Company: Alfred J. Hitchcock Productions
Distributor(s): NBC
Writer(s): Avram Davidson, Morton S. Fine, & David Friedkin
Starring: Alfred Hitchcock, Ron Randell, & David Carradine
Episode Description: A detective's fiancée vanishes just before the wedding.

177. Title: *The Fugitive*; "A.P.B." S2E28
Air Date: April 6, 1965
Genre: Crime
Duration: 60mins
VG's Role: Mrs. Ross
Director(s): William D. Gordon
Producer(s): Alan A. Armer
Production Company: Quinn Martin Productions
Distributor(s): ABC
Writer(s): Daniel B. Ullman & Roy Huggins
Starring: David Janssen, Paul Richards, & Lou Antonio
Episode Description: A pair of escaped convicts (Paul Richards & Lou Antonio) take "Kimble" (David Janssen) hostage inside the home of a woman (Virginia Gregg) and her daughter (Shirley Knight).

178. Title: *The Legend of Jesse James*; "Three Men from Now" S1E1
Air Date: September 13, 1965
Genre: Western

Duration: 30mins
VG's Role: Mrs. Haynes
Director(s): James B. Clark
Producer(s): Don Siegel
Production Company: Twentieth Century Fox Television
Distributor(s): ABC
Writer(s): Anthony Spinner
Starring: Christopher Jones, Allen Case, & Robert J. Wilke
Episode Description: *Unavailable

179. Title: *My Three Sons*; "Red Tape Romance" S6E2
Air Date: September 23, 1965
Genre: Family
Duration: 30mins
VG's Role: Miss Miller
Director(s): James V. Kern
Producer(s): Edmund L. Hartmann
Production Company: Don Fedderson Productions
Distributor(s): CBS
Writer(s): George Tibbles
Starring: Fred MacMurray, William Demarest, & Don Grady
Episode Description: "Steve" (Fred MacMurray) considers adopting "Ernie" (Barry Livingston), but "Uncle Charley" (William Demarest) criticizes the idea.

180. Title: *My Three Sons*; "Brother, Ernie" S6E3
Air Date: September 30, 1965
Genre: Family
Duration: 30mins
VG's Role: Miss Miller
Director(s): James V. Kern
Producer(s): Edmund L. Hartmann
Production Company: Don Fedderson Productions

Distributor(s): CBS
Writer(s): George Tibbles
Starring: Fred MacMurray, William Demarest, & Don Grady
Episode Description: The adoption process gets sticky when the family finds out there must be a lady of the house in order for "Ernie" (Barry Livingston) to stay.

181. **Title:** *Camp Runamuck*; "Today is Parent's Day" S1E9
Air Date: November 12, 1965
Genre: Comedy
Duration: 30mins
VG's Role: Mrs. Radibble
Director(s): David Swift
Producer(s): *Unavailable
Production Company: Runamuck Productions
Distributor(s): NBC
Writer(s): David Swift
Starring: David Ketchum, Arch Johnson, & Leonard Stone
Episode Description: Parent's Day is rained out, but one camper's parents come anyway, and the camp staff must entertain them.

182. **Title:** *Perry Mason*; "The Case of the Silent Six" S9E11
Air Date: November 21, 1965
Genre: Crime
Duration: 60mins
VG's Role: Flo Oliver
Director(s): Jesse Hibbs
Producer(s): Arthur Marks & Art Seid
Production Company: CBS Television Network
Distributor(s): CBS
Writer(s): Erle Stanley Gardner, William Bast, & Ernest Frankel
Starring: Raymond Burr, Barbara Hale, & William Hopper

Episode Description: "Perry" (Raymond Burr) gets involved in the case of "Susan Wolfe" (Chris Noel) who is badly beaten while her neighbors turn a blind eye.

183. Title: *The Addams Family*; "Feud in the Addams Family" S2E11
Air Date: November 26, 1965
Genre: Comedy
Duration: 30mins
VG's Role: Mrs. Courtney
Director(s): Sidney Lanfield
Producer(s): Nat Perrin
Production Company: Filmways Television
Distributor(s): ABC
Writer(s): Rick Richards, Jerry Gottler, & David Levy
Starring: Carolyn Jones, John Astin, & Jackie Coogan
Episode Description: The Addams' family is in a feud with well-known socialite "Abigail Addams" unbeknownst to the Courtney family who try to get to know "Gomez" and "Morticia" in order to meet "Abigail."

184. Title: *Ben Casey*; "In Case of Emergency, Cry Havoc" S5E16
Air Date: January 3, 1966
Genre: Drama
Duration: 60mins
VG's Role: *Unavailable
Director(s): Harvey Hart
Producer(s): *Unavailable
Production Company: Bing Crosby Productions
Distributor(s): ABC
Writer(s): James E. Moser, Howard Browne, & Steven W. Carabatsos
Starring: Vince Edwards, Henry Beckman, & Geraldine Brooks

Episode Description: "Dr. Casey" (Vince Edwards) tries to convince a woman to let him perform life-saving surgery on her husband rather than trying a "miracle" drug she heard about.

185. Title: *Ben Casey*; "Meantime, We Shall Express Our Darker Purpose" S5E17
Air Date: January 10, 1966
Genre: Drama
Duration: 60mins
VG's Role: Mrs. Graham
Director(s): John Meredyth Lucas
Producer(s): *Unavailable
Production Company: Bing Crosby Productions
Distributor(s): ABC
Writer(s): James E. Moser, Steven W. Carabatsos, & Ben Fox
Starring: Vince Edwards, Robert Burr, & Vincent Gardenia
Episode Description: "Dr. Casey" (Vince Edwards) gets caught up in a drama involving a hit-and-run driver and a priest.

186. Title: *Ben Casey*; "For San Diego, You Need a Different Bus" S5E18
Air Date: January 17, 1966
Genre: Drama
Duration: 60mins
VG's Role: Mrs. Graham
Director(s): Harry Landers
Producer(s): *Unavailable
Production Company: Bing Crosby Productions
Distributor(s): ABC
Writer(s): James E. Moser, Howard Dimsdale, & Barry Oringer
Starring: Vince Edwards, Indus Arthur, & Wolfe Barzell
Episode Description: *Unavailable

187. Title: *Ben Casey*; "Smile, Baby, Smile, It's Only Twenty Dols of Pain" S5E19
Air Date: January 24, 1966
Genre: Drama
Duration: 60mins
VG's Role: Mrs. Graham
Director(s): Gerald Mayer
Producer(s): *Unavailable
Production Company: Bing Crosby Productions
Distributor(s): ABC
Writer(s): James E. Moser & Harold Gast
Starring: Vince Edwards, Indus Arthur, & Sidney Blackmer
Episode Description: "Dr. Casey" (Vince Edwards) tries to help a settlement worker (Dana Wynter) who is hooked on pain pills.

188. Title: *Ben Casey*; "Fun and Games and Other Tragic Things" S5E20
Air Date: January 31, 1966
Genre: Drama
Duration: 60mins
VG's Role: Mrs. Graham
Director(s): Alan Crosland Jr.
Producer(s): John Meredyth Lucas
Production Company: Bing Crosby Productions
Distributor(s): ABC
Writer(s): James E. Moser, Howard Dimsdale, & Chester Krumholz
Starring: Vince Edwards, Bettye Ackerman, & Frank Aletter
Episode Description: "Dr. Casey" (Vince Edwards) gets romantically involved with a patient in order to observe her symptoms.

189. Title: *Gunsmoke*; "Sanctuary" S11E23
Air Date: February 26, 1966
Genre: Western

Duration: 60mins
VG's Role: Miss Howell
Director(s): Harry Harris
Producer(s): Philip Leacock
Production Company: CBS Television Network
Distributor(s): CBS
Writer(s): Calvin Clements Sr., Paul Savage, & Norman MacDonnell
Starring: James Arness, Milburn Stone, & Amanda Blake
Episode Description: A wounded outlaw takes hostages inside a church while "Doc Adams" (Milburn Stone) treats his injures.

190. **Title:** *Dr. Kiladare*; "Travel a Crooked Road" S5E54
Air Date: March 22, 1966
Genre: Drama
Duration: 30mins
VG's Role: Dr. Dunning
Director(s): John Brahm
Producer(s): Douglas Benton
Production Company: Arena Productions
Distributor(s): NBC
Writer(s): Edward J. Lakso
Starring: Richard Chamberlain, Raymond Massey, & Diane Varsi
Episode Description: A nurse learns her husband, whom she believed had been killed, is alive and returning home just before she goes into surgery.

191. **Title:** *The Girl from U.N.C.L.E.*; "The Danish Blue Affair" S1E7
Air Date: October 25, 1966
Genre: Adventure
Duration: 60mins
VG's Role: Granny
Director(s): Mitchell Leisen
Producer(s): Douglas Benton

Production Company: Arena Productions
Distributor(s): NBC
Writer(s): Sam Rolfe & Arthur Weingarten
Starring: Stefanie Powers, Noel Harrison, & Leo G. Carroll
Episode Description: *Unavailable

192. Title: *The Big Valley*; "The Stallion" S2E20
Air Date: January 30, 1967
Genre: Western
Duration: 60mins
VG's Role: Libby
Director(s): Paul Henreid
Producer(s): Arthur Gardner, Arnold Laven, & Jules V. Levy
Production Company: Four Star Productions
Distributor(s): ABC
Writer(s): Gabrielle Upton, A.I. Bezzerides, & Louis F. Edelman
Starring: Richard Long, Peter Breck, & Lee Majors
Episode Description: "Nick" (Peter Breck) is almost killed when trying to round up a wild stallion, in part due to an older ranchhand's negligence.

193. Title: *Dragnet*; "The Candy Store Robberies" S1E8
Air Date: March 9, 1967
Genre: Crime
Duration: 30mins
VG's Role: Mrs. Jean Hardy
Director(s): Jack Webb
Producer(s): Jack Webb
Production Company: Mark VII Ltd.
Distributor(s): NBC
Writer(s): Robert C. Dennis & Jack Webb
Starring: Jack Webb, Harry Morgan, & Merry Anders

Episode Description: After several candy stores are robbed at gunpoint, "Sgt. Friday" (Jack Webb) and "Officer Gannon" (Harry Morgan) investigate.

194. Title: *Dragnet*; "The Jade Story" S1E10
Air Date: March 23, 1967
Genre: Crime
Duration: 30mins
VG's Role: Mrs. Francine Graham
Director(s): Jack Webb
Producer(s): Jack Webb
Production Company: Mark VII Ltd.
Distributor(s): NBC
Writer(s): Bill O'Hallaren & Jack Webb
Starring: Jack Webb, Harry Morgan, & Virginia Gregg
Episode Description: "Sgt. Friday" (Jack Webb) and "Officer Gannon" (Harry Morgan) investigate when a wealthy woman (Virginia Gregg) reports her expensive jewelry stolen.

195.Title: *The Road West*; "The Agreement" S1E28
Air Date: April 24, 1967
Genre: Western
Duration: 60mins
VG's Role: Lavinia Bishop
Director(s): *Unavailable
Producer(s): Norman MacDonnell & James Duff McAdams
Production Company: Universal Television
Distributor(s): NBC
Writer(s): *Unavailable
Starring: Barry Sullivan, Andrew Prine, & Brenda Scott
Episode Description: *Unavailable

196. Title: *The Herculoids* "The Beaked People/The Raider" S1E3
Air Date: September 23, 1967
Genre: Animation
Duration: 30mins
VG's Role: Tarra (voice)
Director(s): Bill Perez & Paul Sommer
Producer(s): *Unavailable
Production Company: Hanna-Barbera Productions
Distributor(s): CBS
Writer(s): *Unavailable
Starring: Ted Eccles, Virginia Gregg, & Don Messick
Episode Description: *Unavailable

197. Title: *The Guns of Will Sonnett*; "A Son for a Son" S1E7
Air Date: October 20, 1967
Genre: Western
Duration: 30mins
VG's Role: Mrs. Murdock
Director(s): Richard C. Sarafian
Producer(s): Aaron Spelling
Production Company: Thomas/Spelling Productions
Distributor(s): ABC
Writer(s): Richard Carr & Aaron Spelling
Starring: Walter Brennan, Dack Rambo, & Royal Dano
Episode Description: A farmer and his family help nurse "Jeff" (Dack Rambo) back from a fever, but the farmer's wife (Virginia Gregg), stricken with grief, believes "Jeff" is her son who was killed.

198. Title: *The Herculoids* "Mekkano, the Machine Master/Tiny World of Terror" S1E7
Air Date: October 21, 1967
Genre: Animation
Duration: 30mins

VG's Role: Tarra (voice)
Director(s): *Unavailable
Producer(s): *Unavailable
Production Company: *Unavailable
Distributor(s): *Unavailable
Writer(s): *Unavailable
Starring: Ted Eccles, Virginia Gregg, & Don Messick
Episode Description: *Unavailable

199. **Title:** *The Herculoids;* "The Gladiators of Kyanite/Temple of Trax S1E8
Air Date: October 28, 1967
Genre: Animation
Duration: 30mins
VG's Role: Tarra (voice)
Director(s): Joseph Barbera & William Hanna
Producer(s): Joseph Barbera & William Hanna
Production Company: *Unavailable
Distributor(s): *Unavailable
Writer(s): *Unavailable
Starring: Ted Eccles, Virginia Gregg, & Don Messick
Episode Description: *Unavailable

200. **Title:** *The Virginian;* "Bitter Autumn" S6E8
Air Date: November 1, 1967
Genre: Western
Duration: 60mins
VG's Role: Hattie McLain
Director(s): Don McDougall
Producer(s): Joel Rogosin
Production Company: Universal Television
Distributor(s): NBC
Writer(s): Ken Finley, Andy Lewis, & David E. Lewis

Starring: Charles Bickford, Doug McClure, & Clu Gulager
Episode Description: A young man accidentally shoots and kills a woman (Virginia Gregg) visiting Medicine Bow with her son.

201. Title: *Run for Your Life*; "Cry Hard, Cry Fast: Part 1" S3E11
Air Date: November 22, 1967
Genre: Drama
Duration: 60mins
VG's Role: Trudy Krissell
Director(s): Michael Ritchic
Producer(s): Jo Swerling Jr.
Production Company: Roncom Films
Distributor(s): NBC
Writer(s): John D. MacDonald & Luther Davis
Starring: Ben Gazzara, James Farentino, & Charles Aidman
Episode Description: A bank robber's heist is interrupted by a fatal car crash.

202. Title: *Dragnet*; "The Pyramid Swindle" S2E12
Air Date: November 30, 1967
Genre: Crime
Duration: 30mins
VG's Role: Bonnie Bates
Director(s): Jack Webb
Producer(s): Jack Webb
Production Company: Mark VII Ltd.
Distributor(s): NBC
Writer(s): Norman Lessing & Jack Webb
Starring: Jack Webb, Harry Morgan, & Virginia Gregg
Episode Description: "Bonnie Bates" (Virginia Gregg) is a successful evangelical saleswoman who takes advantage of people through her pyramid scheme until "Sgt. Friday" (Jack Webb) and "Officer Gannon" (Harry Morgan) investigate.

203. Title: *Daniel Boone*; "The Witness" S4E17
Air Date: January 25, 1968
Genre: Western
Duration: 60mins
VG's Role: Nettie Pike
Director(s): William Wiard
Producer(s): Barney Rosenzweig
Production Company: Twentieth Century Fox Television
Distributor(s): Goldhil Entertainment
Writer(s): Ricky Husky
Starring: Fess Parker, Patricia Blair, & Darby Hinton
Episode Description: "Israel" (Darby Hinton) is witness to a murder, but no one believes him until the murderer comes after him.

204. Title: *Dragnet*; "The Big Clan" S2E21
Air Date: February 8, 1968
Genre: Crime
Duration: 30mins
VG's Role: Dallas Andrews
Director(s): Jack Webb
Producer(s): Jack Webb
Production Company: Mark VII Ltd.
Distributor(s): NBC
Writer(s): Stephen Downing & Jack Webb
Starring: Jack Webb, Harry Morgan, & Virginia Gregg
Episode Description: "Sgt. Friday" (Jack Webb) and "Officer Gannon" (Harry Morgan) go undercover to bust a ring of gypsy operations.

205. Title: *Dragnet*; "The Big Gambler" S2E27
Air Date: March 21, 1968
Genre: Crime
Duration: 30mins
VG's Role: Norma Pendleton

Director(s): Jack Webb
Producer(s): Jack Webb
Production Company: Mark VII Ltd.
Distributor(s): NBC
Writer(s): Robert Soderberg & Jack Webb
Starring: Jack Webb, Harry Morgan, & Vic Perrin
Episode Description: "Sgt. Friday" (Jack Webb) and "Officer Gannon" (Harry Morgan) investigate when a business owner reports an embezzlement.

206. Title: *Insight*; "The Ghetto Trap" S1E203
Air Date: May 26, 1968
Genre: Drama
Duration: 30mins
VG's Role: Anya
Director(s): Hal Cooper
Producer(s): John Meredyth Lucas
Production Company: Paulist Productions
Distributor(s): *Unavailable
Writer(s): Maureen Daly
Starring: Ellwood Kieser, James Westerfield, & Virginia Gregg
Episode Description: An immigrant family struggles with changing life in America.

207. Title: *The Outcasts*; "Take Your Lover in the Ring" S1E5
Air Date: October 28, 1968
Genre: Western
Duration: 60mins
VG's Role: Odette
Director(s): Leo Penn
Producer(s): Jon Epstein
Production Company: Screen Gems
Distributor(s): ABC

Writer(s): Ben Brady, Leon Tokatyan, & Anthony Lawrence
Starring: Don Murray, Otis Young, & John Dehner
Episode Description: A man wins a woman in a card game and gives her to his friend who falls in love with her.

208. Title: *The Virginian;* "Ride to Misadventure" S7E8
Air Date: November 6, 1968
Genre: Western
Duration: 60mins
VG's Role: Ma Daggert
Director(s): Michael Caffey
Producer(s): James Duff McAdams
Production Company: Universal Television
Distributor(s): NBC
Writer(s): Gerald Sanford, Charles Marquis Warren, & Owen Wister
Starring: John McIntire, Doug McClure, & David Hartman
Episode Description: "The Virginian" (James Drury) and a bounty hunter go after a gang of thieves.

209. Title: *Dragnet;* "Training: DR-18" S3E9
Air Date: November 21, 1968
Genre: Crime
Duration: 30mins
VG's Role: Dorothy Lee
Director(s): Jack Webb
Producer(s): Jack Webb
Production Company: Mark VII Ltd.
Distributor(s): NBC
Writer(s): Robert C. Dennis & Jack Webb
Starring: Jack Webb, Harry Morgan, & Virginia Gregg
Episode Description: A writer (Virginia Gregg) does a story on female police cadets in the academy, and "Sgt. Friday" (Jack Webb) is her escort.

210. Title: *Dragnet*; "Public Affairs: DR-14" S3E10
Air Date: November 28, 1968
Genre: Crime
Duration: 30mins
VG's Role: Lisa Ruby
Director(s): Jack Webb
Producer(s): Jack Webb
Production Company: Mark VII Ltd.
Distributor(s): NBC
Writer(s): Alf Harris & Jack Webb
Starring: Jack Webb, Harry Morgan, & Del Moore
Episode Description: "Sgt. Friday" (Jack Webb) and "Officer Gannon" (Harry Morgan) meet with business owners about protecting themselves and their businesses from crime.

211.Title: *Mod Squad*; "Twinkle, Twinkle Little Starlet" S1E11
Air Date: December 17, 1968
Genre: Crime
Duration: 60mins
VG's Role: Mrs. Petree
Director(s): George McCowan
Producer(s): Tony Barrett & Harve Bennett
Production Company: Thomas/Spelling Productions
Distributor(s): ABC
Writer(s): Jerome Ross, Buddy Ruskin, & Tony Barrett
Starring: Michael Cole, Clarence Williams III, & Peggy Lipton
Episode Description: "Julie" (Peggy Lipton) goes undercover to investigate when several young actresses are reported murdered.

212. Title: *Bewitched*; "Samantha's Super Maid" S5E14
Air Date: January 2, 1969
Genre: Comedy
Duration: 30mins

VG's Role: Leslie Otis
Director(s): R. Robert Rosenbaum
Producer(s): William Asher
Production Company: Screen Gems
Distributor(s): ABC
Writer(s): Peggy Chantler Dick, Douglas Dick, & Sol Saks
Starring: Elizabeth Montgomery, Dick York, & Agnes Moorehead
Episode Description: "Samantha's" mother-in-law (Mabel Albertson) hires a maid for her.

213. Title: *Gunsmoke*; "The Twisted Heritage" S14E15
Air Date: January 6, 1969
Genre: Western
Duration: 60mins
VG's Role: Jessie Copperton
Director(s): Bernard McEveety
Producer(s): Joseph Dackow
Production Company: CBS Television Network
Distributor(s): CBS
Writer(s): Paul Savage, Arthur Rowe, & Robert Heverly
Starring: James Arness, Milburn Stone, & Amanda Blake
Episode Description: After "Kitty" (Amanda Blake) saves a man's life, she gets caught up in his family's twisted history.

214. Title: *Mod Squad*; "A Hint of Darkness, a Hint of Light" S1E18
Air Date: February 11, 1969
Genre: Crime
Duration: 60mins
VG's Role: Helen Kane
Director(s): Earl Bellamy
Producer(s): Tony Barrett & Harve Bennett
Production Company: Thomas/Spelling Productions
Distributor(s): ABC

Writer(s): Edward J. Lakso, Buddy Ruskin, Tony Barrett, Harve Bennett, & Sammy Hess
Starring: Michael Cole, Clarence Williams III, & Peggy Lipton
Episode Description: The trio investigates when a mysterious man repeatedly attacks a blind girl (Gloria Foster).

215. **Title:** *Dragnet*; "Juvenile: DR-32" S3E24
Air Date: March 27, 1969
Genre: Crime
Duration: 30mins
VG's Role: Mrs. Smith
Director(s): Jack Webb
Producer(s): Jack Webb
Production Company: Mark VII Ltd.
Distributor(s): NBC
Writer(s): Jack Barrett, James Doherty, & Jack Webb
Starring: Jack Webb, Harry Morgan, & Shannon Farnon
Episode Description: When a little girl is bitten by a dog, "Sgt. Friday" (Jack Webb) and "Office Gannon" (Harry Morgan) must act fast.

216. **Title:** *The Big Valley*; "Point and Counterpoint" S4E26
Air Date: May 19, 1969
Genre: Western
Duration: 60mins
VG's Role: Sarah Clark
Director(s): James F. Lichtman
Producer(s): Lou Morheim
Production Company: Four Star Productions
Distributor(s): ABC
Writer(s): A.I. Bezzerides, Arthur Browne Jr., & Louis F. Edelman
Starring: Richard Long, Peter Breck, & Lee Majors

Episode Description: A dying convict tells his son to kill the people he believes are responsible for his death.

217. **Title:** *The Bold Ones: The New Doctors*; "To Save a Life" S1E1
Air Date: September 14, 1969
Genre: Drama
Duration: 60mins
VG's Role: Dorothy
Director(s): Don McDougall
Producer(s): Robert Prince
Production Company: Harbour Productions Unlimited
Distributor(s): NBC
Writer(s): Richard H. Landau, Paul Mason, Steven Bochco, & Irv Pearlberg
Starring: E.G. Marshall, David Hartman, & John Saxon
Episode Description: A young man is injured in a car crash and another patient anxiously awaits a kidney transplant.

218. **Title:** *Dragnet*; "Personnel: The Shooting" S4E1
Air Date: September 18, 1969
Genre: Crime
Duration: 30mins
VG's Role: Virginia Miller
Director(s): Jack Webb
Producer(s): Jack Webb
Production Company: Mark VII Ltd.
Distributor(s): NBC
Writer(s): Stephen Downing & Jack Webb
Starring: Jack Webb, Harry Morgan, & Virginia Gregg
Episode Description: "Sgt. Friday" (Jack Webb) and "Officer Gannon" (Harry Morgan) go to the hospital when two police officers are injured in the line of duty.

219. Title: *Dragnet*; "Homicide: The Student" S4E2
Air Date: September 25, 1969
Genre: Crime
Duration: 30mins
VG's Role: Ada Beale
Director(s): Jack Webb
Producer(s): Jack Webb
Production Company: Mark VII Ltd.
Distributor(s): NBC
Writer(s): Jack Smith & Jack Webb
Starring: Jack Webb, Harry Morgan, & Virginia Gregg
Episode Description: "Sgt. Friday" (Jack Webb) and "Officer Gannon" (Harry Morgan) suspect a young man who likes to read after two people are murdered for sport.

220. Title: *Mannix*; "Color Her Missing" S3E2
Air Date: October 4, 1969
Genre: Crime
Duration: 60mins
VG's Role: Liz Boone
Director(s): Michael Caffey
Producer(s): Ivan Goff & Ben Roberts
Production Company: Paramount Television
Distributor(s): CBS
Writer(s): Richard Levinson, William Link, & Bruce Geller
Starring: Mike Connors, Gail Fisher, & Jason Evers
Episode Description: "Mannix" (Mike Connors) takes on a case involving the man who is accused of killing one of his colleagues.

221. Title: *Ironside*; "Eye of the Hurricane" S3E4
Air Date: October 9, 1969
Genre: Crime
Duration: 60mins

VG's Role: Mrs. Leydon
Director(s): Don McDougall
Producer(s): Winston Miller
Production Company: Harbour Productions Unlimited
Distributor(s): NBC
Writer(s): Collier Young & Donn Mullally
Starring: Raymond Burr, Don Galloway, & Barbara Anderson
Episode Description: "Ironside" (Raymond Burr) and "Mark" (Don Mitchell) are held hostage at a prison by three convicts plotting escape.

222. Title: *Adam-12;* "Log 54: Impersonation" S2E16
Air Date: February 7, 1970
Genre: Crime
Duration: 30mins
VG's Role: Mrs. Dunkit
Director(s): Joseph Pevney
Producer(s): James Doherty & Herman S. Saunders
Production Company: Mark VII Ltd.
Distributor(s): Universal Studios
Writer(s): Robert A. Cinader, Jack Webb, & Robert I. Holt
Starring: Martin Milner, Kent McCord, & Virginia Gregg
Episode Description: A detective is accused of cheating a fight promoter.

223. Title: *The Virginian;* "A Time of Terror" S8E19
Air Date: February 11, 1970
Genre: Western
Duration: 60mins
VG's Role: Mary McMasters
Director(s): Joseph Pevney
Producer(s): Paul Freeman
Production Company: Universal Television

Distributor(s): NBC
Writer(s): Edward J. Lakso, Charles Marquis Warren, & Owen Wister
Starring: John McIntire, Doug McClure, & Tim Matheson
Episode Description: A family seeks revenge on "the Graingers'" friend and Congressional candidate (Joseph Cotten).

224. Title: *Dragnet;* "Missing Persons: The Body" S4E20
Air Date: March 5, 1970
Genre: Crime
Duration: 30mins
VG's Role: Mrs. Campbell
Director(s): Jack Webb
Producer(s): Jack Webb
Production Company: Mark VII Ltd.
Distributor(s): NBC
Writer(s): Robert C. Dennis & Jack Webb
Starring: Jack Webb, Harry Morgan, & Anthony Eisley
Episode Description: The body of a woman is found with no ID. "Sgt. Friday" (Jack Webb) and "Officer Gannon" (Harry Morgan) have a ring as the only clue to her identity.

225.Title: *Dragnet;* "I.A.D.: The Receipt" S4E23
Air Date: March 26, 1970
Genre: Crime
Duration: 30mins
VG's Role: Agnes Emerson
Director(s): Jack Webb
Producer(s): Jack Webb
Production Company: Mark VII Ltd.
Distributor(s): NBC
Writer(s): Stephen Downing & Jack Webb
Starring: Jack Webb, Harry Morgan, & Virginia Gregg

Episode Description: Two detectives are accused of stealing from a dead man, but "Sgt. Friday" (Jack Webb) and "Officer Gannon" (Harry Morgan) think the man's caretaker (Virginia Gregg) may know more than she lets on.

226. Title: *Dragnet;* "Burglary: Baseball" S4E25
Air Date: April 9, 1970
Genre: Crime
Duration: 30mins
VG's Role: Mrs. Mascall
Director(s): Jack Webb
Producer(s): Jack Webb
Production Company: Mark VII Ltd.
Distributor(s): NBC
Writer(s): Robert C. Dennis & Jack Webb
Starring: Jack Webb, Harry Morgan, & G.D. Spradlin
Episode Description: "Sgt. Friday" (Jack Webb) and "Officer Gannon" (Harry Morgan) investigate reports of a safecracker's work.

227. Title: *Ironside;* "A Killing Will Occur" S4E1
Air Date: September 17, 1970
Genre: Crime
Duration: 60mins
VG's Role: Mrs. Borrow
Director(s): Don Weis
Producer(s): Joel Rogosin
Production Company: Harbour Productions Unlimited
Distributor(s): NBC
Writer(s): Collier Young & Alvin Sapinsley
Starring: Raymond Burr, Don Galloway, & Barbara Anderson
Episode Description: "Ironside" (Raymond Burr) receives disturbing calls from an anonymous caller about killings that will occur.

228. Title: *The Bold Ones: The New Doctors*; "Killer on the Loose" S2E2
Air Date: October 11, 1970
Genre: Drama
Duration: 60mins
VG's Role: Nurse Anne Turner
Director(s): Abner Biberman
Producer(s): Joel Rogosin
Production Company: Harbour Productions Unlimited
Distributor(s): NBC
Writer(s): Richard H. Landau, Paul Mason, & Steven Bochco
Starring: E.G. Marshall, David Hartman, & John Saxon
Episode Description: An unknown virus takes over the hospital and doctors scramble to get it under control.

229. Title: *Adam-12*; "Log 75: Have a Nice Weekend" S3E7
Air Date: November 7, 1970
Genre: Crime
Duration: 30mins
VG's Role: Anne White
Director(s): Oscar Rudolph
Producer(s): Herman S. Saunders
Production Company: Mark VII Ltd.
Distributor(s): NBC
Writer(s): Robert A. Cinader, Jack Webb, & Robert I. Holt
Starring: Martin Milner, Kent McCord, & Virginia Gregg
Episode Description: A distraught woman (Virginia Gregg) with a gun confronts "Reed" (Kent McCord), a fight breaks out at church over which songs should be used in a service, and burglaries begin to occur to only female victims in a bridge club.

230. Title: *The Bold Ones: The Lawyers*; "The People Against Doctor Chapman" S2E4
Air Date: December 6, 1970

Genre: Crime
Duration: 60mins
VG's Role: Angela Woodly
Director(s): Jeannot Szwarc
Producer(s): Jo Swerling Jr.
Production Company: Roy Huggins-Public Arts Productions
Distributor(s): NBC
Writer(s): Roy Huggins & Jerry Bredouw
Starring: Burl Ives, Joseph Campanella, & Monte Markham
Episode Description: "Brian's" (Joseph Campanella) client is accused of practicing medicine without a license after a patient of his dies.

231. Title: *Bracken's World*; "Will Freddy's Real Father Please Stand Up?" S2E13
Air Date: December 11, 1970
Genre: Drama
Duration: 60mins
VG's Role: Rita Preston
Director(s): *Unavailable
Producer(s): Stanley Rubin
Production Company: Twentieth Century Fox Television
Distributor(s): NBC
Writer(s): Dorothy Kingsley
Starring: Leslie Nielsen, Peter Haskell, & Elizabeth Allen
Episode Description: A child actor is hired in the studio for a television show, and his troubled family situation soon interferes with the job.

232. Title: *Mannix*; "The Color Murder" S4E22
Air Date: February 27, 1971
Genre: Crime
Duration: 60mins
VG's Role: Jenny Loman

Director(s): Barry Crane
Producer(s): Ivan Goff & Ben Roberts
Production Company: Paramount Television
Distributor(s): CBS
Writer(s): Richard Levinson, William Link, Bruce Geller, & Harold Medford
Starring: Mike Connors, Gail Fisher, & Diane Keaton
Episode Description: *Unavailable

233. **Title:** *Mod Squad*; "Welcome to Our City" S3E21
Air Date: March 2, 1971
Genre: Crime
Duration: 60mins
VG's Role: Hattie
Director(s): John Llewellyn Moxey
Producer(s): Tony Barrett
Production Company: Thomas/Spelling Productions
Distributor(s): ABC
Writer(s): Shirl Hendryx, Tony Barrett, Buddy Ruskin, Harve Bennett, & Sammy Hess
Starring: Michael Cole, Clarence Williams III, & Peggy Lipton
Episode Description: The trio helps a little boy searching for his father.

234. **Title:** *The Interns*; "The Choice" S1E24
Air Date: March 26, 1971
Genre: Drama
Duration: 60mins
VG's Role: Mrs. Tebbetts
Director(s): David Lowell Rich
Producer(s): Bob Claver
Production Company: Screen Gems
Distributor(s): CBS

Writer(s): Richard Frede, Walter Newman, David Swift, William Blinn, Elinor Karpf, Stephen Karpf, & Charles Larson
Starring: Stephen Brooks, Christopher Stone, & Hal Frederick
Episode Description: "Dr. Lydia Thorpe" (Sandra Smith) struggles with the decision to be a fulltime homemaker or continue in medicine.

235. Title: *Insight*; "The Immigrant"
Air Date: June 26, 1971
Genre: Drama
Duration: 30mins
VG's Role: Anya
Director(s): Hal Cooper
Producer(s): John Meredyth Lucas
Production Company: Paulist Productions
Distributor(s): *Unavailable
Writer(s): Maureen Daly
Starring: William Bassett, John Dennis, & Geoffrey Deuel
Episode Description: An immigrant family struggles with changing life in America.

236. Title: *O'Hara, U.S. Treasury*; "Operation: Time Fuse" S1E5
Air Date: October 15, 1971
Genre: Drama
Duration: 60mins
VG's Role: Mrs. Adams
Director(s): Lawrence Dobkin
Producer(s): Leonard B. Kaufman
Production Company: Mark VII Ltd.
Distributor(s): CBS
Writer(s): William P. McGivern, James E. Moser, & Jack Webb
Starring: David Janssen, James Wainwright, & Sian Barbara Allen

Episode Description: "O'Hara" (David Janssen) goes undercover to bust a grassroots terrorist group after they plant a bomb in order to extort money from a publisher.

237. Title: *Mission: Impossible*; "Encounter" S6E7
Air Date: October 30, 1971
Genre: Adventure
Duration: 60mins
VG's Role: Smitty
Director(s): Barry Crane
Producer(s): Laurence Heath
Production Company: Paramount Television
Distributor(s): CBS
Writer(s): Bruce Geller & Howard Berk
Starring: Peter Graves, Greg Morris, & Peter Lupus
Episode Description: "Lisa" (Lynda Day George) goes undercover as a mobster's alcoholic wife, but the operation places her at great risk.

238. Title: *The D.A.*; "The People vs. Lindsey" S1E7
Air Date: November 5, 1971
Genre: Crime
Duration: 30mins
VG's Role: Anne Grady
Director(s): *Unavailable
Producer(s): *Unavailable
Production Company: Mark VII Ltd.
Distributor(s): NBC
Writer(s): *Unavailable
Starring: Robert Conrad, Jack Bailey, & Virginia Gregg
Episode Description: "Deputy D.A. Paul Ryan" (Robert Conrad) struggles to get a conviction out in an alleged child abuse case.

239. Title: *O'Hara, U.S. Treasury*; "Operation: Crystal Springs" S1E11
Air Date: December 3, 1971
Genre: Crime
Duration: 60mins
VG's Role: Elinor Hoxie
Director(s): Alan Crosland Jr.
Producer(s): Norman Jolley
Production Company: Mark VII Ltd.
Distributor(s): CBS
Writer(s): James E. Moser, Gilbert Ralston, & Jack Webb
Starring: David Janssen, David Friedkin, & Lorraine Gary
Episode Description: "O'Hara" (David Janssen) becomes a target in a small town when he stumbles upon a corrupt system in a tax violation investigation.

240. Title: *Owen Marshall, Counselor at Law*; "The Triangle" S1E14
Air Date: December 30, 1971
Genre: Crime
Duration: 60mins
VG's Role: Frank's Mother
Director(s): David Lowell Rich
Producer(s): Jon Epstein
Production Company: Groverton Productions
Distributor(s): ABC
Writer(s): David Victor, Jerry McNeely, & William Driskill
Starring: Arthur Hill, Lee Majors, & Joan Darling
Episode Description: A police officer is charged when his wife's lover is murdered.

241. Title: *Emergency!*; "The Wedsworth-Townsend Act" S1E1
Air Date: January 15, 1972
Genre: Drama

Duration: 60mins
VG's Role: Wilma Jacobs, R.N.
Director(s): Jack Webb
Producer(s): Robert A. Cinader & Edwin Self
Production Company: Mark VII Ltd.
Distributor(s): NBC
Writer(s): Harold Jack Bloom & Robert A. Cinader
Starring: Robert Fuller, Julie London, & Bobby Troup
Episode Description: New LACFD paramedics must prove themselves to "Dr. Brackett" as a state bill pends to approve their positions.

242. Title: *Emergency!*; "Botulism" S1E2
Air Date: January 29, 1972
Genre: Drama
Duration: 60mins
VG's Role: Wilma Jacobs, R.N.
Director(s): Herschel Daugherty
Producer(s): Robert A. Cinader
Production Company: Mark VII Ltd.
Distributor(s): NBC
Writer(s): Harold Jack Bloom, Robert A. Cinader, & Stephen Downing
Starring: Robert Fuller, Julie London, & Bobby Troup
Episode Description: *Unavailable

243. Title: *Ironside*; "And Then There Was One" S5E19
Air Date: January 20, 1972
Genre: Crime
Duration: 60mins
VG's Role: Miss Wilson
Director(s): Arnold Laven
Producer(s): Albert Aley

Production Company: Harbour Productions Unlimited
Distributor(s): NBC
Writer(s): Collier Young & Fred Freiberger
Starring: Raymond Burr, Don Galloway, & Don Mitchell
Episode Description: "Ironside" (Raymond Burr) uses "Ed" (Don Galloway) as bait in an investigation into the attacks of three Vietnam veterans.

244. Title: *Marcus Welby, M.D.*; "I'm Really Trying" S3E19
Air Date: February 1, 1972
Genre: Drama
Duration: 60mins
VG's Role: Dr. Martha Heider
Director(s): Leo Penn
Producer(s): David J. O'Connell
Production Company: Universal Television
Distributor(s): ABC
Writer(s): David Victor, Margaret Schneider, & Paul Schneider
Starring: Robert Young, James Brolin, & Elena Verdugo
Episode Description: A father (Gary Collins) won't admit his son (Sean Kelly) has brain damage.

245. Title: *Alias Smith and Jones*; "Which Way to the O.K. Corral?" S2E20
Air Date: February 10, 1972
Genre: Western
Duration: 60mins
VG's Role: Emma McIntyre
Director(s): Jack Arnold
Producer(s): Glen A. Larson
Production Company: Roy Huggins-Public Arts Productions
Distributor(s): MCA Television
Writer(s): Roy Huggins & Glen A. Larson

Starring: Ben Murphy, Roger Davis, & Neville Brand
Episode Description: A wealthy rancher hires "Curry" (Ben Murphy) and "Heyes" (Roger Davis) to find a man who can testify to the rancher's innocence in a murder case.

246. Title: *Emergency!*; "Cook's Tour" S1E3
Air Date: February 12, 1972
Genre: Drama
Duration: 60mins
VG's Role: 3rd Nurse
Director(s): Christian Nyby
Producer(s): Robert A. Cinader
Production Company: Mark VII Ltd.
Distributor(s): NBC
Writer(s): Harold Jack Bloom, Robert A. Cinader, & Daryl Henry
Starring: Robert Fuller, Julie London, & Bobby Troup
Episode Description: *Unavailable

247. Title: *Love, American Style*; "Love and the Happy Days/Love and the Newscasters" S3E22
Air Date: February 25, 1972
Genre: Comedy
Duration: 60mins
VG's Role: Mrs. Nestrock
Director(s): Marc Daniels & Gary Nelson
Producer(s): Donald R. Boyle, Carl Kleinschmitt, & Alan Rafkin
Production Company: Paramount Television
Distributor(s): ABC
Writer(s): Garry Marshall, R.S. Allen, & Harvey Bullock
Starring: John Astin, Carl Ballantine, & Ric Carrott
Episode Description: A family of the 1950s gets their first television set, and the son, "Ritchie's" (Ron Howard) friend and "Potsie" (Anson Williams) believe the tv can be used to get girls.

248. Title: *The ABC Saturday Superstar Movie*; "Gidget Makes the Wrong Connection" S1E11
Air Date: November 18, 1972
Genre: Animation
Duration: 60mins
VG's Role: Barbara Hightower (voice)
Director(s): Charles A. Nichols
Producer(s): Joseph Barbera, William Hanna, & Iwao Takamoto
Production Company: Filmation Associates
Distributor(s): ABC
Writer(s): *Unavailable
Starring: Kathy Gori, Denny Evans, & Don Messick
Episode Description: "Gidget" (Kathy Gori) comes upon a band of gold smuggling pirates.

249. Title: *Emergency!*; "Musical Mania" S2E11
Air Date: December 9, 1972
Genre: Drama
Duration: 60mins
VG's Role: Edith (uncredited)
Director(s): Christian I. Nyby II
Producer(s): Robert A. Cinader
Production Company: Mark VII Ltd.
Distributor(s): NBC
Writer(s): Harold Jack Bloom, Robert A. Cinader, & Kenneth Dorward
Starring: Robert Fuller, Julie London, & Bobby Troup
Episode Description: The station is annoyed by "Gage's" (Randolph Mantooth) musical interest. Rescue calls come in for frostbite and a man trapped below his house.

250. Title: *The Sixth Sense*; "Gallows in the Wind" S2E11
Air Date: December 16, 1972

Genre: Drama
Duration: 60mins
VG's Role: Thelma Young
Director(s): Alan Crosland Jr.
Producer(s): Stanley Shpetner
Production Company: Universal Television
Distributor(s): ABC
Writer(s): Don Ingalls & Anthony Lawrence
Starring: Gary Collins, Rod Serling, & Meg Foster
Episode Description: A young woman (Meg Foster) has deathly premonitions during a hurricane that others in her group don't know how to interpret.

251. **Title:** *Hec Ramsey*; "Mystery of the Yellow Rose" S1E4
Air Date: January 28, 1973
Genre: Western
Duration: 60mins
VG's Role: Mrs. Lambert
Director(s): Douglas Benton & Charles Ziarko
Producer(s): Douglas Benton
Production Company: Mark VII Ltd.
Distributor(s): NBC
Writer(s): Harold Jack Bloom, John Meston, William R. Cox, & Douglas Benton
Starring: Richard Boone, Rick Lenz, & Diana Muldaur
Episode Description: "Hec" (Richard Boone) chases a forger to New Mexico where he runs into an old flame then must act as attorney to help a friend from being framed.

252. **Title:** *Chase*; "Pilot" S1E1
Air Date: March 24, 1973
Genre: Crime
Duration: 60mins

VG's Role: Judge Mary Foreman
Director(s): Jack Webb
Producer(s): Jack Webb
Production Company: Mark VII Ltd.
Distributor(s): NBC
Writer(s): Stephen J. Cannell
Starring: Mitchell Ryan, Reid Smith, & Michael Richardson
Episode Description: *Unavailable

253. Title: *Kung Fu;* "The Third Man" S1E14
Air Date: April 26, 1973
Genre: Western
Duration: 60mins
VG's Role: Martha
Director(s): Charles S. Dubin
Producer(s): Jerry Thorpe
Production Company: Warner Brothers Television
Distributor(s): ABC
Writer(s): Ed Spielman, Herman Miller, & Robert Lewin
Starring: David Carradine, Ed Nelson, & Fred Beir
Episode Description: "Caine" (David Carradine) dares a murderer to be his own judge while his victim's grieving widow accepts the judgment.

254. Title: *Butch Cassidy;* "The Scientist" S1E1
Air Date: September 8, 1973
Genre: Animation
Duration: 30mins
VG's Role: Voice
Director(s): *Unavailable
Producer(s): Joseph Barbera & William Hanna
Production Company: Hanna-Barbera Productions
Distributor(s): *Unavailable

Writer(s): *Unavailable
Starring: Chip Hand
Episode Description: The group's Belgrovia gig is a cover for smuggling out a hostage.

255. Title: *Yogi's Gang*; "Dr. Bigot" S1E1
Air Date: September 8, 1973
Genre: Animation
Duration: 30mins
VG's Role: (credit only)
Director(s): Charles A. Nichols
Producer(s): Joseph Barbera, William Hanna, Art Scott, & Iwao Takamoto
Production Company: Hanna-Barbera Productions
Distributor(s): ABC
Writer(s): Neal Barbera, Alan Dinehart, Neal Israel, Bill Lutz, R.T. McGee, Jack Mendelsohn, Sloan Nibley, Bob Ogle, Ray Parker, & Dick Robbins
Starring: Daws Butler, Josh Albee, & Julie Bennett
Episode Description: From their secret blimp, "Dr. Bigot" and his gang cause trouble for "Mr. Cheerful" and "Yogi Bear."

256. Title: *Cannon*; "He Who Digs a Grave" S3E1
Air Date: September 12, 1973
Genre: Crime
Duration: 60mins
VG's Role: Dr. Emma Savonka
Director(s): Richard Donner
Producer(s): Adrian Samish
Production Company: Quinn Martin Productions
Distributor(s): CBS
Writer(s): David Delman, Edward Hume, & Stephen Kandel
Starring: William Conrad, Anne Baxter, & Barry Sullivan

Episode Description: "Cannon" (William Conrad) investigates a murder-suicide that involves wealthy, prestigious families in a small town.

257. **Title:** *Adam-12*; "Dirt Duel" S5E1
Air Date: September 13, 1972
Genre: Drama
Duration: 30mins
VG's Role: Mrs. McKay
Director(s): Carl Barth
Producer(s): Herman S. Saunders
Production Company: Mark VII Ltd.
Distributor(s): NBC
Writer(s): Robert A. Cinader, Jack Webb, Stephen Downing, & Stephen J. Cannell
Starring: Martin Milner, Kent McCord, & Micky Dolenz
Episode Description: A motorcycle club helps "Malloy" (Martin Milner) and "Reed" (Kent McCord) catch up with purse-snatching motorcycle riders.

258. **Title:** *Emergency!*; "Alley Cat" S3E3
Air Date: October 6, 1973
Genre: Drama
Duration: 60mins
VG's Role: Zelda Zack
Director(s): Alan Crosland Jr.
Producer(s): Edwin Self
Production Company: Mark VII Ltd.
Distributor(s): NBC
Writer(s): Harold Jack Bloom, Robert A. Cinader, & Charlene Sukins
Starring: Robert Fuller, Julie London, & Bobby Troup
Episode Description: *Unavailable

259.Title: *Adam-12*; "Capture" S6E9
Air Date: November 14, 1973
Genre: Drama
Duration: 30mins
VG's Role: Diane Cooper
Director(s): Lawrence Doheny
Producer(s): Tom Williams
Production Company: Mark VII Ltd.
Distributor(s): NBC
Writer(s): Robert A. Cinader, Jack Webb, Leo Gordon, & Bryan Joseph
Starring: Martin Milner, Kent McCord, & Jed Allan
Episode Description: "Malloy" (Martin Milner) and "Reed" (Kent McCord) pursue a wild dog and burglar.

260. Title: *Yogi's Gang*; "Lotta Litter" S1E12
Air Date: November 24, 1973
Genre: Animation
Duration: 30mins
VG's Role: (credit only)
Director(s): Charles A. Nichols
Producer(s): Joseph Barbera, William Hanna, Art Scott, & Iwao Takamoto
Production Company: Hanna-Barbera Productions
Distributor(s): ABC
Writer(s): Neal Barbera, Alan Dinehart, Neal Israel, Bill Lutz, R.T. McGee, Jack Mendelsohn, Sloan Nibley, Bob Ogle, Ray Parker, & Dick Robbins
Starring: Daws Butler, Josh Albee, & Julie Bennett
Episode Description: "Lotta Litter" tricks "Yogi" and friends into trashing Jellystone Park.

261. Title: *Yogi's Gang*; "Mr. Hothead" S1E15
Air Date: December 15, 1973

Genre: Animation
Duration: 60mins
VG's Role: (credit only)
Director(s): Charles A. Nichols
Producer(s): Joseph Barbera, William Hanna, Art Scott, & Iwao Takamoto
Production Company: Hanna-Barbera Productions
Distributor(s): ABC
Writer(s): Neal Barbera, Alan Dinehart, Neal Israel, Bill Lutz, R.T. McGee, Jack Mendelsohn, Sloan Nibley, Bob Ogle, Ray Parker, & Dick Robbins
Starring: Daws Butler, Josh Albee, & Julie Bennett
Episode Description: "Yogi's" gang is turned into a group of grumps after "Mr. Hothead" zaps them with his "Hothead Zapper."

262. Title: *Chase*; "Right to an Attorney" S1E13
Air Date: January 8, 1974
Genre: Crime
Duration: 60mins
VG's Role: Customer
Director(s): Alan Crosland Jr.
Producer(s): James Schmerer
Production Company: Mark VII Ltd.
Distributor(s): NBC
Writer(s): Stephen J. Cannell & James Basler
Starring: Mitchell Ryan, Wayne Maunder, & Reid Smith
Episode Description: *Unavailable

263. Title: *The Six Million Dollar Man*; "Population: Zero" S1E1
Air Date: January 18, 1974
Genre: Crime
Duration: 60mins
VG's Role: Mrs. Nelson

Director(s): Jeannot Szwarc
Producer(s): Donald R. Boyle & Sam Strangis
Production Company: Silverton Productions
Distributor(s): ABC
Writer(s): Elroy Schwartz
Starring: Lee Majors, Richard Anderson, & Don Porter
Episode Description: "Steve Austin" (Lee Majors) investigates when an entire town's population is knocked out by a mysterious device.

264. **Title:** *Police Story*; "The Ripper" S1E15
Air Date: February 12, 1974
Genre: Crime
Duration: 60mins
VG's Role: Mrs. Mooney
Director(s): Gary Nelson
Producer(s): Stanley Kallis
Production Company: David Gerber Productions
Distributor(s): NBC
Writer(s): Joseph Wambaugh, Don Ingalls, & E. Jack Neuman
Starring: Darren McGavin, Kathie Browne, & Leslie Parrish
Episode Description: "Hallett" (Darren McGavin) investigates when a serial killer targets gay men.

265. **Title:** *Cannon*; "Bobby Loved Me" S3E22
Air Date: February 27, 1974
Genre: Crime
Duration: 60mins
VG's Role: Mrs. Kester
Director(s): Lawrence Dobkin
Producer(s): Winston Miller
Production Company: Quinn Martin Productions
Distributor(s): CBS
Writer(s): Joel Murcott & Edward Hume

Starring: William Conrad, Jon Cypher, & Pippa Scott
Episode Description: "Cannon" (William Conrad) is hired to find the killer of a con man.

266. Title: *Adam-12*; "A Clinic on 18th Street" S6E24
Air Date: March 13, 1974
Genre: Crime
Duration: 30mins
VG's Role: Miss Brown
Director(s): Jack Webb
Producer(s): Jack Webb
Production Company: Mark VII Ltd.
Distributor(s): NBC
Writer(s): Robert A. Cinader, Jack Webb, & Joseph Calvelli
Starring: Martin Milner, Kent McCord, & Ed Nelson
Episode Description: "Malloy" (Martin Milner) and "Reed" (Kent McCord) investigate a doctor who seems to be at the epicenter of fraud.

267. Title: *Apple's Way*; "The Accident" S1E11
Air Date: May 5, 1974
Genre: Drama
Duration: *Unavailable
VG's Role: Mrs. McDougal
Director(s): *Unavailable
Producer(s): *Unavailable
Production Company: Lorimar Productions
Distributor(s): CBS
Writer(s): Earl Hamner Jr.
Starring: Ronny Cox, Frances Lee McCain, & Malcolm Atterbury
Episode Description: After "George Apple" (Ronny Cox) pushes for better traffic signals at a busy intersection, "Steven Apple" (Eric Olson) gets hurt at the site.

268. Title: *These are the Days;* "Sensible Ben" S1E1
Air Date: September 7, 1974
Genre: Animation
Duration: 30mins
VG's Role: Voice
Director(s): *Unavailable
Producer(s): Joseph Barbera, William Hanna, & Iwao Takamoto
Production Company: Hanna-Barbera Productions
Distributor(s): *Unavailable
Writer(s): *Unavailable
Starring: *Unavailable
Episode Description: *Unavailable

269. Title: *Police Woman;* "The Beautiful Die Young" S1E2
Air Date: September 20, 1974
Genre: Crime
Duration: 60mins
VG's Role: Astrid
Director(s): Barry Shear
Producer(s): Douglas Benton
Production Company: David Gerber Productions
Distributor(s): NBC
Writer(s): Robert L. Collins, Edward DeBlasio, & Douglas Benton
Starring: Angie Dickinson, Earl Holliman, & Charles Dierkop
Episode Description: A modeling agency is a front for the porn industry, and "Sgt. Pepper" (Angie Dickinson) and "Sgt. Crowley" (Earl Holliman) use a decoy to go undercover in the bust.

270. Title: *Happy Days;* "Who's Sorry Now?" S2E3
Air Date: September 24, 1974
Genre: Comedy
Duration: 30mins
VG's Role: Mrs. Nestrock

Director(s): Jerry Paris
Producer(s): William Bickley
Production Company: Miller-Milkis Productions
Distributor(s): ABC
Writer(s): Garry Marshall & Michael Leeson
Starring: Ron Howard, Marion Ross, & Anson Williams
Episode Description: An old flame of "Richie's" (Ron Howard), "Arlene" (Tannis G. Montgomery), is back in town, but he must find a way to break things off amicably.

271. **Title:** *Cannon*; "Voice from the Grave" S4E3
Air Date: September 25, 1974
Genre: Crime
Duration: 60mins
VG's Role: Kay Ryan
Director(s): William Wiard
Producer(s): Anthony Spinner
Production Company: Quinn Martin Productions
Distributor(s): CBS
Writer(s): Robert Hamner & Edward Hume
Starring: William Conrad, Robert Webber, & Jason Evers
Episode Description: "Cannon" (William Conrad) investigates an old nightclub murder after another detective becomes a target.

272. **Title:** *The Six Million Dollar Man*; "The Pal-Mir Escort" S2E4
Air Date: October 4, 1974
Genre: Crime
Duration: 60mins
VG's Role: Sarah
Director(s): Lawrence Dobkin
Producer(s): Joe L. Cramer & Lionel E. Siegel
Production Company: Silverton Productions
Distributor(s): ABC

Writer(s): Margaret Schneider, Paul Schneider, & Martin Caidin
Starring: Lee Majors, Richard Anderson, & Anne Revere
Episode Description: Assassins interfere with "Steve Austin's" (Lee Majors) help of a prime minister who needs a heart implant.

273. **Title:** *Ironside*; "The Last Cotillion" S8E7
Air Date: October 31, 1974
Genre: Crime
Duration: 60mins
VG's Role: Ellen
Director(s): Alvin Ganzer
Producer(s): Norman Jolley
Production Company: Harbour Productions Unlimited
Distributor(s): NBC
Writer(s): Collier Young & Walter Black
Starring: Raymond Burr, Don Galloway, & Don Mitchell
Episode Description: A wealthy aristocrat (Kim Hunter) is suspected of murdering two of her former lovers, but "Ironside" (Raymond Burr) believes she is innocent.

274. **Title:** *Marcus Welby, M.D.;* "The Last Rip-Off" S6E11
Air Date: November 26, 1974
Genre: Drama
Duration: 60mins
VG's Role: Janet Kenderdine
Director(s): William Asher
Producer(s): David J. O'Connell
Production Company: Universal Television
Distributor(s): ABC
Writer(s): Norman Hudis, David Victor, & Harold H. Harnum
Starring: Robert Young, James Brolin, & Elena Verdugo

Episode Description: "Dr. Welby" (Robert Young) and "Dr. Kiley" (James Brolin) uncover an unethical funeral director (Richard Basehart).

275. **Title:** *Kolchak: The Night Stalker*; "The Spanish Moss Murders" S1E9
Air Date: December 6, 1974
Genre: Horror
Duration: 60mins
VG's Role: Dr. Hollenbeck
Director(s): Gordon Hessler
Producer(s): Cy Chermak
Production Company: Francy Productions
Distributor(s): ABC
Writer(s): Jeffrey Grant Rice, Alvin R. Friedman, & David Chase
Starring: Darren McGavin, Simon Oakland, & Keenan Wynn
Episode Description: An experiment on dreams brings a monster covered in Spanish moss to life.

276. **Title:** *The Streets of San Francisco*; "Letters from the Grave" S3E16
Air Date: January 16, 1975
Genre: Crime
Duration: 60mins
VG's Role: Phyllis Stebbins
Director(s): Virgil W. Vogel
Producer(s): John Wilder
Production Company: Quinn Martin Productions
Distributor(s): ABC
Writer(s): Tom Cannan, Edward Hume, & Carolyn Weston
Starring: Karl Malden, Michael Douglas, & Peter Strauss
Episode Description: A murder victim is found in the ruins of Alcatraz.

277. Title: *Emergency!*; "905-Wild" S4E22
Air Date: March 1, 1975
Genre: Drama
Duration: 60mins
VG's Role: Rosa Bernardi
Director(s): Jack Webb
Producer(s): *Unavailable
Production Company: Mark VII Ltd.
Distributor(s): NBC
Writer(s): Harold Jack Bloom, Robert A. Cinader, & Buddy Atkinson
Starring: Robert Fuller, Julie London, & Bobby Troup
Episode Description: Emergencies involving animals cause the LA County Animal Control and Station 51 to work together.

278. Title: *The Rockford Files*; "Roundabout" S1E22
Air Date: March 7, 1975
Genre: Crime
Duration: 60mins
VG's Role: Eleanor
Director(s): Lou Antonio
Producer(s): Stephen J. Cannell
Production Company: Roy Huggins-Public Arts Productions
Distributor(s): NBC
Writer(s): Roy Huggins, Stephen J. Cannell, & Mitch Lindemann
Starring: James Garner, Noah Beery Jr., & Jesse Welles
Episode Description: "Jim" (James Garner) must make a delivery to a woman who is caught up in a dangerous situation yet refuses help.

279. Title: *Adam-12*; "Something Worth Dying for: Part 1" S7E23
Air Date: May 13, 1975
Genre: Crime

Duration: 30mins
VG's Role: Matron
Director(s): Hollingsworth Morse
Producer(s): Tom Williams
Production Company: Mark VII Ltd.
Distributor(s): NBC
Writer(s): Robert A. Cinader, Jack Webb, & David H. Vowell
Starring: Martin Milner, Kent McCord, & Sian Barbara Allen
Episode Description: "Reed" (Kent McCord) moves to the narcotics squad but is dissatisfied with the change.

280. Title: *The Six Million Dollar Man*; "The Return of the Bionic Woman: Part 2" S3E2
Air Date: September 21, 1975
Genre: Crime
Duration: 60mins
VG's Role: Mrs. Raymond
Director(s): Dick Moder
Producer(s): Kenneth Johnson
Production Company: Silverton Productions
Distributor(s): ABC
Writer(s): Kenneth Johnson, Richard Carr, & Martin Caidin
Starring: Lee Majors, Richard Anderson, & Lindsay Wagner
Episode Description: "Steve Austin" (Lee Majors) tries to help "Jaime Sommers" (Lindsay Wagner) recover her memory by giving her a challenging mission.

281. Title: *Run, Joe, Run*; "The Hitchhiker" S2E8
Air Date: October 25, 1975
Genre: Drama
Duration: *Unavailable
VG's Role: Hannah Deaks
Director(s): Robert Jones

Producer(s): William P. D'Angelo & Dick O'Connor
Production Company: William P. D'Angelo Productions
Distributor(s): *Unavailable
Writer(s): Martin Donovan & Richard H. Landau
Starring: Paul Frees, Virginia Gregg, & Sid Haig
Episode Description: *Unavailable

282. Title: *Bronk*; "Deception" S1E12
Air Date: December 7, 1975
Genre: Crime
Duration: 60mins
VG's Role: Maxine
Director(s): Corey Allen
Producer(s): Leigh Vance
Production Company: Carnan-Becker Productions
Distributor(s): CBS
Writer(s): Carroll O'Connor, Larry Forrester, & Ed Waters
Starring: Jack Palance, Henry Beckman, & Tony King
Episode Description: A young cop struggles with coming forward with damning information or remaining silent to protect his position.

283. Title: *The Streets of San Francisco*; "The Honorable Profession" S4E16
Air Date: January 15, 1976
Genre: Crime
Duration: 60mins
VG's Role: Martha Travis
Director(s): Harry Falk
Producer(s): William Robert Yates
Production Company: Quinn Martin Productions
Distributor(s): ABC
Writer(s): Paul Robert Coyle, Edward Hume, & Carolyn Weston

Starring: Karl Malden, Michael Douglas, & Robert Reed
Episode Description: A robbery case's star witness vanishes.

284. Title: *The Waltons*; "The Fledgling" S4E23
Air Date: February 26, 1976
Genre: Drama
Duration: 60mins
VG's Role: Mrs. Butterworth
Director(s): Harry Harris
Producer(s): Robert L. Jacks
Production Company: Lorimar Productions
Distributor(s): CBS
Writer(s): Earl Hamner Jr.
Starring: Richard Thomas, Ralph Waite, & Michael Learned
Episode Description: "John-Boy Walton" wants to open his own newspaper.

285. Title: *S.W.A.T.*; "Dragons and Owls" S2E21
Air Date: March 6, 1976
Genre: Crime
Duration: 60mins
VG's Role: Mrs. Hill
Director(s): Bernard McEveety
Producer(s): Gene Levitt
Production Company: Spelling-Goldberg Productions
Distributor(s): ABC
Writer(s): Robert Hamner, Rick Husky, Bob Mitchell, & Esther Mitchell
Starring: Steve Forrest, Robert Urich, & Rod Perry
Episode Description: S.W.A.T. gets involved after reports of a gang stealing vans and attacking women.

286. Title: *Clue Club*; "The Paper Shaper Caper" S1E1
Air Date: August 14, 1976
Genre: Animation
Duration: 30mins
VG's Role: (voice)
Director(s): Charles A. Nichols
Producer(s): Joseph Barbera, William Hanna, & Iwao Takamoto
Production Company: Hanna-Barbera Productions
Distributor(s): CBS
Writer(s): Herb Armstrong, Haskell Barkin, Dick Conway, Jack Fox, Gordon Glasco, Orville H. Hampton, Duane Poole, Dick Robbins, James Schmerer, & Lee Sheldon
Starring: Joan Gerber, Virginia Gregg, & Bob Hastings
Episode Description: Someone sabotages a newspaper's printing press and leaves behind a strange, singular clue.

287. Title: *Clue Club* "The Case of the Lighthouse Mouse" S1E2
Air Date: August 21, 1976
Genre: Animation
Duration: 30mins
VG's Role: (voice)
Director(s): Charles A. Nichols
Producer(s): Joseph Barbera, William Hanna, Alex Lovy, & Iwao Takamoto
Production Company: Hanna-Barbera Productions
Distributor(s): CBS
Writer(s): Herb Armstrong, Haskell Barkin, Dick Conway, Jack Fox, Gordon Glasco, Orville H. Hampton, Duane Poole, Dick Robbins, James Schmerer, Jeffrey Scott, & Lee Sheldon
Starring: Joan Gerber, Virginia Gregg, & Bob Hastings
Episode Description: More and more of the museum's jewels disappear.

288. Title: *Rich Man, Poor Man – Book II*; "Chapter I" S1E1
Air Date: September 21, 1976
Genre: Drama
Duration: 120mins
VG's Role: Miss McPherson
Director(s): Lou Antonio
Producer(s): Jon Epstein, Michael Gleason, & Carl Vitale
Production Company: Universal Television
Distributor(s): ABC
Writer(s): Millard Lampell & Irwin Shaw
Starring: Peter Strauss, Susan Blakely, & Gregg Henry
Episode Description: A U.S. Senator (Peter Strauss) tires of politics in his concern for family matters.

289. Title: *Police Woman*; "The Lifeline Agency" S3E7
Air Date: November 23, 1976
Genre: Crime
Duration: 60mins
VG's Role: Nurse Harris
Director(s): Corey Allen
Producer(s): Douglas Benton
Production Company: David Gerber Productions
Distributor(s): NBC
Writer(s): Robert L. Collins, Gabe Essoe, & Edward DeBlasio
Starring: Angie Dickinson, Earl Holliman, & Charles Dierkop
Episode Description: "Sgt. Pepper" (Angie Dickinson) and "Sgt. Crowley" (Earl Holliman) go undercover to bust a black-market child adoption ring.

290. Title: *The Streets of San Francisco*; "Hang Tough" S5E16
Air Date: February 17, 1977
Genre: Crime
Duration: 60mins

VG's Role: Emma Doyle
Director(s): William Hale
Producer(s): Will Lorin
Production Company: Quinn Martin Productions
Distributor(s): ABC
Writer(s): Norman Lessing, Edward Hume, & Carolyn Weston
Starring: Karl Malden, Richard Hatch, & Ned Beatty
Episode Description: A narcotics department member interferes with "Lt. Mike Stone's" (Karl Malden) investigation of a murder.

291. **Title:** *Man from Atlantis*; "Man from Atlantis" S1E1
Air Date: March 4, 1977
Genre: Adventure
Duration: 90mins
VG's Role: Whale scientist
Director(s): Lee H. Katzin
Producer(s): Robert H. Justman
Production Company: Solow Production Company
Distributor(s): NBC
Writer(s): Mayo Simon
Starring: Patrick Duffy, Belinda Montgomery, & Dean Santoro
Episode Description: One survivor of a sunken city remains: an amphibious man (Patrick Duffy).

292. **Title:** *Police Woman*; "The Buttercup Killer" S4E6
Air Date: December 13, 1977
Genre: Crime
Duration: 60mins
VG's Role: Mother Superior
Director(s): Michael Mann
Producer(s): Douglas Benton, Edward DeBlasio, David Gerber, Abram S. Ginnes, & George Lehr
Production Company: David Gerber Productions

Distributor(s): NBC
Writer(s): Robert L. Collins & Gabe Essoe
Starring: Angie Dickinson, Earl Holliman, & Charles Dierkop
Episode Description: "Sgt. Pepper" (Angie Dickinson) and "Sgt. Crowley" (Earl Holliman) investigate when a Greek immigrant family is being murdered one member at a time, yet refuse police involvement.

293. Title: *Captain Caveman and the Teen Angels*; "The Mystery Mansion Mix-Up" S1E15
Air Date: December 17, 1977
Genre: Animation
Duration: 10mins
VG's Role: (additional voices)
Director(s): Charles A. Nichols
Producer(s): Joseph Barbera, William Hanna, Alex Lovy, Lewis Marshall, Art Scott, & Iwao Takamoto
Production Company: Hanna-Barbera Productions
Distributor(s): ABC
Writer(s): Joe Ruby & Ken Spears
Starring: Michael Bell, Joe Besser, & Mel Blanc
Episode Description: During a magic show at Farthington Mansion, jewels go missing and "Captain Caveman" and "the Teen Angels" must investigate.

294. Title: *The Waltons*; "The Ordeal" S6E19
Air Date: February 16, 1978
Genre: Family
Duration: 60mins
VG's Role: Ada Corley
Director(s): Lawrence Dobkin
Producer(s): Andy White
Production Company: Lorimar Productions

Distributor(s): CBS
Writer(s): Earl Hamner Jr. & Paul West
Starring: Ralph Waite, Michael Learned, & Will Greer
Episode Description: "Elizabeth Walton" (Kami Cotler) falls and injures her leg. When doctors say she may not walk again, friend "Aimee Godsey" (Rachel Longaker) tries to help by recruiting a mountain medicine woman to tend to "Elizabeth" (Virginia Gregg) against the advice of doctors.

295. Title: *Sam*; "Episode #1.1" S1E1
Air Date: March 14, 1978
Genre: Drama
Duration: 30mins
VG's Role: Mrs. Foster
Director(s): Robert M. Leeds
Producer(s): Leonard B. Kaufman
Production Company: Mark VII Ltd.
Distributor(s): CBS
Writer(s): Robert I. Holt
Starring: John Berwick, John Colton, & Virginia Gregg
Episode Description: *Unavailable

296. Title: *Richie Brockelman, Private Eye*; "A Title on the Door and a Carpet on the Floor" S1E3
Air Date: March 31, 1978
Genre: Crime
Duration: 60mins
VG's Role: *Unavailable
Director(s): Arnold Laven
Producer(s): Peter S. Fischer
Production Company: Bunky Productions
Distributor(s): NBC
Writer(s): Steven Bocho & Stephen J. Cannell

Starring: Dennis Dugan, Robert Hogan, & Barbara Bosson
Episode Description: While "Richie Brockelman" (Dennis Dugan) investigates in an infidelity case, his agency gets bought out by a major organization.

297. Title: *Project U.F.O.*; "Sighting 4004: The Howard Crossing Incident" S1E4
Air Date: March 19, 1978
Genre: Sci-Fi
Duration: 60mins
VG's Role: Greta Marshall
Director(s): Robert M. Leeds
Producer(s): William Coleman
Production Company: Mark VII Ltd.
Distributor(s): NBC
Writer(s): Harold Jack Bloom, Lester Wm. Berke, & Donald L. Gold
Starring: William Jordan, Caskey Swaim, & Leif Erickson
Episode Description: "Major Gatlin" (William Jordan) and "Sgt. Fitz" (Caskey Swaim) investigate after receiving reports that Wyoming ranchers believed they were attacked by aliens.

298. Title: *Project U.F.O.*; "Sighting 4013: The St. Hilary Incident" S1E13
Air Date: June 4, 1978
Genre: Sci-Fi
Duration: 60mins
VG's Role: Sister Superior
Director(s): Robert M. Leeds
Producer(s): William Coleman
Production Company: Mark VII Ltd.
Distributor(s): NBC
Writer(s): Harold Jack Bloom, Robert Blees, & James E. Moser
Starring: William Jordan, Caskey Swaim, & Pamela Franklin

Episode Description: "Major Gatlin" (William Jordan) and "Sgt. Fitz" (Caskey Swaim) investigate after two nuns report alien sightings.

299. Title: *Yogi's Space Race*; "The Saturn 500" S1E1
Air Date: September 9, 1978
Genre: Animation
Duration: 30mins
VG's Role: (voice)
Director(s): Ray Patterson & Carl Urbano
Producer(s): Joseph Barbera, William Hanna, Art Scott, & Iwao Takamoto
Production Company: Hanna-Barbera Productions
Distributor(s): NBC
Writer(s): Herb Armstrong, George Atkins, Haskell Barkin, Jack Bonestell, Douglas Booth, Chuck Couch, Mark Fink, Gary Greenfield, George Greer, Andy Heyward, Len Janson, Mark Jones, Glenn Leopold, Ray Parker, Samuel Roeca, Jim Ryan, & Misty Stewart-Taggart
Starring: Roger Behr, Joe Besser, & Mel Blanc
Episode Description: "Yogi" and friends must face the "Abominable Ice Man, Snow Bear, and Goobly" people during a race around Saturn's rings.

300. Title: *Yogi's Space Race*; "The Neptune 9000" S1E2
Air Date: September 16, 1978
Genre: Animation
Duration: 30mins
VG's Role: (voice)
Director(s): Ray Patterson & Carl Urbano
Producer(s): Joseph Barbera, William Hanna, Art Scott, & Iwao Takamoto
Production Company: Hanna-Barbera Productions

Distributor(s): NBC
Writer(s): Herb Armstrong, George Atkins, Haskell Barkin, Jack Bonestell, Douglas Booth, Chuck Couch, Mark Fink, Gary Greenfield, George Greer, Andy Heyward, Len Janson, Mark Jones, Glenn Leopold, Ray Parker, Samuel Roeca, Jim Ryan, & Misty Stewart-Taggart
Starring: Roger Behr, Joe Besser, & Mel Blanc
Episode Description: "Yogi" and friends race around planet Neptune's oceans.

301. **Title:** *Yogi's Space Race*; "The Pongo Tongo Classic" S1E3
Air Date: September 30, 1978
Genre: Animation
Duration: 30mins
VG's Role: (voice)
Director(s): Ray Patterson & Carl Urbano
Producer(s): Joseph Barbera, William Hanna, Art Scott, & Iwao Takamoto
Production Company: Hanna-Barbera Productions
Distributor(s): NBC
Writer(s): Herb Armstrong, George Atkins, Haskell Barkin, Jack Bonestell, Douglas Booth, Chuck Couch, Mark Fink, Gary Greenfield, George Greer, Andy Heyward, Len Janson, Mark Jones, Glenn Leopold, Ray Parker, Samuel Roeca, Jim Ryan, & Misty Stewart-Taggart
Starring: Roger Behr, Joe Besser, & Mel Blanc
Episode Description: "Yogi" and friends visit Nebuloc, a prehistoric planet, and run into "Fred Flintstone."

302. **Title:** *Yogi's Space Race* "Nebuloc-The Prehistoric Planet" S1E4
Air Date: September 30, 1978
Genre: Animation
Duration: 30mins

VG's Role: (voice)
Director(s): Ray Patterson & Carl Urbano
Producer(s): Joseph Barbera, William Hanna, Art Scott, & Iwao Takamoto
Production Company: Hanna-Barbera Productions
Distributor(s): NBC
Writer(s): Herb Armstrong, George Atkins, Haskell Barkin, Jack Bonestell, Douglas Booth, Chuck Couch, Mark Fink, Gary Greenfield, George Greer, Andy Heyward, Len Janson, Mark Jones, Glenn Leopold, Ray Parker, Samuel Roeca, Jim Ryan, & Misty Stewart-Taggart
Starring: Roger Behr, Joe Besser, & Mel Blanc
Episode Description: "Yogi" and friends must face the evil alliance "Phantom Phink" has made with "Medusa."

303. Title: *Little Women*; "Part I" S1E1
Air Date: October 2, 1978
Genre: Drama
Duration: 120mins
VG's Role: Hannah
Director(s): David Lowell Rich
Producer(s): David Victor
Production Company: Groverton Productions
Distributor(s): NBC
Writer(s): Louisa May Alcott & Suzanne Clauser
Starring: Meredith Baxter, Susan Dey, & Ann Dusenberry
Episode Description: Based on Louisa May Alcott's classic of the same name, the March family's four daughters grow up in Civil War New England.

304. Title: *Little Women*; "Part II" S1E2
Air Date: October 3, 1978
Genre: Drama

Duration: 120mins
VG's Role: Hannah
Director(s): David Lowell Rich
Producer(s): David Victor
Production Company: Groverton Productions
Distributor(s): NBC
Writer(s): Louisa May Alcott & Suzanne Clauser
Starring: Meredith Baxter, Susan Dey, & Ann Dusenberry
Episode Description: Based on Louisa May Alcott's classic of the same name, the March family's four daughters grow up in Civil War New England.

305. **Title:** *Yogi's Space Race*; "The Spartikan Spectacular" S1E5
Air Date: October 7, 1978
Genre: Animation
Duration: 30mins
VG's Role: (voice)
Director(s): Ray Patterson & Carl Urbano
Producer(s): Joseph Barbera, William Hanna, Art Scott, & Iwao Takamoto
Production Company: Hanna-Barbera Productions
Distributor(s): NBC
Writer(s): Herb Armstrong, George Atkins, Haskell Barkin, Jack Bonestell, Douglas Booth, Chuck Couch, Mark Fink, Gary Greenfield, George Greer, Andy Heyward, Len Janson, Mark Jones, Glenn Leopold, Ray Parker, Samuel Roeca, Jim Ryan, & Misty Stewart-Taggart
Starring: Roger Behr, Joe Besser, & Mel Blanc
Episode Description: "Scarebear" is offered as a sacrifice to an evil dragon by "Phantom Phink" on a planet much like ancient Rome.

306. **Title:** *Yogi's Space Race*; "The Mizar Marathon" S1E6
Air Date: October 14, 1978

Genre: Animation
Duration: 30mins
VG's Role: (voice)
Director(s): Ray Patterson & Carl Urbano
Producer(s): Joseph Barbera, William Hanna, Art Scott, & Iwao Takamoto
Production Company: Hanna-Barbera Productions
Distributor(s): NBC
Writer(s): Herb Armstrong, George Atkins, Haskell Barkin, Jack Bonestell, Douglas Booth, Chuck Couch, Mark Fink, Gary Greenfield, George Greer, Andy Heyward, Len Janson, Mark Jones, Glenn Leopold, Ray Parker, Samuel Roeca, Jim Ryan, & Misty Stewart-Taggart
Starring: Roger Behr, Joe Besser, & Mel Blanc
Episode Description: On planet Mizar, "Yogi" and friends must face an evil space sorcerer.

307. Title: *The Scooby-Doo/Dynomutt Hour* "The Creepy Case of Old Iron Face" S3E7
Air Date: October 21, 1978
Genre: Animation
Duration: 30mins
VG's Role: (voice)
Director(s): *Unavailable
Producer(s): *Unavailable
Production Company: Hanna-Barbera Productions
Distributor(s): ABC
Writer(s): *Unavailable
Starring: Virginia Gregg, Casey Kasem, & Allan Melvin
Episode Description: "Scooby" and the gang investigate the legend of "Old Iron Face" who is said to haunt an island prison.

308. Title: *Yogi's Space Race* "The Lost Planet of Atlantis" S1E7
Air Date: October 21, 1978
Genre: Animation
Duration: 30mins
VG's Role: (voice)
Director(s): Ray Patterson & Carl Urbano
Producer(s): Joseph Barbera, William Hanna, Art Scott, & Iwao Takamoto
Production Company: Hanna-Barbera Productions
Distributor(s): NBC
Writer(s): Herb Armstrong, George Atkins, Haskell Barkin, Jack Bonestell, Douglas Booth, Chuck Couch, Mark Fink, Gary Greenfield, George Greer, Andy Heyward, Len Janson, Mark Jones, Glenn Leopold, Ray Parker, Samuel Roeca, Jim Ryan, & Misty Stewart-Taggart
Starring: Roger Behr, Joe Besser, & Mel Blanc
Episode Description: "Yogi" and friends travel through the infamous "Archevil Archipelago."

309. Title: *Yogi's Space Race*; "Race Through Oz" S1E8
Air Date: October 28, 1978
Genre: Animation
Duration: 30mins
VG's Role: (voice)
Director(s): Ray Patterson & Carl Urbano
Producer(s): Joseph Barbera, William Hanna, Art Scott, & Iwao Takamoto
Production Company: Hanna-Barbera Productions
Distributor(s): NBC
Writer(s): Herb Armstrong, George Atkins, Haskell Barkin, Jack Bonestell, Douglas Booth, Chuck Couch, Mark Fink, Gary Greenfield, George Greer, Andy Heyward, Len Janson, Mark Jones,

Glenn Leopold, Ray Parker, Samuel Roeca, Jim Ryan, & Misty Stewart-Taggart
Starring: Roger Behr, Joe Besser, & Mel Blanc
Episode Description: While racing through Oz, the gang encounters the wicked "Space Witch of the West."

310. Title: *Yogi's Space Race* "Race Through Wet Galoshes" S1E9
Air Date: November 4, 1978
Genre: Animation
Duration: 30mins
VG's Role: (voice)
Director(s): Ray Patterson & Carl Urbano
Producer(s): Joseph Barbera, William Hanna, Art Scott, & Iwao Takamoto
Production Company: Hanna-Barbera Productions
Distributor(s): NBC
Writer(s): Herb Armstrong, George Atkins, Haskell Barkin, Jack Bonestell, Douglas Booth, Chuck Couch, Mark Fink, Gary Greenfield, George Greer, Andy Heyward, Len
Janson, Mark Jones, Glenn Leopold, Ray Parker, Samuel Roeca, Jim Ryan, & Misty Stewart-Taggart
Starring: Roger Behr, Joe Besser, & Mel Blanc
Episode Description: "Quick Draw McGraw" helps "Yogi" and friends dodge "Phink's" antics on a far western planet.

311. Title: *Yogi's Space Race*; "The Borealis Triangle" S1E10
Air Date: November 11, 1978
Genre: Animation
Duration: 30mins
VG's Role: (voice)
Director(s): Ray Patterson & Carl Urbano
Producer(s): Joseph Barbera, William Hanna, Art Scott, & Iwao Takamoto

Production Company: Hanna-Barbera Productions
Distributor(s): NBC
Writer(s): Herb Armstrong, George Atkins, Haskell Barkin, Jack Bonestell, Douglas Booth, Chuck Couch, Mark Fink, Gary Greenfield, George Greer, Andy Heyward, Len Janson, Mark Jones, Glenn Leopold, Ray Parker, Samuel Roeca, Jim Ryan, & Misty Stewart-Taggart
Starring: Roger Behr, Joe Besser, & Mel Blanc
Episode Description: "Yogi" and friends must confront "Phink's" latest trap: the Diabolical Doomsday Device.

312. Title: *Yogi's Space Race* "Race to the Center of the Universe" S1E11
Air Date: November 18, 1978
Genre: Animation
Duration: 30mins
VG's Role: (voice)
Director(s): Ray Patterson & Carl Urbano
Producer(s): Joseph Barbera, William Hanna, Art Scott, & Iwao Takamoto
Production Company: Hanna-Barbera Productions
Distributor(s): NBC
Writer(s): Herb Armstrong, George Atkins, Haskell Barkin, Jack Bonestell, Douglas Booth, Chuck Couch, Mark Fink, Gary Greenfield, George Greer, Andy Heyward, Len Janson, Mark Jones, Glenn Leopold, Ray Parker, Samuel Roeca, Jim Ryan, & Misty Stewart-Taggart
Starring: Roger Behr, Joe Besser, & Mel Blanc
Episode Description: "Phantom Phink" competes to win a trip to the amusement park Funkyland.

313. Title: *Yogi's Space Race* "Race Through the Planet of the Monsters" S1E12
Air Date: November 25, 1978

Genre: Animation
Duration: 30mins
VG's Role: (voice)
Director(s): Ray Patterson & Carl Urbano
Producer(s): Joseph Barbera, William Hanna, Art Scott, & Iwao Takamoto
Production Company: Hanna-Barbera Productions
Distributor(s): NBC
Writer(s): Herb Armstrong, George Atkins, Haskell Barkin, Jack Bonestell, Douglas Booth, Chuck Couch, Mark Fink, Gary Greenfield, George Greer, Andy Heyward, Len Janson, Mark Jones, Glenn Leopold, Ray Parker, Samuel Roeca, Jim Ryan, & Misty Stewart-Taggart
Starring: Roger Behr, Joe Besser, & Mel Blanc
Episode Description: "Count Cracula" and the "Space Mummy" help "Phantom Phink" to sabotage the race.

314. **Title:** *Lou Grant*; "Skids" S2E23
Air Date: April 2, 1979
Genre: Crime
Duration: 60mins
VG's Role: Dirty Donna
Director(s): Burt Brinckerhoff
Producer(s): Seth Freeman & Gary David Goldberg
Production Company: MTM Enterprises
Distributor(s): CBS
Writer(s): Allan Burns, James L. Brooks, Gene Reynolds, Leon Tokatyan, & Steve Kline
Starring: Edward Asner, Robert Walden, & Linda Kelsey
Episode Description: "Lou" (Edward Asner) investigates reports of a string of stranglings on Skid Row, which lead him to a former doctor of his who is now homeless.

315. Title: *Charlie's Angels*; "Of Ghosts and Angels" S4E13
Air Date: January 2, 1980
Genre: Adventure
Duration: 60mins
VG's Role: Mrs. Craig
Director(s): Cliff Bole
Producer(s): Robert Janes
Production Company: Spelling-Goldberg Productions
Distributor(s): ABC
Writer(s): Ivan Goff, Ben Roberts, & Katharyn Powers
Starring: Jaclyn Smith, Cheryl Ladd, & Shelley Hack
Episode Description: "Tiffany" (Shelley Hack) begins having strange premonitions during a mansion party.

316. Title: *Captain Caveman and the Teen Angels* "Cavey and the Volcanic Villain" S3E3
Air Date: March 22, 1980
Genre: Animation
Duration: 10mins
VG's Role: (additional voices)
Director(s): Charles A. Nichols, Ray Patterson, & Carl Urbano
Producer(s): Joseph Barbera, William Hanna, Don Jurwich, Alex Lovy, Art Scott, & Iwao Takamoto
Production Company: Hanna-Barbera Productions
Distributor(s): ABC
Writer(s): Joe Ruby, Ken Spears, Neal Barbera, Haskell Barkin, Joseph Bonaduce, Larz Bourne, Chuck Couch, Tom Dagenais, Lee Davenport, & Orville H. Hampton
Starring: Marlene Aragon, Michael Bell, & Julie Bennett
Episode Description: "Captain Caveman" and "the Teen Angels" attend a Hawaiian wedding when a treasured pearl vanishes.

317. Title: *Ramblin' Man*; "A Token for Winnie" S1E7
Air Date: March 21, 1981
Genre: Crime
Duration: *Unavailable
VG's Role: Winnie
Director(s): Lawrence Dobkin
Producer(s): *Unavailable
Production Company: *Unavailable
Distributor(s): *Unavailable
Writer(s): Robert W. Lenski
Starring: Julie Cobb, Robert DoQui, & Dan Fitzgerald
Episode Description: *Unavailable

318. Title: *Space Stars*; "Attack of the Space Sharks (Space Ghost)" S1E1
Air Date: September 12, 1981
Genre: Animation
Duration: *Unavailable
VG's Role: Tara (voice)
Director(s): George Gordon, Ray Patterson, & Rudy Zamora
Producer(s): Gerard Baldwin, Joseph Barbera, Oscar Dufau, & William Hanna
Production Company: Hanna-Barbera Productions
Distributor(s): Warner Home Video
Writer(s): *Unavailable
Starring: Michael Bell, Keene Curtis, & Richard Erdman
Episode Description: *Unavailable

319. Title: *Space Stars;* "The Sorceress (Space Ghost)" S1E2
Air Date: September 19, 1981
Genre: Animation
Duration: *Unavailable
VG's Role: Tara (voice)

Director(s): George Gordon, Ray Patterson, & Rudy Zamora
Producer(s): Gerard Baldwin, Joseph Barbera, Oscar Dufau, & William Hanna
Production Company: Hanna-Barbera Productions
Distributor(s): Warner Home Video
Writer(s): *Unavailable
Starring: Michael Bell, Keene Curtis, & Richard Erdman
Episode Description: *Unavailable

320. **Title:** *Space Stars*; "The Antimatter Man (Space Ghost)" S1E3
Air Date: September 26, 1981
Genre: Animation
Duration: *Unavailable
VG's Role: Tara (voice)
Director(s): George Gordon, Ray Patterson, & Rudy Zamora
Producer(s): Gerard Baldwin, Joseph Barbera, Oscar Dufau, & William Hanna
Production Company: Hanna-Barbera Productions
Distributor(s): Warner Home Video
Writer(s): *Unavailable
Starring: Michael Bell, Keene Curtis, & Richard Erdman
Episode Description: *Unavailable

321. **Title:** *Space Stars*; "The Starfly (Space Ghost)" S1E4
Air Date: October 3, 1981
Genre: Animation
Duration: *Unavailable
VG's Role: Tara (voice)
Director(s): George Gordon, Ray Patterson, & Rudy Zamora
Producer(s): Gerard Baldwin, Joseph Barbera, Oscar Dufau, & William Hanna
Production Company: Hanna-Barbera Productions
Distributor(s): Warner Home Video

Writer(s): *Unavailable
Starring: Michael Bell, Keene Curtis, & Richard Erdman
Episode Description: *Unavailable

322. Title: *Space Stars*; "Space Spectre (Space Ghost)" S1E5
Air Date: October 10, 1981
Genre: Animation
Duration: *Unavailable
VG's Role: Tara (voice)
Director(s): George Gordon, Ray Patterson, & Rudy Zamora
Producer(s): Gerard Baldwin, Joseph Barbera, Oscar Dufau, & William Hanna
Production Company: Hanna-Barbera Productions
Distributor(s): Warner Home Video
Writer(s): *Unavailable
Starring: Michael Bell, Keene Curtis, & Richard Erdman
Episode Description: *Unavailable

323. Title: *Space Stars*; "The Toymaker (Space Ghost)" S1E6
Air Date: October 17, 1981
Genre: Animation
Duration: *Unavailable
VG's Role: Tara (voice)
Director(s): George Gordon, Ray Patterson, & Rudy Zamora
Producer(s): Gerard Baldwin, Joseph Barbera, Oscar Dufau, & William Hanna
Production Company: Hanna-Barbera Productions
Distributor(s): Warner Home Video
Writer(s): *Unavailable
Starring: Michael Bell, Keene Curtis, & Richard Erdman
Episode Description: *Unavailable

324. Title: *Space Stars*; "The Shadow People (Space Ghost)" S1E7
Air Date: October 24, 1981
Genre: Animation
Duration: *Unavailable
VG's Role: Tara (voice)
Director(s): George Gordon, Ray Patterson, & Rudy Zamora
Producer(s): Gerard Baldwin, Joseph Barbera, Oscar Dufau, & William Hanna
Production Company: Hanna-Barbera Productions
Distributor(s): Warner Home Video
Writer(s): *Unavailable
Starring: Michael Bell, Keene Curtis, & Richard Erdman
Episode Description: *Unavailable

325. Title: *Space Stars*; "Time Chase (Space Ghost)" S1E8
Air Date: October 31, 1981
Genre: Animation
Duration: *Unavailable
VG's Role: Tara (voice)
Director(s): George Gordon, Ray Patterson, & Rudy Zamora
Producer(s): Gerard Baldwin, Joseph Barbera, Oscar Dufau, & William Hanna
Production Company: Hanna-Barbera Productions
Distributor(s): Warner Home Video
Writer(s): *Unavailable
Starring: Michael Bell, Keene Curtis, & Richard Erdman
Episode Description: *Unavailable

326. Title: *Space Star*; "City in Space (Space Ghost)" S1E9
Air Date: November 7, 1981
Genre: Animation
Duration: *Unavailable
VG's Role: Tara (voice)

Director(s): George Gordon, Ray Patterson, & Rudy Zamora
Producer(s): Gerard Baldwin, Joseph Barbera, Oscar Dufau, & William Hanna
Production Company: Hanna-Barbera Productions
Distributor(s): Warner Home Video
Writer(s): *Unavailable
Starring: Michael Bell, Keene Curtis, & Richard Erdman
Episode Description: *Unavailable

327. **Title:** *Space Stars*; "Eclipse Woman (Space Ghost)" S1E10
Air Date: November 14, 1981
Genre: Animation
Duration: *Unavailable
VG's Role: Tara (voice)
Director(s): George Gordon, Ray Patterson, & Rudy Zamora
Producer(s): Gerard Baldwin, Joseph Barbera, Oscar Dufau, & William Hanna
Production Company: Hanna-Barbera Productions
Distributor(s): Warner Home Video
Writer(s): *Unavailable
Starring: Michael Bell, Keene Curtis, & Richard Erdman
Episode Description: *Unavailable

328. **Title:** *Space Stars*; "The Haunted Space Station (Space Ghost)" S1E11
Air Date: November 21, 1981
Genre: Animation
Duration: *Unavailable
VG's Role: Tara (voice)
Director(s): George Gordon, Ray Patterson, & Rudy Zamora
Producer(s): Gerard Baldwin, Joseph Barbera, Oscar Dufau, & William Hanna
Production Company: Hanna-Barbera Productions

Distributor(s): Warner Home Video
Writer(s): *Unavailable
Starring: Michael Bell, Keene Curtis, & Richard Erdman
Episode Description: *Unavailable

329. **Title:** *Trapper John, M.D.*; "Baby on the Line" S4E13
Air Date: January 9, 1983
Genre: Drama
Duration: 60mins
VG's Role: Contessa
Director(s): Bernard McEveety
Producer(s): Don Brinkley
Production Company: Frank Glicksman Productions
Distributor(s): CBS
Writer(s): Don Brinkley, Frank Glicksman, & Elaine Newman
Starring: Pernell Roberts, Gregory Harrison, & Madge Sinclair
Episode Description: Parents of a baby born with hermaphroditism fight over which gender the baby will be upon surgery.

330. **Title:** *Dynasty;* "The Arrest" S4E1
Air Date: September 28, 1983
Genre: Drama
Duration: 60mins
VG's Role: Nurse
Director(s): Irving J. Moore
Producer(s): Ursula Alexander, Douglas S. Cramer, John B. Moranville, Elaine Rich, Esther Shapiro, Richard Alan Shapiro, Aaron Spelling, & E. Duke Vincent
Production Company: Aaron Spelling Productions
Distributor(s): ABC
Writer(s): Edward DeBlasio, Eileen Pollock, Robert Pollock, Esther Shapiro, & Richard Alan Shapiro
Starring: John Forsythe, Linda Evans, & Pamela Sue Martin

Episode Description: "Mark" (Geoffrey Scott) rescues "Krystle" (Linda Evans) and "Alexis" (Joan Collins) after they are trapped in a burning cabin in the woods.

331. **Title:** *Hanna-Barbera's The Greatest Adventure: Stories from the Bible;* "Samson and Delilah" S1E6
Air Date: December 15, 1985
Genre: Animation
Duration: 25mins
VG's Role: Miriam (voice)
Director(s): Andrea Romano
Producer(s): Joseph Barbera & William Hanna
Production Company: Hanna-Barbera Productions
Distributor(s): *Unavailable
Writer(s): *Unavailable
Starring: Perry King, Linda Purl, & Darleen Carr
Episode Description: The gang travels to the Valley of Sorek where they meet up with an incredibly strong man named "Samson" and a woman named "Delilah" who schemes to find the source of his great strength.

Appendix D: Selected Film Performances of Virginia Gregg with Description

1. Title: *Notorious*
Release Date: September 6, 1946
Genre: Drama/Adventure
Rating: NR
Duration: 102mins
VG's Role: File clerk (uncredited)
Director(s): Alfred Hitchcock
Producer(s): Alfred Hitchcock
Production Company: RKO Radio Pictures
Distributor(s): RKO Radio Pictures
Writer(s): Ben Hecht
Starring: Cary Grant, Ingrid Bergman, & Claude Rains
Description: Following WWII, "Alicia Huberman's" (Ingrid Bergman) German father is convicted of treason against the United States. After his conviction and subsequent suicide, government agent "T.R. Devlin" (Cary Grant) tasks "Alicia" to spy on some of her father's Nazi friends in Brazil. In order to infiltrate the circle in question, "Alicia" must consort with German businessman "Alexander Sebastian" (Claude Rains). Despite the mission requiring her to marry "Sebastian" to conceal her true identity and purpose, "Alicia" and "Devlin" fall in love. Virginia plays an unnamed file clerk uncredited.

2. Title: *Lost Honeymoon*
Release Date: March 29, 1947
Genre: Romance, comedy

Rating: NR
Duration: 71mins
VG's Role: Mrs. Osborne (uncredited)
Director(s): Leigh Jason
Producer(s): Lee S. Marcus
Production Company: Bryan Foy Productions
Distributor(s): Eagle-Lion Films
Writer(s): Joseph Fields
Starring: Franchot Tone, Ann Richards, & Tom Conway
Description: After the death of an Englishwoman, "Tillic Gray" (Ann Richards), her best friend, "Amy Atkins" (also Ann Richards), takes in her orphaned children and together they search for their father architect and former solider "Johnny Gray" (Franchot Tone). Virginia plays a supporting character uncredited.

3. Title: *Gentleman's Agreement*
Release Date: March 1947
Genre: Drama
Rating: NR
Duration: 118mins
VG's Role: Third woman (uncredited)
Director(s): Elia Kazan
Producer(s): Darryl F. Zanuck
Production Company: Twentieth Century Fox
Distributor(s): Twentieth Century Fox
Writer(s): Laura Z. Hobson & Moss Hart
Starring: Gregory Peck, Dorothy McGuire, & John Garfield
Description: Writer "Philip Green" (Gregory Peck) goes undercover as a Jewish man to investigate first-hand anti-Semitism in America for a magazine piece on the subject with the help of his Jewish friend, "Dave Goldman" (John Garfield). Throughout the project, his relationship with love interest "Kathy Lacy" (Dorothy McGuire) is affected. Virginia plays a supporting, unnamed character uncredited.

4. Title: *Body and Soul*
Release Date: November 11, 1947
Genre: Drama
Rating: NR
Duration: 104 min
VG's Role: Irma (uncredited)
Director(s): Robert Rossen
Producer(s): Bob Roberts
Production Company: Enterprise Productions
Distributor(s): United Artists
Writer(s): Abraham Polonsky
Starring: John Garfield, Lilli Palmer, & Hazel Brooks
Description: Boxer "Charley Davis" (John Garfield) faces challenges in the pursuit of success in career and love with the influence of his manager "Quinn" (William Conrad), promoter "Roberts" (Lloyd Gough), and love interest "Peg" (Lilli Palmer). Virginia counted this performance as her first in film as liberated vixen "Irma," roommate of Peg.

5. Title: *Casbah*
Release Date: April 1948
Genre: Crime
Rating: NR
Duration: 94mins
VG's Role: Madeline
Director(s): John Berry
Producer(s): Nat C. Goldstone
Production Company: Marston Productions
Distributor(s): Universal Pictures
Writer(s): Leslie Bush-Fekete, Arnold Manoff, Erik Charell, & Henri La Barthe
Starring: Yvonne De Carlo, Tony Martin, & Peter Lorre

Description: "Pepe Le Meko" (Tony Martin) is a notorious jewel thief living in Algiers after his exile from France to avoid imprisonment. "Detective Slimane" (Peter Lorre) must lure him into captivity, but a love's tryst complicates matters when "Pepe" falls for "Gaby" (Marta Toren) in spite of his relationship with "Inez" (Yvonne DeCarlo). Virginia plays "Madeline," the traveling companion of "Claude" and "Gaby."

6. Title: *The Amazing Mr. X*
Release Date: July 29, 1948
Genre: Thriller
Rating: NR
Duration: 78mins
VG's Role: Emily
Director(s): Bernard Vorhaus
Producer(s): Benjamin Stoloff
Production Company: Ben Stoloff Productions
Distributor(s): Eagle-Lion Films
Writer(s): Crane Wilbur, Muriel Roy Bolton, & Ian McLellan Hunter
Starring: Turhan Bey, Lynn Bari, & Cathy O'Donnell
Description: A wealthy widow, "Christine Faber," (Lynn Bari) tries to move on with her life after the death of her husband "Paul" (Donald Curtis), but seemingly supernatural events lead her to believe he is contacting her beyond the grave. In search for answers, "Christine" meets a charming psychic named "Alexis" (Turhan Bey) who claims he can help. With "Alexis'" help, "Christine" discovers "Paul" is alive. Virginia plays "Emily," "Christine's" dutiful servant.

7. Title: *The Gay Intruders*
Release Date: September 2, 1948
Genre: Comedy
Rating: NR
Duration: 68mins

VG's Role: Dr. Susan Nash
Director(s): Ray McCarey
Producer(s): Frank N. Seltzer
Production Company: Frank Seltzer Productions
Distributor(s): Twentieth Century Fox
Writer(s): Ray McCarey & Francis Swann
Starring: John Emery, Tamara Geva, & Leif Erickson
Description: *The Gay Intruders* tell the story of successful stage couple "John" (John Emery) and "Maria" (Tamara Geva) who are caught in a cycle of marital trouble. Psychiatrists "Dr. Harold Matson" (Leif Erickson) and "Dr. Susan Nash" (Virginia Gregg) move in with the couple to help settle their differences. The arrangement improves the stage couple's marriage, but the doctors begin bickering.

8. Title: *Flesh and Fury*
Release Date: March 12, 1952
Genre: Drama
Rating: NR
Duration: 83mins
VG's Role: Claire (uncredited)
Director(s): Joseph Pevney
Producer(s): Leonard Goldstein
Production Company: Universal International Pictures
Distributor(s): Universal Pictures
Writer(s): William Alland & Bernard Gordon
Starring: Tony Curtis, Jan Sterling, & Mona Freeman
Description: "Paul Callan" (Tony Curtis) is a deaf boxer in whom the beautiful, gold-digging "Sonya Bartow" (Jan Sterling) becomes interested. As "Paul" grows more and more successful, "Sonya's" influence over him also grows until he encounters journalist "Ann Hollis" (Mona Freeman) interested in doing a story on him. Both women compete for influence over him and his career while "Paul"

struggles to break free of the triangle. Virginia plays "Claire," an uncredited supporting role.

9. Title: *Love is a Many-Splendored Thing*
Release Date: August 18, 1955
Genre: Romance
Rating: NR
Duration: 102mins
VG's Role: Anne Richards
Director(s): Henry King
Producer(s): Buddy Adler
Production Company: Twentieth Century Fox
Distributor(s): Twentieth Century Fox
Writer(s): John Patrick & Han Suyin
Starring: William Holden, Jennifer Jones, & Torin Thatcher
Description: American reporter "Mark Elliot" (William Holden) tours Hong Kong in his war time coverage of the country and meets widowed Eurasian physician, "Dr. Han Suyin" (Jennifer Jones). The two fall in love, but face the challenges of "Mark's" crumbling marriage back in the states, while "Dr. Han Suyin" must grapple with loving an American in the face of her family and country's traditions. Virginia plays supporting character "Anne Richards."

10. Title: *Dragnet*
Release Date: September 4, 1954
Genre: Crime
Rating: NR
Duration: 88mins
VG's Role: Ethel Starkie
Director(s): Jack Webb
Producer(s): Stanley D. Meyer
Production Company: Mark VII Ltd.
Distributor(s): Warner Brothers

Writer(s): Richard L. Breen
Starring: Jack Webb, Ben Alexander, & Ann Robinson
Description: Homicide detectives "Sgt. Joe Friday" (Jack Webb) and "Officer Frank Smith" (Ben Alexander) investigate the brutal murder of mobster "Miller Starkie" (Dub Taylor). "Friday" and "Smith" enlist the help of the attractive "Officer Grace Downey" (Ann Robinson) in their undercover strategy to crack the case. Virginia plays "Miller Starkie's" lush widow, "Ethel."

11. Title: *I'll Cry Tomorrow*
Release Date: December 25, 1955
Genre: Biography
Rating: NR
Duration: 117mins
VG's Role: Ellen
Director(s): Daniel Mann
Producer(s): Lawrence Weingarten
Production Company: MGM
Distributor(s): MGM
Writer(s): Helen Deutsch, Jay Richard Kennedy, Lillian Roth, Mike Connolly, & Gerold Frank
Starring: Susan Hayward, Richard Conte, & Eddie Albert
Description: *I'll Cry Tomorrow* is a biopic of famed American actress and singer Lillian Roth based on her autobiography by the same name. The film tells the tragic story of Lillian's (Susan Hayward) ascent to fame and simultaneous descent into alcoholism, and ultimately her recovery. Virginia plays Lillian's faithful, yet enabling caregiver, "Ellen."

12. Title: *Terror at Midnight*
Release Date: April 27, 1956
Genre: Crime
Rating: NR
Duration: 70mins

VG's Role: Helen Hill
Director(s): Franklin Adreon
Producer(s): Rudy Ralston
Production Company: Republic Pictures
Distributor(s): Republic Pictures
Writer(s): John K. Butler & Irving Shulman
Starring: Scott Brady, Joan Vohs, & Frank Faylen
Description: "Detective Neal "Rick" Rickards'" (Scott Brady) fiancée, "Susan Lang" (Joan Vohs) becomes deeply involved in a web of crime when "Rick" investigates a stolen car racket. Virginia plays "Helen Hill," the wife of "Fred," who is also involved in the operation.

13. Title: *Crime in the Streets*
Release Date: June 10, 1956
Genre: Crime
Rating: NR
Duration: 91 mins
VG's Role: Mrs. Dane
Director(s): Don Siegel
Producer(s): Vincent M. Fennelly
Production Company: Lindbrook Productions
Distributor(s): Allied Artists Pictures
Writer(s): Reginald Rose
Starring: James Whitmore, John Cassavetes, & Sal Mineo
Description: Social worker "Ben Wagner" (James Whitmore) gets caught in a web of crime when trying to befriend members of a street gang. Virginia plays "Mrs. Dane," the slum mother of "Frankie Dane" (John Cassavetes), the leader of the gang.

14. Title: *The Fastest Gun Alive*
Release Date: July 6, 1956
Genre: Western
Rating: NR

Duration: 89mins
VG's Role: Rose Tibbs
Director(s): Russell Rouse
Producer(s): Clarence Greene
Production Company: MGM
Distributor(s): MGM
Writer(s): Frank D. Gilroy & Russell Rouse
Starring: Glenn Ford, Jeanne Crain, & Broderick Crawford
Description: In a small western town, local shopkeeper "George Temple" (Glenn Ford) is hiding a secret past. When gunmen learn of "Temple's" secret, he and his wife "Dora" (Jeanne Crain) plan to leave town, but "Temple" is challenged to a shootout to ultimately save his family and his town. Virginia plays townslady "Rose Tibbs."

15. Title: *The D.I.*
Release Date: May 30, 1957
Genre: Drama
Rating: NR
Duration: 106mins
VG's Role: Mrs. Charles D. Owens
Director(s): Jack Webb
Producer(s): Jack Webb
Production Company: Mark VII Ltd.
Distributor(s): Warner Brothers
Writer(s): James Lee Barrett
Starring: Jack Webb, Don Dubbins, & Jackie Loughery
Description: "Gunnery Sgt. Jim Moore" (Jack Webb) must make a Marine out of the young, faltering recruit "Pvt. Owens" (Don Dubbins). "Pvt. Owens" finds it difficult to meet "Sgt. Moore's" demands due in part to his family history. Virginia plays "Pvt. Owens'" mother, "Mrs. Charles D. Owens," who surprises "Sgt. Moore" with her response to her son's difficulties in training.

16. Title: *Portland Expose*
Release Date: August 11, 1957
Genre: Crime
Rating: NR
Duration: 72mins
VG's Role: Clara Madison
Director(s): Harold D. Schuster
Producer(s): Lindsley Parsons
Production Company: Lindsley Parsons Picture Corporation
Distributor(s): Allied Artists Pictures
Writer(s): Jack DeWitt
Starring: Edward Binns, Carolyn Craig, & Virginia Gregg
Description: Tavern owner "George Madison" (Edward Binns) and his family get caught up in a ring of seedy operations related to a gang war. Virginia plays "George's" wife "Clara."

17. Title: *Hi, Grandma!* (TV Movie)
Release Date: May 7, 1958
Genre: Horror
Rating: NR
Duration: 30 mins
VG's Role: *Unavailable
Director(s): Arch Oboler
Producer(s): Jerry Fairbanks & Arch Oboler
Production Company: Arch Oboler Productions
Distributor(s): *Unavailable
Writer(s): Arch Oboler
Starring: Ronald Anton, Jeanne Bates, & Terry Burnham
Description: An inventor develops a recording machine that plays voices of dead people, and his evil grandmother uses the machine to haunt her family. Virginia plays an unlisted supporting role.

18. Title: *Twilight for the Gods*
Release Date: August 6, 1958
Genre: Drama
Rating: NR
Duration: 120mins
VG's Role: Myra Pringle
Director(s): Joseph Pevney
Producer(s): Gordon Kay
Production Company: Universal International Pictures
Distributor(s): Universal Pictures
Writer(s): Ernest K. Gann
Starring: Rock Hudson, Cyd Charisse, & Arthur Kennedy
Description: "Captain Bell" (Rock Hudson) is a former navy sergeant who commands a leaking ship named the *Cannibal*. Passengers and crew plead with "Bell" to change course to prevent the ship's sinking, but tension aboard causes the decision to be difficult for "Bell." Virginia plays passenger "Myra Pringle."

19. Title: *The Hanging Tree*
Release Date: February 11, 1959
Genre: Western
Rating: NR
Duration: 107mins
VG's Role: Edna Flaunce
Director(s): Delmer Daves, Karl Malden, & Vincent Sherman
Producer(s): Martin Jurow & Richard Shepherd
Production Company: Baroda
Distributor(s): Warner Brothers
Writer(s): Wendell Mayes, Halsted Welles, & Dorothy M. Johnson
Starring: Gary Cooper, Maria Schell, & Karl Malden
Description: "Dr. Joseph Frail" (Garry Cooper) takes control of a local thief's (Ben Piazza) life after he saves him from a mob. "Dr.

Frail" heals him on the condition that he remain his bondservant. Virginia plays prudish storekeeper "Edna Flaunce."

20. Title: *Hound-Dog Man*
Release Date: November 1959
Genre: Drama
Rating: NR
Duration: 87mins
VG's Role: Amy Waller
Director(s): Don Siegel
Producer(s): Jerry Wald
Production Company: Twentieth Century Fox
Distributor(s): Twentieth Century Fox
Writer(s): Fred Gipson & Winston Miller
Starring: Fabian, Stuart Whitman, & Carol Lynley
Description: Based on Fred Gipson's novel of the same name, *Hound-Dog Man* tells the story of the two "McKinney" brothers who go on a hunting trip with their friend, "Blackie Scantling" (Stuart Whitman), a notorious womanizer interested in the "McKinney's" sister. Virginia plays "Cora McKinney," the children's mother who is skeptical of "Blackie's" engagement with her family.

21. Title: *Operation Petticoat*
Release Date: December 24, 1959
Genre: Comedy
Rating: NR
Duration: 124mins
VG's Role: Maj. Edna Heywood, R.N.
Director(s): Blake Edwards
Producer(s): Robert Arthur
Production Company: Granart Company
Distributor(s): Universal Pictures

Writer(s): Stanley Shapiro, Maurice Richlin, Paul King, & Joseph Stone

Starring: Cary Grant, Tony Curtis, & Joan O'Brien

Description: An aging submarine is commissioned at the beginning of WWII and commanded by the straightlaced "Lt. Commander Sherman" (Cary Grant). During its operation, "Sherman" contends with various antics aboard that threaten the vessel's true mission including playboy "Lt. JG Nicholas Holden" (Tony Curtis) and a group of female Army nurses who unexpectedly board the all-male vessel. Virginia plays the leader of the Army nurses, "Edna Heywood."

22. Title: *Psycho*

Release Date: September 8, 1960

Genre: Horror

Rating: R

Duration: 109mins

VG's Role: Norma Bates (voice, uncredited)

Director(s): Alfred Hitchcock

Producer(s): Alfred Hitchcock

Production Company: Shamley Productions

Distributor(s): Paramount Pictures

Writer(s): Joseph Stefano & Robert Bloch

Starring: Anthony Perkins, Vera Miles, & John Gavin

Description: Secretary "Marion Crane" (Janet Leigh) is on the run after making off with $40,000 of her employer's money. On her way to start a new life, "Marion" checks in to a highway motel managed by "Norman Bates" (Anthony Perkins), a man of many secrets. Virginia plays the role of "Norman's" mother, "Norma Bates," uncredited.

23. Title: *All the Fine Young Cannibals*

Release Date: September 22, 1960

Genre: Drama

Rating: NR

Duration: 112mins
VG's Role: Ada Davis
Director(s): Michael Anderson
Producer(s): Pandro S. Berman
Production Company: Avon Productions
Distributor(s): MGM
Writer(s): Rosamond Marshall & Robert Thom
Starring: Robert Wagner, Natalie Wood, & George Hamilton
Description: After the town minister dies, his son "Chad" (Robert Wagner) learns his girlfriend "Sarah" (Natalie Wood) is pregnant. With "Chad's" future uncertain, "Sarah" leaves town on an Eastbound train where she meets Yale student "Tony" (George Hamilton). "Tony" and "Sarah" soon marry, though she conceals the pregnancy and relationship with "Chad." In "Sarah's" absence, "Chad" begins a new life for himself as well. Virginia plays the supporting role of "Ada Davis."

24. Title: *Man-Trap*
Release Date: September 20, 1961
Genre: Thriller
Rating: NR
Duration: 93mins
VG's Role: Ruth
Director(s): Edmond O'Brien
Producer(s): Stanley Frazen & Edmond O'Brien
Production Company: Tiger Productions
Distributor(s): Paramount Pictures
Writer(s): Ed Waters & John D. MacDonald
Starring: Jeffrey Hunter, David Janssen, & Stella Stevens
Description: "Matt Jameson" (Jeffery Hunter) and "Vince Biskay" (David Janssen), two Korean War veterans reunite to commandeer money from a Central American dictator and run away with the loot

at the San Francisco airport. However, while on the run, "Vince" is wounded with a gunshot, and they both are racing the clock. Virginia plays the supporting role of "Ruth."

25. Title: *House of Women*
Release Date: April 11, 1962
Genre: Drama
Rating: NR
Duration: 85mins
VG's Role: Mrs. Edith Hunter
Director(s): Walter Doniger
Producer(s): Bryan Foy
Production Company: Bryan Foy Productions
Distributor(s): Warner Brothers
Writer(s): Crane Wilbur
Starring: Shirley Knight, Andrew Duggan, & Constance Ford
Description: "Erica Hayden" (Shirley Knight) is sentenced to five years in prison, though she is innocent. She is imprisoned while carrying her unborn child. With the prison conditions becoming unbearable, she is worried about the future of her child and is unexpectedly supported by warden "Frank Cole" (Andrew Duggan), who helps her prove her innocence to avoid being separated from her child. Virginia plays "Edith Hunter," a hard-nosed official who is taken hostage.

26. Title: *Shootout at Big Sag*
Release Date: June 1, 1962
Genre: Western
Rating: NR
Duration: 64mins
VG's Role: Sarah Treadway Hawker
Director(s): Roger Kay
Producer(s): Andy Brennan

Production Company: Brennan Productions
Distributor(s): Parallel Film Distributors Inc.
Writer(s): Walter J. Coburn & Roger Kay
Starring: Walter Brennan, Leif Erickson, & Luana Patten
Description: A range war breaks out between neighbors in Big Sag territory, but things take an interesting turn when the feuding families' children fall in love with each other. Virginia plays the shrewish role of "Sarah Treadway Hawker," wife of "Preacher Hawker" (Walter Brennan).

27. Title: *Spencer's Mountain*
Release Date: May 16, 1963
Genre: Drama
Rating: NR
Duration: 118mins
VG's Role: Miss Parker
Director(s): Delmer Daves
Producer(s): Delmer Daves
Production Company: Warner Brothers
Distributor(s): Warner Brothers
Writer(s): Earl Hamner Jr. & Delmer Daves
Starring: Henry Fonda, Maureen O'Hara, & James MacArthur
Description: Hardworking father of nine, "Clay Spencer" (Henry Fonda), helps a minister revive his congregation after the two experience a bit of trouble. "The Spencer's" large family struggles against the intersection of education and religion in their quest for a brighter future. Virginia plays the role of "Miss Parker," the children's teacher.

28. Title: *The Kiss of the Vampire*
Release Date: September 11, 1963
Genre: Horror
Rating: NR

Duration: 88mins
VG's Role: Rosa Stangher
Director(s): Don Sharp
Producer(s): Anthony Hinds
Production Company: Hammer Films
Distributor(s): Universal Pictures
Writer(s): Anthony Hinds
Starring: Clifford Evans, Edward de Souza, & Noel Willman
Description: After newlyweds "Gerald and Marianne Harcourt" (Edward de Souza & Jennifer Daniel) break down near a small, remote European village, a well-to-do family offers to help them. Little do they know accepting the family's help will lead to dangerous consequences. Virginia plays supporting character "Rose Stangher" in the US television version.

29. Title: *Gorath*
Release Date: May 15, 1964
Genre: Sci-Fi
Rating: NR
Duration: 88mins
VG's Role: Voice, uncredited
Director(s): Ishirô Honda
Producer(s): Tomoyuki Tanaka
Production Company: Toho Company
Distributor(s): MGM
Writer(s): Takeshi Kimura, Jôjirô Okami, & John Meredyth Lucas
Starring: Ryô Ikebe, Yumi Shirakawa, & Akira Kubo
Description: A giant planetoid named Gorath is on a collision course with Earth. Scientists desperately try to formulate a plan to move Earth out of Gorath's path before it destroys all of mankind. Virginia provides uncredited voiceover performances in this film.

30. Title: *Two on a Guillotine*
Release Date: January 13, 1965
Genre: Horror
Rating: NR
Duration: 107mins
VG's Role: Dolly Bast
Director(s): William Conrad
Producer(s): William Conrad
Production Company: William Conrad Productions
Distributor(s): Warner Brothers
Writer(s): Henry Slesar & John Kneubuhl
Starring: Connie Stevens, Dean Jones, & Cesar Romero
Description: Daughter (Connie Stevens) of renown magician "The Great Duquesne" (Cesar Romero), learns her father has passed away, and in order to inherit his estate, she must stay in his mysterious mansion for seven nights. She comes to learn more and more about her family's strange history and encounters colorful people as the week in his home progresses. Virginia plays the role of "Dolly Bast," "The Great Duquesne's" fiercely loyal caretaker.

31. Title: *Joy in the Morning*
Release Date: May 5, 1965
Genre: Romance
Rating: GP
Duration: 103mins
VG's Role: Mrs. Lorgan
Director(s): Alex Segal
Producer(s): Henry T. Weinstein
Production Company: MGM
Distributor(s): MGM
Writer(s): Betty Smith, Sally Benson, Alfred Hayes, & Norman Lessing
Starring: Richard Chamberlain, Yvette Mimieux, & Arthur Kennedy

Description: Young couple "Carl Brown" (Richard Chamberlain) and "Annie McGairy" (Yvette Mimieux) marry while "Carl" is still attending college. The two face many difficulties as young newlyweds contending with their parents and obligations on campus. Virginia plays the role of supporting character "Mrs. Lorgan."

32. Title: *A Big Hand for the Little Lady*
Release Date: May 31, 1966
Genre: Western
Rating: NR
Duration: 95mins
VG's Role: Mrs. Drummond
Director(s): Fielder Cook
Producer(s): Fielder Cook
Production Company: Eden Productions Inc.
Distributor(s): Warner Brothers
Writer(s): Sidney Carroll
Starring: Henry Fonda, Joanne Woodward, & Jason Robards
Description: Family man, "Meredith" (Henry Fonda), bets more than he can pay in a poker game on his way to settle in Texas. Unfortunate events follow his decision, and his wife "Mary" (Joanne Woodward) must sit in for him in another big game. Virginia plays supporting role "Mrs. Drummond."

33. Title: *The Bubble*
Release Date: December 21, 1966
Genre: Sci-Fi
Rating: PG
Duration: 112mins
VG's Role: Ticket cashier
Director(s): Arch Oboler
Producer(s): Arch Oboler & Marvin J. Chomsky
Production Company: Arch Oboler Productions

Distributor(s): Arch Oboler Productions
Writer(s): Arch Oboler
Starring: Michael Cole, Deborah Walley, & Johnny Desmond
Description: A couple carrying their first child becomes stranded due to strange atmospherics on a flight. An emergency plane landing in a zombie-like area causes panic as the couple sees no escape. Virginia plays the supporting role of a ticket cashier.

34. Title: *Prescription: Murder*
Release Date: February 20, 1968
Genre: Crime
Rating: PG
Duration: 100mins
VG's Role: Miss Petrie
Director(s): Richard Irving
Producer(s): Richard Irving
Production Company: Universal Television
Distributor(s): MCA-TV
Writer(s): Richard Levinson & William Link
Starring: Peter Falk, Gene Barry, & Katherine Justice
Description: Psychiatrist "Dr. Ray Flemming" (Gene Barry) enlists the help of his mistress "Joan Hudson" (Katherine Justice) to kill his wife who is suing for divorce. LAPD Lt. Columbo (Peter Falk) dismantles "Flemming's" alibi and learns the truth. Virginia plays supporting character "Miss Petrie."

35. Title: *Madigan*
Release Date: March 29, 1968
Genre: Crime
Rating: TV-14
Duration: 101mins
VG's Role: Esther Newman
Director(s): Don Siegel

Producer(s): Frank P. Rosenberg
Production Company: Universal Pictures
Distributor(s): Universal Pictures
Writer(s): Howard Rodman, Abraham Polonsky, & Richard Dougherty
Starring: Richard Widmark, Henry Fonda, & Inger Stevens
Description: "Detective Daniel Madigan" (Richard Widmark) and "Detective Rocco Bonaro" (Harry Guardino) are given 72 hours to track and locate a killer in Brooklyn. Virginia plays the supporting role of "Esther Newman."

36. Title: *The Night Before Christmas* (TV Movie)
Release Date: December 1968
Genre: Animation
Rating: G
Duration: 30mins
VG's Role: Gretchen (voice)
Director(s): Jim Pabian
Producer(s): Bill Turnbull
Production Company: Elba Productions
Distributor(s): EastWest Entertainment
Writer(s): Clement Clarke Moore, Bill Turnbull, Louise Turnbull, & Dick Woellhaf
Starring: Olan Soule, Barbara Eiler, & Hal Smith
Description: The animated fictional account of how Clement Clarke Moore came to write the classic "A Visit from St. Nicholas." Virginia voices supporting character "Gretchen."

37. Title: *Dragnet 1966* (TV Movie)
Release Date: January 27, 1969
Genre: Crime
Rating: NR
Duration: 100min

VG's Role: Mrs. Eve Kruger
Director(s): Jack Webb
Producer(s): Jack Webb
Production Company: Mark VII Ltd.
Distributor(s): NBC
Writer(s): Richard L. Breen
Starring: Jack Webb, Harry Morgan, & Vic Perrin
Description: "Sgt. Joe Friday" (Jack Webb) is assigned to a missing person's case with "Officer Bill Gannon" (Harry Morgan). Little is known about the missing person, "J. Johnson," and the pair is given varying descriptions of the man complicating their search. During the investigation, three female models also come up missing, leaving "Friday" and "Gannon" with even more puzzle pieces that don't seem to fit. Virginia plays the role of "Eve Kruger," the eccentric owner of a matchmaking service.

38. Title: *Heaven with a Gun*
Release Date: June 13, 1969
Genre: Western
Rating: NR
Duration: 101mins
VG's Role: Mrs. Patterson
Director(s): Lee H. Katzin
Producer(s): Frank King & Maurice King
Production Company: King Brothers Productions
Distributor(s): MGM
Writer(s): Richard Carr
Starring: Glenn Ford, Carolyn Jones, & Barbara Hershey
Description: In a small western town, a preacher who gave up gunslinging (Glenn Ford) is caught in a tense range war. Virginia plays supporting character "Mrs. Patterson."

39. Title: *The Great Bank Robbery*

Release Date: September 10, 1969
Genre: Western
Rating: PG
Duration: 98mins
VG's Role: Townswoman (voice, uncredited)
Director(s): Hy Averback
Producer(s): Malcolm Stuart
Production Company: Malcolm Stuart Productions
Distributor(s): Warner Brothers/Seven Arts
Writer(s): William Peter Blatty & Frank O'Rourke
Starring: Zero Mostel, Kim Novak, & Clint Walker
Description: Based on Frank O'Rourke's novel by the same name, *The Great Bank Robbery*, tells the story of three different heists planned for the same small-town bank in 1880s Texas. Virginia voices an uncredited townswoman.

40. Title: *Along Came a Spider* (TV Movie)
Release Date: February 3, 1970
Genre: Drama
Rating: NR
Duration: 75mins
VG's Role: Dr. Sylvia Newman
Director(s): Lee H. Katzin
Producer(s): William D. Faralla
Production Company: Twentieth Century Fox Television
Distributor(s): ABC
Writer(s): Leonard Lee & Barry Oringer
Starring: Suzanne Pleshette, Ed Nelson, & Andrew Prine
Description: After a lab experiment goes wrong resulting in the death of a scientist, his widow "Janet Furie" (Suzanne Pleshette) goes undercover to prove foul play was involved. Virginia plays supporting character "Dr. Sylvia Newman."

41. Title: *Quarantined* (TV Movie)
Release Date: February 24, 1970
Genre: Drama
Rating: NR
Duration: 74mins
VG's Role: Nurse Nelson
Director(s): Leo Penn
Producer(s): Lou Morheim
Production Company: Paramount Television
Distributor(s): ABC
Writer(s): Norman Katkov
Starring: Gary Collins, John Dehner, & Susan Howard
Description: A group of doctors find themselves up against a cholera epidemic at their medical center with a host of patient responses. Virginia plays supporting character "Nurse Nelson."

42. Title: *A Walk in the Spring Rain*
Release Date: April 9, 1970
Genre: Romance
Rating: GP
Duration: 98mins
VG's Role: Ann Cade
Director(s): Guy Green
Producer(s): Stirling Silliphant
Production Company: Columbia Pictures
Distributor(s): Columbia Pictures
Writer(s): Rachel Maddux & Stirling Silliphant
Starring: Anthony Quinn, Ingrid Bergman, & Fritz Weaver
Description: Married couple, "Roger and Libby Meredith" (Fritz Weaver & Ingrid Bergman) take a trip to the Great Smoky Mountains for a sabbatical. The couple's mountain neighbor, "Will Cade" (Anthony Quinn), falls in love with "Libby" at first sight.

"Libby" is equally taken by him, but their romance is interrupted. Virginia plays supporting character "Ann Cade."

43. Title: *The Other Man* (TV Movie)
Release Date: October 19, 1970
Genre: Thriller
Rating: NR
Duration: 97mins
VG's Role: Mrs. Baird
Director(s): Richard A. Colla
Producer(s): William Frye
Production Company: Universal Television
Distributor(s): NBC
Writer(s): Michael Blankfort, Eric Bercovici, & Margaret Lynn
Starring: Roy Thinnes, Arthur Hill, & Joan Hackett
Description: "Kathy Maitland" (Joan Hackett) wife of a district attorney falls in love with an ex-convict, "Johnny Brant" (Roy Thinnes), who her husband sent to prison. When "Johnny" is found murdered, "Kathy" must find his killer. Virginia plays supporting character "Mrs. Baird."

44. Title: *Crowhaven Farm* (TV Movie)
Release Date: November 24, 1970
Genre: Horror
Rating: NR
Duration: 74mins
VG's Role: Mercy Lewis
Director(s): Walter Grauman
Producer(s): Walter Grauman
Production Company: Aaron Spelling Productions
Distributor(s): ABC
Writer(s): John McGreevey
Starring: Hope Lange, Paul Burke, & Lloyd Bochner

Description: When young married couple "Ben and Maggie Porter" (Paul Burke and Hope Lange) inherit a farm, they find the land haunted by restless spirits. Virginia plays supporting character "Mercy Lewis."

45. Title: *D.A.: Conspiracy to Kill* (TV Movie)
Release Date: January 11, 1971
Genre: Crime
Rating: NR
Duration: 120mins
VG's Role: Judge Virginia Adamson
Director(s): Paul Krasny
Producer(s): Robert Forward
Production Company: Mark VII Ltd.
Distributor(s): NBC
Writer(s): Stanford Whitmore
Starring: Robert Conrad, William Conrad, & Belinda Montgomery
Description: A pharmacist claims self-defense after shooting and killing an armed robber claiming, but D.A. "Paul Ryan" (Robert Conrad) believes there is more to the case. Virginia plays the supporting role of "Judge Virginia Adamson."

46. Title: *The Night Stalker* (TV Movie)
Release Date: January 11, 1972
Genre: Horror
Rating: NR
Duration: 74mins
VG's Role: Mrs. Brandon (uncredited)
Director(s): John Llewellyn Moxey
Producer(s): Dan Curtis
Production Company: ABC Circle Films
Distributor(s): ABC
Writer(s): Richard Matheson & Jeffrey Grant Rice

Starring: Darren McGavin, Carol Lynley, & Simon Oakland
Description: Hardnosed reporter, "Carl Kolchak" (Darren McGavin), investigates an unusual series of slayings with evidence of vampire involvement. Virginia plays supporting character "Mrs. Brandon," uncredited.

47. Title: *All My Darling Daughters* (TV Movie)
Release Date: November 22, 1972
Genre: Romance
Rating: NR
Duration: 90mins
VG's Role: Witness
Director(s): David Lowell Rich
Producer(s): David J. O'Connell
Production Company: Groverton Productions
Distributor(s): ABC
Writer(s): John Gay, Robert Presnell Jr., & Stan Dreben
Starring: Robert Young, Raymond Massey, & Eve Arden
Description: Widower "Judge Charles Raleigh" (Robert Young) has four daughters who marry on the same day. Virginia plays the supporting role of witness.

48. Title: *The Stranger* (TV Movie)
Release Date: February 26, 1973
Genre: Sci-Fi
Rating: NR
Duration: 100mins
VG's Role: Ward E Administrator
Director(s): Lee H. Katzin
Producer(s): Alan A. Armer
Production Company: Bing Crosby Productions
Distributor(s): NBC
Writer(s): Gerald Sanford

Starring: Glenn Corbett, Cameron Mitchell, & Sharon Acker
Description: Astronaut "Neil Stryker" (Glenn Corbett) finds himself on a parallel Earth called Terra with three moons. He wakes up imprisoned by an Orwellian government called "The Perfect Order." "Stryker" tries desperately to break away from his captors and return home. Virginia plays the supporting role of the "Ward E Administrator."

49. Title: *Airport 1975*
Release Date: October 18, 1974
Genre: Thriller
Rating: PG
Duration: 107mins
VG's Role: Lily – Passenger (uncredited)
Director(s): Jack Smight
Producer(s): William Frye
Production Company: Universal Pictures
Distributor(s): Universal Pictures
Writer(s): Arthur Hailey & Don Ingalls
Starring: Charlton Heston, Karen Black, & George Kennedy
Description: A 747 collides with another aircraft with no pilot. "Nancy Pryor" (Karen Black), a flight attendant and her boyfriend, "Alan Murdock" (Charlton Heston), miraculously keep the 747 in the air, but panic ensues onboard as they determine how to land the plane safely. Virginia plays the uncredited role of a flight passenger.

50. Title: *Attack on Terror: The FBI vs. the Ku Klux Klan*
Release Date: February 20, 1975
Genre: Drama
Rating: NR
Duration: 215mins
VG's Role: Commissioner Miller
Director(s): Marvin J. Chomsky

Producer(s): Philip Saltzman
Production Company: Quinn Martin Productions
Distributor(s): CBS
Writer(s): Calvin Clements Sr. & Don Whitehead
Starring: Ned Beatty, John Beck, & Billy Green Bush
Description: Three young civil rights workers are arrested by "Deputy Sheriff Cecil Price" in Mississippi. Shortly after they are released, the Ku Klux Klan capture and murder them. The FBI attempts to identify the killers after their bodies are found, with only one vague clue. Virginia plays supporting role of "Commissioner Miller."

51. Title: *You Lie So Deep, My Love*
Release Date: February 25, 1975
Genre: Drama
Rating: NR
Duration: 78mins
VG's Role: The maid
Director(s): David Lowell Rich
Producer(s): David Lowell Rich
Production Company: Universal Television
Distributor(s): ABC
Writer(s): Robert Hamner, John Neufeld, & William L. Stuart
Starring: Don Galloway, Barbara Anderson, & Angel Tompkins
Description: "Neal Collins" (Don Galloway) is a married man who wants the best of both his worlds: his mistress's affection and his wife's wealth. "Collins" stops at nothing to get what he wants including murder. Virginia plays the supporting role of the maid.

52. Title: *Mobile Two* (TV Movie)
Release Date: September 2, 1975
Genre: Drama
Rating: NR

Duration: 90mins
VG's Role: Uncredited
Director(s): David Moessinger
Producer(s): William Bowers
Production Company: Mark VII Ltd.
Distributor(s): ABC
Writer(s): James M. Miller, David Moessinger, & Leo Pipkin
Starring: Jackie Cooper, Julie Gregg, & Mark Wheeler
Description: TV reporter "Peter Campbell" (Jackie Cooper) ruins his career and personal life with his alcoholism, but suddenly gets a second chance to prove himself after being hired by a new television program. Virginia plays an uncredited, unnamed role.

53. Title: *No Way Back*
Release Date: April 23, 1976
Genre: Crime
Rating: R
Duration: 103mins
VG's Role: Mildred Pickens
Director(s): Fred Williamson
Producer(s): Fred Williamson
Production Company: Po'Boy Productions
Distributor(s): Atlas Films
Writer(s): Fred Williamson
Starring: Fred Williamson, Charles Woolf, & Tracy Reed
Description: Private detective and former policeman "Jesse Crowder" (Fred Williamson) investigates when a woman asks him to help find her lost husband on the run. The case becomes complicated when "Crowder's" investigation leads him into hot water with gangsters. Virginia plays the role of "Mildred Pickens."

54. Title: *State Fair*
Release Date: May 14, 1976

Genre: Drama
Rating: NR
Duration: 55mins
VG's Role: Miss Detweiler
Director(s): David Lowell Rich
Producer(s): Robert L. Jacks
Production Company: Twentieth Century Fox Television
Distributor(s): Twentieth Century Fox Television
Writer(s): Richard Fielder
Starring: Vera Miles, Tim O'Connor, & Mitch Vogel
Description: "Jim and Melissa Bryant" (Tim O'Connor and Vera Miles) live in Iowa with their children. Their son, "Wayne," is a talented singer and guitarist who has big dreams. The family enters the Iowa State Fair according to "Wayne's" career aspirations. Virginia plays supporting character "Miss Detweiler."

55. Title: *A Flintstone Christmas*
Release Date: December 7, 1977
Genre: Animation
Rating: NR
Duration: 60mins
VG's Role: (additional voices)
Director(s): Sid Marcus, Charles A. Nichols, Alex Lovy, Gerry Chiniquy, & Hawley Pratt
Producer(s): Joseph Barbera, William Hanna, Alex Lovy, & Iwao Takamoto
Production Company: Hanna-Barbera Productions
Distributor(s): NBC
Writer(s): Duane Poole, Dick Robbins, Willie Gilbert, David Detiege, John W. Dunn, Friz Freleng, Larry Siegel, & John Barrett
Starring: Mel Blanc, Lucille Bliss, & Henry Corden
Description: On Christmas Eve Day, "Fred" (Mel Blanc) is finally convinced to play Santa Claus for a good cause, but late that night,

the real Santa Claus is injured falling off "Fred's" roof, and "Fred" must finish Santa's route. Virginia voices several different characters.

56. Title: *Goodbye, Franklin High*
Release Date: April 1978
Genre: Comedy
Rating: PG
Duration: 94mins
VG's Role: Nurse
Director(s): Mike MacFarland
Producer(s): Mike MacFarland
Production Company: Cal-Am Productions
Distributor(s): Cal-Am Artists
Writer(s): Stu Krieger
Starring: Lane Caudell, Julie Adams, & William Windom
Description: During his senior year, "Will Armer" (Lane Caudell) wrestles with the decision to either go to college or to pursue a career in baseball after graduation. Virginia plays the supporting role of school nurse.

57. Title: *Evita Peron*
Release Date: February 23, 1981
Genre: Historical drama
Rating: TV-PG
Duration: 200mins
VG's Role: Radio actress
Director(s): Marvin J. Chomsky
Producer(s): Marvin J. Chomsky
Production Company: Hartwest Productions
Distributor(s): NBC
Writer(s): John Barnes, Nicholas Frazer, & Ronald Harwood
Starring: Faye Dunaway, James Farentino, & Pedro Armendáriz Jr.

Description: Based on the true story of actress Eva Duarte, *Evita Peron* tells the story of her career, marriage to Argentina dictator, Juan Peron, and how her selfish ambition brings about her undoing. Virginia voices an unnamed radio actress.

58. Title: *S.O.B.*
Release Date: July 1, 1981
Genre: Comedy
Rating: R
Duration: 122mins
VG's Role: Funeral home owner's wife
Director(s): Blake Edwards
Producer(s): Tony Adams & Blake Edwards
Production Company: Artista Management
Distributor(s): Paramount Pictures
Writer(s): Blake Edwards
Starring: Julie Andrews, William Holden, & Marisa Berenson
Description: Film producer "Tim Culley's" (William Holden) latest film is a flop, so in an effort to save his industry reputation he recreates the film as an erotica whose leading lady is a well-known family-friendly celebrity. Virginia plays the role of the funeral home owner's wife.

59. Title: *Forbidden Love*
Release Date: October 18, 1982
Genre: Drama
Rating: NR
Duration: 100mins
VG's Role: Henny Brandywine
Director(s): Steven Hillard Stern
Producer(s): Marcy Gross & Ann Weston
Production Company: Gross-Weston Productions
Distributor(s): CBS

Writer(s): Priscilla English & Laurian Leggett
Starring: Yvette Mimieux, Andrew Stevens, & Lisa Lucas
Description: "Dr. Casey Wagner" (Andrew Stevens) falls for his hospital superior, "Joanna Bittan" (Yvette Mimieux), who is several years older than he is. Others in their lives struggle to accept their relationship due to the age difference. Virginia plays supporting character "Henny Brandywine."

60. Title: *Heidi's Song*
Release Date: November 19, 1982
Genre: Animation
Rating: G
Duration: 94mins
VG's Role: Aunt Dete (voice)
Director(s): Robert Taylor
Producer(s): Joseph Barbera, William Hanna, & Iwao Takamoto
Production Company: Hanna-Barbera Productions
Distributor(s): Paramount Pictures
Writer(s): Joseph Barbera, Jameson Brewer, Robert Taylor, & Johanna Spyri
Starring: Lorne Greene, Sammy Davis Jr., & Margery Gray
Description: This animated musical is based on Johanna Spyri's novel by the same name that tells the story of orphan girl "Heidi" (Margery Gray) who goes to live with her grandfather (Lorne Greene) in the Swiss Alps. Soon after, "Heidi" is taken away to be a playmate for an official's injured daughter, but she tries to find a way back to her grandfather and friends on the mountain. Virginia voices the character "Aunt Dete."

61. Title: *The 25ᵗʰ Man*
Release Date: 1982
Genre: Crime
Rating: NR

Duration: 60mins
VG's Role: Mrs. Taylor
Director(s): Daniel Haller
Producer(s): William Stark
Production Company: Universal Television
Distributor(s): Universal Television
Writer(s): Stephen Downing
Starring: Michael Andrew, Michael Bell, & Howard Culver
Description: "Lynn Taylor" (Ellen Regan) is the Los Angeles Police Academy's only female recruit. She suddenly finds herself in danger when a strange man begins to stalk her. The other academy recruits come to her aid in determining who this man is and how they can keep "Lynn" safe. Virginia plays supporting character "Mrs. Taylor."

62. Title: *Psycho II*
Release Date: June 3, 1983
Genre: Horror
Rating: R
Duration: 113mins
VG's Role: Norma Bates (voice, uncredited)
Director(s): Richard Franklin
Producer(s): Hilton A. Green
Production Company: Universal Pictures
Distributor(s): Universal Pictures
Writer(s): Tom Holland & Robert Block
Starring: Anthony Perkins, Vera Miles, & Meg Tilly
Description: Psychopath "Norman Bates" (Anthony Perkins) has been in psychiatric care for the last twenty-two years, and upon his release, he tries to resume his life. His demons soon catch up to him again. Virginia voices "Norma Bates" uncredited.

63. Title: *Hanna-Barbera's The Greatest Adventure: Stories from the Bible: Samson and Delilah*

Release Date: April 25, 1986
Genre: Animation
Rating: G
Duration: 30mins
VG's Role: Miriam (voice)
Director(s): Ray Patterson
Producer(s): Kay Wright
Production Company: Hanna-Barbera Productions
Distributor(s): VTI Home Video
Writer(s): Harvey Bullock
Starring: Perry King, Linda Purl, & Darleen Carr
Description: Animated interpretation of the Old Testament story of "Samson and Delilah." Virginia voices supporting character "Miriam."

64. Title: *Psycho III*
Release Date: July 2, 1986
Genre: Horror
Rating: R
Duration: 93mins
VG's Role: Norma Bates (voice, uncredited)
Director(s): Anthony Perkins
Producer(s): Hilton A. Green
Production Company: Universal Pictures
Distributor(s): Universal Pictures
Writer(s): Charles Edward Pogue & Robert Bloch
Starring: Anthony Perkins, Diana Scarwid, & Jeff Fahey
Description: "Norman Bates" (Anthony Perkins) becomes smitten with a strange nun staying at the Bates Motel. Virginia voices "Norma Bates" uncredited.

Bibliography

1. Burton, R. (1956, May). Hollywood report: Aline Mosby. *Press-Courier*, p. 16.
2. *Don't Touch That Dial* with Bobb Lynes and Barbara Sunday September 19, 1982.
3. Actors and actresses could perform in multiple roles within the same script until the 1950s when the American Federation of Radio Artists (AFRA) developed the limitation of no more than two roles per individual per script.
4. SPERDVAC CBS Panel Interview August 1982.
5. Page, D. (1958, December). Virginia Gregg tailor-made actress. *The Los Angeles Times*, 78, p. 5.
6. *Don't Touch That Dial* with Bobb Lynes and Barbara Sunday September 19, 1982.
7. A phase often used by "Richard Diamond" on NBC's Richard Diamond, Private Detective in which Virginia played the witty gumshoe's Park Avenue girlfriend "Helen Asher."
8. SPERDVAC CBS Panel Interview August 1982.
9. Rehearsals for the *Dragnet* radio shows were actually pretty rare. Jack preferred cold reads to give an extra layer of realism to the story. Many times, actors and actresses had not even completed a read-through before going on-air in a Jack Webb production.
10. Virginia's attempt to ease the tension is in no way related to anti-Semitism. When considering the context of this story, it would be analogous today to saying about a friend whom everyone knew to be a devout Catholic, "Well obviously he did blank because of his Buddhist faith." The joke was in the sarcasm and absurdity of what Virginia called Jack that she knew was not true, rather than the ethnoreligious group of Jewish people itself.

She could have substituted any other people group to which she knew Jack did not belong and it would still have had the desired effect: humor in the face of distress. This was no insult, but an attempt at levity that apparently worked for everyone present – including true Jewish cast and crew members. Virginia had not a prejudice bone in her body and had great respect for all humans regardless of status, race, ethnicity, or religion.

11. United Press International. (1982, December). Jack Webb, Sgt. Joe Friday of 'Dragnet,' dies. *The Sacramento Bee*, 250(41,613), A3.

12. Other radio and television shows to follow Jack's lead in the crime drama genre were *Tales of the Texas Rangers, 21st Precinct,* and *Nightwatch*. A more contemporary production that continued in this trend is *Law & Order: Special Victims Unit,* which premiered in 1999 and is now in its 22nd season as of 2020, making it the longest running drama in television history. Before *Law & Order: SVU, Gunsmoke* was the longest running television drama. Screenwriter Charles Marquis Warren adapted the legendary radio show *Gunsmoke* to television beginning in 1955 and it ran for twenty seasons. Virginia was a regular on both the radio and television series.

13. The LAPD gifted Jack a badge (badge number 714, which was his on *Dragnet*) with the inscription: "To Jack Webb, the best reel cop from the best real cops." (UPI, 1982).

14. Aside from the *Dragnet* franchise productions Jack produced, he also involved Virginia in countless other series he created and/or produced including, but not limited to *77 Sunset Strip, Temple Houston, O'Hara U.S. Treasury, Emergency!, Hec Ramsey, Adam-12, Project U.F.O.*

15. SPERDVAC CBS Panel Interview August 1982.

16. The episode is called "The Big Show;" Season 2, Episode 11.

17. Page, D. (1958, December). Virginia Gregg tailor-made actress. *The Los Angeles Times*, 78, p. 5.

18. The Staff of the Mitchell-Carnegie Public Library. (1934). A history of Saline County. *Journal of the Illinois State Historical Society (1908-1984), 27*(1), 31-54. http://www.jstor.org/stable/40187821

19. Ferguson, G. (2007). "Harrisburg's founding fathers: Real estate developers in pioneer Illinois." *Journal of the Illinois State Historical Society, 100*(2), 110-127. https://search-proquest-com.library.capella.edu/docview/232490317?pq- origsite=summon

20. Deneal, T. (2017, February). River-ravaged region. *Harrisburg Register.* https://www.dailyregister.com/news/20170208/river-ravaged-region

21. Groeninger, A. & Haggerty, R. (2012, March). "Harrisburg comes together after deadly tornado. *Chicago Tribune.* https://www.chicagotribune.com/news/breaking/chi-harrisburg-cleans-up-tornado- damage-20120302-story.html

22. Groeninger, A. & Haggerty, R. (2012, March). "Harrisburg comes together after deadly tornado. *Chicago Tribune.* https://www.chicagotribune.com/news/breaking/chi-harrisburg-cleans-up-tornado- damage-20120302-story.html

23. DeNeal, G. (1998). *A knight of another sort: Prohibition days and Charlie Birger.* Southern Illinois University Press.

24. DeNeal, G. (1998). *A knight of another sort: Prohibition days and Charlie Birger.* Southern Illinois University Press.

25. DeNeal, G. (1998). *A knight of another sort: Prohibition days and Charlie Birger.* Southern Illinois University Press.

26. DeNeal, G. (1998). *A knight of another sort: Prohibition days and Charlie Birger.* Southern Illinois University Press.

27. Eschner, K. (2017, December). "Why the Ku Klux Klan flourished under Prohibition. Smithsonian Magazine." https://www.smithsonianmag.com/smart-news/why-racism-   flourished-under-prohibition-180967406/

28. DeNeal, G. (1998). *A knight of another sort: Prohibition days and Charlie Birger.* Southern Illinois University Press.

29. DeNeal, G. (1998). *A knight of another sort: Prohibition days and Charlie Birger*. Southern Illinois University Press.

30. DeNeal, G. (1998). *A knight of another sort: Prohibition days and Charlie Birger*. Southern Illinois University Press.

31. n.a. (1965, June). City has had commission form of government for fifty years. *The Daily Register, 51*(1), p. 58.

32. The Gregg family home was located at 326 E Poplar Street in Harrisburg. The Gregg's eldest son T.D. and his wife Elsie lived in the home after Virginia's grandparents, William and Neila, died. The home no longer stands today. The site is a parking lot across from the popular local Italian bistro "Morello's."

33. Murray, J.F. (2004). A century of tuberculosis. *American Journal of Respiratory and Critical Care Medicine, 169*(11), 1182-1186. doi: 10.1164/rccm.200402-140OE

34. n.a. (1959, October). Virginia Gregg is kept busy by TV producers; appears in new series. *The Daily Register, 45*(81), p. 7.

35. n.a. (1933, April). Schoolhouse quiz ordered. *The Los Angeles Times, 52*, p. 2.

36. Mead, T. (1979, February). TV mailbag. *Five Cities Times-Press-Recorder, 91*(63), p. 12.

37. Pasadena Junior College Annual, 1933.

38. Ruth was buried in the Mountain View Cemetery and Mausoleum in Altadena, California where from Virginia's mother is buried.

39. Lane, L. (1959, October). Hollywood beauty: Discipline is the answer to a weight problem. *The Press Democrat*, p. 15.

40. n.a. (1937, May). Fete winners on programs. *The Pasadena Post, 18*(240), p. 8.

41. Architecture: Pasadena Playhouse. (n.d.). https://www.visitpasadena.com/directory/pasadena-playhouse/

42. n.a. (1934, June). Youth kills mother and brother in L.A. horror. *Santa Rosa Republican, 9*(10), p. 1.

43. n.a. (1933, January) Driver who killed woman is fined $200. *St. Louis Post-Dispatch, 85*(123), p. 13A.

44. n.a. (1934, June) Axe-youth mystified by motive. *The Pasadena Post, 15*(271), p. 1.

45. n.a. (1935, February). Louis Rude Payne is now in asylum. *The Californian, 1*(1), p. 1.

46. n.a. (1934, July). Epilepsy blamed for youth's ax murders. *The Fresno Bee, 24*(4198), p. 3A.

47. Swed, M. (2013, November). A new direction for Pasadena? *The Los Angeles Times*, D, p. 25.

48. n.a. (1936, April). Police show to be varied. *The Los Angeles Times*, 55, Part I, p. 11.

49. n.a. (1959, October). Virginia Gregg is kept busy by TV producers; appears in new series. *The Daily Register, 45*(81), p. 7.

50. n.a. (1937, November). Singing Strings of radio. *The Los Angeles Times*, 56, Part I, p. 14.

51. n.a. (1959, October). Virginia Gregg is kept busy by TV producers; appears in new series. *The Daily Register, 45*(81), p. 7.

52. Others filmed in Echo Park include the 1974 film *Chinatown* starring Jack Nicholson and Faye Dunaway, the 2001 film *The Fast and the Furious* starring Paul Walker and Vin Diesel, and most recently the 2018 film *A Star is Born* with Bradley Cooper and Lady Gaga.

53. Artist Ada Mae Sharpless sculpted "Lady of the Lake" in the 1930s and it was installed at Echo Park in 1935 as a donation piece to the city of Los Angeles. The statue has undergone many restoration phases since, but is still a notable presence in the area today.

54. n.a. (1917, May). Tell 'solid seven' today what you think of Billboard Trust. *Los Angeles Evening Express, 47*(54), p. 3.

55. Epstein, D.M. (1993). *Sister Aimee: The life of Aimee Semple McPherson*. Harvest Books.

56. Epstein, D.M. (1993). *Sister Aimee: The life of Aimee Semple McPherson*. Harvest Books.

57. The first female to ever be given a broadcasting license was Marie Zmmerman in the same year "Sister Aimee" was granted hers: 1922. Marie was the first woman to own a radio station.

58. In Daniel Mark Epstein's biography of Aimee Semple McPherson, he describes another abduction that occurred at the hands of the KKK in June of 1922. By most accounts, the May 1926 disappearance was in fact "Sister Aimee's" second "abduction."

59. United Press. (1926, June). Kidnappers were Americans, says Aimee; Dope used with ruse when she was taken from beach; Had many privations while in Mexico. *Woodland Daily Democrat*, p. 1.

60. Epstein, D.M. (1993). *Sister Aimee: The life of Aimee Semple McPherson*. Harvest Books.

61. Epstein, D.M. (1993). *Sister Aimee: The life of Aimee Semple McPherson*. Harvest Books.

62. Banks, D. (1945, June). What's new from coast to coast. *Radio Mirror*, p. 8.

63. Schaden, C. (March 14, 1984). Virginia Gregg interview. http://www.speakingofradio.com/interviews/

64. Schaden, C. (March 14, 1984). Virginia Gregg interview. http://www.speakingofradio.com/interviews/

65. Schaden, C. (March 14, 1984). Virginia Gregg interview. http://www.speakingofradio.com/interviews/

66. Basten, F.E. (2012). *Max Factor: The man who changed the faces of the world*. Arcade.

67. Basten, F.E. (2012). *Max Factor: The man who changed the faces of the world*. Arcade.

68. Newton, D. (1954, February). Day and night with radio and television. *The San Francisco Examiner*, p. 26.

69. Newton, D. (1954, February). Day and night with radio and television. *The San Francisco Examiner*, p. 26.

70. Actor Leo Carrillo who later starred in the *Cisco Kid* television series that premicred in 1950 and ran for six seasons was a first

cousin to Jaime del Valle. He was known as "Leo Carrillo the Movie Star."

71. *Cisco Kid* episodes were often still being written during their live radio performances.

72. Newton, D. (1954, February). Day and night with radio and television. *The San Francisco Examiner*, p. 26.

73. Rasmussen, C. (2001, November). del Valle family played a starring role in early California. *The Los Angeles Times*, p. B4.

74. Danson, T.E. (1949, January). Yours truly, Virginia Gregg. *Press-Telegram Radio Editor*.

75. n.a. (1947, March). San Fernando Valley's chronological history. *Valley Times*, 11(54), p. 2.

76. Rasmussen, C. (2001, November). del Valle family played a starring role in early California. *The Los Angeles Times*, p. B4.

77. Hayes-Bautista, D.E., Firebaugh, M.A., Chamberlin, C.L., & Gamboa, C. (2006). Reginaldo Francisco del Valle: UCLA's forgotten forefather. *Southern California Quarterly*, 88(1), 1-35. doi: 10.2307/41172295

78. Danson, T. E. (1953, September). Radiologic: What's new in radio and television. *Daily News-Post and Monrovia News-Post*, p. 7.

79. Danson, T. E. (1953, September). Radiologic: What's new in radio and television. *Daily News-Post and Monrovia News-Post*, p. 7.

80. Newton, D. (1954, January). Day and night with radio and television. *The San Francisco Examiner*, p. 12.

81. n.a. (1948, December). Today's personality. *Daily News*.

82. SPERDVAC CBS Panel Interview August 1982.

83. SPERDVAC CBS Panel Interview August 1982.

84. Lane, L. (1959, October). Hollywood beauty: Discipline is the answer to a weight problem. *The Press Democrat*, p. 15.

85. Adler, S. (2000). *The art of acting*. Applause Books.

86. A particularly great example of this submerging-withholding dichotomy can be seen in Virginia's portrayal of "Sheila

Cromwell" on the witness stand in *Perry Mason's* "The Case of the Cautious Coquette" from season one.

87. Burton, R. (1956, May). Aline Mosby. *Press-Courier*, p. 16.

88. Burton, R. (1958, December). Aline Mosby. *The Los Angeles Times*, p. 16.

89. Witbeck, C. (1959, February). Virginia Gregg has been in many shows. *The Manhattan Mercury*, p. 1.

90. n.a. (1959, December). Alimony reminds him of the fact. *Reno-Gazette-Journal*, p. 1.

91. n.a. (1959, December). Virginia Gregg granted divorce. *News-Pilot San Pedro*, p. 2.

92. Smith, J.W. (2009). *The psycho file: A comprehensive guide to Hitchcock's classic shocker.* McFarland.

93. Radio did not die globally in 1962. Great Britain and South Africa audiences were slower to abandon radio compared to those in the United States.

94. Burton, R. (1956, May). Hollywood report: Aline Mosby. *Press-Courier*, p. 16.

95. While Robert Keith played the dying "Jason Foster," in this episode, coincidentally it was his last performance before his death in 1966.

96. n.a. (1965, April). *Press-Telegram* p. A6.

97. n.a. (1965, April). *Press-Telegram* p. A6.

98. *Gunsmoke* "Phoebe Strunk" (1962) S8E9

99. *Lou Grant* (1979) "Skids" S2E23

100. *Dragnet* (1954)

101. *Dragnet* "The Pyramid Swindle" (1967) S2E12

102. *Gunsmoke* "The Twisted Heritage" (1969) S14E15

103. *The Waltons* "The Ordeal" (1978) S6E19

104. Lowrie, K. (1981, October). Mug shots. *Los Angeles Times*, p. 24.

105. Lane, L. (1959, October). Hollywood beauty: Discipline is the answer to a weight problem. *The Press Democrat*, p. 15.

106. Christensen, R. (1982, March 6). Actors request new warnings on health risks of cigarettes. *The News and Observer*, Raleigh, North Carolina. Section C.

107. n.a. (1986, September 17). "Versatile character actress Virginia Gregg dies at 70." *LA Times*, Part I, p. 23.

108. Lane, L. (1959, October). Hollywood beauty: Discipline is answer to a weight problem. *The Press Democrat*, p. 15.

109. OTRCAT.com/p/first-nighter

110. Dunning, J. (1976). *Tune in yesterday: The ultimate encyclopedia of old-time radio 1925-1976.* Prentice-Hall, Inc.

111. Goldin, J.D. (2021). "Children's hour, but not for children." https://radiogoldin.library.umkc.edu/Home/Radio Goldin_Records?searchString=Gr egg,%20Virginia&type=Artists&count=1260

112. Brooks, M. (2005). *The American family on television: A chronology of 121 shows, 1948-2004.* McFarland & Company Publishers.

Index